LIBRARY OF NEW TESTAMENT STUDIES

341

Formerly The Journal For The Study Of The New Testament Supplement Series

Editor
Mark Goodacre

RHETORICAL TEXTURE AND NARRATIVE TRAJECTORIES OF THE LUKAN GALILEAN MINISTRY SPEECHES

Hermeneutical Appropriation by Authorial Readers of Luke-Acts

PATRICK E. SPENCER

t&t clark

Published by T&T Clark
A Continuum imprint
The Tower Building, 11 York Road, London SE1 7NX
80 Maiden Lane, Suite 704, New York, NY 10038

www.tandtclark.com

British Library Cataloguing-in-Publication Data
A catalogue record for this book is available from the British Library

ISBN-10: 0-567-03130-6 (hardback)
ISBN-13: 978-0567-0313-03 (hardback)

Typeset by Data Standards Limited, Frome, Somerset, UK
Printed on acid-free paper in Great Britain by Biddles Ltd, King's Lynn,
Norfolk

CONTENTS

Acknowledgements   xi
Abbreviations   xiii

PART ONE: CURRENT STATUS OF RESEARCH AND A METHODOLOGICAL
FOUNDATION

CHAPTER 1: UNDERSTANDING TODAY'S SCHOLARLY LANDSCAPE:
JESUS' FOUR LUKAN GALILEAN MINISTRY SPEECHES   3
  I. Previous Investigation of the Four Galilean Ministry Speeches   5
    A. The First Galilean Speech (4.14-30)   6
    B. The Second Galilean Speech (6.17-49)   6
    C. The Third Galilean Speech (7.24-35)   8
    D. The Fourth Galilean Speech (8.4-18)   8
  II. Investigation of the Narrative Discourse of Luke-Acts   9
    A. Formalism Lays the Foundation: Narrative Criticism   10
    B. Early Attempts to Go Beyond Formalism: Sociological
    Explorations   14
    C. Moving beyond Formalism: Integrating Reader-Response
    Criticism   16
    D. Other Narrative, Sociological, and Reader-Response
    Investigations   18
      1. Characterization   18
      2. Investigation of Narrative Redundancies and Intertextuality   20
    E. Embracing an Integrated Hermeneutic: Ideological Systems
    and Location   21
  III. Concluding Summary   27

CHAPTER TWO: A METHODOLOGICAL FOUNDATION FOR INVESTIGATION:
TOWARDS READING AS CONDUCTION   28
  I. Constructing Meaning: Combination, Selection, and the
  Imaginary   29
    A. Reading (Listening) Dynamics, the Implied Reader, and
    Authorial Readers   29
      1. Theophilus: Literary Patronage   31
      2. Extratextual and Intratextual Repertoire   33
      3. Authorial Readers and Ideological Location   33

B. Processing Texts: Consistency and Coherency   35
   1. Rhetorical Argument   36
   2. Intertextual Echoes and Weaving   37
   3. Constructing Plot, Theme, Characterization, and Motifs
   (Topoi)   38
C. Interpretation as Conduction: The Fictive and Imaginary   42
II. Concluding Summary   44

CHAPTER THREE: GRECO-ROMAN RHETORICAL ARGUMENT:
DELINEATING RHETORICAL TEXTURE   46
I. Greco-Roman Handbook Rhetoric   46
   A. Rhetorical Invention, Arrangement, and Style   47
   B. Rhetorical Handbooks and New Testament Rhetoric   48
II. Delineating the Parameters of Rhetorical Texture   50
   A. Rhetorical Proof: Logos, Pathos, and Ethos   52
   B. Rhetorical Questioning   52
   C. Maxims   53
   D. Enthymemes   54
III. Speeches in Ancient Greco-Roman Narrative   58
IV. Concluding Summary   59

PART TWO: RHETORICAL TEXTURE OF THE FOUR LUKAN GALILEAN
MINISTRY SPEECHES

CHAPTER FOUR: THE FIRST GALILEAN MINISTRY SPEECH (4.14-30):
HOMETOWN SYNAGOGUE REJECTS NEW PATRONAL BOUNDARIES   63
I. Rhetorical Situation   63
II. Rhetorical Texture   64
   A. An Amplified Chreia   65
   B. Introduction: Narrative Introduction, Quaestio, and
   Digressio (4.18-20)   66
   C. Statement of Case: Chreia (4.21-22)   67
   D. Body of Argument: Statements by Analogy and Example
   (4.23-27)   68
   E. Missing Conclusion/Exhortation (4.28-30)   69
III. Concluding Summary   70

CHAPTER FIVE: THE SECOND GALILEAN MINISTRY SPEECH (6.17-49):
A NEW ETHICAL MODE OF (NON-RECIPROCAL) BENEFACTION   71
I. Rhetorical Situation   71
II. Rhetorical Argument   73
III. Rhetorical Texture   74
   A. Introduction (6.20-26)   75
      1. First Three Pair of Blessing/Woe Clusters   76

2. Final Blessing/Woe Cluster   77
3. Enthymematic Argument Generates Rhetorical Texture   78
B. Statement of Case (6.27-31)   81
  1. Overarching Topos: Loving Your Enemies (6.27-28)   82
  2. What It Means to Love Your Enemies (6.29-30)   84
  3. Rationale for the Statement of Case (6.31)   86
C. Body of Argument (6.32-45)   87
  1. Unconditional Patronage: First Segment (6.32-36)   88
  2. Friendship without Boundaries: Second Segment (6.37-42) 92
  3. Rationale for the Body: Third Segment (6.43-45)   96
D. Conclusion (6.46-49)   98
IV. Concluding Summary   100

CHAPTER SIX: THE THIRD GALILEAN MINISTRY SPEECH (7.24-35):
JESUS, JOHN THE BAPTIST, AND THEIR DISCIPLES AND OPPONENTS   101
I. Rhetorical Situation   101
II. Rhetorical Texture   102
A. An Amplified Chreia   103
B. Narrative Introduction: Quaestio and Chreia (7.24-27)   105
C. Statement of Case: Rationale (7.28)   106
D. Narrative Aside: Digressio (7.29-30)   107
E. Body of Argument: Statement by Analogy and Example
(7.31-34)   108
F. Conclusion (7.35)   110
III. Concluding Summary   113

CHAPTER SEVEN: THE FOURTH GALILEAN MINISTRY SPEECH (LK. 8.4-18):
SOWING CHARACTER TAXONOMIES FOR THE IMPLIED READER   114
I. Rhetorical Situation   114
II. Rhetorical Texture   116
A. Introduction (8.5-8a)   116
B. Statement of Case (8.9-10)   118
C. Body of Argument (8.11-15)   119
  1. First Example: Sowing Along the Path   121
  2. Second Example: Sowing on the Rock   121
  3. Third Example: Sowing Among the Thorns   122
  4. Fourth Example: Sowing into the Good Soil   123
D. Conclusion (8.16-18)   124
E. Inclusio: 8.1-3 and 8.19-20   126
III. Concluding Summary   127

PART THREE: NARRATIVE TRAJECTORIES AND HERMENEUTICAL
APPROPRIATION BY AUTHORIAL READERS

CHAPTER EIGHT: RHETORICAL TEXTURE AND NARRATIVE TRAJECTORIES:
GENERATION OF PLOT, CHARACTERIZATION, AND TOPOI   131
  I. A Methodological Basis and Framework   132
  II. Framing the Narrative Discourse: Lukan Prologue   134
  III. The First Galilean Ministry Speech   135
    A. Constructing Meaning from the Rhetorical Texture   135
    B. Narrative Trajectories Engender Characterization   137
      1. Details on Jesus' Characterization   137
      2. Jesus' Hometown Synagogue and Those Who Repudiate
      'Salvation'   137
    C. Narrative Trajectories Engender Topoi   138
      1. Forgiveness of Sin and Jubilee Legislation   138
      2. A Type Scene: A Paradigm of Proclamation   139
  IV. The Second Galilean Ministry Speech   140
    A. Constructing Meaning from the Rhetorical Texture   140
    B. Narrative Trajectories Engender Characterization   141
      1. Jesus: Embodiment of Moses, Elijah, and Elisha   141
      2. Opponents of Jesus   142
      3. True Disciples   142
    C. Narrative Trajectories Engender Topoi   143
      1. Reversal of Fortunes   143
      2. Material Benefaction   143
      3. A New Mode of Benefaction: Ethical Comportment of
      Disciples   144
      4. Discipleship Equals Action   145
      5. Ethical Actions Derive From the Heart   145
  V. The Third Galilean Ministry Speech   146
    A. Constructing Meaning from the Rhetorical Texture   146
    B. Narrative Trajectories Engender Characterization   149
      1. Characterization of John the Baptist   149
      2. Characterization of Jesus   150
      3. Characterization of the Pharisees and Lawyers   151
      4. Characterization of All the People and the Tax Collectors   152
    C. Narrative Trajectories Engender Topoi   152
  VI. The Fourth Galilean Ministry Speech   153
    A. Constructing Meaning from the Rhetorical Texture   153
    B. Narrative Trajectories Engender Characterization   155
      1. The First Sowing Example: Sowing Along the Path   156
      2. The Second Sowing Example: Sowing on the Rock   157
      3. The Third Sowing Example: Sowing Among the Thorns   157
      4. The Fourth Sowing Example: Sowing into the Good Soil   158

C. Narrative Trajectories Engender Topoi 160
  1. Maturation, Production of Fruit, and the Importance of
  'Doing' 161
  2. Condemnation of and Triumph over Divination and
  Magic 161
  3. Repudiation and Persecution Results in Apocalyptic
  Condemnation 161
  4. Discipleship and the 'Heart' (Καρδία) 162
VII. Concluding Summary 162

CHAPTER NINE: HERMENEUTICAL APPROPRIATION BY AUTHORIAL
READERS AND THEIR IDEOLOGICAL TRANSFORMATION 164
  I. Getting from Implied Reader to Authorial Readers 165
  II. Appropriation by Authorial Readers 166
  III. Identifying Different Authorial Readers 166
  IV. Authorial Readers and Ideological Transformation 168
    A. Defamiliarization of Honor and Shame Protocols 168
      1. Honor and Shame and the Narrative Discourse of the
      First Galilean Ministry Speech 169
      2. Honor and Shame and the Narrative Discourse of the
      Second Galilean Ministry Speech 170
      3. Honor and Shame and the Narrative Discourse of the
      Third Galilean Ministry Speech 171
      4. Honor and Shame and the Narrative Discourse of the
      Fourth Galilean Ministry Speech 172
    B. Reshaping Material Benefaction 172
    C. Expansion of Religious and Ethnic Boundaries 174
    D. Jesus, John the Baptist, and Their Disciples 176
    E. Evaluation of Gender and the Narrative Discourse 177
  V. Concluding Summary 179

PART FOUR
CONCLUDING SUMMARY – FROM GALILEE TO ROME

CHAPTER TEN: CONCLUSION: RHETORICAL TEXTURE, NARRATIVE
TRAJECTORIES, AND APPROPRIATION BY AUTHORIAL READERS 183
  I. Concluding Comments on Rhetorical Texture 184
    A. The First Galilean Ministry Speech 184
    B. The Second Galilean Ministry Speech 184
    C. The Third Galilean Ministry Speech 185
    D. The Fourth Galilean Ministry Speech 185
    E. Assessing the Rhetorical Texture of the Four Galilean
    Ministry Speeches 185
  II. Concluding Comments on Narrative Trajectories 187

A. Theme and Plot   187
B. Characterization   188
  1. Jesus   188
  2. The 'Poor'   188
  3. Opponents of Jesus and His Disciples   188
  4. Failed Disciples   189
  5. Four Sowing Activities Delimit Four Character
    Taxonomies   189
C. Topoi   190
  1. Topoi Overlapping All Four Galilean Ministry Speeches 190
  2. Topoi Found in One Speech Only   190
III. Concluding Comments on Redactional Indicators   191
IV. Luke-Acts Unity   193
V. Representation of the Jewish People   194
  A. The First Galilean Ministry Speech   195
  B. The Second Galilean Ministry Speech   195
  C. The Third Galilean Ministry Speech   195
  D. The Fourth Galilean Ministry Speech   196
VI. The Lukan Community   197
VII. Methodological Implications   200
  A. Redaction Criticism and the Integrated Hermeneutic   200
  B. Rhetorical Texture and Narrative Trajectories   201
  C. Ideological Systems and Hermeneutical Transformation 201
  D. Authorial Readers and Hermeneutical Appropriation   202
VIII. Concluding Summary   203

Figure 1: A Hermeneutical Model: Reading as Conduction   204
Figure 2: Sowing Character Taxonomies   205

Bibliography   206

Index of References   237

Index of Authors   245

ACKNOWLEDGMENTS

The 'way' from Galilee to Jerusalem to Rome is a lengthy, event-filled, often treacherous journey that plots a map of unrelenting endurance. Regardless of the protagonist who is on the 'way', Jesus and his disciples in the Gospel of Luke and then Peter, Paul, and others in the Book of Acts, the journey is propelled by actions of non-reciprocal benefaction. In many ways, the journey of this study, which is a revision of my doctoral dissertation at the University of Durham, parallels the journeys in Luke and Acts: in both length and non-reciprocal benefaction.

Wherever I have found myself, I have been blessed with Lukan-like non-reciprocal benefaction. My greatest expression of gratitude is to Stephen C. Barton, who, as my advisor, not only graciously agreed to work with me as a doctoral candidate in 1998 but showed great degrees of patience and insight during the writing of the dissertation. Indeed, without his unwavering direction, I assuredly would have gotten lost somewhere along the 'way'.

I am indebted to many other 'patrons' – teachers and students – from the time I spent at the Graduate Theological Union. The methodological approach of the study emerged from a Newhall Fellowship research grant on which I worked with Herman C. Waetjen, for whom I have great admiration as both scholar and human being. Special thanks is due to Joel B. Green, who, at the time of my studies at the Graduate Theological Union, served as advisor, friend, and mentor and continued to provide ongoing guidance. Numerous other professors and students, at Abilene Christian University, the Graduate Theological Union, and the University of Durham, too many to mention by name, helped make my studies a stimulating and enriching experience.

Parts of the dissertation were written with my daughter, Kendalia Teng Lei Spencer, either sitting on my lap in front of the computer or working at her table in my office – memories that are sure to last long after those of the actual research and writing processes. And mention of my parents, Eugene and Linda Spencer, who have shown Lukan-like benefaction to neighbors as long as I can remember, must be included. The beginnings of my journey would not have been possible without my uncle, Shane Sullivan, getting me started on the 'way' by introducing me to the gospel story.

I would like to offer my appreciation to Mark Mullins and Wesley

Weed, for their friendship as well as insightful critique and edits during the final phases of the manuscript. Special thanks is also due to my friends at the NAVAJO Company, especially graphic designer Robert Cerrato, who helped in designing figures 1 and 2.

My acknowledgments would not be complete without mention of my wife, Wan-Yun Lei, who has shown exceptional patience and sacrifice, often putting her professional and personal ambitions on hold, as I have slowly inched forward in my academic endeavors. I am forever grateful for her love, encouragement, and companionship.

ABBREVIATIONS

AB	Anchor Bible
BARev	*Biblical Archaeology Review*
BBR	*Bulletin for Biblical Research*
BETL	Bibliotheca ephemeridum theologicarum lovaniensium
Bib	*Biblica*
BibInt	*Biblical Interpretation: A Journal of Contemporary Approaches*
BTB	*Biblical Theology Bulletin*
BZNW	Beihefte zur ZNW
CBQ	*Catholic Biblical Quarterly*
CBR	*Currents in Biblical Research*
CurTM	*Currents in Theology and Mission*
ETL	*Ephemerides theologicae lovanienses*
ETR	*Etudes théologiques et religieuses*
ExpTim	*Expository Times*
FFNT	Foundations and Facets: New Testament
FTS	Frankfurter theologische Studien
HeyJ	*Heythrop Journal*
HTKNT	Herders theologischer Kommentar zum Neuen Testament
HTR	*Harvard Theological Review*
IBS	*Irish Biblical Studies*
Int	*Interpretation*
JAAR	*Journal of the American Academy of Religion*
JBL	*Journal of Biblical Literature*
JHC	*Journal of Historical Criticism*
JR	*Journal of Religion*
JSNT	*Journal for the Study of the New Testament*
JSNTSup	Journal for the Study of the New Testament, Supplement Series
JSOTSup	Journal for the Study of the Old Testament, Supplement Series
JTS	*Journal of Theological Studies*
LD	Lectio divina
Neot	*Neotestamentica*
NICNT	New International Commentary on the New Testament

NIGTC	The New International Greek New Testament Commentary
NovT	*Novum Testamentum*
NovTSup	Supplements to Novum Testamentum
NTAbh	Neutestamentliche Abhandlungen
NTS	*New Testament Studies*
OBT	Overtures to Biblical Theology
PTMS	Pittsburgh Theological Monograph Series
RB	*Revue biblique*
SANT	Studien zum Alten und Neuen Testaments
SBL	Society of Biblical Literature
SBLDS	SBL Dissertation Series
SBLMS	SBL Monograph Series
SBLRBS	SBL Resources for Biblical Study
SBLSP	SBL Seminar Papers
SBLSymS	SBL Symposium Series
SNTSMS	Society for New Testament Studies Monograph Series
SNTSU	Studien zum Neuen Testament und seiner Umwelt
SP	Sacra Pagina
TynBul	*Tyndale Bulletin*
WBC	Word Biblical Commentary
ZNW	*Zeitschrift für die neutestamentliche Wissenschaft*

PART ONE: CURRENT STATUS OF RESEARCH AND A
METHODOLOGICAL FOUNDATION

CHAPTER ONE: UNDERSTANDING TODAY'S SCHOLARLY LANDSCAPE: JESUS' FOUR LUKAN GALILEAN MINISTRY SPEECHES

Articles and monographs on literary and sociological aspects of the Gospels and the Book of Acts have proliferated in recent years. Discussion of narrative, rhetorical, sociological, and reader-response criticisms fills their pages, as each study attempts to unearth previously unknown facets of the narrative contained therein.[1] Recent investigative forays into Luke-Acts have brought forth some interesting insights into the narrative of the two volumes in areas such as plot, characterization, and rhetorical strategies[2] and how these, in turn, shape the construal of the narrative. Most inquiries stop at this point, however, manifesting the formalistic tendencies in their methodological approaches. Hence, the manner in which the narrative shapes the ideological location of ancient readers (or, more appropriately, listeners in the case of ancient narrative) remains outside the purview of most studies.[3]

Growing interest in Greco-Roman rhetoric has produced a number of articles and monographs that assess the invention, arrangement, and style of the speeches in the Gospels and Acts. Since Acts contains more speeches, and since its speeches conform more closely to the patterns delineated in the rhetorical handbooks than the Gospels,[4] it has received the bulk of scholarly

---

1. A good example is the compilation of articles from the journal, *Interpretation*, found in *Gospel Interpretation: Narrative-Critical & Social-Science Approaches*, ed. Jack D. Kingsbury (Harrisburg: Trinity Press International, 1997).

2. One of the first to attempt a thoroughgoing literary analysis of the narrative in Luke-Acts was Charles H. Talbert in *Literary Patterns, Theological Themes, and the Genre of Luke-Acts* (SBLMS, 20; Missoula: Scholars Press, 1974). He followed this initial exploration with *Reading Luke: A Literary and Theological Commentary on the Third Gospel* (New York: Crossroad, 1982). Robert C. Tannehill built upon Talbert's work in *The Narrative Unity of Luke-Acts: A Literary Interpretation*, 2 vols. (Philadelphia and Minneapolis: Fortress Press, 1986, 1990), which opened the floodgates for a stream of publications on a wide range of subjects related to plot, characterization, rhetoric, and narrative in Luke-Acts.

3. The most well-known critic of biblical scholars as 'formalistic' is Stephen D. Moore (*Literary Criticism and the Gospels: The Theoretical Challenge* [New Haven and London: Yale University Press, 1989], *passim*). Certain feminist scholars have made the plea for critical reading over the past two decades as well. For an overview of feminist biblical criticism, see the collection of essays in Elizabeth Schüssler Fiorenza (ed.), *Searching the Scriptures: A Feminist Introduction*, 2 vols. (New York: Crossroad, 1993, 1994).

4. The one exception would be the Gospel of Matthew, as its five speeches have been long recognized as integral components of the Gospel (see David R. Bauer, *The Structure of*

attention, with various inquiries to locate the rhetorical texture of each individual speech and, to a lesser extent, how they contribute to the plot and characterization of the narrative.[5] Nevertheless, though it contains a number of fairly lengthy speeches by Jesus and is considered – by most – as the predecessor to Acts,[6] Luke has garnered little attention in terms of the rhetorical argument and narrative impact of its speeches. My argument, however, is that the speeches in Luke are as integral as the ones in Acts and are, in certain ways, more important to the narrative discourse. Specifically, I propose that Jesus' four speeches from the Galilean ministry (4.14-30, 6.17-49, 7.24-35, 8.4-18) serve a vital function in shaping narrative trajectories and how authorial readers appropriate the narrative.[7]

Most scholars recognize that the narrative transition in Lk. 9.51 marks a major turning point in Luke-Acts, as Jesus turns his face towards Jerusalem, and the narrative audience and implied reader embark with him on the fateful journey to his death.[8] The initial stages of Jesus' ministry in 4.14–9.50 pave the way for the construal of later events. Within this context the four speeches of the Galilean ministry establish a foundation upon which the implied reader builds plot and characterization and sketches out narrative trajectories that result in the construction of thematic motifs (or

---

Matthew's Gospel: A Study in Literary Design [Bible and Literature Series, 15; Sheffield: Almond Press, 1988]), though only passing attention has been paid to their rhetorical invention, arrangement, and style in relationship to plot and characterization of the narrative. However cf. Greg Alan Camp, 'Woe to You Hypocrites! Law and Leaders in the Gospel of Matthew' (Ph.D. diss, University of Sheffield, 2003).

5. See, e.g., Marion L. Soards, *The Speeches in Acts: Their Content, Context, and Concerns* (Louisville: Westminster/John Knox Press, 1994); Ben Witherington III, *The Acts of the Apostles: A Socio-Rhetorical Commentary* (Grand Rapids/Cambridge: William B. Eerdmans Publishing Company, 1997) *passim*, esp. 39–50; Philip E. Satterthwaite, 'Acts Against the Background of Classical Rhetoric', in Bruce W. Winter (ed.), *The Book of Acts in Its Ancient Literary Setting, Volume 1: Ancient Literary Setting* (The Book of Acts in Its First Century Setting; Grand Rapids: William B. Eerdmans Publishing Company, 1993), pp. 337–80.

6. However cf. Mikeal Parsons and Richard Pervo, *Rethinking the Unity of Luke and Acts* (Minneapolis: Fortress Press, 1993).

7. Every text assumes readers who are cognizant of cultural codes, literary and rhetorical devices, other texts, and so on. This readerly entity best corresponds with what Peter J. Rabinowitz describes as the 'authorial audience' (in contrast to Umberto Eco's 'mock reader' and Wolfgang Iser's 'implied reader'). Rabinowitz contends that real, flesh-and-blood readers join the authorial audience by assuming the beliefs, engagements, commitments, and prejudices of the authorial audience ('Truth in Fiction: A Reexamination of Audiences', *Critical Inquiry* 4 [1977], pp. 121–41; idem, *Before Reading: Narrative Conventions and the Politics of Interpretation* [Ithaca and London: Cornell University Press, 1987], *passim*, esp. pp. 15–47; idem, 'Whirl Without End: Audience-Oriented Criticism', in G. Douglas Atkins and Laura Morrow (eds), *Contemporary Literary Theory* [Amherst: University of Massachusetts Press, 1989], pp. 81–100).

8. See Joel B. Green, *The Gospel of Luke* (NICNT; Grand Rapids: William B. Eerdmans Publishing Company, 1997), pp. 394–99, for an overview of Lk. 9.51 as a turning point in the plot of the Gospel.

topoi). These components of the narrative discourse are the matrix within which hermeneutical appropriation occurs.[9]

The present study is divided into four major sections. The first section, consisting of this chapter and the two that follow, surveys prior research, describes a comprehensive methodological approach, and provides an overview of ancient Greco-Roman rhetoric. The second section, consisting of a total of four chapters, investigates the rhetorical texture of the four Galilean ministry speeches in Luke from the standpoint of ancient Greco-Roman rhetoric. The third section examines the ramifications of this rhetorical analysis for how narrative trajectories from each of the four speeches guide the implied reader in the construction of theme, plot, characterization, and thematic motifs (or *topoi*). It also sketches out how the authorial audience – comprised of varying individuals and groups with different social, gender, religious, and political locations – appropriates meaning. The final section, a concluding chapter, offers reflections on the preceding analysis, proposes areas for future investigation, and points out how my analysis contributes to issues currently under discussion in Lukan studies.

I. *Previous Investigation of the Four Galilean Ministry Speeches*

The only scholar to approach the speeches of Jesus in the Galilean ministry from the perspective of how they fit – as a coherent whole – into the overall narrative discourse of Luke-Acts is Jeffrey A. Staley. Performing a close reading of the entire narrative in Lk. 4.14–9.62, Staley proposes that the three speeches in 4.14-30, 6.17-49, and 8.4-18 inscribe plot developments for the narrative units that follow them, and these units end where the next speech begins.[10] Each of the speeches demarcates a new phase in the ministry of Jesus, and the episodes that follow each reflect thematic motifs established in that earlier speech. One omission in Staley's analysis is that he does not recognize the third speech (7.24-35) as a speech at all, and, as a result, does not explain how it fits into narrative discourse of the section. In addition, his argument only goes 'halfway' towards answering whether an ancient reader would recognize his proposed tripartite 'geometric' structure. He is on the right track when he suggests that ancient Greco-Roman literature embodies repetitive 'stereotypical scenes and motifs' – and thus presupposes an audience that would easily identify his proposed divisions.

9. It is more accurate to speak of the audiences of the Gospels and Acts as *listeners* rather than *readers* because of the low literacy levels in antiquity and because reading was conducted as a presentation before an audience. For more on the oral/audible nature of first-century Greco-Roman society, see Paul J. Achtemeier, '*Omne verbum sonat*: The New Testament and the Oral Environment of Late Western Antiquity', *JBL* 109 (1990), pp. 3–27.

10. 'Narrative Structure (Self Stricture) in Luke 4:14-9:62: The United States of Luke's Story World', *Semeia* 72 (1995), pp. 173–213. For an earlier version of this paper, see '"With Power of the Spirit": Plotting the Program and Parallels of Luke 4:14-37 in Luke-Acts', in Kent H. Richards (ed.), 32 (SBLSP, 32 Atlanta: Scholars Press, 1993), pp. 281–302.

He fails, however, to bolster his position by noting parallels between the roles and functions of speeches in ancient narrative and those in Luke-Acts. And while Staley is able to correlate various narrative trajectories between the three speeches and the narrative sections between each, his focus on narrative texture does not consider rhetorical texture – an element I shall argue plays an important role in the construction of narrative discourse and even in the appropriation of it by the authorial audience.

A. *The First Galilean Speech (4.14-30)*

Of the four speeches in the Galilean ministry, the inaugural speech in 4.14-30 has received, by far, most of the scholarly attention. Like the first two chapters in the Gospel,[11] it is seen as programmatic in terms of plot and characterization. Because of its significant position in the sequence of the narrative – that is, the first public teaching appearance of Jesus, the presence of analeptic and proleptic references, and subsequent summaries of Jesus' ministry that allude back to the speech[12] – this first speech defines the basis for Jesus' ministry and message in Luke and that of the church in Acts.[13] When it comes to understanding the rhetorical texture of the speech within the context of ancient Greco-Roman rhetoric and its rhetorical orientation in relation to the larger narrative discourse, however, the scholarly literature contains only a smattering of references. Instead, scholars concentrate on the intertextuality of the speech – its direct and indirect references to LXX passages – and intratextuality within the overall narrative – its analeptic and proleptic connections. The present study builds upon these investigations by examining the rhetorical texture of the speech within the context of Greco-Roman rhetoric, and the ways in which its rhetorical argument affects the overarching narrative discourse of Luke-Acts as a two-volume work.

B. *The Second Galilean Speech (6.17-49)*

Most scholars consider the Sermon on the Mount in Mt. 5.3–7.27 as exhibiting greater redaction than the Sermon on the Plain in Lk. 6.17-49. Therefore, many view the parallel in Luke as a 'wayward stepchild', and so

11. Scholarly consensus has overturned the argument of Hans Conzelmann that chs 1–2 are peripheral to the rest of the narrative in Luke-Acts (*The Theology of Luke* [trans. G. Buswell; New York: Harper & Row, 1960], pp. 118–20, 172). It is now believed the narrative of Luke-Acts is firmly rooted in the discourse of chs 1–2. The first to challenge Conzelmann's conclusion was Paul S. Minear, 'Luke's Use of the Birth Stories', in Leander E. Keck and J. Louis Martyn (eds), *Studies in Luke-Acts* (Philadelphia: Fortress Press, 1966), pp. 111–30. More recently, see Joseph B. Tyson, 'The Birth Narratives and the Beginnings of Luke's Gospel', *Semeia* 52 (1991), pp. 103–20.

12. Green, *Gospel of Luke*, p. 207, provides a detailed list of reasons why Lk. 4.14–30 is of central importance to the overall narrative of Luke-Acts.

13. For a summary of scholarship, see Christopher J. Schreck, 'The Nazareth Pericope: Luke 4:16-30 in Recent Study', in Frans Neirynck (ed.), *L'Evangile de Luc – The Gospel of Luke* (BETL, 100; Leuven: Leuven University Press, 1989), pp. 399–471.

focus most of their attention on the Matthean 'firstborn'. In addition, few recognize the overall rhetorical relevance of Lk. 6.17-49 to the rest of Luke-Acts, and they only make passing note of intertextual connections and intratextual referents.[14]

Nevertheless, three scholars have attempted to describe the rhetorical species and taxis of this second speech, though agreement does not exist in regard to either. George A. Kennedy identifies 6.20-26 and 6.39-49 as epideictic in species: a celebration of the poor and actions to help the poor, and condemnation of the rich and inaction on their part to assist the poor. He places 6.27-38 in the vein of deliberative species, as an attempt to elicit a decision for future action.[15] He concludes that 6.17-49 'is not a very good speech', and that whatever persuasive power it holds is with the ethos – the authority – of Jesus.[16] Hans Dieter Betz, in an appendix to his study on the Matthean Sermon on the Mount, though he does not specify the species of the speech, identifies three rhetorical sections: an exordium (6.20-26), a main body consisting of three consecutive units (6.27-45), and a conclusio (6.46-49).[17] For the middle section, which he does not identify with a standard Greco-Roman speech structure, Betz posits a threefold division: discussion of the conduct of a disciple in relation to the outside world (vv. 27-38), rules concerning conduct within the community (vv. 39-42), and conduct towards oneself (vv. 43-45). His examination ends at this point, as he does not examine the speech in its larger narrative context. S. John Roth highlights the four references to Jesus' auditors in 6.20, 6.27, 6.39, and 7.1 as integral to understanding the species, taxis, and style of the speech, arguing that 6.20-26 is epideictic, 6.27-38 is deliberative, and 6.39-49 marks a return to epideictic.[18] Roth's discussion is embedded in a larger overview of characterization – that of the character type of the blind, lame, and poor (collectively, 'marginalized') – in which he contends the speech moves along the plotline established in 4.16-30, specifically providing the implied reader with information for better understanding the character group of the marginalized.

Yet Kennedy, Betz, and Roth all fail to consider the rhetorical impact of speeches in Greco-Roman antiquity – particularly those placed at the inaugural stages of narrative – on narrative discourse. In addition, while Roth does argue that 4.14-30[19] and 6.17-49 contribute to the construction of

---

14. For an overview, see Green, *Gospel of Luke*, pp. 260–81, and Tannehill, *Luke-Acts*, vol. 1, pp. 206–10.

15. *New Testament Interpretation Through Rhetorical Criticism* (Chapel Hill and London: University of North Carolina Press, 1984), pp. 63–67.

16. *Rhetorical Criticism*, p. 67.

17. *The Sermon on the Mount: A Commentary on the Sermon on the Mount, including the Sermon on the Plain (Matthew 5:3-7:27 and Luke 6:20-49)* (Hermenia; Minneapolis: Fortress Press, 1995), pp. 571–640.

18. *The Blind, the Lame, and the Poor: Character Types in Luke-Acts* (JSNTSup, 144; Sheffield: Sheffield Academic Press, 1997) pp. 164–71, esp. p. 165.

19. *Character Types*, pp. 152–64.

plot and characterization (though he does not consider the unit as a speech), he only considers the two units in the context of the character group of the marginalized. Despite their deficiencies, however, these prior efforts have laid the foundation for my inquiry, which attempts a thorough analysis of the speech in terms of rhetorical texture and how it contributes to narrative trajectories and the narrative discourse.

C. *The Third Galilean Speech (7.24-35)*

Investigation of the speech in 7.24-35 typically partitions the unit into several redactional segments, with little attention in regard to its relationship to the rest of the narrative in Luke-Acts. Its overall coherence as a rhetorical unit is thus largely overlooked.[20] Regardless, several have attempted to locate the narrative unit within the context of the larger narrative. For example, John A. Darr argues that it plays a pivotal role in the characterization of John the Baptist – establishing a means for comparing the ministry of John the Baptist to that of Jesus.[21] Roth subsequently pinpoints various connections between its rhetorical argument and characterization of the marginalized elsewhere in Luke-Acts. Specifically, by means of intertextual linkages with the LXX and intratextual connections with earlier episodes in the narrative, he posits that the implied author expands upon the characterization of Jesus as an agent of salvation to a broad canvas of character groups, including sinners – a group outside the parameters of those associated with the Messiah.[22] Roth goes on to comment on the rhetorical style of the narrative in the speech, one representative of brevity, rhyming, and rhythm that heightens the import of Jesus' words. Despite the analyses of these scholars, more remains to be said regarding the rhetorical texture of the speech. Moreover, aside from passing reference to the characterization of John the Baptist, such as that by Darr, analyses of the speech do not consider larger issues such as plot, characterization, and thematic motifs (topoi).

D. *The Fourth Galilean Speech (8.4-18)*

At present, the rhetorical texture of the speech in 8.4-18 has not been surveyed in terms of ancient rhetoric, and most interpretive endeavors neglect its connection to the larger narrative discourse, focusing instead on its coherence as an internal unit and its analeptic and proleptic echoes. In

---

20. An exception is Ron Cameron, '"What Have You Come Out to See?" Characterizations of John and Jesus in the Gospels', *Semeia* 49 (1990), pp. 35–69. See Chapter six for a discussion of his rhetorical analysis of Lk. 7.18–35.

21. *On Character Building: The Reader and the Rhetoric of Characterization in Luke-Acts* (Literary Currents in Biblical Interpretation; Louisville: Westminster/John Knox Press, 1992), pp. 75–78. Cf. also Walter Wink, 'Jesus' Reply to John: Matt 11.2-6/Luke 7.18-35', *Forum* 5 (1989), pp. 121–28.

22. *Character Types*, pp. 173–77.

contrast, much more attention has been paid to its parallel in Mk 4.1-34. Most notably, Mary Ann Tolbert argues that this passage from Mark is the primary key for 'unlocking' the construal of characterization throughout the Marcan narrative discourse, providing a grid from which individual characters and character groups are evaluated.[23] A corresponding evaluation of the Lukan successor has not been made. It is my contention that the speech, though its overall role and significance in the overall narrative discourse is slightly less than with its parallel in Mark, the speech serves a comparable function in Luke-Acts.

II. *Investigation of the Narrative Discourse of Luke-Acts*

In the field of biblical studies, the influence of New Criticism, in the form of composition and narrative criticism – which began with a smattering of publications in the 1970s and showed dramatic growth in the 1980s and early 1990s – and subsequently of reader-response criticism – beginning in the 1980s and extending into the 1990s – created a burgeoning interest in plot and characterization in biblical narrative.[24] Inquiries into the narrative of Luke-Acts date back to Charles H. Talbert and Norman Petersen in the 1970s. Talbert, under the descriptive term of 'architectural analysis', argues that Luke-Acts is connected by structural patterns, such as parallelism, chiastic arrangement, and other literary devices. He supplements his work with what he designates as 'genre criticism', comparing the structural patterns of Luke-Acts with characteristics of biographical accounts of philosophers from Greco-Roman antiquity.[25] Petersen approaches the narrative of Luke-Acts from the perspective of poetic function and, using the work of Roman Jakobson as his methodological basis, focuses on how linear elements and repetitive cycles form the narrative's plot.[26]

Beginning with Robert C. Tannehill, scholarship began to move towards a more encompassing methodology termed 'narrative criticism'.[27] These investigations examine the narrative as an interactive whole in terms of plotlines, gaps, redundancies, characterization, irony, narrative points of view, and more – terminology drawn from the literary criticism known as

---

23. *Sowing the Gospel: Mark's World in Literary-Historical Perspective* (Minneapolis: Fortress Press, 1989), pp. 148–64; idem, 'How the Gospel of Mark Builds Character', *Int* 47 (1993), pp. 347–57.

24. For an overview of literary investigation of the narrative in Luke-Acts, see F. Scott Spencer, 'Acts and Modern Literary Approaches', in *The Book of Acts in Its Ancient Literary Setting*, pp. 381–414.

25. *Literary Patterns*; idem, *Reading Luke*; idem, *Reading Acts: A Literary and Theological Commentary on the Book of Acts* (New York: Crossroad, 1984).

26. *Literary Criticism for New Testament Critics* (New Testament Series; Philadelphia: Fortress Press, 1978), pp. 81–92.

27. *Unity of Luke-Acts*, 2 vols.

'narratology'.[28] Subsequent permutations of narrative criticism delve into aspects of reader-response criticism, whereby the extratext – historical and social information of the milieu from which Luke-Acts derives – is melded with intratextual features from which the implied reader builds plot and characterization.[29] Recently, Lukan scholarship has seen a few attempts to read the narrative in terms of ideological discourse or deconstructionism, though such approaches have yet to make significant inroads into the mainstream of scholarly discussion.[30]

A. *Formalism Lays the Foundation: Narrative Criticism*

Tannehill is one of the first scholars to broach issues related to plot and characterization in Luke-Acts. He views characterization from the stand-point of narratology, focusing primarily on intratextual elements – such as narrative point of view, repetition, and type scenes – with sporadic mentions of intertextual referents.[31] Based on the premise that Jesus serves as the protagonist in the narrative, Tannehill's analysis delineates different character groups in terms of their relationship to Jesus. In particular, he notes a tendency throughout the narrative to introduce characters who will figure prominently later in the narrative as minor characters: Mary Magdalene, Barnabas, Stephen, Philip, Saul, and James all make their entrance into the story in this manner. Tannehill also sees a close relationship between plot and characterization, with characterization subservient to plot, helping to move the narrative along to closure. Hence, characterization is construed in terms of how characters respond to Jesus in Luke and subsequently his followers in Acts. Tannehill breaks Lukan characterization into categories that parallel several major character groups that appear throughout the narrative of Luke-Acts – the crowds or people, Jewish authorities, disciples, and followers.

In regard to the plot of Luke-Acts, Tannehill argues that it revolves around the purpose of God, a dynamic force adjusting to recurrent conflicts and the arrival of new opportunities. Lk. 4.16-30 is programmatic, and Tannehill believes it establishes the basis for Jesus' ministry and message

---

28.   E.g., Mieke Bal, *Narratology: Introduction to the Theory of Narrative* (trans. Christine van Boheemen; Toronto: University of Toronto Press, 1985).

29.   Much has been written in this area during the past decade and a half (see Todd Penner, 'Contextualizinng Acts', in Todd Penner and Caroline Vander Stichele (eds), *Contextualizing Acts: Lukan Narrative and Greco-Roman Discourse* [SBLSS, 20; Atlanta: SBL, 2003], pp. 1–22; Joseph B. Tyson, 'From History to Rhetoric and Back: Assessing New Trends in Acts Studies', in *Contextualizing Acts*, pp. 23–42; F. Scott Spencer, *Journeying Through Acts: A Literary-Cultural Reading* [Peabody, Mass.: Hendrickson Publishers, 2004], esp. pp. 13–32; idem, 'Literary Approaches', pp. 396–405, 410–14).

30.   The most prominent work in this area is that of Stephen D. Moore, *Mark and Luke in Poststructuralist Perspectives: Jesus Begins to Write* (New Haven: Yale University Press, 1992). Most recently, Jonathan Knight, *Luke's Gospel* (New Testament Readings; New York and London: Routledge Press, 1998), pp. 147–60.

31.   *Unity of Luke-Acts*, 2 vols.

and then that of the early church. Specifically, he identifies the tragic characterization of Israel as the overarching plotline, noting that the prior promises of salvation to Israel are left unfulfilled.[32] Regarding the characterization of the disciples, he argues that the faults of the disciples in Luke are overcome in the narrative of Acts by those who adhere to Jesus' message and ministry set forth in Luke. The crowds serve as a means for moving the narrative forward and are, for the most part, depicted in a positive light. As a result, the crowd's rejection of Jesus before Pilate at the end of Luke is a tragic mistake – one inspiring pity and fear at their tragic error. The final group, the marginal and oppressed, encompasses a potpourri of characters that appear and then disappear.

Tannehill's inquiry is helpful in that it establishes a foundation for further investigation into characterization in Luke-Acts. He recognizes the importance of Jesus' initial speech in Lk. 4.16-30 for the construction of plot and characterization throughout the rest of the narrative. Nevertheless, he makes only passing reference to the two speeches in Lk. 6.17-49 and 8.4-18 and no reference to the one in 7.24-35 in relation to the larger issues of the narrative discourse. Moreover, his discussion is primarily oriented towards intratextual features, with sparse references to intertextual connections and echoes and little mention of extratextual connotations.[33]

Almost the opposite is true of David Gowler's examination of the Pharisees.[34] He employs a methodological approach consisting of a mixture of literary features – ancient and modern – and cultural scenarios. Though he demonstrates a significant awareness of literary theory, he fails to formulate a methodological framework for his investigation, becoming lost in the details of cultural codes that occupy the bulk of his analysis. Perhaps the greatest weakness of his analysis is that it gives precedence to cultural codes at the expense of any framework to explain how the reader processes data in the narrative in a way that might determine construction of plot and characterization.[35] This leads him to conclude that the characterization of the Pharisees in Luke is largely negative, whereas their characterization in Acts is largely positive. This incongruity in characterization results from a lack of methodological coherence and consistency.

Mark Allan Powell argues that the religious leaders (Sadducees,

---

32. 'Israel in Luke-Acts', *JBL* 104 (1985), pp. 69–85; idem, 'Rejection by Jews and Turning to Gentiles: The Pattern of Paul's Mission in Acts', in Joseph B. Tyson (ed.), *Luke-Acts and the Jewish People: Eight Critical Perspectives* (Minneapolis: Augsberg Press, 1988), pp. 83–101.

33. This is Spencer's criticism, 'Literary Approaches', pp. 393–96, 413–14. In some of his recent publications, Tannehill takes greater account of intertextuality and extratextual referents (e.g., *Luke* [Abingdon New Testament Commentaries; Nashville: Abingdon Press, 1996], esp. pp. 27–31).

34. *Host, Enemy, and Friend: Portraits of the Pharisees in Luke and Acts* (Emory Studies in Early Christianity, 2; New York: Peter Lang, 1991). Cf. also his 'Characterization in Luke: A Socio-Narratological Approach', *BTB* 19 (1989), pp. 57–62.

35. For a criticism of Gowler's methodological approach, see Darr, *Character Building*, pp. 187 n. 4, 190–91 n. 24.

Pharisees, lawyers, scribes, et al.) form a distinct character group, with the similarities outweighing the differences between the individual characters.[36] He contends the character trait of self-righteousness pervades the characterization of the religious leaders throughout the narrative. He also suggests that the characterization of the religious leaders is not absolute, concluding that individual characters, such as Zechariah and Joseph of Arimathea, embody characteristics counter to representations elsewhere in the narrative. The strongest aspect of Powell's argument is his delineation of various character traits attributed to the religious leaders. His examination of the narrative, however, is restricted to the characterization of the Pharisees and stops at the end of Luke, failing to consider the effects of the narrative discourse of Acts on the characterization of the religious leaders.[37]

Jack Dean Kingsbury identifies two separate plotlines: one pertaining to the conflict between Jesus and the Jewish authorities and the other to the conflict between Jesus and the disciples.[38] The former plotline revolves around the question of authority – that is, whether Jesus and his followers or the Jewish authorities have the right to lead a reconstituted Israel. The latter plotline involves the inability of the disciples to recognize Jesus and embody his teaching in their actions. Kingsbury acknowledges that the conflict between Jesus and the Jewish authorities continues in Acts, with the Jewish authorities remaining as the antagonists and the followers of Jesus simply replacing him as the protagonist in the narrative.[39] The plotline representing the struggle between Jesus and his disciples comes to a completion at the end of Luke and ceases to exist in Acts. Kingsbury also performs a brief overview of the crowds and people as one character group, concluding that while they are well disposed toward Jesus, they lack the faith required to respond in an appropriate manner.[40] There are a number of minor characters in the narrative as well, which Kingsbury argues serve either as foils for other characters or as examples of negative or positive traits.[41] While informative, Kingsbury's analysis is exceedingly formalistic in its approach and exhibits weaknesses similar to those of Tannehill, exhibiting detailed attention to literary aspects while showing little concern for intertextual matters and no regard for extratextual connotations.

Combining historical criticism and narrative criticism – with the latter including intertextuality – in a series of articles and essays, Swiss scholar

36. 'The Religious Leaders in Luke: A Literary-Critical Study', *JBL* 109 (1990), pp. 93–110; idem, *What Is Narrative Criticism?* (Minneapolis: Fortress Press, 1990), pp. 61, 63, 65, 67.

37. Powell ('Religious Leaders in Luke', p. 108) seemingly believes the characterization of the religious leaders in Luke remains the same in the narrative of Acts.

38. *Conflict in Luke: Jesus, Authorities, Disciples* (Minneapolis: Fortress Press, 1991), *passim*; idem, 'The Plot of Luke's Story of Jesus', *Int* 48 (1994), pp. 369–78.

39. 'The Pharisees in Luke-Acts', in F. Van Segbroeck, et al. (eds), *The Four Gospels 1992*, vol. 2 (Leuven: Leuven University Press, 1992), pp. 1497–1511.

40. *Conflict in Luke*, pp. 28–31. Also, cf. Joseph B. Tyson, 'The Jewish Public in Luke-Acts', *NTS* 30 (1984), pp. 574–83.

41. *Conflict in Luke*, pp. 31–34.

Daniel Marguerat addresses various aspects of the narrative of Luke-Acts.[42] In regard to methodology, he concludes that Luke-Acts 'must be evaluated according to the *point of view of the historian* which controls the writing of the narrative, the *truth* that the author aims to communicate, and *the need for identity* to which the work of the historian responds'.[43] Through his analysis of the narrative discourse, he contends that the portrayal of the Jewish people and interactions within the Christian community on the topic of Jewish-Gentile relations reflect a post-70 CE readership wrestling with issues of identity and animosity between Jews and Gentiles. He further proposes that the presence of various descriptions with dual meanings – one for a Jewish readership and another for a Gentile readership – points in the direction of a mixed ethnic readership for Luke-Acts. Specifically, Marguerat proposes that the separation of the early church from the Jewish synagogue had already taken place for the readership, and this reality prompts much of the rhetoric typically identified as anti-Semitic in the narrative discourse. Regarding Acts, Marguerat contends that the narrative presents the ideal social setting as one in which Jews and Christians live in harmony with each other (citing the school of Tyrannus and the house of Paul in Rome as examples).

Central to Marguerat's investigation is his construal of the enigmatic ending in Acts 28.17-31, and his contention that narrative closure must be completed by the reader. Context for the conclusion is established by the preceding narrative scenes: Acts 27 presents Paul in heroic deliverance from evil powers (using the Greco-Roman sea voyage-type scene); Acts 28.1-16 attests a chain of events that demonstrate divine favor towards Paul; and Acts 28.17-28 is an inverted trial, one in which Paul (rather than his accusers) summons the defense. Marguerat concludes that the enigmatic ending of Acts – resembling a rhetorical device found in other Greco-Roman narrative designated as 'narrative suspension' – is an attempt by the implied author to reinterpret Paul's martyrdom by inverting the structure of the expected trial and moreover by depicting it as perpetuating his missionary work up to the day of the authorial audience.[44]

---

42. A compilation of Marguerat's essays and articles orginally appeared in French – *La première histoire du Christianisme (Actes des apôtres)* (LD, 180; Paris, Cerf, and Geneva: Labor et Fides, 1999). An English translation was published in 2002 – *The First Christian Historian: Writing the 'Acts of the Apostles'* (SNTSMS, 121; Cambridge: Cambridge University Press, 2002).

43. *Christian Historian*, pp. 6–7 (emphasis in original).

44. Originally presented in 'The End of Acts (28,16-31) and the Rhetoric of Silence', in Stanley E. Porter and Thomas H. Olbricht (eds), *Rhetoric and the New Testament: Essays from the 1992 Heidelberg Conference* (JSNTSup, 90; Sheffield: Sheffield Academic Press, 1993), pp. 74–89. A revision of this initial article was subsequently published as 'The Enigma of the Silent Closing of Acts (28:16-31)', in David P. Moessner (ed.), *Jesus and the Heritage of Israel: Luke's Narrative Claim upon Israel's Legacy* (Harrisburg, PA: Trinity Press International, 1999), pp. 284–304.

Of all the continental scholars, Marguerat presents the most thorough literary investigation of Luke-Acts.[45] His examination falls short, however, in that it does not probe beyond narrative texture, showing little or no interest in the presence of sociological systems and ways in which the narrative discourse is appropriated by readers. In addition, he does not consider the entirety of the narrative of Luke-Acts, but rather focuses on select sections, mostly contained within Acts.

B. *Early Attempts to Go Beyond Formalism: Sociological Explorations*

Phillip Esler, combining social-science criticism and redaction criticism, argues that social and political factors, rather than theological issues, shape the narrative discourse of Luke-Acts.[46] He reaches three general conclusions regarding the readership of Luke-Acts. First, he finds that Luke-Acts addresses a readership in need of legitimization in contradistinction to the Jewish synagogue and to wider Hellenistic society. The readership consists of Jewish and Gentile Christians, with the latter deriving from the ranks of Godfearers. The thematic motif of table fellowship serves to corroborate solidarity between Jews and Gentiles – both for the narrative audience and for the actual readership. Second, for Roman Christians, the narrative discourse provides reassurance that Christianity is not incompatible with allegiance to Rome. Finally, in regard to the motif of material benefaction, Esler suggests the readership of Luke-Acts was experiencing social stratification and economic disparity, a situation threatening their fellowship. For corroboration, he identifies the paraenetic emphasis in the narrative discourse surrounding the importance of material benefaction from the rich to the poor.

While widely acknowledged for demonstrating the importance of sociological interpretation for Lukan studies, Esler's methodological approach has been criticized on various grounds. Foremost is his assumption that each major theme of the narrative discourse represents issues confronting a hypothetical sectarian community; it requires a huge methodological leap to conclude that a narrative focus explicitly reveals a problem facing the readership. A second problem concerns Esler's tendency to portray early Christianity in terms of a purely defined sect-church typology, an approach that is too simplistic and delineates a static, formalistic sociological entity.[47]

---

45.   Also, cf. the literary approach of J.-N. Aletti, *Quand Luc raconte: Le récit comme théologie* (Lire la Bible, 115; Paris: Cerf, 1998).

46.   *Community and Gospel in Luke-Acts: The Social and Political Motivations of Lucan Theology* (SNTSMS, 57; Cambridge: Cambridge University Press, 1987).

47.   For this criticism, see Stephen C. Barton, 'Sociology and Theology', in I. Howard Marshall and David Peterson (eds), *Witness to the Gospel: The Theology of Acts* (Grand Rapids and Cambridge: William B. Eerdmans Publishing Company, 1998), p. 469. Also, cf. Barton's earlier examination of the sect-church taxonomy ('Early Christianity and the Sociology of the Sect', in Francis Watson (ed.), *The Open Text: New Directions for Biblical Studies?* [London: SCM Press, 1993], pp. 140–62).

Though much of continental scholarship remains focused on source and redactional issues, several scholars have pushed their investigative approaches beyond formalistic methodological parameters. In addition to Betz's in-depth rhetorical analysis of the Sermon on the Plain (Lk. 6.20-49),[48] several German scholars have explored elements of Greco-Roman rhetoric in relationship to the larger Lukan narrative discourse.[49] Scandanavian scholar Halvor Moxnes, like Esler, utilizes social-scientific criticism to identify various aspects of the social system of the Lukan implied readership.[50] He concludes that the question of material benefaction forms a central theme, with a call to enact economic redistribution in which the needy are cared for and the wealthy give without expectation of return. The Pharisees stand in contradistinction to this reciprocity ethic, in that they are characterized by the implied author as using material benefaction as a means of achieving higher social status. Moxnes further asserts that Luke-Acts addresses both a Jewish-Christian and a Hellenistic-Christian readership, one searching to resolve questions about the social interaction of the two ethnic groups.[51] Regarding the issue of women, he asserts that their depiction in the Lukan narrative – as independent of their husbands, with means of their own – serves as a prescription for women as disciples, even though the representation is based on male ideals. Moxnes concludes the meal settings for the Christian community serve as the means in Luke-Acts (and thus for the readership) for the break with traditional social systems related to benefaction, honor and shame, and ethnicity. Despite opening up new directions in the discussion over the narrative discourse of Luke-Acts, Moxnes' analysis is limited in that he primarily focuses on Luke and pays passing attention to the narrative of Acts. The scope of his investigation is also restricted, as he merely looks at one of a number of narrative threads (viz., material benefaction).[52]

48. *Sermon on the Mount*, pp. 571-640.

49. Specifically, Manfred Diefenbach, *Die Komposition des Lukasevangeliums unter Berücksichtigung antiker Rhetorikelemente* (FTS; Frankfurt am Main: Verlag Josef Knacht, 1993); Robert Morgenthaler, *Lukas und Quintilian: Rhetorik als Erzählkunst* (Zurich: Gotthelf-Verlag, 1993).

50. *The Economy of the Kingdom: Social Conflict and Economic Relations in Luke's Gospel* (OBT; Minneapolis: Fortress Press, 1988); idem, 'Social Relations and Economic Interaction in Luke's Gospel', in Peter Luomanen (ed.), *Luke-Acts: Scandinavian Perspectives* (Göttingen: Vandenhoeck & Ruprecht, 1991), pp. 58–75.

51. Specifically, see 'The Social Context of Luke's Community', *Int* 49 (1994), pp. 379–89.

52. David Wenham uses a similar methodology to reconstruct the historical and sociological context addressed by Luke-Acts ('The Purpose of Luke-Acts: Israel's Story in the Context of the Roman Empire', in Craig G. Bartholomew, Joel B. Green, and Anthony C. Thiselton (eds), *Reading Luke: Interpretation, Reflection, Formation* [Scripture and Hermeneutics Series, 6; Grand Rapids: Zondervan, 2005], pp. 79–103, esp. pp. 95–102). However cf. F. Scott Spencer, 'Preparing the Way of the Lord: Introducing and Interpreting Luke's Narrative: A Response to David Wenham', in *Reading Luke*, pp. 104–24.

C. *Moving Beyond Formalism: Integrating Reader-Response Criticism*

Examining the dynamic voice of narrator, William S. Kurz proposes that
Luke-Acts consists of four different narrators that operate in solidarity with
each other to produce a unified narrative.[53] Kurz's examination of Luke-
Acts is perhaps the most comprehensive in terms of plot in that he suggests
that three separate plotlines constitute the narrative – promise and
fulfillment, conflict, and the journey motif – all of which move the narrative
along to closure. In particular, he argues that the implied author uses Sir.
48.1-16 to establish all three plotlines via intertextual allusions, contending
the pattern of Israel rejecting both the prophet and his successor and hence
being evicted from its land – as described in Sir. 48.1-16 – parallels the
Lukan portrayal of the Jewish rejection of Jesus and his apostolic
successors.[54] In regard to characterization in Luke-Acts, Kurz proposes
that the implied author draws on Hellenistic rhetorical conventions, creating
characterization that provides both positive and negative examples of
behavior.[55] Kurz's approach to Luke-Acts is helpful in that it demonstrates
how the narrative discourse incorporates paradigmatic frameworks found
elsewhere in Greco-Roman narrative – in terms of characterization,
structure, and argument – and how the implied author uses these to shape
the rhetorical discourse of the narrative. Indeed, in many ways Kurz moves
the scholarly investigation of Luke-Acts further than his narrative and
reader-response contemporaries by going beyond narrative texture to the
ideological underpinnings of the implied author via identification of
intertextual connections – both LXX and extra-biblical. The weakness of
Kurz's approach lies in his demarcation of the implied reader as a one-
dimensional textual construct and his lack of attention to ideological issues
related to the narrative discourse. In contrast, recent research on the
audiences of Greco-Roman narrative (as I will discuss in greater detail in
Chapter two) calls for a much more complex, multidimensional understanding of the appropriation process.

In what is probably the most thoroughgoing study of characterization in
Luke-Acts (and perhaps all the New Testament), John A. Darr proposes
that characterization is a construction of the authorial audience, which

---

53. *Reading Luke-Acts: Dynamics of Biblical Narrative* (Louisville: Westminster/John
Knox, 1993); also, cf. 'Narrative Approaches to Luke-Acts', *Bib* 68 (1987), pp. 195–220.
Kurz identifies four narrators in Luke-Acts: (1) *histor*, 'I' in the prologue of Luke; (2) an
unobtrusive, omniscient narrator speaking in the third person through most of Luke-Acts;
(3) a marginal observant and participant, 'we' narrator appearing in sections of Acts after
16.10; and (4) character voices of stories within stories such as the call conversion narratives
of Paul in Acts 22 and 26.
54. 'Intertextual Use of Sir. 48.1-16 in Plotting Luke-Acts', in Craig A. Evans and W.
Richard Stegner (eds), *The Gospels and Scriptures of Israel* (JSNTSup, 104; Sheffield:
Sheffield Academic Press, 1994), pp. 308–24.
55. 'Narrative Models for Imitation in Luke-Acts', in David L. Balch, Everett Ferguson,
and Wayne A. Meeks (eds), *Greeks, Romans, and Christians* (Festschrift Abraham J.
Malherbe; Minneapolis: Fortress Press, 1990), pp. 171–89.

builds characterization by a sequential compilation of intratextual referents, coupled with intertextual allusions and extratextual details.[56] He concludes evaluation of characters in Luke-Acts is predicated on perception and response: certain characters understand Jesus' message or that of his followers and act upon that understanding, while other characters – though they carefully observe the words of Jesus or his followers – remain unperceptive and, as a result, fail to act. Darr focuses on three different character groups: John the Baptist, the paradigmatic model for response to Jesus; the Pharisees, the paradigmatic prototype of everything the implied author rejects; and King Herod, the embodiment of tyrants – biblical and extra-biblical.[57] Darr's investigation of the narrative discourse is the most complete at this point, incorporating intratextual data, intertextual echoes, and extratextual codes into its construction of characterization. His analysis falls short in three areas: (1) it only considers three different character groups; (2) its methodological basis – seeing the reading process, as determined by anticipation – is flawed (i.e., he does not consider retrospection a valid part of the reading process);[58] and (3) it does not move beyond formalism to account for the ideological effects of characterization on the authorial audience.[59]

Roth draws upon Darr's methodological approach, arguing that intratextual, intertextual, and extratextual information assists the authorial audience in constructing the character group of the blind, lame, and poor.[60] He suggests that Jesus' inaugural speech in Lk. 4.14-30 establishes the foundation and that the LXX supplies the intertextual repertoire. Through repetition in the narrative, the authorial audience builds a stereotype for a character group that typically remains anonymous, powerless, and vulnerable. This character group is to be distinguished from the sinners. Specifically, Roth contends that the authorial audience would be predisposed to a sympathetic reaction to a character group embodying characteristics of the blind, lame, and poor, but antipathetic towards sinners.

---

56. *Character Building*, passim.

57. On the latter character type, see John A. Darr, *Herod the Fox: Audience Criticism and Lukan Characterization* (JSNTSup, 163; Sheffield: Sheffield Academic Press, 1998), *passim*.

58. Green criticizes Darr's categorical reading of the Pharisees, arguing that he fails to account for the possibility that the reading process is both anticipatory and retrospective, thus providing the means for reevaluation of character groups (*Gospel of Luke*, pp. 301–02, 307, 537; idem, *The Theology of the Gospel of Luke* [New Testament Theology; Cambridge: Cambridge University Press, 1995], pp. 72–75). Darr responds with the contention that anticipatory effects of the reading process take precedence over those of retrospection. Hence, subsequent characterization of the Pharisees is colored by that which comes before in the narrative ('Irenic or Ironic? Another Look at Gamaliel before the Sanhedrin [Acts 5:33-42]', in Richard P. Thompson and Thomas E. Phillips (eds), *Literary Studies in Luke-Acts* [Festschrift Joseph B. Tyson; Macon: Mercer University Press, 1998], p. 133 n. 33).

59. Darr is one of the first biblical scholars to adopt the heuristic construct of the 'authorial audience' in contrast to that of the 'implied reader', though his classification is essentially semantic, in that his 'reader' remains a one-dimensional construct.

60. *Character Types*, passim.

Jesus' programmatic ministry to the former character group corroborates the implied author's equation of Jesus as the Messiah. The character group disappears in Acts because its existence is no longer necessary. However, connecting threads between Luke and Acts remain, as Jesus' ministry to the character group of the sinners is paralleled in the ministry of the apostles. Roth pinpoints a number of very interesting insights regarding the narrative discourse in relationship to characterization. The primary weakness of his analysis springs from his construct of a one-dimensional audience and his lack of interest in examining potential ways of appropriation by the authorial reader. In addition, *pace* Roth, the implied author's interest in the stereotypical character group ('the marginalized') does not fall completely from purview in the narrative of Acts (cf. 2.41-47; 4.32–5.11; 6.1-7; 9.36-43; 11.27-30).

D. *Other Narrative, Sociological, and Reader-Response Investigations*

Various studies on the characterization of God, Peter, Paul, and even the Holy Spirit in Luke-Acts have appeared over the past decade. Two other significant areas of examination revolve around identification of narrative redundancies and type scenes and their overarching impact on the narrative discourse and intertextual connections with extra-biblical texts. These queries largely parallel the above studies in their methodological approaches by considering intratextual, extratextual, and intertextual features. A survey of some of the more influential of these studies follows.

1. *Characterization*

Robert L. Brawley and William H. Shepherd, Jr. both attempt to construct characterization for the divine. Despite detailed narrative analysis, both of these attempts are largely unsuccessful. Brawley traces the characterization of God throughout the narrative of Luke-Acts, but concludes the character of God is elusive and difficult to fix from the narrative.[61] Shepherd argues from a framework similar to that of Brawley, except that – rather than construing the Holy Spirit as embodiment of God in the earthly realm, he proposes that the Holy Spirit and God are two separate characters, with the Holy Spirit as the on-stage representative of God.[62] However, as Brawley argues, Shepherd's proposed dichotomy between God and the Holy Spirit is

---

61. *Centering on God: Method and Message in Luke-Acts* (Literary Currents in Biblical Interpretation; Louisville: Westminster/John Knox Press, 1990), pp. 111–24. Also, see his 'The God of Promises and the News in Luke-Acts', in *Literary Studies in Luke-Acts*, pp. 279–96.

62. *The Narrative Function of the Holy Spirit as a Character in Luke-Acts* (SBLDS, 147; Atlanta: Scholars Press, 1994). Cf. also Ju Hur, *A Dynamic Reading of the Holy Spirit in Luke-Acts* (JSNTSup, 211; Sheffield: Sheffield Academic Press, 2001).

questionable.[63] The most compelling investigation of the characterization of God and the Holy Spirit is that of François Bovon, who sees no boundary between God and the Holy Spirit, contending the implied author constructs a new aspect of the characterization of God in Luke-Acts, one in which God becomes a God of all – ceasing to be a God of direct descendants of Israel only.[64] The intervention of God in the narrative does not obviate human responsibility: divine providence does not control human actions, but rather God provides direction through human mediations – which, through prayer, are open to divine direction.[65]

Attempts to construct characterization of Peter and Paul are more persuasive than those of God. Characterization of Peter in Luke-Acts has received less attention than that in Mark, Matthew, and even John. In Luke-Acts, the tragic downfall of Peter is reversed in Acts, where he ascends to an exemplary status. This is made possible by means of the resurrection, which enables the disciples to gain a full understanding of Jesus' message and subsequently act upon it. Peter's words and deeds in Acts parallel those of Jesus in Luke, thereby leading the reader to the conclusion that Jesus' ministry continues in the form of early church leaders such as Peter.[66] Characterization of Paul has been the subject of several monographs and articles over the past several years. John C. Lentz draws on rhetorical categories to construct a characterization of Paul, concluding that Paul garners respect when viewed through the lens of classical virtues of Greco-Roman antiquity.[67] Jerome H. Neyrey comes to a similar conclusion through a reading of Paul's characterization from the standpoint of social status.[68]

In a recent examination of characterization of Jewish believers in the Book of Acts, Richard P. Thompson suggests the narrative discourse of Acts prompts readers to compare the depiction of the Jewish-Christian

---

63. 'God of Promises', 280–81.

64. 'The God of Luke', in *New Testament Traditions and Apocryphal Narratives* (PTMS, 36; Allison Park, Pa.: Pickwick, 1995), pp. 67–80.

65. 'The Importance of Mediations in Luke's Theological Plan', in *New Testament Traditions*, pp. 51–66. For a similar approach to the characterization of God and the Holy Spirit, cf. Marguerat, *Christian Historian*, pp. 85–108.

66. See, e.g., David P. Moessner, '"The Christ must suffer": New Light on the Jesus-Peter, Stephen, Paul Parallels in Luke-Acts', *NovT* 28 (1986), pp. 220–56; Robert W. Wall, 'Successors to the "Twelve" according to Acts 12.1-17', *CBQ* 53 (1991), pp. 628–43.

67. *Luke's Portrait of Paul* (Cambridge: Cambridge University Press, 1993), *passim*.

68. 'Luke's Social Location of Paul: Cultural Anthropology and the Status of Paul in Acts', in Ben Witherington III (ed.), *History, Literature and Society in the Book of Acts*, (Cambridge: Cambridge University Press, 1999) pp. 251–79. Also, cf. the argument of Marie-Eloise Rosenblatt that the characterization of Paul is twofold: the heroic apostle to the Gentiles, as the equal of Peter (based on the parallels between the ministries of Peter and Paul), and, on the other hand, the archetypal representative for beleaguered missionary teachers (*Paul the Accused: His Portrait in the Acts of the Apostles* [Collegeville: Liturgical Press, 1995]).

believers to that of the Jewish religious leaders.[69] He finds Jewish-Christian believers are shown as faithful to the Jewish law and religious practices; those among whom the presence of God is found, united in the face of controversy, and forthright in helping those who are in material and/or spiritual need. The portrayal of the Jewish religious leaders is in direct contrast: they are beyond the presence of God, united together in jealousy and opposition to Jewish-Christian believers, and a divisive group intent on dividing the Jewish people. Thompson lays the groundwork for his investigation with a thorough methodological discussion that spans the spectrum from ancient rhetoric to modern reading theories. The first problem with his analysis is his limited focus – characterization of the Christian community in Acts – while the second involves the formalistic nature of his study, as he only touches on the plausible effects of the narrative upon the recipients of Luke-Acts and largely ignores the ways in which such effects might impact the appropriation by the authorial audience (to which Thompson refers as the 'implied reader').

2. Investigation of Narrative Redundancies and Intertextuality
Interest in understanding the various redundancies scattered throughout the narrative of Luke-Acts dates back to the groundbreaking work of Talbert. His inquiry not only addresses intertextual parallels but intratextual parallels, with the former focusing on structural and thematic correspondence between the ministries of Elijah and Elisha, on the one hand, and that of Jesus and, on the other, narrative patterns that extend from Jesus, to Peter, to Paul.[70] This concern for repetition extends to structural redundancies in the narrative – an aspect that has received increased attention over the past decade. The greatest attention has been paid to the two versions of the 'Conversion of Cornelius' in Acts 10–11[71] and the three versions of 'Saul's Conversion' in Acts 9, 22, and 26.[72] Variants in the

69. 'Christian Community and Characterization in the Book of Acts: A Literary Study of the Lukan Concept of the Church' (Ph.D diss., Southern Methodist University, 1996); idem, 'Believers and Religious Leaders in Jerusalem: Contrasting Portraits of Jews in Acts 1-7', in *Literary Studies in Luke-Acts*, 327–44.

70. *Literary Patterns, passim*. Also, see Susan Marie Praeder, 'Jesus-Paul, Peter-Paul, and Jesus-Peter Parallelisms in Luke-Acts: A History of Reader Response', in Kent H. Richards (ed.), (SBLSP, 23 Chico, California: Scholars Press, 1984), pp. 23–39.

71. Ronald D. Witherup, 'Cornelius Over and Over Again: "Functional Redundancy" in the Acts of the Apostles', *JSNT* 49 (1993), pp. 45–66; William S. Kurz, 'Effects of Variant Narrators in Acts 10-11', *NTS* 43 (1997), pp. 570–86.

72. Ronald D. Witherup, 'Functional Redundancy in the Acts of the Apostles', *JSNT* 48 (1992), pp. 67–86; Daniel Marguerat, 'Saul's Conversion (Acts 9-22-26) and the Multiplication of Narrative in Acts', in Christopher Tuckett (ed.), *Luke's Literary Achievement* (JSNTSup, 116; Sheffield: Sheffield Academic Press, 1995), pp. 127–55. Also, see David Lertis Matson, *Household Conversion Narratives in Acts: Pattern and Interpretation* (JSNTSup, 123; Sheffield: Sheffield Academic Press, 1996), who contends that Jesus' speech to the seventy disciples in Lk. 10.1-24 establishes a household conversion pattern that is replicated throughout Acts.

repetitive scenes serve different rhetorical purposes for the implied author in shaping the narrative discourse. While these investigations prove quite valuable in understanding the narrative discourse of Luke-Acts better, they fall short in that they fail to go beyond the boundaries of author and text to that of reader.

There is increasing recognition that Luke-Acts – particularly the narrative of Acts – contains not only numerous intertextual connections with and echoes of the LXX[73] but also various intertextual connections with extra-biblical narrative. While most of the initial explorations of this issue concentrate on Acts 27.1–28.10,[74] a number expand the investigation to a much broader expanse of texts. These studies suggest a greater degree of potential meanings through the presence of this expanded intertextuality.[75] In particular, the appropriation of these intertextual connections – both in the congruence and incongruence of the texts – produces new meaning encompassing aspects of the narrative such as plot, characterization, and thematic motifs.

E. *Embracing an Integrated Hermeneutic: Ideological Systems and Location*

Approaches to the narrative discourse through narrative and reader-response criticisms have laid the foundation for recent investigations that aim to move beyond the textual surface to deeper nuances ranging from ideological systems embraced or repudiated by the implied author to ways in which the narrative discourse might shape the social, gender, and political systems of the plausible recipients of the two-volume work. One of the first to move the discussion in this direction is Joseph B. Tyson. Though his earlier work focuses on narrative nuances of Luke-Acts – and is best known for its analysis of the Jewish people[76] – his later work aims to disclose the ideological location of the implied reader and the potential ways in which the implied reader might construe the narrative discourse.[77] Tyson

---

73. The amount of research on LXX intertextuality in Luke-Acts is significant. For an overview, see Kenneth Duncan Litwak, *Echoes of Scripture in Luke-Acts: Telling the History of God's People Intertextually* (JSNTSup, 282; London: T&T Clark, 2005).

74. See, e.g., Susan Marie Praeder, 'Acts 27,1-28.16: Sea Voyages in Ancient Literature and the Theology of Luke-Acts', *CBQ* 46 (1984), pp. 683–706.

75. Perhaps the most notable is the work of Dennis R. MacDonald, 'Luke's Emulation of Homer: Acts 12:1-17 and Illiad 24', *Forum* 3 (2000), pp. 197–205; idem, 'The Shipwrecks of Odysseus and Paul', *NTS* 45 (1999), pp. 88–107; idem, 'Luke's Eutychus and Homer's Elphenor: Acts 20:7-12 and Odyssey 10-12', *JHC* 1 (1994), pp. 4–24.

76. See, e.g., 'Jewish Public', pp. 574–83.

77. Specifically, *Images of Judaism in Luke-Acts* (Columbia: University of South Carolina Press, 1992) esp. pp. 19–41; idem, 'Jews and Judaism in Luke-Acts: Reading as a Godfearer', *NTS* 41 (1995), pp. 19–38. Cf. Vernon K. Robbins ('The Social Location of the Implied Author of Luke-Acts', in Jerome H. Neyrey (ed.), *The Social World of Luke-Acts: Models for Interpretation* [Peabody, Mass.: Hendrickson Publishers, 1991], pp. 305–32), who employs a similar methodological approach in delineating the 'social location' of the implied author, though he does not restrict the identification of the implied reader to Godfearers.

concludes, based on seven observations about the implied reader that he gleans from a close reading of the Lukan text, that the implied reader most closely coincides with the personages designated as Godfearers. He specifically argues that the various Godfearers in the narrative stand as 'intratextual representations of the implied reader' in Luke-Acts.[78] The primary effect of the narrative discourse, which Tyson sees as anti-Semitic based on his understanding of the characterization of the Jewish people, is to wean the implied reader away from any tendencies to associate with Jews and to convince the implied reader that Christianity, rather than Judaism, embodies the values that initially led the implied reader to embrace Judaism. While notable for its attempt to move the discussion of Luke-Acts beyond formalism, Tyson's argument falls short in regard to its methodological underpinnings. First, a predisposition by the implied author to favor Godfearers through positive characterization and an extratextual repertoire that coincides with the ideological location of an implied reader are inadequate evidence to deem the implied reader as a Godfearer. Second, as will be discussed in greater detail in Chapter two, the processes associated with the publication of Greco-Roman narratives, which resulted in a broad distribution through literary patronage, militates against the identification of a one-dimensional, analogous group of recipients.

Günter Wasserberg, building upon the work of Kingsbury, Tannehill, and Tyson on the ethnicity of the readership and the ideological nature of the narrative discourse, combines synchronic and diachronic concerns.[79] Unlike most German scholarship, which concentrates on source, redactional, and historical elements,[80] Wasserberg focuses on narrative and readerly aspects. He argues these help reveal ideological systems and the ways in which they shape the narrative discourse of Luke-Acts. As Luke-Acts shows significant interest in portraying certain Jews in a positive light,[81] Wasserberg contends that Tyson's designation of the implied reader ('impliziten Leserkreise') as a

---

78. *Images of Judaism*, p. 37.

79. *Aus Israels Mitte – Heil für die Welt: Eine narrativ-exegetische Studie zur Theologie des Lukas* (BZNW, 92; Berlin and New York: Walter de Gruyter, 1998).

80. See, e.g., Heinz Schürmann, *Das Lukasevangelium*, 2 vols. (HTKNT; Freiburg: Herder, 3rd edn, 1994).

81. See Wasserberg's comments (*Israels Mitte*, pp. 64–65):
    Die von Lukas intendierte Adressatenschaft kann, wie wir oben gesehen haben, nicht allein auf den Kreis 'Gott fürchtender' ἔθνη beschränkt werden. Zwar ist durchaus ein erzählerisches Gefälle in Lk-Act von Juden hin zu ἔθνη, zumal solchen, die sich explizit gottesfürchtig verhalten, zu beobachten, aber daraus zu folgern, in letzteren *allein* den von Lukas intendierten Leserkreis auszumachen, übersieht die positive Zeichnung auch *judenchristlicher* (Petrus; Paulus) und selbst *jüdischer* (z.B. Zacharias Lk 1; Siemon Lk 2) Frömmigkeit. Sind solche judenchristlichen Frömmigkeitsprofile wie das der Urgemeinde inklusive Pauli lediglich eine – nunmehr obsolete – Vorstufe heidenchristlicher Frömmigkeit? Ein narrativ-exegetisches Herangehen, das dem gesamten Erzählduktus Rechnig tragen will, muß *alle* möglichen impliziten Leserkreise in Erwägung ziehen, folglich auch Judenchristen.

Godfearer is too exclusive and does not accurately reflect the narrative discourse when it is considered in its entirety. Consequently, he suggests that the intended readership ('intendierten Leserkreis') encompasses a much broader matrix – both Gentiles and Jews already instructed in the Christian message.

Wasserberg goes on to propose that the narrative of Acts must account for the interpretive models set forth in Luke and the various redundancies and parallels that exist between the two works. He identifies 'salvation of God to all peoples' as the primary theological theme of Luke-Acts – initially set forth by Simeon (Lk. 2.29-35) and then elaborated upon throughout the narrative. In regard to the depiction of the Jewish people, Wasserberg asserts that it is inaccurate to categorize the narrative of Luke-Acts as anti-Semitic, pointing out that the representation of the Pharisees is ambivalent, with the Pharisees absent from the Jewish groups present at Jesus' trial and crucifixion (Lk. 22–23) and even coming to the defense of the Christian movement at various junctures (Acts 5.33-39; 22.3; 23.1-10).[82] In addition, he argues the close of Acts (28.17-31) is open-ended, with 'salvation of God' available to all people who embrace the Christian message – both Jew and Gentile.[83]

Wasserberg's examination of Luke-Acts is a valuable contribution in that it pushes the discussion of implied reader and the 'hypothetical/intended' readership beyond the formalistic parameters of the text. The most glaring weakness of his investigation is his failure to delimit a clear methodological approach. While he includes a section on methodology, he does not build the basis for his methodological inquiry on primary literature but rather on secondary sources. As such, he merely reviews the interpretive approaches of Kingsbury, Tannehill, and Tyson – specifically in regard to narrative elements such as plot, characterization, and implied reader – and posits the need for a methodological approach that includes both synchronic and diachronic concerns.[84] Similarly, his methodological foundation is deficient in that issues central to a narrative investigation with the implied reader at the forefront, such as repetition (ranging from verbal to type scenes), intertextuality, extratextual repertoire, point of view, and so forth, are absent. A third weakness is his lack of interest in exploring sociological aspects of the narrative – specifically how these might affect appropriation of the narrative by the implied reader. Finally, as Wasserberg's analysis is limited to the narrative topic of 'salvation of God to all peoples' and its relationship to the question of whether the narrative discourse is anti-Semitic, his work does not encompass the narrative of Luke-Acts in its entirety.

One of the most comprehensive methodological approaches to Luke-Acts is that of Joel B. Green, who integrates hermeneutical frameworks from new

---

82. *Israels Mitte*, pp. 179–90.
83. *Israels Mitte*, pp. 71–115, 352–54.
84. *Israels Mitte*, pp. 32–35.

historicism[85] – from which he seeks to gain deeper insights into the ideological nuances of the narrative discourse and its meaning-making potentials – with narrative and reader-response criticisms. Corresponding with what he designates 'discourse analysis' (taken from the field of linguistics), he breaks his investigative approach into three areas: (1) co-text – the string of linguistic data within which the text is set (viz., intratextuality); (2) intertext – the location of the text within the larger linguistic frame of reference on which it consciously or unconsciously draws for meaning (viz., intertextuality); and (3) context – the socio-historical realities to which the text gives witness as well as that of the narrative itself (viz., extratextuality).[86] Integral to Green's approach is his understanding of the reading process as both prospective and retrospective – the reader projects expectations while concurrently re-examining prior events. Also important to Green's hermeneutical framework is a recognition that the narrative discourse feeds theological discovery, which, in the case of Luke-Acts, Green posits as 'Salvation to the Ends of the Earth' as the overarching theme,[87] supplemented with various theological motifs such as non-reciprocal benefaction, discipleship, poverty and wealth, and so forth.[88] Green criticizes most interpretations of the textual fabric of Luke-Acts for erroneously assuming that authors and their texts are wholly determined by their socio-historical contexts. Instead, he contends the narrative discourse exhibits both conformity and non-conformity with its socio-historical location.[89] Through an integrated hermeneutic that embraces an assortment of methodologies, Green contributes notable advances to the study of Luke-Acts; his approach, however, has two weaknesses. The first is terminological: since discourse analysis has not gained widespread acceptance as a *modus operandi* in biblical studies, Green's threefold methodological framework adopted from discourse analysis – co-text, intertext, and context – could be expressed just as easily using the taxonomies of intratextuality, intertextuality, and extratextuality, concepts with more widespread acceptance both inside and outside the field of biblical studies. The second weakness is the absence of an in-depth examination of socio-historical readerly concerns focused on a multivalent authorial audience: Green looks at the potential meaning-making dimensions of the narrative discourse largely from that of a one-dimensional construct (the 'model reader' as

85. For an overview, see, e.g., Paul Hamilton, *Historicism* (London and New York: Routledge, 1996), pp. 150–204.

86. *Gospel of Luke*, pp. 11–20. For an in-depth overview of 'discourse analysis', see his 'Discourse Analysis and New Testament Interpretation', in Joel B. Green (ed.), *Hearing the New Testament: Strategies for Interpretation* (Grand Rapids, Mich.: William B. Eerdmans Publishing Company, 1995), pp. 175–96.

87. '"Salvation to the End of the Earth" (Acts 13:47): God as Saviour in the Acts of the Apostles', in *Witness to the Gospel*, pp. 83–106.

88. *Theology of the Gospel, passim.*

89. See, e.g., 'The Social Status of Mary in Luke 1,5-2,52: A Plea for Methodological Integration', *Bib* 73 (1992), pp. 457–72.

defined by Umberto Eco) rather from that of an audience encompassing different economic, religious, gender, and other cultural frameworks.

Inquiries into (and debate over) the generic conventions of Luke-Acts have spurred a spate of studies on generic parallels between Luke-Acts and Greco-Roman narrative, ranging from historiography, to novels, to epics, to biographies. Correspondence between the rhetorical argument of Luke-Acts and Greco-Roman narrative provides a framework for uncovering rhetorical strategies and ideological systems of author and reader. Perhaps the scholar who has pursued this investigation the furthest is Loveday C. A. Alexander.[90] She argues that the prologues of Luke and Acts – which coincide most closely with scientific technical treatises situated on the periphery of historiography – play a crucial role in prompting the reader to place the text within a socio-historical setting that demarcates rhetorical strategies and ideological parameters for the initial readers. The focus and direction of the rhetorical argument of the narrative discourse also feed into her construction of the apologetic aims of the narrative as well as the ideological location of Theophilus and the earliest recipients of Luke-Acts. She concludes Luke-Acts is directed towards the Diaspora Jewish community – perhaps the one in Rome – with the apologetic aim of persuading its various constituents to afford the Christian movement a fair hearing.[91]

A key part of Alexander's argument identifying the Jewish community as the target audience of Luke-Acts centers on the enigmatic ending of Acts (28.17-31). Alexander, along with several other scholars over the past decade, highlights the open-ended conclusion as a hermeneutical key to the narrative, a rhetorical device that prompts the reader to analeptically reevaluate the preceding discourse.[92] She also contends that enigmatic endings are a common literary device in Greco-Roman narrative, a rhetorical tool that prods the reader to complete the story in conjunction with the narrative discourse; moreover, she notes a number of rhetorical threads in the closing scene that incite intratextual connections with earlier scenes and activities – ranging from linkages to Lk. 3–4 (particularly 4.16-30), to the citation of Isa. 6.9-10, to the theme of salvation. Alexander carries this argument a step further by suggesting the closing scene serves as a 'framing' device that guides the reader to reevaluate earlier narrative

90. Starting with *The Preface to Luke's Gospel: Literary Convention and Social Context in Luke 1.1-4 and Acts 1.1* (SNTSMS, 78; Cambridge: Cambridge University Press, 1993), *passim*. Also, 'Formal Elements and Genre: Which Greco-Roman Prologues Most Closely Parallel the Lukan Prologues?' *Heritage of Israel*, pp. 9–26.

91. 'The Acts of the Apostles as an Apologetic Text', in Mark Edwards, et al. (eds), *Apologetics in the Roman Empire: Pagans, Jews, and Christians* (Oxford: Oxford University Press, 2000), pp. 15–44.

92. See, especially, Loveday C. A. Alexander, 'Reading Luke-Acts From Back to Front', in J. Verheydon (ed.), *The Unity of Luke-Acts* (BETL, 112; Leuven: Leuven University Press, 1999), pp. 419–46. Also, cf. Marguerat, 'End of Acts (28,16-31)', pp. 74–89; idem, 'Silent Closing', pp. 284–304; William F. Bosend, II, 'The means of absent ends', in *History, Literature and Society*, pp. 348–62; Wasserberg, *Israels Mitte*, pp. 71–115, 352–54.

discourse and brings the narrative world closer to that of the reader.[93] This recent investigation by Alexander into the retrospective activity that the ending of Acts induces will play an important role in my analysis in Chapter eight, which highlights ways in which the narrative discourse – as established by the four speeches of Jesus in the Galilean ministry – brings about prospective and retrospective appropriation.

Despite general acceptance of Alexander's views, her separation of Luke-Acts from the genre of ancient historiography and her designation of the scientific treatise as the generic tradition behind the two-volume work exists have been challenged. First, similarities between Luke-Acts and the scientific treatise start and end with the prologues; apart from the prologues, Luke and Acts primarily consist of narrative discourse, whereas the scientific treatise traditions consist of expository and descriptive discourse.[94] Second, in contrast to earlier claims of marked discrepancies between the Lukan prologue (1.1-4) and those found in ancient historiography, several scholars have pointed out closer correspondence (viz., Plutarch,[95] Dionysius,[96] and Jewish Hellenistic historians[97]) than previously thought. Third, there is increasing recognition of the fluidity between different narrative genres in late antiquity, thus making it quite possible that Luke-Acts is representative of two or more generic categories.[98] Finally, as argued by David E. Aune, the distinction between prologues in historiography and in the scientific treatise tradition is quite possibly a false dichotomy.[99]

---

93. 'Reading Luke-Acts', pp. 419–46.

94. See David E. Aune, 'Luke 1.1-4: Historical or Scientific *Prooimion*?', in Alf Christophersen, et al. (eds), *Paul, Luke and the Graeco-Roman World* (Festschrift Alexander J. M. Wedderburn; JSNTSup, 217; Sheffield: Sheffield Academic Press, 2003), pp. 138–48.

95. David L. Balch, 'ΜΕΤΑΒΟΛΗ ΠΟΛΙΤΕΙΩΝ: Jesus as Founder of the Church in Luke-Acts: Form and Function', in *Contextualizing Acts*, pp. 142–49, drawing on the analysis of Timothy E. Duff (*Plutarch's Lives: Exploring Virtue and Vice* [New York: Oxford University Press, 1999], pp. 14–20, 66), argues that the narratives of Plutarch resemble both the biographical and historiographical generic taxonomies. Also, cf. Balch's earlier essay, 'Septem Sapientium Convivium (*Moralia* 146B-164D)', in Hans Dieter Betz (ed.), *Plutarch's Ethical Writings and Early Christian Literature* (Studia ad Corpus Hellenisticum Novi Testamenti; Leiden: Brill Publishers, 1978), pp. 51–105.

96. For parallels with Dionysius, see David L. Balch, 'Comments on the Genre and a Political Theme of Luke-Acts: A Preliminary Comparison of Two Hellenistic Historians', in Kent H. Richards (ed.), (SBLSP, 28 Atlanta: Scholars Press, 1989), pp. 343–61; idem, 'ΜΕΤΑΒΟΛΗ ΠΟΛΙΤΕΙΩΝ', pp. 139–88.

97. For parallels with Hellenistic Jewish historiography, see Gregory E. Sterling, *Historiography and Self-Definition: Josephus, Luke-Acts, and Apologetic Historiography* (NovTSup, 64; Leiden: Brill, 1992).

98. Thomas E. Phillips ('The Genre of Acts: Moving Toward a Consensus?' *CBR* 4 [2006], pp. 365–96) contends the tendency of scholarship appears to be moving in the direction of viewing Acts as a mixture of genres. Cf. Loveday C. A. Alexander ('Fact, Fiction and the Genre of Acts', *NTS* 44 [1998], pp. 380–99), who suggests Acts contains elements of both the ancient novel and ancient historiography.

99. 'Luke 1.1-4', pp. 145–47.

III. *Concluding Summary*

Several aspects of Luke-Acts studies become apparent from the preceding analysis. First and foremost is the lack of attention paid to the speeches found in the Lukan Galilean ministry. The lack of cohesive, comprehensive readings of plot and characterization has perhaps contributed to this neglect, with most investigation focusing on individual narrative units or specific character groups apart from the larger narrative. Second, the relevance of Greco-Roman rhetoric for understanding the rhetorical texture of and identifying the trajectories that extend from the four speeches of the Galilean ministry is ignored by most interpreters. In addition, the few who give some time to understanding the rhetorical argument of the four speeches generally play down their importance by criticizing Luke's employment of 'second-class' rhetoric. Third, the majority of methodological approaches construe the narrative in silos, focusing on one of three interpretive frames – author, text, and audience – without considering the intertwined relationship of all three.[100] Fourth, investigation largely follows a formalistic line of inquiry, failing to evaluate the narrative discourse in terms of better understanding the potential ways in which it coheres or does not cohere with ideological systems. Finally, for the most part, those who propose ways in which the narrative discourse shapes new horizons for the earliest readers – or, for that matter, readers throughout history – assume a one-dimensional model that does not ask how the ideological systems of different readers might impact the appropriation process.

---

100. David P. Moessner (' "Ministers of Divine Providence": Diodorus Siculus and Luke the Evangelist on the Rhetorical Significance of the Audience in Narrative "Arrangement" ', in Sharon H. Ringe and H. C. Paul Kim (eds), *Literary Encounters with the Reign of God* [Festschrift Robert C. Tannehill; New York: T&T Clark, 2004], pp. 304–23; ' "Managing the Audience: Diodorus Siculus and Luke the Evangelist on Designing Authorial Intent" ', in R. Bieringer, G. Van Belle, and J. Verheyden (eds), *Luke and His Readers* [Festschrift A. Denaux; BETL, 182; Leuven: Leuven University Press/Peeters, 2005], pp. 61–80) argues the intertwining of the constructs of author, text, and audience have their premise within the rhetorical argument of Greco-Roman antiquity ('trialectic hermeneutic').

CHAPTER TWO: A METHODOLOGICAL FOUNDATION FOR
INVESTIGATION: TOWARDS READING AS CONDUCTION

The field of biblical studies is strewn with various methodological attempts to mine the biblical text for new insights and to uncover previously hidden meanings. The text of Luke-Acts has not gone untouched in this flurry of investigation, as initial queries into its literary nuances in the late 1980s quickly developed into a rush of inquiries using narrative, reader-response, rhetorical, and sociological criticisms in the 1990s. As discussed in the previous chapter, most of the investigation during the 1990s remained formalistic, concentrating on intratextual and intertextual elements contributing to the construction of plot, characterization, and point-of-view. This was supplemented by a separate, largely unrelated interest in extratextual features – cultural information on beliefs and actions related to hospitality, gender, honor and shame, home, sex, business, and more. In both instances, the result is an interpretive experience that predominantly does not probe beyond autonomous, intrinsic forms and primarily focuses on one of the three elements of the hermeneutical process – author, text, or reader.[1] My criticism of these approaches lies in the fact that – while some very interesting insights have been pinpointed – they largely fail to discuss and subsequently evaluate the rhetorical impact these characteristics have on the ideological location of what literary critics designate as the 'authorial audience' (see below for more detail on this heuristic construct).[2]

I propose to move beyond this paradigm to a methodology that is more encompassing, one that not only considers how the implied reader identifies and constructs plot, characterization, theme, and motifs (topoi), but how the authorial audience enacts hermeneutical appropriation through ideological systems engendered by the narrative discourse. This hermeneutical mode – designated by Wayne C. Booth as 'conduction'[3] – necessitates an understand-

---

1. The hermeneutical triad of that in front of the text (reader), that within the text (text), and that behind the text (author) was first proposed by M. H. Abrams, *The Mirror and the Lamp: Romantic Theory and Critical Tradition* (London and Oxford: Oxford University Press, 1953), pp. 3–29.

2. Initially proposed by Peter J. Rabinowitz, *Before Reading*, 15–42; idem, 'Whirl without End', pp. 81–100; idem, 'Truth in Fiction', pp. 121–41.

3. *The Company We Keep: An Ethics of Fiction* (Berkeley and Los Angeles: University of California Press, 1988), pp. 70–75, for a detailed description of 'conduction'. 'Conduction' is a mode of critical re-reading, an approach in which a reader probes the text for deeper meanings and for a better understanding of the principles or structures that determine the author's act of composition.

ing that authors work within literary and social constraints resulting from their historical milieu yet also remain autonomous enough to challenge these same constraints. Consequently, my proposed methodological approach not only asks about the conditions that shape a particular text but also ways these conditions did not shape it, instances where a text embodies ideological systems that alter or confront cultural assumptions of the status quo.[4]

I. *Constructing Meaning: Combination, Selection, and the Imaginary*

Appropriation of texts occurs in what many describe as the realm of the imaginary, that is, the subject's conceptualization (or ideation) of the object. Wolfgang Iser observes that 'the imaginary is not a self-activating potential', but instead must be brought into play from outside itself, propagated by the to-and-fro movement between the realms of text and reader.[5] This occurs in three interacting functions, which Iser identifies as combination, selection, and the 'as-if' construction (i.e., the set of attitudes represented in the world of the text).[6] Each of these heuristic functions represents an assortment of interpretive strategies from which to examine the multidimensional meaning potentialities of a text.

A. *Reading (Listening) Dynamics, the Implied Reader, and Authorial Readers*

Every text contains various social, historical, cultural, gender, religious, economic, and literary systems that exist as referential fields (or presupposition pools) outside the text.[7] According to Peter J. Rabinowitz, these '... are not in the text waiting to be uncovered, but in fact precede the text and make discovery possible in the first place'.[8] Hence, in order for readers to engage certain meaning-producing dimensions of a text, they must decode portions of the referential fields that are presupposed by the text.[9] Since the

---

4. Cf. Robert Wuthnow, *Communities of Discourse: Ideology and Social Structure in the Reformation, the Enlightenment, and European Socialism* (Cambridge and London: Harvard University Press, 1989), pp. 1–21.

5. *The Fictive and the Imaginary: Charting Literary Anthropology* (Baltimore and London: Johns Hopkins University Press, 1993), pp. 222–3. Cf. also Paul Ricoeur, *From Text to Action: Essays in Hermeneutics, II* (trans. Kathleen Blamey and John B. Thompson; Evanston, Ill.: Northwestern University Press, 1991), pp. 168–187.

6. For a discussion, see Iser, *Fictive and the Imaginary*, pp. 2–21, 222–38.

7. Cf. Rabinowitz (*Before Reading*, p. 19): 'an author cannot begin to fill up a blank page without making assumptions about the readers' beliefs, knowledge, and familiarity with conventions'.

8. Rabinowitz, *Before Reading*, p. 27.

9. Rabinowitz (*Before Reading*, pp. 29–36) points out that readers must possess some knowledge of the extratext in order to move beyond reading, which he describes as 'authorial reading', to look at the work critically from some perspective other than the one called for by the author. He thus concludes that '... while authorial reading without further critique is

act of selection involves inclusion and exclusion on the part of authors, readers view the present through what is absent, and the absent through what is present; in doing so, readers are able to construct meaning from the text, bringing it life. The hypothetical audience that is able to recognize rhetorical conventions, intertextual referents, and extratextual connotations coincides with the heuristic construct of what Rabinowitz calls the 'authorial audience' – a designation that has gained widespread acceptance in the past decade, including in the field of biblical studies.[10] In addition, though the term 'reader' is normally employed in the analysis of biblical texts, it is more accurate to speak in terms of audiences or, more specifically, because of the low literacy levels in antiquity, coupled with the fact that reading was conducted as a presentation (a means of entertainment) before an audience, listeners.[11]

An underlying premise of this study is that the authorial audience is a somewhat elusive heuristic construct. In order to ascertain the precise hermeneutical effects of the narrative discourse of Luke-Acts, a social, religious, ethnic, and gender orientation must be assumed on the part of the authorial audience. The resulting reading/listening location partially determines hermeneutical appropriation of the narrative discourse. In this context, ideology designates the systems of representation – ideas, beliefs, and feelings – through which authorial readers of different cultural backgrounds order reality.[12] Because any authorial audience consists of disparate cultural systems, we must speak of the narrative discourse as producing multidimensional effects.[13] Consequently, though somewhat intertwined, a difference exists between the implied reader and the authorial audience. Whereas the implied reader is a text-based function, the authorial audience is an extratextual entity consisting of various, multidimensional listeners. The analysis of rhetorical texture in chapters four, five, six, and seven and then narrative trajectories in Chapter eight – as largely embedded within narrative and readerly concerns – employs the implied reader as the

---

often incomplete, so is a critical reading without an understanding of the authorial audience at its base'. (32) Also, cf. Robert Scholes (*Protocols of Reading* [New Haven and London: Yale University Press, 1989], pp. 1–88).

10.   *Before Reading*, pp. 15–42; idem, 'Whirl without End', pp. 81–100; idem, 'Truth in Fiction', pp. 121–41.

11.   For more on the oral/aural nature of first-century CE Greco-Roman society, see Paul J. Achtemeier, '*Omne verbum sonat*', pp. 3–27.

12.   See, e.g., James H. Kavanagh, 'Ideology', in Frank Lentricchia and Thomas McLaughlin (eds), *Critical Terms for Literary Study* (Chicago and London: University of Chicago Press, 2nd ed., 1995), pp. 306–20.

13.   See Robert C. Tannehill, ' "Cornelius" and "Tabitha" Encounter Luke's Jesus', *Int* 48 (1994), pp. 347–56, for an initial attempt to read Luke-Acts from differing ideological locations. Also, cf. Ingrid Rosa Kitzberger, 'Mary of Bethany and Mary of Magdala – Two Female Characters in the Johannine Passion Narrative: A Feminist, Narrative-Critical, Reader-Response', *NTS* 41 (1995), pp. 564–86, who approaches the narrative discourse of the Gospel of John – through the characterization of Mary of Bethany and Mary of Magdala – from the heuristic construct of a female authorial reader.

listenerly/readerly construct standing in parallel to the implied author.[14] The investigative approach of Chapter nine, however, which aims to understand better the ideological impact of the rhetorical texture and narrative trajectories, focuses the authorial audience (or more accurately different readers/listeners comprising the authorial audience).[15]

1. *Theophilus: Literary Patronage*

Unfortunately, it is impossible to pinpoint the precise contours of the authorial audience of Luke-Acts due to the historical distance in time and equivocal nature of the narrative regarding the identity of the recipients. In particular, the identity of Theophilus has elicited significant discussion. Some scholars find a possible symbolic description of the authorial audience in the etymological meaning of Theophilus as 'dear to God' or 'lover of God', with the audience consisting of any who would align themselves with the message found within Luke-Acts.[16] However, there are several compelling reasons that militate against considering Theophilus as merely symbolic: (1) Theophilus is a common name, extant in various papyri and inscriptions; (2) the appellation 'most excellent' is usually employed in reference to Roman political officials, individuals with advanced power and prestige; and (3) symbolic dedications in other Greco-Roman literary works from antiquity do not exist.

Having concluded the above, however, we should not assume that Theophilus represents the Lukan community or that Theophilus is the only desired audience.[17] Concerning the former, there is growing consensus that the Gospels were not addressed simply to one group of individuals. In addition, endeavors to uncover the world behind the text are extremely reductionistic in nature, running the risk of a 'superficial kind of sociological allegorization'.[18] For the latter, while Theophilus is certainly recognized as

14. For the purposes of interpreting ancient Greco-Roman texts, including the New Testament documents, it would be more accurate to speak in terms of 'implied listener' versus 'implied reader'. However, since implied reader is used widely in literary criticism and biblical studies, and not wanting to introduce new terminology that could potentially confuse readers of this study, I will employ implied reader throughout.

15. See Patrick E. Spencer, 'Narrative Echoes in John 21: Intertextual Interpretation and Intratextual Connection', *JSNT* 75 (1999), pp. 49–68, esp. pp. 64–67.

16. See, e.g., John Nolland, *Luke 1-9:20* (WBC, 35a; Dallas: Word Books, 1989) xxxii-xxxiii, 10, who concludes: 'A symbolic significance for the name cannot be entirely ruled out. Much about Luke-Acts would well suit Cornelius-like readers' (p. 10).

17. Cf. the argument of Robert R. Creech, 'The Most Excellent Narratee: The Signficance of Theophilus in Luke-Acts', in Raymond H. Keathley (ed.), *With Steadfast Purpose Essays on Acts* (Festschrift Henry Jackson Flanders, Jr.; Waco: Baylor University Press, 1990), pp. 107–26, as well as that of Witherington, *Acts*, pp. 63–65. Perhaps the most thoroughgoing attempt to identify the audience of Luke-Acts with one community is that of Esler, *Community and Gospel, passim*, esp. pp. 30–45.

18. Stephen C. Barton, 'Can We Identify the Gospel Audiences?' in Richard Bauckham (ed.), *The Gospels for All Christians: Rethinking the Gospel Audiences* (Grand Rapids: William B. Eerdmans Publishing Company, 1997), pp. 173–94 (quote: p. 179). However cf.

the literary patron by the writer, it is not an attempt on the part of the writer to secure monetary support for multiplication or distribution or even to acknowledge monetary remuneration during the writing of Luke and then Acts. Unlike standard forms of patronage in Greco-Roman society, literary patronage was not reciprocal, namely, requiring the writer to become a client indebted to the benefactor.[19] Rather, the literary patron – in the case of Luke-Acts Theophilus – served as the conduit for circulation; the release of each volume to Theophilus allowed for its entree to a wider audience. Loveday C. A. Alexander explains:

> This system – with all of its developments and ramifications – had the potential to offer an author an entree into a different social network of the patron's own peers, whether by oral performance within the patron's house, or by the disposition of a presentation copy of a book in the patron's private library. Once there, a book would implicitly be available to any of the patron's friends who wished to read or copy it.[20]

The social networks of Theophilus, as a result, likely formed the avenues through which Luke-Acts circulated.[21] Though several scholars have questioned the classification recently,[22] many believe that the nature of the prologues in Lk.1.1-4 and Acts 1.1-2, coupled with the style of the larger narrative, suggests a group of recipients belonging to the social matrix between upper literary classes and lower social levels, most likely free artisans and small businessmen and -women.[23] Nevertheless, attempts to go

---

Margaret M. Mitchell, 'Patristic Counter-Evidence to the Claim that "The Gospels Were Written for All Christians"', *NTS* 51 (2005), pp. 36–79; Edward W. Klink, 'The Gospel Community Debate: State of the Question', *CBR* 3 (2004), pp. 60–85.

19. See Barbara K. Gold, *Literary Patronage in Greece and Rome* (Chapel Hill: University of North Carolina Press, 1987), *passim.*

20. 'Ancient Book Production and the Circulation of the Gospels', in *Gospels for All*, p. 98.

21. Alexander comments ('Book Production', pp. 103–04):

> Where the patron is somehow seen as facilitating the 'publication' of the book, this should be associated ... with the ancient conventions whereby the aristocracy were expected to provide a 'hearth' for the public performance ... , as well as a meeting place for wandering scholars and teachers .... the patron could provide another, equally valuable kind of hospitality for an author's work in his library, where the text could be 'deposited' for consultation and copying by his friends. Such a role could well make sense for Theophilus, whom we could see as an equivalent to the patrons of house churches known from the Pauline letters: his library, in this case, could well have become the basis of the church's library.

22. See, e.g., Penner ('Civilizing Discourse', p. 67) notes that '... while the content and style of a book such as Acts may still be distinct on certain levels when compared to Tacitus, Livy, or Dionysius of Halicarnassus, on many fronts it is now perceived as fully consonant with the so-called high culture of antiquity'.

23. Those of more 'high-browed' literary traditions looked upon technical and professional writing of those who worked with their hands with contempt; this seemingly eliminates the upper literary class from view (see, e.g., Alexander, *Preface*, pp. 200–5). This

beyond this conclusion into greater granularity – in terms of geography, politics, ethnicity, gender, religious beliefs, and more – will gain little consensus, pursuits that will remain evasive. Further, considering the oral/ aural nature of communications in Greco-Roman antiquity, the multiple contexts in which texts were read, and the diverse way in which early Christians gathered, it is groundless to propose a precise setting in which Luke and Acts were heard.[24]

2. *Extratextual and Intertextual Repertoire*

Despite the above caveats, we can say some things about certain expectations the implied author imposes on the authorial audience. Darr lists the following as constitutive elements of the extratext: (1) language; (2) social norms and cultural scripts; (3) classical or canonical literature; (4) literary conventions such as genres, type scenes, standard plots, rhetorical devices, and prototypes of characterization; (5) reading rules on how to categorize, rank, and process various kinds of textual data; and (6) commonly known historical and geographical facts.[25] These referential fields divide into two schemas: extratextual and intertextual. Extratextual repertoire equates to the knowledge of political, social, and religious beliefs and assumptions the implied author assumes the authorial audience possesses. Interaction of elements in this complex web of presuppositions serves as the basis for meanings engendered by the authorial audience. As to the four Galilean ministry speeches of Jesus, the implied author assumes extratextual knowledge of material benefaction, honor/shame protocols, agriculture, common rhymes, and more. Intertextual repertoire involves the referential interpretation of a previous text, in which one discourse becomes 'the theme viewed from the standpoint of the other, and vice versa. This iterative movement enables old meanings to become material for new; it opens up long-established borders, and allows excluded meanings to enter and challenge the meanings that had excluded them.'[26] Regarding the narrative discourse of the four speeches of Jesus in the Galilean ministry, significant knowledge of the LXX is presupposed by the implied author.[27]

3. *Authorial Readers and Ideological Location*

Though caution must be shown in doing so, it is possible to delineate the basic contours of the authorial audience of Luke-Acts. To begin, the

---

corresponds with recent assessments that early Christianity was composed of a large number of free artisans and small business owners (see, e.g., Carolyn Osiek and David L. Balch, *Families in the New Testament World: Households and House Churches* [Louisville: Westminster/John Knox Press, 1997], pp. 91–102).

24. See F. Gerald Downing, 'Theophilus's First Reading of Luke-Acts', in Tuckett (ed.), *Luke's Literary Achievement*, pp. 91–109.

25. *Character Building*, p. 22; idem, *Herod the Fox*, pp. 34–6.

26. Iser, *Fictive and the Imaginary*, p. 227.

27. See Litwak, *Echoes of Scripture*.

authorial audience falls within the social network of Theophilus. The authorial audience therefore encompasses a broad spectrum of personages across society that would have included men and women, masters and slaves, patrons and clients, Gentile and Jew, the powerful and weak, and Roman citizens and non-citizens. Exclusion of any of the above from the authorial audience is reductionistic and narrows the possibilities for evaluation beyond the boundaries of what can be validated through that found in the text of Luke-Acts. Second, we can speak of an authorial audience located in a Hellenistic urban setting.[28] Corroborating this claim is the widely held view that first-century and early second-century CE Christianity was largely an urban-based movement, coupled with descriptions within the narrative of Luke-Acts of housing, culture, and landscape indicative of a Hellenistic urban environment.[29] Third, considering the widespread understanding that the Lukan prologue (1.1-4) and the recapitulation of Acts (1.1-2) contains language typical of narrative popular among artisans and small business owners,[30] plus the widespread understanding of the early Christian movement as being most prevalent among the labor classes (i.e., those who work with their hands),[31] I propose a social location for the authorial audience that excludes the upper and lower classes.[32] Finally, while Godfearers – Gentiles attracted to the tenets and practices of Jewish religious life – may have comprised part of the authorial audience, the conclusions of some scholars that the authorial audience is comprised exclusively, or even primarily, of Godfearers is unlikely.[33] The

28.   See the argument of Moxnes, 'The Social Context of Luke's Community', pp. 379–89. However cf. Jim Grimshaw, 'Luke's Market Exchange District: Decentering Luke's Rich Urban Center', *Semeia* 86 (1999), pp. 33–51.

29.   See, e.g., Richard L. Rohrbaugh, 'The Pre-Industrial City in Luke-Acts', in Jerome H. Neyrey (ed.), *The Social World of Luke-Acts* (Peabody: Hendrickson Publishers, 1991), pp. 125–49.

30.   Alexander reaches this conclusion on the basis that the prologues of Luke and Acts correspond with those found in technical and scientific treatises (*Preface*, pp. 29–36; eadem, 'Luke's Preface in the Context of Greek Preface-Writing', *NovT* 28 [1986], pp. 60–61). However cf. Aune, 'Luke 1.1-4', pp. 138–48, who argues that Alexander draws a false dichotomy between the prologues found in the historical and scientific traditions. Regardless of the generic argument, most scholars acknowledge that the style of the language and composition of Luke-Acts does not coincide with narrative written for the upper class.

31.   See Osiek and Balch, *Households and House Churches*, pp. 91–102, for an overview. Also, see Abraham J. Malherbe, *Social Aspects of Early Christianity* (Philadelphia: Fortress Press, 2nd edn., 1983), pp. 29–59, and Wayne A. Meeks, *The First Urban Christians: Social World of the Apostle Paul* (New Haven: Yale University Press, 1983), pp. 51–79.

32.   The narrative discourse of Luke-Acts (e.g., Lk. 12.16-21; 16.19-31) militates against the elite rich, portraying them as outsiders, eliciting a negative judgment against such societal groups by the authorial audience (see Moxnes, *Economy*, pp. 163–65). Also, see Gerd Theissen, *Social Reality and the First Christians: Theology, Ethics, and the World of the New Testament* (Edinburgh: T&T Clark, 1992), pp. 270–71, who contends the early Christian movement drew its members not from the 'ruling elite', but from the 'fringe elite'.

33.   Contra Tyson, *Images of Judaism*, pp. 35–39; idem, 'Reading as a Godfearer', pp. 19–38; Esler, *Community and Gospel*, pp. 15–36.

function of the literary patron as a social network for circulation and distribution purposes inveighs against this conclusion. Instead, Luke-Acts was not written for a monolithic community but rather a network of communities consisting of various ideological systems.

Based on the above, coupled with information from the narrative itself, several other aspects of the extratextual repertoire of the authorial audience can be identified: (1) knowledge of Greek and Roman coinage; (2) knowledge of Greco-Roman religious beliefs and practices; (3) understanding of the larger Greco-Roman political and historical landscape, including key political and historical figures and events; (4) familiarity with eastern Mediterranean geography, including the boundaries of Roman provinces and basic configuration of major cities such as Ephesus, Athens, Corinth, and Jerusalem;[34] (5) awareness of social codes of patronage;[35] (6) knowledge of social interaction during meal settings;[36] (7) understanding of social codes denoting appropriate and inappropriate behavior, including male–female interaction in public venues;[37] (8) knowledge of ancient rhetoric and oratory practices; (9) familiarity with names, stories, characters, and wording from the LXX; and (10) knowledge of Hellenistic texts and the traditions that ensued from them.[38]

B. *Processing Texts: Consistency and Coherency*

Readers process texts by drawing on various schematic conventions, which interact to corroborate or limit one another as meaning is engendered by the reader.[39] This is accomplished by means of 'bottom-up' processing and 'top-

34. The most complete discussion of geographical perspectives in relation to the narrative of Luke-Acts is in J. M. Scott, 'Luke's Geographical Horizon', in D. W. J. Gill and Conrad Gempf (eds), *The Book of Acts in Its First Century Setting: Graeco-Roman Setting* (Grand Rapids: William B. Eerdmans Publishing Company, 1994), pp. 483–544.

35. For a thorough description of patron-client relationships in Luke-Acts, see Halvor Moxnes, 'Patron-Client Relations and the New Community in Luke-Acts', in *Social World of Luke-Acts*, pp. 241–70.

36. For an overview of meal settings in Luke-Acts and the various social connotations surrounding them, see Jerome H. Neyrey, 'Ceremonies in Luke-Acts: The Case of Meals and Table-Fellowship', in *Social World of Luke-Acts*, pp. 361–88. Also, cf. Dennis E. Smith, 'Table Fellowship as a Literary Motif in the Gospel of Luke', *JBL* 106 (1987), pp. 613–38.

37. See Bruce J. Malina and Jerome H. Neyrey, 'Honor and Shame in Luke-Acts: Pivotal Values in the Mediterranean World', in *Social World of Luke-Acts*, pp. 25–65.

38. The following contain various facets belonging to the social and ideological location of the authorial audience: Robbins, 'Implied Author of Luke-Acts', pp. 305–32; Tyson, *Images of Judaism*, pp. 19–42; idem, 'Reading as a Godfearer', pp. 19–38; Moxnes, 'Social Context', pp. 379–89.

39. Rabinowitz (*Before Reading*, pp. 15–46) delineates four categories that guide readers in the construction of meaning: (1) rules of notice; (2) signification; (3) configuration; and (4) coherence.

down' processing.[40] Bottom-up processing takes place by induction, moving from the parts to the whole and encompassing elements such as lexicon, syntax, and texture. These elements begin with the connotations of the actual words contained in the text and move to aspects such as delineation of textual units and interconnection of textual units. Top-down processing, in contrast, is deductive, moving from the whole to the parts, encompassing elements such as theme, motifs, plot, characterization, genre, intertextual connotations, and extratextual referents. These two modes of processing texts correspond with the description of rhetorical argument as inductive and deductive in Greco-Roman rhetoric.[41]

1. *Rhetorical Argument*

A profound interest in Greco-Roman rhetorical handbooks is shown towards the use of rhetorical devices, focusing on persuasion and moving the audience to make certain judgments. Since the fundamental characteristic of discourse in antiquity was oral, for the ear more than for the eye, many of the devices delineated pertain to auditory reception.[42] For example, Demetrius' *On Style* begins by addressing basic grammatical issues of word choice, structure of sentences, use of clauses, and development of periods (combination of clauses and phrases) and then moves to a broader overview focused on style. The most often-used rhetorical category is repetition, whether in the context of smaller units or the text as a whole.[43] The ultimate aim of reading (and listening) was to build consistency in a text by fitting everything into a consistent pattern.[44] Because readers process texts in a linear fashion, the reading experience is both sequential and holistic: the reader supplies missing information and clarifies ambiguities both sequentially and retrospectively through the extratextual repertoire, intertextual

---

40.   See Jerry Camery-Hoggatt (*Speaking of God: Reading and Preaching the Word of God* [Peabody, Massachusetts: Hendrickson Publishers, 1995], pp. 91–113) and Green ('Practice of Reading', pp. 420–1) for a discussion of 'bottom-up' and 'top-down' reading strategies.

41.   Aristotle, *Rhetoric*, 1.2.7–1.2.22.

42.   The majority of classical scholars hold the view that reading in Greco-Roman antiquity was done aloud and very rarely in silence (e.g., Rosalind Thomas, *Literacy and Orality in Anicent Greece* [Cambridge: Cambridge University Press, 1992], *passim*; Achtemeier, '*Omne verbum sona*', pp. 3–27). However cf. A. K. Gavrilov, 'Reading Techniques in Classical Antiquity', *Classical Quarterly* 47 (1997), pp. 56–73, who contends silent reading was a common practice in classical Athens. Hence, in contrast to much of scholarly opinion, reading in antiquity was not much unlike that of modernity: texts were read aloud as well as silently. Also, see Frank D. Gilliard, 'More Silent Reading in Antiquity: *Non omne verbum sonat*', *JBL* 112 (1993), pp. 689–96.

43.   Repetition includes elements such as *pleonasm* (redundancy), *homoioteleuton* (similar end sounds), *onomatopoeia* (words that express similar sounds), *parachesis* (repetition of the same sound in consecutive words), *chiasmus* (crosswise repetition), and *anaphora* (repetition of the same word at the beginning of clauses).

44.   See, e.g., Aristotle, *Poetics*, 1451a–1451b; Longinus, *On the Sublime*, 11.1–12.1; Lucian, *How to Write History*, 55.

connections, and intratextual information.[45] Repetition – and the importance of building consistency – plays an important role in the rhetorical
analysis of Jesus' four Galilean ministry speeches in chapters four, five, six,
and seven and then the subsequent discussion of narrative trajectories in
Chapter eight.

2. *Intertextual Echoes and Weaving*

Though other modes of intertextuality can be discussed in relation to the
hermeneutical process – such as reading Luke against Mark or reading the
beheading of John the Baptist in conjunction with artistic characterizations[46] – I suggest that all texts are built from and assume other texts. The
intertextual web – direct and indirect, intentional and unintentional –
consists of stock forms, recognizable story patterns, and various uses of
language. As a result, every text is an intertextual field of transpositions
from various signifying systems; an absorption and transformation of the
precursor.[47] This produces an intersection of texts that assist the implied
reader in the construction of elements such as plot and characterization
while simultaneously prompting the authorial audience to create new
ideological horizons.[48] The narrative of Luke-Acts is replete with the
interplay of other texts, networked systems of references forming the
intertextual repertoire of the implied reader. The interplay of other texts
serves as invitations to the implied reader to hear the current narrative
through reverberations and continuations of previous texts.[49]

Both Jewish and Hellenistic texts comprise the intertextual repertoire of
Luke-Acts. The most obvious intertext is the LXX, with particular
familiarity with Deutero-Isaiah. The narrative discourse is replete with

45. For a description of how readers build consistency by means of supplying missing
information and/or disambiguation, see Wolfgang Iser, *The Act of Reading: A Theory of
Aesthetics* (Baltimore and London: Johns Hopkins University Press, 1978), pp. 163–74.

46. See, e.g., Robert M. Fowler, *Let the Reader Understand: Reader-Response Criticism
and the Gospel of Mark* (Minneapolis: Fortress Press, 1991), pp. 237–60, who reads Matthew
against Mark.

47. The mode of uniting one text ('hypertext') with an earlier text ('hypotext') is
designated as hypertextuality by Gerard Genette, *Palimpsests: Literature in the Second
Degree* (trans. Channa Newman and Claude Doubinsky; Lincoln, Nebraska: University of
Nebraska Press, 1997), pp. 5–9. For an overview of intertextuality, see Julia Kristeva, *Desire
in Language: A Semiotic Approach to Literature and Art* (trans. T. Gora, A. Jardine, and L.
Roudiez; New York: Columbia University Press, 1980), and Jay Clayton and Eric Rothstein,
'Figures in the Corpus: Theories of Influence and Intertextuality', in Jay Clayton and Eric
Rothstein (eds), *Influence and Intertextuality in Literary History* (Madison: University of
Wisconsin Press, 1991), pp. 3–36.

48. The meaning created by the interplay of texts is described as the 'dialogic
imagination' by Mikhail M. Bakhtin, *The Dialogic Imagination* (trans. Caryl Emerson and
Michael Holquist; Austin: University of Texas Press, 1981).

49. The first two chapters of Luke are perhaps the most well-known New Testament texts
in terms of intertextuality (see Joel B. Green, 'The Problem of a Beginning: Israel's Scriptures
in Luke 1-2', *BBR* 4 [1996], pp. 61-86; idem, *Gospel of Luke*, pp. 52–58).

quotations, direct references, and indirect allusions. Nevertheless, while the LXX is by far the most predominant intertext, there are numerous instances where knowledge of basic themes, plotlines, modes of characterization, and literary motifs in ancient Greco-Roman historiography, novels, and biographies are necessitated.[50] The implied reader constructs meaning from these intertextual networks in a number of ways: (1) direct citations, with or without an introductory formula; (2) summaries of LXX history and teaching; (3) use of type scenes that constitute repetition in wording, scenery, motifs, and event sequences; and (4) allusions or linguistic echoes.[51] The interplay of meaning not only occurs through the similarities between two or more texts, but through the differences; the implied reader makes judgments about the reasons for the exclusion or modification of the intertext. The rhetorical analysis of each speech, in addition to the overarching narrative trajectories that extend from each speech, will account for these intertextual networks.

3. Constructing Plot, Theme, Characterization, and Motifs (Topoi)
The tendency in scholarly circles to dismiss Greco-Roman characterization as devoid of personality and thus lacking the capacity for development has been somewhat reversed in recent years. While, admittedly, the use of jargon and methodological approaches based on modern characterization has been overdone by some, the reverse has also been true; others overstate the claim – based on information from Aristotle that devalues the role and depiction of characterization – that character development was unknown in ancient Greco-Roman narrative. Indeed, it is virtually impossible to read/listen to a narrative from Greco-Roman antiquity, including Luke-Acts, without constructing personages for the various character types. Frederick W. Burnett elaborates on this nuance: 'From what appears to us as a minimum of characterization may have been read in maximal terms by contemporary auditors and readers'.[52]
    The difference between ancient and modern characterization can be explained better in terms of psychological and individual development. In particular, the very nature of the listening process requires that the implied reader make judgments about the actions of characters based on their

50.   There is growing recognition of Greco-Roman intertextuality in Luke-Acts; see, e.g., Saundra Schwartz, 'The Trial Scene in the Greek Novels and in Acts', in *Contextualizing Acts*, pp. 105–33; MacDonald, 'Emulation of Homer', pp. 197–205; idem, 'Shipwrecks', pp. 88–107; idem, 'Eutychus and Homer's Elphenor', pp. 4–24; Marianne Palmer Bonz, *The Past as Legacy: Luke-Acts and Ancient Epic* (Minneapolis: Fortress Press, 2000).
51.   See Richard B. Hays and Joel B. Green, 'The Use of the Old Testament by New Testament Writers', *Hearing the New Testament: Strategies for Interpretation*, pp. 226–29, for a similar delineation.
52.   'Characterization and Reader Construction of Characters in the Gospels', in Barry Callen (ed.), *Listening to the Word of God* (Festschrift Boyce W. Blackwelder; Anderson, Ind.: Warner Press, 1990), p. 77. Also, cf. the later adaptation, 'Characterization and Reader Construction of Characters in the Gospels', *Semeia* 63 (1993), pp. 1–29.

words, actions, and relationships, as well as narrative asides vis-à-vis the narrator.[53] Because narrative cannot and does not contain all of the information the implied reader needs to understand plot and characterization,[54] the implied reader must make inferences to construct and evaluate individual characters and character groups. The implied reader constructs characterization from information within and outside of the narrative, building consistency from accumulation of intratextual features, importing of extratextual information, and deciphering of intertextual echoes. Few of these are obvious to the implied reader, who must go through a process of construction. This results in positive, negative, or ambivalent judgments about the actions and words of characters. These take place on the continuum of three levels, per Aristotle's division of character into the taxonomies of ethos, logos, and pathos.[55] Naturally, when the heuristic construct of culturally situated authorial readers is considered, the nuanced psychological effects of the narrative become even more patent.[56]

While nearly all scholars agree that characterization is subservient to plot in ancient narrative, I demur from the tendency of some scholars to dismiss characterization as a peripheral consideration. Characterization functions as a role within the unfolding plotlines of the narrative; actions and characters form a conceptual network from which the implied reader derives plot. This paradigm permits us to speak of characterization in terms of differing degrees, with certain characters or character groups playing larger roles in the plot of the narrative than others and vice versa. In addition, because the reading process is cumulative in nature, consisting of proleptic and analeptic construction, characterization is not a static entity; rather, characters are capable of ideological transformation, as the implied reader is constantly engaged in retrospective evaluation.[57] Similarly, though character groups

53.   For an overview, see the discussion in Robert Scholes and Robert Kellogg, *The Nature of Narrative* (London and New York: Oxford University Press, 1966), pp. 161–239. Specifically, they contend, per Greco-Roman rhetoricians, that characterization ensues from ethos, certain traits about a character or character group from words and actions – that is, in contrast to attitudes or motives in modern narrative, elements lacking in ancient narrative.

54.   Note the comment of Demetrius, *On Style* 222: 'Some points should be left to the comprehension and inference of the hearer, who when he perceives what you have left unsaid becomes not only your hearer but your witness'. Narrative providing too much information was considered exhausting work, and thus narrative requiring activity on the part of the hearer was preferential (e.g., cf. Dionysius, *Letter to Gnaeus Pompeius* 3, who states that Herodotus' work is preferable to that of Thucydides because the latter lacks selectivity and thereby exhausts the reader).

55.   *Rhetoric* 1.2.3–1.2.6.

56.   See, e.g., Petri Merenlahti, 'Characters in the Making: Individuality and Ideology in the Gospels', in David Rhoads and Kari Syreeni (eds), *Characterization in the Gospels: Reconceiving Narrative Criticism* (JSNTSup, 184; Sheffield: Sheffield Academic Press, 1999), pp. 49–72.

57.   James Phelan (*Reading People, Reading Plots: Character, Progression, and the Interpretation of Narrative* [Chicago and London: University of Chicago Press, 1989], p. 115) explains: 'the text contains not just the patterns of instabilities, tensions, and resolutions but

embody a matrix of traits the implied reader constructs from the elements contained in the intratextual, extratextual, and intertextual repertoires, this does not necessitate that all members of a character group manifest the same characteristics. Instead, in sporadic instances narrators introduce new information that results in different understanding.[58]

In Greco-Roman antiquity narrative consists of actions or events comprised of a beginning, middle, and end.[59] These events or actions form a line of reversal and recognition, usually in the context of conflict between differing characters or character groups, which results in the formation of a plotline. When done so in an effective manner, the presence of characterization permits plot to come to life. To use an illustration; characterization serves as the flesh and muscle that cause the skeletal bones of the narrative plot to function. The four speeches of Jesus in the Galilean ministry play a pivotal role in the characterization of Luke-Acts: (1) providing valuable information for judgments – analeptic and proleptic – about the speakers themselves; (2) revealing aspects concerning the characterization of antagonists and protagonists regarding what is said about each as well as how each respond to the actual speech and speaker; and (3) establishing interpretive frameworks from which preceding and subsequent actions of characters and character groups are evaluated.[60] All three of these will be considered in Chapter eight's discussion of characterization.

While a diversity of opinion exists on other issues related to the narrative of Luke-Acts, recent Lukan scholarship repeatedly identifies 'salvation' as the primary theme of Luke-Acts.[61] Scholars argue that salvation in Luke-Acts is predicated on the concept of benefaction, on the one hand, in which members of the state are expected to exercise their powers for the benefit of their subjects and, on the other hand, the depiction of God in the LXX as a savior of his people. In this sense, 'salvation' denotes a wide range of

---

also the authorial audience's responses to those patterns .... We might say that progression involves not only the developing pattern of instabilities and tensions but also the accompanying sequence of attitudes that the authorial audience is asked to take toward that pattern.' Also, cf. Christopher Gill, 'The *Ethos/Pathos* Distinction in Rhetorical and Literary Criticism', *Classical Quarterly* 34 (1984), pp. 149–66; idem, 'The Character-Personality Distinction', in Christopher Pelling (ed.), *Characterization and Individuality in Greek Literature* (Oxford: Clarendon Press, 1990), pp. 1–31.

58.   Green makes this assertion regarding the characterization of the Pharisees and disciples (*Gospel of Luke*, passim; *Theology of the Gospel*, pp. 72–75).

59.   Aristotle, *Poetics*, 1450a–1451b.

60.   Among other examples, see Stephen V. Tracy, *The Story of the Odyssey* (Princeton: Princeton University Press, 1990), who demonstrates the pivotal role the speeches in Homer's *Odyssey* play in the construction of characterization – for both protagonists such as Telemachus, Odysseus, Penelope, and others as well as antagonists such as Antinoos, Leokritos, and others.

61.   Cf. the various essays in Marshall and Peterson (eds), *Witness to the Gospel*.

activity, whereby role reversal occurs – inclusion of the marginalized as members of the divine community, empowerment of those without power due to social and religious maladies, and the call for followers of Jesus to bestow 'salvation' – within the context of the patron-client paradigm – to Christians and non-Christians alike.[62] This use of theme refers to something different from plot, motif (*topos*), or characterization. Hence, for example, whereas plot, characterization, and motifs (*topoi*) are linked to particular events and topics commensurate with a set of concrete entities, theme only involves general, abstract realities such as ideas, thoughts, beliefs, and so forth.[63] Accordingly, while salvation unifies the overall discourse of Luke-Acts, these elements – more indicative of the discourse – enable the narrative to shape authorial readers through ideological confirmation, reinterpretation, and disorientation. For motifs (or *topoi* in accordance with Greco-Roman rhetoric[64]), they occur in repeated instances throughout narrative: events, scenes, and actions that contribute to the identification of plotlines and the construction of characterization.[65] Motifs are the subjects around which the implied author constructs narrative discourse (e.g., non-reciprocal benefaction); maxims and enthymemes are used as vehicles for persuasion.[66]

62. Green, 'Salvation to the End of the Earth', pp. 83–106; idem, *Theology of the Gospel*, pp. 76–121. Also, cf. Ben Witherington III, 'Salvation and Health in Christian Antiquity: The Soteriology of Luke-Acts in its First Century Setting', in *Witness to the Gospel*, pp. 145–65; Gary Gilbert, 'Roman Propaganda and Christian Identity in the Worldview of Luke-Acts', in *Contextualizing Acts*, pp. 233–56.

63. This understanding derives from Gerald Prince, *Narrative as Theme: Studies in French Fiction* (Lincoln and London: University of Nebraska Press, 1992), pp. 1–27. The identification of theme, or, as Prince describes it, 'theming', is connected to the context of the 'themer' ('To put it even more bluntly, I always make the work I theme' [p. 11]). The subjective nature of reading is the reason for disagreement among scholars regarding what constitutes theme in any narrative.

64. For a discussion of *topos* in Greco-Roman rhetoric, see Carolyn R. Miller, 'The Aristotelian *Topos*: Hunting for Novelty', in Alan G. Gross and Arthur E. Walzer (eds), *Rereading Aristotle's Rhetoric* (Carbondale and Edwardsville: Southern Illinois University Press, 2000), pp. 130–48; David E. Aune, 'Topos', in *The Westminster Dictionary of New Testament & Early Christian Literature & Rhetoric* (Louisville and London: Westminster John Knox Press, 2003), p. 476.

65. *Topoi* refer to (1) commonplaces ('themes'); (2) stock arguments or ready-made arguments for speakers to use for rhetorical situations; and (3) abstract argumentative structure or pattern. In the case of the above argument, *topoi* signify motifs such as table fellowship, healing, promise/fulfillment, wealth/possessions, conversion, and more. None of these can be considered overarching themes, as they do not hold the narrative discourse together, but rather are elements that contribute to the overall theme of salvation and moreover move plotlines along and provide fodder for the construction of characterization. In a sense, certain *topoi* (motifs) in narrative correspond with what can be described as intratextual type-scenes (cf. Robert Alter, 'How Convention Helps Us Read: The Case of the Bible's Annunciation Type Scene', *Prooftexts* 3 [1983], pp. 115–30; idem, *The Art of Biblical Narrative* [New York: Basic Books, 1981], pp. 47–62).

66. For an overview of *topoi* and their relationship to maxims and enthymemes in ancient Greco-Roman rhetoric, see Aristotle, *Rhetoric*, 1.2.19–1.2.22; 2.22.13–2.23.30.

Chapter eight shows that rhetorical texture and narrative trajectories are inextricably tethered in the case of the four Lukan Galilean ministry speeches.

C. *Interpretation as Conduction: The Fictive and Imaginary*

Readers perform a double operation of imagining and interpreting when engaging a text; the result is the formation of the text in terms of an imaginary 'as-if' construction. Evolving from this is the act of ideation: readers step out of their world by configuring the textual world emerging from the functions of selection and combination into coherent modes of 'imaginary' existence. A dialectical tension develops between the horizon of the text and that of the reader, resulting in the confirmation, amplification, or modification of the reader's self-understanding. This act of ideation occurs by both the implied reader and real, flesh-and-blood readers. The difference between the implied reader and real, flesh-and-blood readers is the ability of real, flesh-and-blood readers to assess the narrative discourse from the perspective of conduction, whereby judgments are made regarding narrator, plot, theme, topoi, and characterization. This mode of assessment by real readers can even extend to authorial readers, a step covered in Chapter nine.

Drawing upon the hermeneutical framework of Iser, we are able to identify several ways in which ideological systems of authorial readers experience metamorphosis.[67] 'Gaps' are places where readers must supply missing information in order to make sense of the narrative. These include abrupt changes in geographical location, failure to comment on the response of characters to actions in the narrative, open-ended plotlines, and various breaks or intrusions in the narrative. The four Lukan speeches in the Galilean ministry contain a number of textual 'gaps' that prompt the implied reader to engender meaning through interpretive decisions, ranging from geographical changes at the beginning of the speeches, to repetition, to rhetorical play, to narrative asides.

'Blanks' are places where readers must connect openings between textual perspectives (e.g., narrator, characters, plot, etc.). Use of irony is perhaps the most frequent use of this device in biblical narrative, whereby the implied reader is privy to information not available to the characters in the story through narrative asides or even previous information in the narrative. Irony plays an important role in the four speeches in that the implied reader possesses information of which the narrative audience is not aware. This aids the implied reader in building judgments about various characters and character groups comprising the narrative audience; their reactions to Jesus' speeches disclose aspects of their ethos.

---

67. *Prospecting: From Reader Response to Literary Anthropology* (Baltimore and London: Johns Hopkins University Press, 1989), pp. 33–41; idem, *Act of Reading*, pp. 163–239.

'Negations' constitute places where familiar elements or knowledge are invoked but then canceled out, prompting the various constituents of the authorial audience to modify their position in relation to the text. An important component in this interpretive approach is the premise that authors work within the constraints of their historical and social milieu yet also remain autonomous enough to challenge some of these constraints. My investigation of the narrative discourse pushes beyond the boundaries of the text to establish linkages to the ideological systems from which the text was produced.[68] Robert Wuthnow explains the process:

> [Individual texts] draw resources, insights, and inspiration from their social environment: they reflect it, speak to it, and make themselves relevant to it. And yet they also remain autonomous enough from their social environment to acquire a broader, even universal and timeless appeal. The process of articulation is thus characterized by a delicate balance between the products of culture and the social environment in which they are produced.[69]

In this model, certain meaning-making dimensions of a text simply correspond with the social and historical framework from which the author is operating, while other meaning-making dimensions may challenge or disorient particular facets of this framework.[70]

Of the three meaning-making dimensions, 'negations' have received the least amount of attention in biblical studies, and the examination of the four Lukan Galilean ministry speeches of Jesus are no exception. Chapter nine explores instances of sociological 'negation', places where the ideological systems represented in the narrative discourse extend, alter, or even challenge those of the authorial audience. Specifically, the

---

68. See the hermeneutical questions Stephen Greenblatt contends need to be posed ('Culture', in *Critical Terms*, p. 226):

> What kinds of behavior, what models of practice, does this work seem to enforce? Why might readers at a particular time and place find this work compelling? Are there differences between my values and the values implicit in the work I am reading? Upon what social understandings does the work depend? Whose freedom of thought or movement might be constrained implicitly or explicitly by this work? What are the larger social structures with which these particular acts of praise or blame might be connected?

69. *Communities of Discourse*, p. 3. Also, see Richard Freadman and Seumas Miller, *Re-Thinking Theory: A Critique of Contemporary Literary Theory and an Alternative Account* (Cambridge: Cambridge University Press, 1992), p. 233: '... authors and their texts are not wholly determined by their socio-historical context: though some textual meanings will be so conditioned, others will reflect the fact that authors can to some extent transcend their socio-historical contexts'. For the application to the Gospel narratives, see James L. Resseguie, 'Defamiliarization and the Gospels', *BTB* 20 (1990), pp. 147–53.

70. This approach is taken by Green in respect to the characterization of Mary, the mother of Jesus, in the Lukan prologue ('Social Status of Mary', 457–71).

discourse of the four speeches does not simply mirror the ideological systems of the authorial audience, but rather concurrently expands upon, reinterprets, and even challenges those same systems. Additionally, appropriation of the rhetorical texture of the speeches and the different narrative trajectories differs based on the ideological location of the authorial reader; the effect is that the meaning produced may vary. For example, authorial readers with material possessions construe the hermeneutical implications of the second speech (6.20–49) differently than authorial readers lacking in material possessions.

II. *Concluding Summary*

The hermeneutical process of conduction opens up new horizons, as flesh-and-blood readers engage the attitudes that the narrative discourse imposes upon the implied reader. Afterwards, authorial readers encounter the otherness of what the text represents. This engenders the formation of new modes of ethical, social, political, and religious being.[71] Biblical texts are comprised of a variety of perspectives that delineate the implied author's view and provide authorial readers with the means to engage the 'otherness' of the text. In terms of the narrative discourse in Luke-Acts, this study identifies six different perspectives: (1) narrators – both the first-person narrator present in much of the narrative and the we-narrator that appears at the latter end of Acts (point-of-view); (2) plot – which, as discussed, in ancient narrative parallels theme; (3) characterization; (4) *topoi* (or motifs); (5) the implied reader – a text-based function that is guided by the implied author; and (6) the authorial audience – the hypothetical audience as represented by an extratextual heuristic construct embodying various cultural systems.[72]

The encounter by authorial readers with these perspectives produces an intertwined network of relationships, which results in the ideation of new horizons. Authorial readers move in and out of these new horizons in order to reflect upon and even to assess their own reactions. My conductive reading of the narrative discourse of Luke-Acts – through narrative trajectories generated by the rhetorical texture of the four speeches found in the Lukan Galilean ministry (Lk. 4.14–9.50) – critically evaluates each of these perspectives and their appropriation by the authorial audience. The goal of the analysis is to move the discussion about the narrative discourse of Luke-

---

71. This is called for in the secular reading of texts by Jane P. Tompkins, 'The Reader in History: The Changing Shape of Literary Response', in Jane P. Tompkins (ed.), *Reader-Response: From Formalism to Post-Structuralism* (Baltimore and London: Johns Hopkins University Press, 1980), pp. 224-26. Also, see Stephen E. Fowl and L. Gregory Jones, *Reading in Communion: Scripture and Ethics in Christian Life* (Grand Rapids and London: William B. Eerdmans Publishing Company, 1991).

72. See Iser, *Prospecting*, pp. 33-41, for a similar delineation.

Acts – specifically in regard to the four Galilean ministry speeches of Jesus – towards a deeper understanding of those who first heard the narrative read and, in particular, some of the potential ways in which the narrative confirms, reinterprets, and challenges the ideological locations of those earliest readers/listeners.

CHAPTER 3: GRECO-ROMAN RHETORICAL ARGUMENT: DELIMITING RHETORICAL TEXTURE

That the New Testament is imbued with Greco-Roman rhetorical argument is now widely acknowledged.[1] Various articles and books have been written on the ways that New Testament letters – and, to a lesser extent, the Gospels[2] – exhibit a close affinity with rhetorical forms and devices. As regards to Luke-Acts, numerous scholars have acknowledged the presence of Greco-Roman rhetoric. The speeches in Acts have received the preponderance of attention, with particular focus on the three defense speeches of Paul in chapters 22, 25, and 26. The most in-depth rhetorical analysis of Acts is the recent commentary on Acts by Witherington, who explores the narrative discourse from the lens of Greco-Roman rhetorical categories.[3] The use of ancient rhetorical conventions in the narrative of Luke, however, in contrast to that of Acts, though examined in passing, has not been thoroughly investigated.[4]

I. *Greco-Roman Handbook Rhetoric*

In the 1980s, a significant contingent of biblical scholars embarked on a search to locate rhetorical patterns – as primarily delineated in the ancient rhetorical handbooks – within the New Testament. At the core of their rhetorical investigation was the seminal work of George A. Kennedy, who – based on the ancient Greco-Roman rhetorical handbooks – proposed a five-

1. See among others, Vernon K. Robbins, 'The Present and Future State of Rhetorical Analysis', *The Rhetorical Analysis of Scripture*, pp. 32–41; Jan Lambrecht, S. J., 'Rhetorical Criticism and the New Testament', *Bijdragen* 50 (1989), pp. 239–53; C. Clifton Black II, 'Keeping up with Recent Studies: Rhetorical Criticism and Biblical Interpretation', *ExpTim* 100 (1988/89), pp. 252–58.
2. For the relationship of narrative and rhetoric in Greco-Roman antiquity, see Vernon K. Robbins, 'Narrative in Ancient Rhetoric and Rhetoric in Ancient Narrative', in Kent H. Richards (ed.) SBLSP, 35 (Atlanta: Scholars Press, 1996), pp. 368–84. Cf. also Satterthwaite, 'Classical Rhetoric', pp. 337–79.
3. *Acts*, esp. 39–50. Also, see Soards, *Speeches in Acts, passim*.
4. This is also the observation of Mikeal C. Parsons, 'Luke and the *Progymnasmata*: A Preliminary Investigation into the Preliminary Exercises', in *Contextualizing Acts*, p. 44: 'Nonetheless, with some notable exceptions scholars have been reluctant to apply these insights to the Gospel of Luke and the narrative portions of Acts'. Two exceptions are Diefenbach, *Komposition des Lukasevangeliums* and Morgenthaler, *Lukas und Quintilian*.

stage approach in examining texts from antiquity: (1) definition of the rhetorical unit; (2) delineation of the rhetorical situation; (3) identification of the rhetorical disposition and arrangement; (4) examination of rhetorical techniques and style; and (5) evaluation of rhetorical criticism as a synchronic whole.[5] Application of Kennedy's model is widespread, ranging from the rhetorical structure and argumentation of the Pauline and non-Pauline letters to the speeches of the four Gospels as well as those of Acts.

A. *Rhetorical Invention, Arrangement, and Style*

According to Kennedy, when delimiting the rhetorical situation, the focus must be on the premises of the ascribed text as appeal or argument – the complex of persons, events, and relations generating the basis for a verbal response. The situation controls the rhetorical response, the question controls the answer, and the problem controls the solution.[6] Kennedy defines rhetorical disposition and arrangement as 'what subdivisions a text falls into, what the persuasive effect of these parts seems to be, and how they work together – or fail to do so – to some unified purpose in meeting the rhetorical situation'.[7] Rhetorical invention, according to the handbooks, consists of three different species: judiciary, deliberative, and epideictic. Judicial speeches, with the law court as their setting, focus on the speaker's desire to convince the audience of past actions by means of accusation or defense. Deliberative speeches, with legislative settings as their contextual frame, pertain to future events, with the speaker aspiring to persuade or dissuade the audience about a course of action intended for the future. Epideictic speeches, with the public assembly as their setting, refer to present events, drawing on praise or blame in an attempt to bring about honor or shame on the individual or group of individuals in question.[8]

Greco-Roman oratory, as taught in the tertiary phases of education, consists of five parts: (1) invention – the planning of a discourse and the arguments used in it;[9] (2) arrangement – the composition of the different

5. *Through Rhetorical Criticism*, pp. 33–38.
6. Kennedy follows Lloyd F. Bitzer's understanding of the argumentative or rhetorical situation ('The Rhetorical Situation', *Philosophy and Rhetoric* 1 [1968], pp. 1–14). Bitzer contends that 'a particular discourse comes into existence because of some specific condition or situation that invites utterance. The situation controls the rhetorical response in the same sense that the question controls the answer and the problem controls the solution'. (4–6)
7. *Through Rhetorical Criticism*, p. 37.
8. Because most of the New Testament letters and speeches do not easily fall into one of the three species, a number of scholars contend there is often a utilization of more than one species. Note the comment of Kennedy: 'In a single discourse there is sometimes more than one species, and the definition of the species as a whole can become very difficult, but a discourse usually has one dominant species that reflects the author's major purpose in speaking or writing' (*Through Rhetorical Criticism*, p. 19).
9. For an overview of 'invention' in ancient rhetoric, see Malcolm Heath, 'Invention', in Stanley E. Porter (ed.), *Handbook of Classical Rhetoric in the Hellenistic Period 330 B.C. - A.D. 400* (Leiden, New York, and Köln: Brill Publishing, 1997), pp. 89–119.

parts into a whole;[10] (3) style – the choice of words and the placement of them into sentences, including the use of figures;[11] (4) memory – the preparation for delivery; and (5) delivery – the control of the voice and use of gestures.[12] Most who draw upon the rhetorical handbooks utilize the first three parts, though there has been an increasing amount of attention paid to the latter two, particularly in regard to the fact that reading in Greco-Roman society was an oral/aural experience and certain rhetorical conventions in the New Testament coincide with presentation requirements surrounding memory and delivery.[13]

Judicial speeches consist of five basic parts. An exordium (or proem) seeks to obtain the goodwill and attention of the audience; the narratio (or statement of facts) specifies the objectives of the speech; the proof details the speaker's arguments, with a refutation of opposing views; and the conclusio (or epilogue) summarizes the speech's primary arguments and seeks to bring about a judgment or action on the part of the audience. The deliberative speech has the same elements, minus the refutation. An epideictic speech also reflects a similar arrangement, with the addition of ecphrasis (vivid description) and synkrisis (comparison) in the rhetorical argument.

B. *Rhetorical Handbooks and New Testament Rhetoric*

Difficulties in a carte blanche use of rhetorical frameworks contained within the ancient rhetorical handbooks to analyze the New Testament writings began to be recognized in the 1990s.[14] The breakdown revolves around the

10.   For an overview of 'arrangement' in ancient rhetoric, see Wilhelm Wuellner, 'Arrangement', in *Handbook*, pp. 51–88.

11.   For an overview of 'style' in ancient rhetoric, see Galen O. Rowe, 'Style', in *Handbook*, pp. 121–57.

12.   For an overview of 'memory' and 'delivery' in ancient rhetoric, see Thomas H. Olbricht, 'Delivery and Memory', in *Handbook*, pp. 159–70.

13.   See, e.g., Birger Gerhardsson, *Memory and Manuscript: Oral Tradition and Written Transmission in Rabbinic Judaism and Early Christianity* (Grand Rapids: William B. Eerdmans Publishing Company, 1998), pp. 163–68; Ray Nadeau, 'Delivery in Ancient Times: Homer to Quintilian', *Quarterly Journal of Speech* 50 (1964), pp. 53–60. Also, cf. Whitney Shiner, *Proclaiming the Gospel: First-Century Performance of Mark* (Harrisburg, Pa.: Trinity Press International, 2003), *passim*, for an analysis of memory and delivery in relationship to the Gospel of Mark.

14.   The most prominent and thorough criticism of those who use the rhetorical handbooks for analyzing the New Testament is that of Philip H. Kern, *Rhetoric and Galatians: Assessing an approach to Paul's epistle* (SNTSMS, 101; Cambridge: Cambridge University Press, 1998). He places rhetoric into four separate categories: (1) level one rhetoric: effective communication that draws on universal rhetorical strategies; (2) level two rhetoric: persuasive speech that aims to persuade the audience to accept a new position; (3) level three rhetoric: a form of verbal discourse that conforms to specific patterns of expression determined by the group to which the speaker belongs; and (4) level four: rhetorical discourse deployed in specific venues. As the venues for the New Testament writings and classical handbooks are disparate, Kern argues that it is impossible to examine New Testament texts as a mirror image of the rhetorical argument found in the rhetorical

contextual differences between the rhetoric of the ancient handbooks and that of the New Testament. Ancient oratory and the rhetoric of the New Testament epistles are not of the same genre and, while rhetorical texture is found in epistolary conventions, this does not necessitate that they be viewed as the same – a conclusion reached by many who took up rhetorical criticism in the 1980s and 1990s.[15] In particular, the category of rhetoric in the ancient handbooks is formulated for formal oratory settings – judiciary, deliberative, and epideictic – and not for written communication to specific communities.[16] In addition, rhetorical study in antiquity focused on court and assembly oratory (viz., guidelines for public speaking). Those who received training in the rhetoric of the ancient handbooks, as a result, were a very small group, and, therefore, the likelihood that any of the New Testament writers received formal rhetorical training is doubtful.[17] Conversely, for those who contend that most were exposed to rhetoric in the vein of the handbooks – and the New Testament writers, as a result, simply drew upon this assimilated knowledge – it is unlikely that the bulk of the populace attended court and public assemblies, the two venues where handbook rhetoric would have been practiced.[18]

The lynchpin holding together analysis of New Testament letters using ancient handbook rhetoric involves the contention that letter writing and oratory were not disparate enterprises. It is becoming increasingly evident, however, that the two were not integrated until centuries after the first

---

handbooks. Instead, he concludes that while the rhetorical handbooks represent level four rhetoric, the New Testament simply coincides as level- two rhetoric; rhetorical analysis of the New Testament should examine the texts using rhetorical categories with universal appeal. While I concur with Kern's contention that the rhetoric of the New Testament does not fit the parameters of handbook rhetoric, I disagree on the categorization of the New Testament as level two rhetoric. Rather, as the New Testament is enmeshed within the constraints of Greco-Roman antiquity, a presupposition pool upon which the implied author and implied reader draw, I contend that it more closely coincides with level three rhetoric.

I would like to thank Professor Loveday C. A. Alexander for calling my attention to this monograph and to credit Professor Alexander and Professor John M. G. Barclay for their recommendations to re-evaluate my initial analysis of the four Lukan Galilean speeches, though neither is responsible for deficiencies or errors in my theoretical formulation and subsequent rhetorical analysis.

15. Stanley E. Porter ('Paul of Tarsus and His Letters', in *Handbook*, pp. 533–86) raises four cautionary observations: (1) rhetorical interpretations yield different results as to the genre and arrangement of individual documents; (2) the Roman and Greek rhetorical sources are used in an opportunistic manner; (3) the amount of epistolary material considered by each scholar as rhetorical widely varies from scholar to scholar; and (4) rhetorical and epistolary structures often do not coincide, thereby creating a 'stumbling block' for most interpreters (p. 561).

16. For an in-depth discussion, see Kern, *Rhetoric and Galatians*, pp. 12–38.

17. However cf. Jerome H. Neyrey, 'The Social Location of Paul: Education as the Key', in David B. Gowler, L. Gregory Bloomquist, and Duane F. Watson (eds), *Fabrics of Discourse* (Festschrift Vernon K. Robbins; Harrisburg: Trinity Press International, 2003), pp. 157–64.

18. Kern, *Rhetoric and Galatians*, pp. 61–66.

century CE.[19] Letter writing was not of interest to the rhetoricians; rather, the rhetorical handbooks occasionally refer to epistolary conventions in order to highlight differences in the arena of style – with invention and arrangement not in purview.[20]

A final issue relates to the literary level of early Christian communication. The rhetorical argument of the New Testament and, for the most part, early Christianity does not fall into the vein of that deemed as classical rhetoric.[21] The closest resembling the upper hierarchy would be the Epistle to the Hebrews and the prefaces to Luke (1.1-4) and Acts (1.1-2), though all fall beneath the most prestigious classical modes of rhetoric. The remainder of the New Testament reflects the language of the general population, a literary level, while far from the bottom of the literary hierarchy, that certainly does not coincide with the invention, arrangement, and style typically associated with classical rhetoric.[22]

II. *Delineating the Parameters of Rhetorical Texture*

The aforementioned differences between the New Testament and the Greco-Roman rhetorical handbooks, however, do not result in a complete estrangement. Rather than examining New Testament texts based on rhetorical invention and arrangement and, to a lesser extent, rhetorical style, as defined within the handbook tradition, we can do so in terms of rhetorical texture. A rhetorical analysis of the New Testament – or in the case of this study, Luke-Acts – does not place the rhetorical conventions of the handbooks alongside New Testament text with the anticipation of mirrored structures or patterns coming into immediate focus. Instead, rhetorical texture, comprised of argument with a goal of persuasion, is a more appropriate methodological approach. It does not adhere to a rigid mode of invention and arrangement but aspects of argumentation – deductive and inductive. Derivation comes from standard modes of argumentation, topoi ('commonplace' arguments) not only found in the handbooks but various other texts as well. Further, concern is less with genre and structure and

19. See Edward P. J. Corbett, *Classical Rhetoric and the Modern Student* (Oxford: Oxford University Press, 1965), p. 20.

20. See, e.g., Stanley E. Porter, 'The Theoretical Justification for Application of Rhetorical Categories to Pauline Epistolary Literature', in *Rhetoric and the New Testament*, pp. 108–16.

21. The basis for pinpointing the differences in Hellenistic Greek and New Testament Greek is the work of Adolf Deissmann, 'Hellenistic Greek with Special Consideration of the Greek Bible', in Stanley E. Porter (ed.), *The Language of the New Testament: Classic Essays* (Sheffield: Sheffied Academic Press, 1991), pp. 39–59.

22. See the conclusions of Kern, *Rhetoric and Galatians*, pp. 247–55. Also, see Thomas H. Olbricht, 'An Aristotelian Rhetorical Analysis of 1 Thessalonians', in *Greeks, Romans, and Christians*, pp. 216–36, who argues that early Christianity developed its own distinctive rhetorical topoi.

more with effective argumentation – namely, the use of rhetorical topoi familiar to the audience.

As the rhetorical analysis of the four Lukan Galilean ministry speeches shows, these topoi involve all three textual dimensions: intertextual, intratextual, and extratextual. Of the rhetorical proofs found in the rhetorical handbooks, the most relevant for the study of the New Testament is that of style, as its primary concern is with the ways in which the audience appropriate rhetorical argument.[23]

As scholars search for alternative sources to analyze New Testament rhetoric, one group of texts receiving significant scrutiny in recent years are the handbooks of the progymnasmata – exercises used in the secondary schools (usually boys between the age of twelve and fifteen) of Greco-Roman antiquity for preliminary rhetorical training.[24] The curriculum in the progymnasmata features a series of pedagogical exercises that served as the basis for written and oral expression, with a focus on how to engage effectively in dialectical debate. Issues related to invention and arrangement, which receive significant attention in the rhetorical handbooks, do not garner mention in the progymnasmata. Instead, the exercises examine rhetorical conventions useful in persuasive argument within the context of three modes of communication: the chreia, fable, and narration. Overlap with the rhetorical handbooks occurs on the level of rhetorical style and its use in successful argumentation, ranging from maxim, to enthymeme, to repetition, to ecphrasis (vivid description), to synkrisis (comparison).

It now is commonly held that all texts are ideologically located – reflecting social, political, religious, gender, and other biases. Narrative discourse is inescapably enmeshed within certain cultural constructs, with the implied author – both intentionally and unintentionally – using rhetorical texture as a vehicle for bringing about a response on the part of the authorial audience. In this context, rhetorical texture affects the ways in which authorial readers might actualize the narrative discourse – namely, ways in which the narrative discourse reinforces, reinterprets, and confronts the ideological beliefs of the authorial audience.[25] This study begins by examining the

---

23. This assessment of style, as opposed to the less universal categories of invention and arrangement, coincides with that of Rowe ('Style', p. 121): '... the ancient precepts on style apply to any verbal expression and not simply to that which is used to persuade. These precepts inform poetry as well as prose, historical writings, philosophical essays, and letters as well as political and forensic speeches .... The criteria, the so-called virtues (ἀρεταί/ *virtutes*) of correctness, clarity, ornamentation, and propriety, form the basis of the entire classical theory.'

24. For an introduction and translation to the progymnasmata, see George A. Kennedy, *Progymnasmata: Greek Textbooks and Prose Composition and Rhetoric* (Writings from the Greco-Roman World, 10; Leiden and Boston: Brill, 2003). There are four extant progymnasmata: Aelius Theon (late first century BCE), Hermogenes of Tarsus (second century CE), Aphthonius the Sophist (fourth century CE), and Nicolaus the Sophist (fifth century CE).

25. Cf. Wilhelm Wuellner who has been pivotal in helping to push classical rhetorical analysis into the realms of discourse and ideological systems and the ways in which these

rhetorical texture of the four Lukan Galilean ministry speeches on the basis of argumentative style and conventions. It thereafter probes the discourse for its ideological rhetoric, ways in which the rhetorical texture persuades authorial readers to make certain judgments about plot, theme, characterization, and topoi.

A. *Rhetorical Proof: Logos, Pathos, and Ethos*

One nuance of rhetorical texture that largely transcends the rhetorical handbooks is Aristotle's delineation of rhetorical proof as consisting of logos, pathos, and ethos. The latter refers to character and establishes the credibility of the speaker. It serves an important role in the characterization of Jesus in Luke and the characterization of the major protagonists in Acts. Negative caricatures in Luke-Acts also draw upon the proof of ethos. Pathos refers to the ability of the speaker to evince an emotive response from the audience. Of the three rhetorical proofs, pathos is the least relevant for Luke-Acts, though there are places where it is evident. Logos is the most encompassing rhetorical proof, consisting of both inductive and deductive reasoning. Inductive argument uses examples and stories as well as various rhetorical devices to persuade or dissuade the audience. One aspect of doing so – since ancient rhetoric was done for the ear and not for the eye, aural and not visual – was by means of sound, whereby the use of repetition was used to elicit a response from the audience. Deductive argumentation utilizes rhetorical questioning, maxims, and enthymemes. The argumentation of the latter two (viz., maxims and enthymemes) involves topoi (or motifs) embedded within the rhetorical discourse.[26] The four Galilean speeches in Luke include significant deductive and inductive argument, aspects of their rhetorical texture covered in the next four chapters.

B. *Rhetorical Questioning*

Rhetorical questioning typically assumes that the audience agrees with the presupposed answer. The response to the question is often left unanswered. It is assumed that the audience – both the narrative audience and implied reader – answers correctly.[27] The use of logos in rhetorical questioning serves as a form of power: the implied reader is prompted to view the protagonist in a positive light, as one who speaks with authority and uses logical proofs, and the antagonist in a negative light, as one who lacks

---

exercise persuasive power during the mode of hermeneutical appropriation – both for readers in antiquity and readers today (see, e.g., 'Hermeneutics and Rhetorics: From "Truth and Method" to "Truth and Power"', *Scriptura* 3 [1989], pp. 1–54; idem, 'Where is Rhetorical Criticism Taking Us?' *CBQ* 49 [1987], pp. 448–63).

26. Aristotle, *Rhetoric*, 2.22.13–2.23.30. Also, see the *progymnasmata*: Theon, 96–106; Hermogenes, 8c–10; Aphthonius, 25b–27b; Nicolaus, 25–29a.

27. Demetrius, *On Style*, 278–279; *Rhetorica ad Herennium*, 4.16; Quintilian, *Institutio Oratoria*, 9.3.90–9.3.98; Cicero, *De Oratore*, 3.54.207.

authority and fails to speak with logical proofs. The implied author of Luke-Acts uses rhetorical questioning to demarcate differences in characterization – specifically about the characterization of Jesus and his disciples in contrast with their opponents. Hence, for the implied reader, the argument of Jesus and his disciples coincides with the logical protocols of the world and life, whereas the argument of their opponents runs counter to the norms of the world and life.

When rhetorical questioning is delineated in an uninterrupted series, the result is a heightening of the aural/oral impact. A series of rhetorical questions also serve to illustrate (in the case of the implied reader) the utter lack of logos on the part of the opponents of Jesus and his disciples (viz., they are not only at odds with one precept of life or the world but commonly accepted standards). Both the second (Lk. 6.20-49) and third (Lk. 7.24-35) speeches of Jesus in the Galilean ministry employ the latter; the result is an incremental gradation in the amplification of argument that reaches its apex with the final rhetorical question (e.g., Jesus' questions regarding John the Baptist in Lk. 7.24-27).

C. *Maxims*

Maxims, in general, are the premise or conclusion of an enthymeme, summarizing general truths based on popular wisdom. Some maxims appear without a reason, whereas others include a reason.[28] Specifically, when maxims state something contrary to general opinion they require a supporting reason. For example, the conclusion 'a student who spends significant time preparing for exams is deceived in thinking she is assured of attaining high grades' requires the accompanying reason: 'painstaking preparation for exams is just one of several factors that determine the performance of a student'. Of course, these types of maxims often blur the lines of demarcation between maxims and enthymemes, as more complex maxims such as this one actually exhibit enthymematic argument.[29]

The rhetorical function of maxims is for the sake of argument and not simply to dispense moral axioms. At the same time, they imbue speeches with ethos (viz., credibility) through their use of commonly accepted opinions (viz., topoi).

---

28. It is unclear as to whether these instances – maxim plus a reason – qualify as actual enthymemes or simply resemble enthymematic argument; cf. Aristotle, *Rhetoric*, 2.21.6: 'As for the maxims that are accompanied by an epilogue (viz., reason), some partake of the nature of, but not of the form of, enthymemes'. Also, see Theon, 96–97; Hermogenes, 8b–10; Aphthonius, 25b–27c; Nicolaus, 25–29, for a discussion of maxim within the progymnasmata.

29. Aristotle, *Rhetoric*, 2.21.1–2.21.16; *Rhetorica ad Herennium*, 4.17; Demetrius, *On Style*, 9.

D. *Enthymemes*

Enthymemes have received a spate of attention in the past decade in New Testament scholarship. David E. Aune recently questioned some of the underlying assumptions of the methodological approach of these investigations. Some of the key reasons he cites include: (1) Aristotle's *Rhetoric*, upon which much of rhetorical investigation of the New Testament is based, was largely unknown during the first century CE; (2) the premises of enthymematic argument are based on probabilities and not certainties (which largely runs counter to most analysis by New Testament scholars); and (3) enthymemes cannot be restricted simply to truncated syllogisms (viz., a conclusion and premise with a missing premise that must be deduced by the audience).[30] As regards to the latter, Aune contends – on the basis of Demetrius and Quintilian – that enthymemes in the first century CE comprised four different forms: (1) a thought; (2) an inference from consequents or contraries; (3) a rhetorical syllogism; and (4) an incomplete (or truncated) syllogism.[31] Aune then proceeds to fault New Testament scholarship on the basis that three of the four enthymematic forms are largely neglected, focusing almost exclusively on the truncated syllogism.

Aune provides a valuable critique of enthymematic investigation in New Testament scholarship, specifically the need to look at enthymematic argument beyond that of incomplete syllogism and the fact that some scholars have pushed the presence of enthymemes beyond the constraints of supporting reason (viz., when the syllogisms are retraced, the reasoning disintegrates). Nevertheless, his analysis is unconvincing on two fronts. First, the dismissal of Aristotelean influence on the Greco-Roman rhetorical handbooks and, moreover, the New Testament writers is nebulous: there is evidence of several first-century CE writers – and quite possibly Demetrius and Quintilian, as well as the progymnasmata handbook of Aelius Theon – who knew of Aristotle's *Rhetoric* and drew upon it.[32] In short, there is a difference between showing appropriate caution in the 'wholesale' application of Aristotle's *Rhetoric* to the New Testament and

---

30. 'The Use and Abuse of the Enthymeme in New Testament Scholarship', *NTS* 49 (2003), pp. 299–320, esp. pp. 302–07; idem, 'Enthymeme', in *Westminster Dictionary*, pp. 150–57.

31. Aune ('Abuse of the Enthymeme', pp. 300–1) posits a fifth enthymematic form in Quintilian (a maxim supported by a reason) but seemingly dismisses it as irrelevant since it is not found in Demetrius. His almost immediate dismissal requires some form of reasoning, which he fails to provide. Further, simply because it is lacking in Demetrius is not sufficient evidence to excise it from purview (viz., on the basis that it was not a common component of rhetorical systems of the first century CE).

32. Cicero, *De inventione*, 1.7; Dionysius, *Epistle ad Ammaeum*, 1.6–9; Demetrius, *On Style*, 34; Theon, 61b. See George A. Kennedy, 'The Composition and Influence of Aristotle's *Rhetoric*', in A. O. Rorty (ed.), *Essays on Aristotle's Rhetoric* (Berkeley, Los Angeles, and London: University of California Press, 1996), pp. 416–24.

dispensing with it as altogether irrelevant.[33] Second, Aune's fourfold distinction between different enthymematic forms is questionable. The passage in Demetrius (*On Style*, 30–33) that Aune concludes specifies four different enthymematic forms is certainly not clear on the matter. Indeed, Demetrius seems to denote the enthymeme as a thought that can be expressed in two different ways: either as a contrast or as a logical consequence (*On Style*, 30). And Demetrius' following reference to the enthymeme as a rhetorical syllogism and incomplete syllogism (*On Style*, 32) is a further definition of the enthymeme (in contrast to the period) and not an additional enthymematic form (or even ways in which they can be expressed). In summary, nowhere is it apparent that Demetrius is delineating four separate forms of the enthymeme.

Aune's examination of the passages from Quintilian also exhibits a tendency to identify a multiplicity of enthymematic forms. In particular, in contrast to Aune, Quintilian, like Demetrius, appears to identify two basic modes of enthymematic expression: as a consequence or as a contrast.[34] Further, construal of the enthymeme as a 'thought' is simply an overarching description and not a mode of expression. Discussion of the form of an enthymeme as a rhetorical syllogism or incomplete syllogism in Quintilian (or, for that matter, a maxim supported by a reason – the enthymematic 'form' Aune identifies as present in Quintilian but not Demetrius) is as explanation of and not in addition to the modes of expression (viz., as a consequence or in contrast). As a result of the above, Aune's division of enthymematic forms in Demetrius and Quintilian is deficient, and thus further scrutiny is required.

With the aforementioned at the forefront, what can be said regarding enthymematic argument and New Testament studies and, most notably, the narrative discourse of Luke-Acts?[35] First, some enthymemes occur as incomplete (or truncated) syllogisms. Here it is important to note that the constructed syllogism must exhibit 'reverse engineering' in which the different parts of the syllogism can be identified: a major premise, minor premise, and conclusion, with one of the three implicit, typically one of the premises – and the requirement for the audience to fill it. The missing premise must be a common notion widely accepted by the audience and is

---

33. Aune's methodological approach is 'muddy' in that he spends significant time detailing enthymematic argument according to Aristotle's *Rhetoric* ('Abuse of the Enthymeme', pp. 302–6) but then quickly dismisses the work as irrelevant for New Testament rhetorical investigation ('Abuse of the Enthymeme', pp. 306–07).

34. Quintilian, *Institutio Oratoria*, 5.10.2; 14.1.1.

35. Though faulty in his overly rigid classification of all clauses with γάρ and ὅτι as minor premises of an enthymematic argument, see Richard B. Vison, 'A Comparative Study of the Use of Enthymemes in the Synoptic Gospels', in Duane F. Watson (ed.), *Persuasive Artistry: Studies in New Testament Rhetoric* (Festschrift George A. Kennedy; JSNTSup, 50; Sheffield: Sheffield Academic Press, 1991), pp. 93–118, for an overview of enthymemes in Luke.

filled through deductive reasoning.[36] The conclusion of the incomplete syllogism must be reached through the combination of the major premise – universal probability and acceptable by definition – and minor premise – more specific but also generally acceptable. The following is a fairly simple, straightforward example of an incomplete syllogism: 'college students who fail to attend class typically do not receive passing grades, because preparation for exams takes place during class sessions'. Reconstruction of the enthymematic argument results in the identification of the conclusion, 'college students who fail to attend class typically do not receive passing grades', and the major premise, 'preparation for exams takes place during class sessions'. Simply implied in the rhetorical argument, the minor premise, a commonly accepted probability (viz., 'exams are a key component of the grading process'), must be filled in by the audience. The four Lukan Galilean ministry speeches each contain examples of this enthymematic form, ranging from the introduction to the first speech (4.18-19), to various aspects of the body of the second speech (6.32-45), to portions of the body of the third speech (7.32-34), to the conclusion of the fourth speech (8.16-18).

Second, enthymemes serve to either refute or demonstrate, with the juxtaposition of two elements as the most popular mode of argumentation.[37] A conjunctive (e.g., ὅτι, γάρ) often separates the two parts of the enthymeme. A syllogistic formula is not a requisite in order for a rhetorical argument to be classified as an enthymeme. Refutative enthymemes draw their conclusions from facts that are disputed (often by an adversary), whereas demonstrative enthymemes draw their conclusions from generally accepted facts (admitted by the adversary). The following is an example of a refutative enthymeme: the conclusion, 'money can be put to bad use and therefore is not good', derives from the combination of the major premise, 'money is not a good thing', and minor premise, 'that which is not good can be put to a bad use'.[38] Refutative enthymemes in the four Galilean ministry speeches are found in the introduction to the second speech (6.20-26) and the body of the third speech (7.31-34). The following is an example of a demonstrative enthymeme: the conclusion, 'a student should spend significant time studying for her exam', results from the combination of the major premise, 'the student received poor grades on prior exams when she failed to study', and minor premise, 'significant time studying results in

---

36. Note the comment of Aristotle (*Rhetoric*, 2.23.30): 'But of all syllogisms, whether refutative or demonstrative, those are specially applauded, the result of which the hearers foresee as soon as they are begun, and not because they are superficial (for as they listen they congratulate themselves on anticipating the conclusion); and also those which the hearers are only so little behind that they understand what they mean as soon as they are delivered'.

37. While Aristotle (*Rhetoric*, 2.23.30) makes the claim that refutative enthymemes are preferable to those that demonstrate because of their use of opposites in the formulation of argumentation, he concurrently posits the use of opposites as one mode of argumentation that can be used when employing a demonstrative enthymeme (*Rhetoric*, 2.23.23).

38. See Quintilian, *Institutio Oratoria*, 5.14.25.

good grades'. The four speeches in the Galilean ministry include a number of demonstrative enthymemes such as the latter part of the body of the second speech (6.43-45) and the conclusion of the fourth speech (8.16-18).

Third, as Aune and others point out, enthymemes also occur in the form of contraries, whereby two opposite statements are juxtaposed. The following is an example of this type of enthymematic argument: the statement, 'rain causes the grass to grow', when combined with the premise, 'grass withers without moisture', results in the following conclusion: 'lack of rainfall produces withered grass'. Within the context of my investigation, the most obvious instance of this form of enthymematic argument is the introduction to the second speech (Lk. 6.20-26). The premise of the third speech also employs two opposites in the form of an enthymematic argument (7.28).

Fourth, enthymematic argument in the New Testament includes the use of abductive reasoning, rhetorical argument that uses transcendent topoi – which cannot be seen – to suggest similarities between the transcendent and the reality of earthly experiences.[39] This is important in that the actions of the divine establish a precedent for humans to emulate. In the context of enthymematic argument, different attributes and actions of the divine stand as major and/or minor premises. For example, the conclusion, 'children of God should show benefaction to the poor without expectation of reciprocity', and the major premise, 'God shows benefaction to the poor without expectation of reciprocity', yield the minor premise (implied), 'children of God emulate the actions of the divine'. The enthymematic argument comprising the enthymematic rationale concluding the first section of the body in the second speech (6.36) corresponds with the abductive form of argument.

Fifth, enthymematic argument is a mode of persuasion through which topoi – symbolic systems representing recognizable premises – provide a means for deductive association or disassociation.[40] The premises of enthymemes are not certainties but rather probabilities expressed through the use of logos, ethos, and pathos.[41] Aristotle cites four sources for enthymematic argument: probabilities, examples, necessary signs, and signs.[42] As they make for more effective argument, most of the enthymemes

39. See Richard L. Lanigan, 'From Enthymeme to Abduction: The Classical Law of Logic and the Postmodern Rule of Rhetoric', in Lenore Langsdorf and Andrew R. Smith (eds), *Recovering Pragmatism's Voice: The Classical Tradition, Rorty, and the Philosophy of Communication* (Albany, New York: SUNY Press, 1995), pp. 49–70; Bruce J. Malina, 'Interpretation: Reading, Abduction, Metaphor', in David Jobling, et al. (eds), *The Bible and the Politics of Exegesis* (Festschrift Norman K. Gottwad; Cleveland, Ohio: Pilgrim Press, 1991), pp. 253–66.

40. See, e.g., Thomas B. Farrell, 'Aristotle's Enthymeme as Tacit Reference', in *Rereading Aristotle's Rhetoric*, pp. 93–106.

41. See Antoine C. Braet, 'Ethos, Pathos, and Logos in Aristotle's '*Rhetoric*': A Reexamination', *Argumentation* 6 (1992), pp. 307–20, who argues that ethos, pathos, and logos comprise enthymematic argument in Aristotle's *Rhetoric*.

42. *Rhetoric*, 2.25.8–2.25.14.

in the four speeches use probabilities and examples as their topoi. Ultimately, enthymematic networks invite the implied reader to search for topoi elsewhere, both within and outside the text (encompassing the intratext, extratext, and intertext).[43] An instance of topoi from outside of the text is the conclusion to the fourth speech (8.16-18), which assumes an extratextual repertoire, requisite knowledge that the narrative audience and implied reader must tap in order to enact coherence. Also, as already mentioned above, abductive argument, topoi from outside of the text involving the disposition and actions of the divine, frequently serves as an enthymematic rationale in New Testament literature (cf. Lk. 6.36). An example of topoi from within the text is the statement of case of the third speech (7.28), which compels the implied reader to draw upon intratextual information from earlier narrative (1.5–2.52) in order to complete the rhetorical construction.

Finally, enthymemes appear as key markers in speeches, serving as stylistic mechanisms for capturing pivotal topoi for the implied reader. In particular, enthymemes round off argument so that the inference cannot be refuted – or, if refuted, with the greatest level of difficulty.[44] An excellent example of the latter is the conclusion to the fourth speech (8.16-18), where the narrative switches from the largely inductive argument of the introduction (8.5-8a), statement of case (8.8b-10), and body (8.11-15) to deduction. Regardless, enthymemes are not be used in overabundance, which detracts from the overall effectiveness of the argumentation.[45] The rhetorical texture in the four speeches corresponds with this approach. For example, the introduction to the second speech (6.20-26) consists of a series of enthymemes that builds for optimal impact through repetition: switches to maxims in the statement of case (6.27-31), moves to a mixture of rhetorical questioning, maxims, and enthymemes in the body (6.32-45), and concludes with inductive examples in the conclusion (6.46-49).

III. *Speeches in Ancient Greco-Roman Narrative*

Speeches in ancient Greco-Roman narrative – ranging from epic, to novels, to historiography, to biography – play a pivotal role in inscribing narrative discourse,[46] providing the framework from which the implied reader generates plotlines, discerns theme and motifs (topoi), and construes characterization. As such, speeches serve as the means through which

43. Thomas M. Conley, 'The Enthymeme in Perspective', *Quarterly Journal of Speech* 70 (1984), pp. 168–87, who argues this point and others regarding the Aristotelean enthymeme.

44. *Rhetorica ad Herennium*, 4.23.26.

45. Aristotle, *Rhetoric*, 3.17.6–3.17.8; Quintilian, *Institutio Oratoria*, 5.14.27–5.14.32.

46. The amount of research on the role of speeches in ancient Greco-Roman narrative is significant; see, e.g., Peter Toohey, *Reading Epic: An Introduction to the Ancient Narratives* (New York: Routledge, 1992); Virginia J. Hunter, *Past and Process in Herodotus and Thucydides* (Princeton: Princeton University Press, 1982).

implied authors communicate information to implied readers, the derivation being the identification of narrative trajectories and then construction of the narrative discourse. In addition, versus modern and postmodern narrative, ancient Greco-Roman narrative is not interested in telling what happened but in explaining why and how with details regarding who. Within this context, speeches typically provide the implied reader with the 'ligaments and muscle' needed to ascertain the specific contours of the narrative skeleton, interpretive grids containing information used to bring coherence and consistency to the narrative and, in turn, to make hermeneutical judgments about the actions of characters and character groups and ideological systems represented by the narrative discourse.

An important framing mechanism, speeches evoke both analeptic and proleptic activity and provide the implied reader with both implicit commentary and explanation on preceding narrative and an interpretive framework for discerning coherence from subsequent narrative. As to the latter, speeches often help propel the narrative forward by introducing changes in plotline(s), adding to or introducing new topoi and laying an 'interpretive filter' from which evaluations can be made regarding the actions of characters (whether protagonists, antagonists, or simply minor characters). Specifically, speeches in the initial stages of narrative – given by both of protagonists and antagonists – play an integral role in the evaluation of later scenes and actions by the implied reader. Likewise speeches at the conclusion of a narrative provide important information that guides the implied reader in bringing the plotline to completion[47] or, in some instances, creates dissonance that spurs hermeneutical appropriation.[48]

IV. *Concluding Summary*

The aforementioned analysis of ancient Greco-Roman rhetoric serves as the foundation for my examination of the speeches of Jesus in the Lukan Galilean ministry. This study begins with the understanding that speeches in

47. Alexander, 'Reading Luke-Acts', pp. 419–46.

48. Among the more notable examples of narratives that have open endings: Homer's *Iliad* and *Odyssey*; Philostratus' *Life of Apollonius*; and the Gospel of Mark (16.8). Luke-Acts fits this scenario as well, with Paul's final speech (Acts 28.17-28) providing both closure and suspension (e.g., Brosend, 'Means of absent ends', pp. 348–62; Marguerat, 'Silent Closing', pp. 284–304; idem, 'End of Acts', pp. 74–89).

While the speeches in Acts have received significant attention as they coincide with these tendencies, the speeches in Luke have garnered little recognition as speeches in their own right and, needless to say, in terms of their rhetorical argument. However, cf. David L. Balch ('ἀκριβῶς ... γράψαι (Luke 1:3): To Write the *Full* History of God's Receiving All Nations', in *Heritage of Israel*, p. 240: n. 41) in regard to the rhetorical examination of Soards (*Speeches in Acts*): '[He] fails to investigate the speeches in the Gospel of Luke or any connection the hymns in the infancy narrative might have to the speeches in Acts, and second, he fails to investigate any relationship to speeches in Greco-Roman historiography beyond formal rhetorical categories'.

ancient Greco-Roman narrative – specifically those placed at the beginning of the narrative – prompt implied readers to delineate core elements of narrative texture, ranging from plot, to theme, to characterization, to topoi. Second, the rhetorical texture – most notably style – helps the implied reader to build overarching narrative coherence. In particular, both deductive (viz., rhetorical questioning, maxims, and enthymemes) and inductive (viz., examples, parables) argumentation guide the implied reader in the creation of meaning from the narrative. Finally, as discussed in greater detail in Chapter nine, rhetorical texture serves an important role in the identification of ideological systems represented by the narrative discourse and the different ways in which rhetorical texture confirms, reinterprets, and confronts the ideological location of authorial readers.

PART TWO: RHETORICAL TEXTURE OF THE FOUR LUKAN GALILEAN MINISTRY SPEECHES

CHAPTER 4: THE FIRST GALILEAN MINISTRY SPEECH (LK. 4.14-30):
HOMETOWN SYNAGOGUE REJECTS NEW PATRONAL BOUNDARIES

Luke 4.14-30 shapes Jesus' ethos by drawing upon the past in the form of Jesus' citation of two LXX examples associated with Elijah and Elisha. Here, Jesus draws similarities between those who rejected Elijah and Elisha in the LXX because of their embrace of Gentiles and those who reject him because of his extension of salvation to those outside of the boundaries of kinship and friendship. Through the narrative discourse the implied author establishes an antagonistic character type – initially comprised of Jesus' hometown synagogue crowd – that the implied reader expands to include other characters and character groups as the narrative progresses.

I. *Rhetorical Situation*

The rhetorical situation for the first speech of the Lukan Galilean ministry (4.14-30) is established in vv. 14-16, which plays an important role in the implied reader's sequential processing. In particular, the narrative transition indicates that Jesus returns from the wilderness to initiate his ministry in Nazareth of Galilee. Verses 14-16 include some key intratextual linkages to the narrative section (1.5–2.52) following the prologue – a self-contained unit, addressing the birth and childhood of Jesus. The unit is comprised of three separate stories that move from the discourse of promise to that of praise response. As all three stories take place in Galilee, the implied reader is led to construe Galilee as a place of spiritual formation and growth. Specifically, the reference that Jesus returned to Galilee (vv. 14-16) prompts the implied reader to construe the rhetorical context of the speech with what has previously taken place in Galilee. This analeptic activity involves the following intratexts. First, in 1.26-38, the Angel Gabriel appears to Mary to announce her miraculous conception (1.26-38). Second, when Jesus and his parents return from Bethlehem to Galilee, the narrator notes that Jesus 'grew and became strong, filled with wisdom (σοφία); and the favor (χάρις) of God was upon him' (2.39-40). Third, after Jesus, who was at the age of twelve, travels with his parents to Jerusalem for the Feast of Passover, the narrator again notes that Jesus returned to Galilee, repeating some of the wording from the second account (2.39-34) – namely, that he 'increased in wisdom (σοφία) and in stature and in favor (χάρις) with God and man' (2.51-52). The geographical space of Galilee, as a result, is a place where the ethos of Jesus advances. The implied reader, therefore, expects similar results when approaching the inaugural speech of Jesus in 4.14-30.

In addition to the connotations represented by the geographical change, there are a number of verbal allusions in 4.14-15 to the preceding narrative, which also help to curry favorable expectations on the part of the implied reader. The implied author has already established that those to whom the Spirit (τοῦ πνεύματος) is attributed (v. 14) are to be viewed positively, as individuals or character groups endowed with special qualities (John the Baptist in 1.15; Elizabeth in 1.41; Zechariah in 1.67; Mary in 1.35; Simeon in 2.25, 27; and Jesus in 3.22). Further, the narrator's insertion that Jesus' attendance in the synagogue was done 'according to his custom' (κατὰ τὸ εἰωθὸς αὐτῷ) (v. 16) hearkens back to the time when Jesus, at the age of twelve, was lost in the temple and was found by his parents – who had searched for three days – at the feet of the teachers via the earlier intratext κατὰ τὸ ἔθος τῆς ἑορτῆς ('according to the custom') in 2.42. As a result, the implied reader anticipates, because of this intratextual linkage, that the earlier success – that is, the 'amazement' that the Jewish teachers displayed at his understanding (2.47) – will continue with the new scene in 4.14-30. Finally, use of the verb ὑποστρέφω (v. 14) hearkens back to 4.1, where the narrator also notes that Jesus 'returned' (ὑπέστρεψεν) endowed with the Spirit. The implied reader, based on this connection, expects Jesus' encounter with his hometown synagogue crowd to parallel the results in his confrontation with Satan in 4.1-15 – a rhetorical (logos) triumph. In sum, the rhetorical situation for the first Galilean speech of Jesus is cloaked in repetitive language reminiscent of earlier narrative that predisposes the implied reader to expect the following: (1) divine activity will likely occur: (2) Jesus will continue to advance his logos and ethos; and (3) the Nazareth synagogue crowd – in a privileged position concerning Jesus' identity – will warmly receive him.

II. *Rhetorical Texture*

The inaugural speech is widely accepted as playing a pivotal role in the establishment of plot and characterization for both Luke and Acts. However, few scholars see 4.14-30 as a speech imbued with rhetorical texture. Instead, most investigations concentrate on underlying source- and redaction-critical issues or the use of the LXX in the narrative scene.[1] Albeit without concern for ancient rhetoric, some recent attempts examine the impact of the speech upon the overall narrative discourse of Luke-Acts, with particular attention to matters such as plot, characterization, and

---

1. See, e.g., François Bovon, *Luke 1: A Commentary on the Gospel of Luke 1:1-9-50* (trans. Christine M. Thomas; Hermenia, Minn.: Fortress Press, 2002), pp. 148–57.

intratextual connections and patterns.[2] This study contends that the construction of narrative trajectories and discourse, as associated with and extending from 4.14-30, is closely tethered to the rhetorical texture of the speech. A thoroughgoing understanding of the speech and its relationship to the overall narrative, as a result, is not possible without first looking at its rhetorical argument.

A. *An Amplified Chreia*

An increasing number of scholars recognize that early Christian literature with sayings' material is often replete with chreiai.[3] The *Progymnasmata* delineates two types of chreia, the abbreviated and the amplified, with the latter consisting of the following parts: a narrative introduction, *digressio*, *quaestio* (seeking rationale), the chreia, a statement from the opposite, a statement from analogy, a statement from example, a statement by an authority, and conclusion/exhortation.[4] Not all of these elements must be present – and in the ascribed order – in order for a sayings' episode to conform as a chreia, but rather only the basic structure needs to be retained. The *Progymnasmata* divide chreiai into three major types: sayings-chreiai, action-chreiai, and mixed-chreiai. The sayings-chreia presents either a statement or a response. A response-chreia may occur in one of five different forms: (1) response to a simple question; (2) a response to an inquiry; (3) an explanatory response to a question; (4) a responsive chreia; and (5) a double chreia (contains statements from two characters).[5]

The inaugural speech resembles an amplified sayings-chreia in the form of a statement. The rhetorical texture is oriented towards the ethos of Jesus within the context of his relationship to his hometown family and friends. Verses 14-15 serve as the narrative introduction, with the prior narrative providing an interpretive framework for the implied reader. The reading from Deutero-Isaiah (vv. 16-19) functions as the quaestio (or rationale). The digressio in v. 20 is not an essential part of the narrative but rather provides suspense and sets the stage for the recitation of the chreia in vv. 21-22. The rationale is found in v. 23. A statement by analogy (v. 24) is followed with two statements by example (vv. 25-27). The conclusion is missing, as the

---

2. Two representative examples include Frans Neirynck, 'Luke 4,16-30 and the Unity of Luke-Acts', in *Unity of Luke-Acts*, pp. 357–95; Jeffrey S. Siker, ' "First to the Gentiles": A Literary Analysis of Luke 4:16-30', *JBL* 111 (1992), pp. 73–90.

3. For an overview of chreia, see Vernon K. Robbins, 'The Chreia', in David E. Aune (ed.), *Greco-Roman Literature and the New Testament* (Atlanta: Scholars Press, 1988), pp. 1–23.

4. For a description of expanded chreia, see Vernon K. Robbins, 'Introduction: Using Rhetorical Discussions of the Chreia to Interpret Pronouncement Stories', *Semeia* 64 (1993), pp. ix, xiii–xvi.

5. See *Progymnasmata: Greek Textbooks of Prose Composition and Rhetoric* (trans. with introductions and notes George A. Kennedy; Leiden and Boston: Brill, 2003), *passim*, esp. pp. ix–xvi, for detail on the chreiai.

narrative audience endeavors to end Jesus' life (vv. 28-30). As a result of the omission, the implied reader recognizes the missing element and must fill the narrative blank, concluding that the narrative audience was so agitated by Jesus' words they did not even allow him to complete his rhetorical argument. The following is a breakdown of the speech's chreia-like arrangement:

1. Narrative Introduction (vv. 14-15)   5. Rationale (v. 23)
2. *Quaestio* (vv. 16-19)   6. Statement by Analogy (v. 24)
3. *Digressio* (v. 20)   7. Statement by Example (vv. 25-27)
4. Chreia (vv. 21-22)   8. Missing Conclusion (vv. 28-30)

B. *Introduction: Narrative Introduction, Quaestio, and Digressio (4.18-20)*

The reading from Isaiah comprises the introduction (vv. 18-20), a passage embraced by many of the character groups from the narrative world of Luke-Acts (particularly the bulk of the Galilean populace) as representative of hope. The narrative aside in v. 22 clarifies any confusion on the part of the implied reader; the introduction serves its purpose: Jesus' audience places him in high regard, to the point of marveling at his gracious words. The introduction is bracketed by parallel actions – in a chiastic pattern – prompting the implied reader to identify it as a separate unit.[6]

    A   Jesus stands up to read
        B   Jesus takes the book from the attendant
            C   Jesus reads from the book
        B'   Jesus hands the book back to the attendant
    A'   Jesus sits down

The center of the chiastic arrangement falls on the reading from Isaiah, prompting the implied reader to identify the intertextual LXX citation as the apex of the introduction. Repetition of the pronoun με in the emphatic position in the first three lines (v. 18ab) and the parallel symmetry of the ensuing three clauses initiated by infinitives largely determine the structure of the introduction (vv. 18c-19). The initial period – consisting of 'The Spirit of the Lord is upon me, because he has anointed me to preach good news to the poor' – is in the form of an enthymeme. The conjunction οὗ εἵνεκεν serves as the link between the minor premise, 'The Spirit of the Lord is upon Jesus', and the conclusion, 'Jesus has been anointed to preach good news to the poor'. The implied reader fills the major premise, namely, 'those who preach good news to the poor are filled with the Holy Spirit'.

---

6. While identification of chiasms in New Testament studies has been abused, chiasm was one component in rhetorical texture of antiquity (e.g., *Rhetorica ad Herennium*, 4.30). See Augustine Stock, 'Chiastic Awareness and Education in Antiquity', *BTB* 17 (1984), pp.70-74. For the chiastic construction of Jesus' actions in Lk. 4.16-30, see H. J. B. Combrink, 'The Structure and Significance of Luke 4:16-30', *Neot* 7 (1973), pp. 27-47; Green, *Gospel of Luke*, pp. 209; Nolland, *Luke*, vol. 1, pp. 191–92.

Conclusion: Jesus has been anointed to preach good news to the poor.
Major Premise: Those who preach good news to the poor are filled with
the Holy Spirit.
Minor Premise: The Holy Spirit is upon Jesus.

The enthymematic argument provides the implied reader with an
interpretive lens: 'preaching good news to the poor' conveys that one
possesses the Holy Spirit. Specific parameters of 'preaching good news to
the poor' are delineated by the three infinitival clauses in vv. 18-19: (1) to
proclaim release (ἄφεσιν) to the captives and sight to the blind; (2) to send
forth the oppressed in release (ἄφεσιν); and (3) to proclaim the year of the
Lord's favor.[7] The repetition of ἄφεσις accentuates the intertextual
connection with jubilary themes present in Deutero-Isaiah – particularly
chs 57 and 61 – as well as the social implications of Jubilee legislation in Lev.
25 (esp. v. 10).[8] Hence, the implied reader defines ἄφεσις through these
intertextual linkages: release from debts.[9]

C. Statement of Case: Chreia (4.21-22)

The statement of case (or thesis) begins with Jesus telling his audience that
the realization of divine benefaction contained in the Isaianic citation (viz.,
the introduction) is fulfilled with the onset of his ministry (v. 21).[10]
Connection between the introduction and statement of case is accentuated
by the narrative aside in v. 20, which heightens narrative suspense and
highlights the first part of the statement of case – or, more specifically, the
chreia – in v. 21 for the implied reader.[11] The use of χάρις to describe the
words spoken on behalf of Jesus in the narrative aside in v. 22 hearkens back
to the two summary statements in 1.40 and 2.52, thereby prodding the
implied reader to equate those from the synagogue on the same level as the

7. See, e.g., Roth, *Character Types*, esp. pp. 152–64.
8. Other Jewish texts exhibit interpretive maneuvering of the jubilary themes of Isaiah
(*11QMelch, Pss. Sol.* 11, Dan. 9.24-27). For a discussion, see, e.g., Robert Sloan, *The
Favorable Year of the Lord: A Study of Jubilary Theology in the Gospel of Luke* (Austin, Tex.:
Schola Press, 1977); Sharon Ringe, *Jesus, Liberation, and the Biblical Jubilee: Images for
Ethics and Christology* (OBT; Philadelphia: Fortress Press, 1985).
9. Note the further intertextual connection with the Year of Jubilee in Lev. 25 that is
suggested by Bovon, *Luke 1:1-9:50*, p. 156: 'The connection between the Year of Jubilee and
the homeland in the LXX is usually forgotten. During this year of forgiveness (Lev. 25:10
LXX) and blessing (Lev. 25:21 LXX), all people should return to their homeland: καὶ
ἕκαστος εἰς τὴν πατρίδα αὐτοῦ ἀπελεύσεσθε ("and each should go off to his or her
fatherland", Lev 25:10 LXX). Thus it is in accordance with the Scriptures that Jesus begins
preaching the year of grace in his hometown.'
10. Siker ('Literary Analysis', pp. 77–79) contends 4.21b ('today this scripture has been
fulfilled in your hearing') stands as the 'final climax' of the section, though on the basis of a
parallel structure between vv. 16-18 and vv. 20-21.
11. Per Siker ('Literary Analysis', p. 78) ἀτενίζω is used in Lukan narrative asides and
functions to slow down narrative time and heighten focus on the subsequent discourse –
speech or action (cf. Lk. 22.56; Acts 1.10; 3.4, 12; 6.15; 7.55; 10.4; 11.6; 13.6; 14.9).

narrator. This perception is transitory, however, as the revulsion those from the synagogue display at the end of the scene (vv. 28-30) quickly deconstructs this image. The implied reader also ascertains – based on previous narrative discourse that clearly identifies Jesus as the 'Son of God' and not the 'son of Joseph' (cf. 2.48-50; 3.21-23) – that the designation of Jesus as 'Joseph's son' by the synagogue audience is not sufficient.[12]

D. *Body of Argument: Statements by Analogy and Example (4.23-27)*

The main body of the speech – or body of argument – begins with a challenge from Jesus to the synagogue crowd in the form of two aphorisms, with the second (v. 24) corroborated by two examples from the prophets. The first aphorism, 'Physician, heal yourself', was a well-known maxim in Greco-Roman and Jewish rhetoric. It would be employed in an argument to implore someone to deliver the same favors to his or her kin and friends as she or he would provide to others beyond the boundaries of kinship and friendship.[13] The implied reader, drawing on this extratextual repertoire, concludes that Jesus will not deliver the patronal blessings his hometown synagogue crowd anticipates. In the case of the second aphorism, the identity of the 'rejected prophet' (v. 24) is given an ironic twist in the narrative discourse: the reaction of the synagogue crowd in vv. 28-29 – in their rejection of Jesus – prompts the implied reader to identify Jesus as the 'rejected prophet'. As a result, Jesus' opponents – rather than diminishing – actually strengthen the ethos of his characterization.

Reference to the deeds Jesus performed in Capernaum in the first aphorism (v. 23) creates a dissonance for the implied reader, as there is no previous reference to this activity in the narrative. Rather, in order for the implied reader to make sense of the text, the ensuing section in 4.31-42 regarding the deeds Jesus performed in Capernaum must be read analeptically. It is a gap in the narrative discourse that cannot be filled until the processing of the subsequent narrative.

The second of the two aphorisms (v. 24) is corroborated in the latter part of the body of argument with two examples from the prophets (inductive argument using examples), one of Elijah from 1 Kgs 17.8-24 and the other of Elisha from 2 Kgs 5.1-19. The second aphorism includes several intratextual

---

12.   The narrative aside in 3.23 at the beginning of Jesus' genealogy ('as some suppose') is a clear indication to the implied reader that those who identify Jesus as the 'son of Joseph' are wrong. Wasserberg (*Israels Mitte*, p. 160) sees an analeptic connection with 2.35 and the prediction contained therein: 'Offenbar geworden ist jetzt erstmals in Anlehnung an die Worte Simeons in Lk 2,35b, welcher Herzen Gedanken die Einwohner Nazarets über den Heilssohn aus ihrer Mitte wirklich hegen'.

13.   See John Nolland, 'Classical Rabbinic Parallels to "Physician, Heal Yourself" (Luke iv 23)', *NovT* 21 (1979), pp. 193–209; S. J. Noorda, '"Cure Yourself, Doctor!" (Luke 4,23): Classical Parallels to an Alleged Saying of Jesus', in Joël Delobel (ed.), *Logia: Les Paroles de Jésus – The Sayings of Jesus* (Festschrift Joseph Coppens; BETL, 59; Leuven: Leuven University, 1982), pp. 459–69.

linkages that serve as analeptic and proleptic pointers for the implied reader. Specifically, the use of δεκτός, προφήτη, and ἐν τῇ πατρίδι αὐτοῦ in the aphorism prompts the implied reader to connect 'the acceptable (δεκτός) year of the Lord' from the introduction (v. 19) with the prophetic ministries of Elisha and Elijah via the two LXX examples in vv. 25-27; this includes extension of πατρίδι beyond Nazareth (insiders) to the Gentiles (outsiders).[14]

Parallelism is a device frequently employed in Greco-Roman rhetoric. The structure of the two LXX examples in the latter part of the body of argument (vv. 25-27) stands in parallel fashion:

A   there were many widows in Israel
   B   in the time of Elijah
      C   yet Elijah was sent to none of them
         D   except to a widow at Zarephath in Sidon.
A'   there were also many lepers in Israel
   B'   in the time of the prophet Elisha
      C'   and none of them were cleansed
         D'   except Naaman the Syrian.[15]

In addition to serving as a mnemonic device for rhetorical performance, this fourfold parallelism accentuates both the needs of those in Israel and the exceptional character of the recipients of divine blessing – namely, the widow of Zarephath and Naaman the Syrian, those outside of the community, the socially and religiously disenfranchised. Elijah is sent to a woman, a non-Jew who is a widow. Elisha is also sent to a non-Jew, a despised Syrian whose disease distanced him from the community of those belonging to God. The implied reader, therefore, concludes that the 'good news to the poor' comes to lowly personages like the widow and unclean such as the Gentile – namely, those of marginal status.

E. *Missing Conclusion/Exhortation (4.28-30)*

Jesus does not have an opportunity to complete the speech due to the violent response of the synagogue crowd. The narrator does not specify the reasons behind their reaction; rather, the implied reader must fill this narrative gap. The legislation in Deut. 13.1-11 – where the Israelite community is instructed to stone those who make false prophetic claims – is a possible intertext upon which the implied reader draws in understanding the actions

---

14. See Siker, 'Literary Analysis', pp. 82–83, for this observation. Also, see Wasserberg (*Israels Mitte*, p. 163) who pinpoints connections between v. 24 and the LXX examples of Elisha and Elijah in vv. 25-27: 'Kein Prophet ist wohlgelitten in seiner Heimatstadt (Lk 4,24), ergo kann auch der Prophet Jesus in Nazaret nur auf Ablehnung stoßen. Daß diese Regel vom Geschick der Propheten sogar schriftgemäß ist, zeigt er mit seinem Verweis auf Elia und Elisa.'

15. See Larrimore C. Crockett, 'Luke 4:25-27 and Jewish-Gentile Relations in Luke-Acts', *JBL* 88 (1969), pp. 177–83, for this fourfold parallelism.

of the synagogue crowd.[16] This intertextual connection is one element, however, as the abrupt interruption to Jesus' speech supplies the bulk of the information. The narrative crowd responds positively to the introduction of the speech. Only after hearing the statement of case and body of argument does the narrative audience display an adverse reaction. The statement of case delineates to the synagogue crowd that Jesus – in contrast to their self-centered expectations through actualization of the initial aphorism in v. 23 by the implied reader – will not bestow the same blessings to them as he did to those in Capernaum.

III. *Concluding Summary*

Despite an almost overwhelming amount of scholarly research on the first speech of the Lukan Galilean ministry, little exists on its rhetorical texture. This chapter attempts to push the discussion further by accounting for the speech in terms of rhetorical argument – specifically within the context of Greco-Roman rhetorical style. When the speech is construed from this lens, new vistas of meaning result through the construction of rhetorical texture by the implied reader – ranging from the presence of rhetorical devices such as chiasm and parallelism, to a speech that does not end (due to the violent reaction of the narrative audience), to inductive argument in the form of two examples from the LXX. As part of the larger rhetorical argument of the speech, all of these parts fit together to form a coherent whole.

---

16. For this intertextual suggestion, see Green, *Gospel of Luke*, 218. Also, cf. 2 Chron. 25.12 (parallel to Lk. 4.29), per Bovon (*Luke 1:1–9:50*, p. 156: n. 41), where 'the people of Judah captured another ten thousand alive, took them to the top of a rock and threw them down (κατεκρήμνιζον – κατακρημνίσαι in Lk. 4.29) from the top of the rock, so that all of them were dashed to pieces'.

CHAPTER 5: THE SECOND GALILEAN MINISTRY SPEECH (LK. 6.17-49):
A NEW ETHICAL MODE OF (NON-RECIPROCAL) BENEFACTION

The second speech is the most detailed of the four speeches contained in the Lukan Galilean ministry. Like the first speech in 4.14-30, the second speech follows one of several narrative episodes (6.12-16) – scattered throughout this section of the Gospel – where Jesus withdraws from the crowds. The narrative scenes between the first and second speeches portray confrontations between Jesus and Jewish interlocutors, those with social, ethnic, and religious boundaries threatened by Jesus' actions and words. Figurative connotations of the selection of twelve disciples prompt the implied reader to associate apocalyptic meaning to the episode; an intertextual derivation suggesting that the restoration of Israel would coincide with the reconstitution of the twelve tribes.[1]

I. *Rhetorical Situation*

The rhetorical situation of the second speech is established in 6.17-19, when Jesus comes down from the mountain to address the disciples who have been traveling with him. The disciples are not confined simply to the twelve apostles Jesus appointed in 6.12-16, but rather to all those who embrace the message of salvation; a larger group of disciples as well as a multitude of people seeking to hear his message and to receive healing from their diseases. This scene is reminiscent of the one when Moses descended from Mount Sinai to deliver the Ten Commandments to the Jewish people (Exod. 19.24; 24.3), leading the implied reader to recognize the similarities and thus impose comparable expectations upon that which is about to take place in the Lukan narrative. The implied reader construes the following narrative discourse through this lens, with the speech in 6.20-49 serving as the basis of Jesus' teaching, just as the law served as the basis for Moses and his predecessors.[2]

1. This trajectory is evident in the narrative discourse such as Lk. 22.30 and the episode in Acts 1.12-26. The extratextual repertoire of the narrative audience and the implied reader is comprised of various intertexts portending the connection between the 'restoration of Israel' and the 'reconstitution of the twelve tribes' (see, e.g., Jacob Jervell, 'The Twelve on Israel's Thrones: Luke's Understanding of the Apostolate', in Jacob Jervell , *Luke and the People of God: A New Look at Luke-Acts* [Minneapolis: Augsburg Press, 1972], pp. 75–112).
2. See, e.g., Luke T. Johnson, *The Gospel of Luke* (SP, 3; Collegeville, Minnesota: Liturgical Press, 1991), pp. 110–11, who posits a connection between 6.17-19 and Moses'

The scene in 6.17-19 mirrors the buttressed scenes in 4.42-44 and 5.1-11, where Jesus – after emerging from seclusion – encounters growing crowds seeking to hear his message and to receive healing from him. In 5.1-11, the implied author employs a type scene,[3] whereby the calling of the three disciples echoes the 'commission story' in Isa. 6.1-10.[4] This information, coupled with the prior appointment of the twelve apostles, prods the implied reader to anticipate similar results: Jesus will continue to expand his coterie of followers. The growth of Jesus' ministry is encapsulated in the notation by the narrator that the great crowd of disciples and the multitude of people came from all of Judea and Jerusalem as well as the seacoast of Tyre and Sidon. The magnitude of the crowd is emphasized by the repetition of the adjective πολύς and the use of ὄχλος and πλῆθος ('a great crowd of his disciples and great multitude of people') in v. 17b. The region has also expanded beyond Galilee to that of all Judea; the regional center is no longer Capernaum but Jerusalem (v. 17c). Further, the inclusion of Tyre and Sidon (v. 17c) hints at the presence of Gentiles – namely, through an analeptic connection with the Sidonian widow from the initial speech (4.26-27). A topos that continues throughout the Lukan corpus, was integral in the initial speech of 4.14-30 (particularly the citation of Isa. 61.1 and 58.6 in 4.18-20), and was a constant in the narrative scenes between the first and second speeches (viz., Peter's mother-in-law in 4.38-39; the multitudes at Capernaum in 4.40-41; the paralytic in 5.17-26; the man with the withered hand in 6.6-11), that of healing people from their diseases, ties the speech to the preceding narrative.[5]

The final part of the period in vv. 17-19 (v. 19) specifies that the crowd was seeking to touch Jesus because δύναμις ('power') came forth from him. Analeptic activity by the implied reader results in the connection of this scene with the transition (4.14-15) preceding Jesus' first speech in the Galilean ministry ('And Jesus returned in the "power" [δυνάμει] of the Spirit into Galilee' – v. 14a). Specifically, the implied reader understands that Jesus' healing activity in 6.19 – resulting from his possession of δύναμις – is a derivative of his endowment of the Holy Spirit. The precise reasons for the crowd seeking to touch Jesus are not noted by the narrator, a gap that the implied reader must fill. Is it because of the healing he is dispensing or

---

descent from Mount Sinai with the law. Richard A. Horsley, 'The Covenant Renewal Discourse: Q 6:20-49', in Richard A. Horsley and Jonathan A. Draper (eds), *Whoever Hears You Hears Me: Prophets, Performance, and Tradition in Q* (Harrisburg, Pa.: Trinity Press International, 1999), pp. 195–227, argues that Q 6.20-49 stands as a coherent speech in Q and functions as a covenantal renewal discourse as reflected in Deut. 28, Exod. 21-23, Lev. 19, and Deut. 22.

3. Recognition of type scenes as a rhetorical device in biblical literature is based on the work of Robert Alter ('Annunciation Type-Scene', pp. 115–30; idem, *Art of Biblical Narrative*, pp. 47–62). The background to a type scene can be based on either intertextual or intratextual referents.

4. See Talbert, *Literary Patterns*, pp. 60–61.

5. See, e.g., Ben Witherington III, 'Salvation and Health', pp. 145–65; John J. Pilch, 'Sickness and Healing in Luke-Acts', in *Social World of Luke-Acts*, pp. 181–209.

because of the fact that he is full of the Spirit? Eventually, a retrospective reading of characterization in Luke-Acts leads the implied reader to the realization that characters who truly embrace discipleship come to Jesus because they are full of the Holy Spirit.

II. *Rhetorical Argument*

Surprisingly, few interpreters of 6.20-49 consider it from the standpoint of ancient Greco-Roman rhetoric, and most see little coherence in the whole as well as between the different parts.[6] The few who do query it for the embodiment of ancient rhetoric largely do so through redactional comparison, using the Sermon on the Mount (Mt. 5.1–7.29) as the basis of their analysis.[7] Kennedy's assessment is representative: 'Luke 6 is not a very good speech. What persuasive power Luke's speech has inheres almost solely in the ethos, or authority, of Jesus. In Matthew too ethos is primary, but more attempt is made to couch statements in logical form, and greater pathos is achieved.'[8] While redactional analysis is helpful in identifying various indicators about the implied author, it is inadequate for explaining how rhetorical argument functions within a narrative's discourse – such as plot, characterization, and topoi. In addition, in contrast to Kennedy's claim that Lk. 6.20-49 lacks the overarching argumentation of Mt. 5.1–7.29 – focusing on the argumentative mode of ethos and largely ignoring logos and pathos – the following examination pinpoints a dialectical texture that encompasses all three modes of argumentation: ethos and logos and, to a lesser extent, pathos.

The rhetorical situation – found in 6.17-19 – situates the scene in a very positive light, providing the implied reader with further corroboration for Jesus' contention in the first speech about the fulfillment of Isa. 61.1-2 and 58.6 (Lk. 4.21). In doing so, the implied author bolsters the ethos of Jesus by demonstrating the authenticity of his words. Jesus' interlocutors, whom he has encountered at almost every turn since escaping from the angry synagogue crowd in his hometown of Nazareth (4.30), are not mentioned by the narrator as present. As a result, it seems, since Jesus is able to complete the speech without interruption (in contrast to his first speech in 4.16-30),

---

6. Jonathan Knight's comments are representative (*Luke's Gospel*, pp. 91–92): 'There follows in 6.37-49 a collection of sayings with no obvious connection between them ... [T]he form of the material even suggests that it depends for its meaning on the provision of subsequent commentary. It is compressed and does not read easily when compared to Luke's pacier narrative.' Knight's assessment is flawed in that he shows no regard to rhetorical elements in the Lukan narrative and moreover ignores its oral/aural nature. In contrast to Knight and others, see Horsley, 'Covenant Renewal', pp. 209–16, who argues that the speech is a coherent whole that is replete with oral/aural patterns.

7. Note Bovon's comment (*Luke 1:1-9:50*, p. 215): 'In both scholarship and the church, the Matthean Sermon on the Mount has crowded out the Lukan Sermon on the Plain, which must be heard in its own guise'.

8. *Through Rhetorical Criticism*, p. 67.

that Jesus' interlocutors are not in attendance. The exact composition of the character group of 'disciples' is open-ended at this point in the narrative; the implied reader infers a connection between those following Jesus and discipleship based on the preceding narrative (e.g., 5.1-11; 5.27-32).

III. *Rhetorical Texture*

Various proposals on the structural dimensions of the speech exist.[9] Those who view the speech through the lens of ancient Greco-Roman rhetoric largely concur that vv. 20-26 forms the exordium and vv. 46-49 resembles a conclusio.[10] The binary argument of the two parts stands in parallel: blessings and woes in the exordium and two contrasting paradigmatic examples in the conclusio. The rhetorical arrangement of the body of the speech (vv. 27-45) is where the uncertainty arises; scholars designate the material as paraenetic in nature and do not place the material within the specific context of ancient rhetorical arrangement.

As discussed in Chapter three, the speeches in the Gospels and Acts largely do not conform to rhetorical invention and arrangement delineated in the rhetorical handbooks. Recognition of a species and structure that coheres with that specified in the handbooks is unlikely – both in terms of a writer fully trained in handbook rhetoric and an audience attentive to the speeches as representations of handbook rhetoric (viz., for the law court or public assembly). While the speech exhibits rhetorical argument that has a coherent structure and style, it is a far reach to claim conformity with the rhetorical invention and arrangement found in the rhetorical handbooks. Fourfold division of the rhetorical texture seems likely. Carefully crafted blessings and woes in vv. 20-26 form the introduction. The implied author establishes the statement of case or purpose of the speech in vv. 27-31. The body of argument in vv. 32-45 is replete with deductive and inductive reasoning that is supported by several analogies. The speech concludes with a longer, more detailed analogy in vv. 46-49.

9. Most proposals reflect form-critical concerns (e.g., Bovon, *Luke 1:1-9:50*, p. 216). However, though not from the basis of ancient Greco-Roman rhetoric, cf. Horsley, 'Covenant Renewal', pp. 195–227, who envisions a fivefold structure reflecting covenantal renewal discourses evinced in the LXX (Lev. 19, Exod. 19 and 24) and Dead Sea Scrolls (*1QS* 3.13–4.26): vv. 20-26, vv. 27-36, vv. 37-42, vv. 43-45, and vv. 46-49.

10. See, e.g., Betz, *Sermon on the Mount*, pp. 571–640, who proposes a threefold structure using ancient Greco-Roman rhetorical categories: exordium in vv. 20-26; paraenetic body in vv. 27-45 (consisting of conduct of disciples to outsiders in vv. 27-38; rules concerning conduct within the community in vv. 39-42; conduct towards oneself in vv. 43-45); and conclusio in vv. 46-49. Cf. also Jacques Dupont, *Les béatitudes: Le problème littéraire: Les deux versions du Sermon sur la Montagne et des Béatitudes*, vol. 1 (Bruges and Louvain: Abbaye de Saint-André/E. Nauwelaerts, 2nd ed., 1958) p. 200, who suggests a fourfold structure consisting of the exordium in vv. 20-26, body in vv. 27-42 (two parts: vv. 27-36 and vv. 37-42), and conclusio in vv. 43-49.

A. *Introduction (6.20-26)*

The introduction (6.20-26) exhibits a balanced fourfold parallelism that contrasts blessings (vv. 20-23) and woes (vv. 24-26), a common mode of argumentation in the LXX and other Jewish texts.[11] The ethos of Jesus is corroborated by the logos of the rhetorical construction,[12] thus prompting the implied reader to construct a positive image of Jesus as a reliable, skilled orator.[13]

A Blessed are the poor,
  for yours is the kingdom of God.
    B Blessed are the hungry now,
      for you shall be satisfied.
        C Blessed are you that weep now,
          for you shall laugh.
            D Blessed are you when men hate you
              and when they exclude you
              and they cast out your name as evil on account of the
              Son of Man.
              Rejoice in that day, and leap for joy,
              for behold, your reward is great in heaven;
              for so their fathers did to the prophets.
A' But woe to the rich,
  for you have received your consolation.
    B' Woe to you, the ones who are full now,
      for you shall hunger.
        C' Woe to you that laugh now,
          for you shall mourn and weep.
            D' Woe to you, when all men speak well of you,
              for so their fathers did to the false prophets.[14]

The anaphoric positioning of μακάριος and οὐαί connects as well as reinforces the impact of the successive series of blessings and then woes, with the conjunctive πλήν serving as the transition between the two. Grammatical comparison of the blessings and woes shows that the latter come across as more direct: the second-person address (ὑμῖν in v. 24 and v. 25 and ὑμᾶς in v. 26) in the first three woes has no corresponding parallel

---

11. Isa. 3.10-11; *1 En.* 96.1-8; 97.1-10; Eccl. 10.16-17; Tob 13.12; *2 Bar.* 10.6-7.

12. Aristotle contends that the ethos of a speaker is internal to the speech, part of the logos, and does not derive from outside of the speech itself (*Rhetoric*, 1.2.4).

13. For an excellent discussion of ethos in Lk. 6.20-49, though from the standpoint of Q and not Luke-Acts, see Shawn Carruth, 'Strategies of Authority: A Rhetorical Study of the Character of the Speaker in Q 6:20-49', in *Conflict and Invention*, pp. 98–115. The introduction of a speech in antiquity is pivotal in establishing the ethos of the speaker; see Quintilian, *Institutio Oratoria*, 3.8.36; Cicero, *De Oratore*, 2.42.182; *Rhetorica ad Herennium*, 1.2.3; *Rhetorica ad Alexandrum*, 15; Quintilian, *Institutio Oratoria*, 4.1.7; Aristotle, *Rhetoric*, 3.14.12.

14. See Green, *Gospel of Luke*, pp. 265–68, for this parallel construction.

in the first three blessings (vv. 20b-21).[15] The direct address in the woe parallels – versus the blessing parallels – prompts the narrative audience and implied reader to place the rhetorical emphasis on them. The presence of a corresponding direct address in the fourth blessing/woe cluster (vv. 22-23 and v. 26) serves as a rhetorical marker for the narrative audience and implied reader; the result being that the fourth blessing and woe cluster receives greater primacy in the overall rhetorical argument. Each of the blessings and woes are in the form of an enthymeme.

1. *First Three Pairs of Blessing/Woe Clusters*
The first three pairs of blessing and woe clusters in the introduction begin with a conclusion followed by the minor premise; the implied author expects the implied reader to deduce the major premise for each. This mode of 'gap filling' shapes the actualization of the narrative discourse and serves as a means for prodding authorial readers to reinterpret ideological beliefs. The enthymematic argument of the three blessing and woe clusters resembles the following:[16]

First Blessing/Woe Cluster: The Poor versus the Rich (vv. 20, 24)

Major Premise: Those who possess the kingdom of God are blessed.	*Major Premise:* Those who have received consolidation are cursed.
Minor Premise: The poor possess the kingdom of God.	*Minor Premise:* The rich have received consolation.
Conclusion: Blessed are the poor, for yours is the kingdom of God.	*Conclusion:* Woe to you who are rich, for you have received your consolation.

Second Blessing/Woe Cluster: The Hungry versus the Full (vv. 21a, 25a)

Major Premise: Those who are satisfied are blessed.	*Major Premise:* Those who are hungry are cursed.
Minor Premise: The hungry shall be satisfied.	*Minor Premise:* The full shall be hungry.
Conclusion: Blessed are you that hunger now, for you shall be satisfied.	*Conclusion:* Woe to you who are full now, for you shall hunger.

Third Blessing/Woe Cluster: The Disconsolate versus the Joyful (vv. 21b, 25b)

Major Premise: Those who laugh are blessed.	*Major Premise:* Those who mourn and weep are cursed.
Minor Premise: The ones mourning shall laugh.	*Minor Premise:* The ones laughing shall mourn and weep.
Conclusion: Blessed are you who weep now, for you shall laugh.	*Conclusion:* Woe to you who laugh now, for you shall mourn and weep.

The major premises of the three blessing and woe clusters are accepted by

---

15. For this observation, see Betz, *Sermon on the Mount*, p. 572.
16. For a different construction of the enthymematic argument, cf. Vernon K. Robbins, 'Pragmatic Relations as a Criterion for Authentic Sayings', *Forum* 1 (1985), p. 51.

the narrative audience and the implied reader; embedded within generally accepted cultural suppositions. The minor premises and the conclusions counter underpinning belief systems (viz., honor and shame constructs) of the Greco-Roman world.[17] The reversal of fortunes is an ongoing Lukan topos – beginning with the Song of Mary (Lk. 1.46-55) and then reoccurring, for example, in the first speech (Lk. 4.16-30), Jesus' instructions on table fellowship (Lk. 14.7-24), the story of the rich man and Lazarus (Lk. 16.19-31), the story of the Pharisee and the toll collector (Lk. 18.9-14), and the crucifixion and exaltation of Jesus (Lk. 22-24).[18] This topos comes to fruition in Acts; fortunes of those pushed to the margins are reversed – for example, the communal sharing of the Jerusalem community (Acts 2.43-47; 4.32-37; 5.1-11), the healing of those afflicted with diseases and unclean spirits (Acts 3.1-10; 5.16; 14.8-18; 16.16-40; 19.11-20), and the inclusion of those from the ethnic, religious, and social margins (Acts 8.9-40; 10.1–11.18; 13.4-12; 16.11-15).

2. Final Blessing/Woe Cluster

The final blessing and woe cluster is different from the preceding three clusters on several accounts. First, the blessing is much more elaborate than the corresponding woe. Second, the blessing actually contains two enthymemes, with one embedded in the other – a rhetorical mode known as intercalation. In this case, the embedded enthymeme bolsters the argument of the one in which it is contained, providing the impetus for the enveloping enthymeme. Third, the subject matter directly pertains to the confrontations Jesus and his disciples encountered in the earlier episodes between the first speech (4.14-30) and the second speech (6.17-49): the authority to forgive sins (5.17-26), the ability to fellowship with tax collectors and sinners (5.27-32), the prerogative to pluck and eat grain on the Sabbath (6.1-5), and the authority to heal on the Sabbath (6.6-11). The two enthymemes comprising the final blessing and woe cluster resemble the following:

Final Blessing/Woe Cluster: The Humble Versus the Proud (vv. 22-23, 26)

Major Premise: The prophets are blessed.

Minor Premise: Those whom men hate, exclude, and revile are like the prophets.

Conclusion: Blessed are you when men hate you, and when they exclude and revile you, for so their fathers did to the prophets.

Major Premise: The false prophets are cursed.

Minor Premise: Those of whom men speak well are like the false prophets.

Conclusion: Woe to you, when men speak well of you, for so their fathers did to the false prophets.

---

17. Though his investigation is not from the standpoint of ancient Greco-Roman argument, see Green, *Gospel of Luke*, pp. 265–66, for an overview of the cultural presuppositions that stand behind the blessing and woe clusters. Also, see Robbins, 'Pragmatic Relations', p. 42; Carruth, 'Strategies of Authority', p. 108.

18. Green, 'Social Status of Mary', pp. 457–72; John O. York, *The Last Shall Be First: The Rhetoric of Reversal* (JSNTSup, 46; Sheffield: Sheffield Academic Press, 1991).

Embedded/Intercalated Descriptive Enthymeme (v. 23)

Major Premise: The reward in heaven is cause for rejoicing and leaping for joy.	*Minor Premise:* The recipients of hate and those who are excluded and reviled have a great reward in heaven.

Conclusion: Rejoice and leap for joy when you are the recipients of hate, excluded, and reviled, for your reward is great in heaven.

3. *Enthymematic Argument Generates Rhetorical Texture*

Symmetry between the four woes and preceding four blessings embodies a carefully crafted rhetorical construction; the subject matter, form, and language of the four blessings mirrors that of the four woes. Some of the most notable general corollaries include: (1) anaphoric use of μακάριος and οὐαί; (2) use of the present tense for the minor premise contained in the first and final blessing and woe pairs;[19] (3) use of the future tense for the minor premises contained in the second and third blessing and woe pairs; (4) repetition of νῦν at the end of the second and third clustered pairs of blessings and woes;[20] (5) repetition of the temporal conjunction, ὅταν, in the final blessing and woe pair; and (6) repetition of the language contained in the minor premises of the final blessing and woe pair. In particular, the implied author employs opposites, a rhetorical device frequently used in Greco-Roman oratory,[21] to demarcate linkage between each of the four blessing and woe clusters. The four blessing and woe clusters break into the following taxonomies:

First Blessing/Woe Pair: The Poor Versus the Rich (vv. 20, 24)

Blessed are you *poor* (πτωχοί), for yours is the kingdom of God.

Woe to you who are *rich* (πλουσίοις), for you have received your consolation.

Second Blessing/Woe Pair: The Hungry Versus the Full (vv. 21, 25)

Blessed are you that *hunger* (πεινῶντες) *now* (νῦν), for you shall be satisfied.

Woe to you who are full *now* (νῦν), for you shall *hunger* (πεινάσετε).

Third Blessing/Woe Pair: The Disconsolate Versus the Joyful (vv. 21, 25)

Blessed are you who *weep* (κλαίοντες) *now* (νῦν), for you shall *laugh* (γελάσετε).

Woe to you who *laugh* (γελάσετε) *now* (νῦν), for you shall mourn and *weep* (κλαύσετε).

Final Blessing/Woe Pair: The Humble Versus the Proud (vv. 22-23, 26)

---

19.   Present tense, indicative of gnomic material (see Carruth, 'Strategies of Authority', pp. 110–11), serves to make the discourse more vivid and closer to actuality (Longinus, *On the Sublime*, 25.1).

20.   The repetition of the same word at the end of clauses is designated as antistrophe (*Rhetorica ad Herennium*, 4.13).

21.   *Rhetorica ad Herennium*, 4.17, 4.59-61; Aristotle, *Rhetoric*, 2.19.1.

Blessed are you *when* (ὅταν) men hate (μισήσωσιν) *you* (ὑμᾶς), and *when* (ὅταν) they exclude (ἀφορίσωσιν) *you* (ὑμᾶς) and revile (ὀνειδίσωσιν) you, and cast out (ἐκβάλωσιν) your name as evil, on account of the Son of man! Rejoice (χάρητε)) in that day, and leap (σκιρτήσατε) for joy, for behold, your reward (μισθός) is great in heaven; *for so their fathers did to the prophets.*

Woe to you (ὑμᾶς), *when* (ὅταν) all men speak well of you, *for so their fathers did to the false prophets.*

The one deviation in symmetry occurs in the fourth blessing and woe pair, where the conclusion of the blessing contains more detail than that of the woe. The intercalation of the two enthymemes in the blessing is an additional distinguishing factor. This differentiation guides the implied reader to the realization that the final blessing has particular importance in the overall narrative discourse (viz., disposition and actions representative of the divine run counter to cultural norms and incur social and religious rejection as corroborated by an LXX intertextual repertoire – Jer. 5.12-13; 6.13-15; Mic. 2.11; Ezek. 2.1-7).[22]

Authenticity of Lk. 6.20-26 is disputed, though most acknowledge a common core lies behind Mt. 5.3-12 and Lk. 6.20-26. It is also widely accepted that the blessings, at least some type of derivation, come from Q. As to the authenticity of the woes in a pre-Lukan source, disagreement exists as to the primacy of Matthew or Luke, though over the past two decades many attribute the reading in Luke as secondary. They conclude that the implied author of Luke (1) changed the third-person pronouns of the blessings to the second person; (2) inserted the ensuing woes;[23] and (3) added the conjunctive νῦν to the second and third blessings.[24]

While resolution of all redaction-critical issues is outside of the purview of my investigation, redactional comparison shows that the speech is more than simply an ad hoc adaptation of a pre-Lukan source by the implied author. First, use of the second person in the Lukan blessings and woes, contra the third person found in the blessings of Matthew, is ambiguous – evoking the narrative audience and the implied reader to equate the second person 'you' with themselves. The overarching theme of discipleship and

22. The importance of the final blessing is further accentuated by the use of *homoioteleuton* (*Rhetorica ad Herennium*, 4.20.28), whereby the three verbs used to describe the actions against faithful disciples end with similar sound (viz., the third person plural [-ωσιν]).

23. However cf. Heinz Schürmann, *Das Lukasevangelium*, vol. 1 (HTKNT, 3; Freiburg: Herder, 3rd ed., 1984), pp. 339–41; Betz, *Sermon on the Mount*, p. 575.

24. The modern derivation of the argument for a secondary reading in Luke goes back to Dupont, *Les Béatitudes*, pp. 297–312; also, cf. Bovon, *Luke 1:1-9:50*, pp. 222–23. Dupont's argument is corroborated largely by those focusing their studies on Q (e.g., John S. Kloppenborg, *Q Parallels: Critical Notes and Concordance* [Sonoma, Calif.: Polebridge Press, 1988], pp. 24–27; James M. Robinson, 'The International Q Project: Work Sessions 12-14 July, 22 November 1991', *JBL* 111 [1992], pp. 501–2; Milton C. Moreland and James M. Robinson, 'The International Q Project: Work Sessions 23-27, 22-26 August, 17-18 November 1994', *JBL* 114 [1995], p. 478).

the call to discipleship recurs throughout the Lukan corpus;[25] the use of the second person forces the narrative audience and implied reader, unlike the use of the indirect third-person addressee by the implied author of Matthew, to directly engage the enthymematic discourse of Lk. 6.20-26.

Second, the blessings in Matthew exhibit a mode of general proposition, whereas the blessing and woe clusters in Luke coincide more closely with the blessings and curses of Deut. 28 as well as the condemnatory speech of the prophets and select intertextual texts (e.g., Hab. 2.6-20; *1 En.* 96.1-8; 97.1-10; Eccl. 10.16-17; Tob 13.12; *2 Bar.* 10.6-7).[26] In particular, inclusion of a reference to the prophets and false prophets in the final blessing and woe cluster evokes images of the LXX (Neh. 9.26; Ezek. 2.1-7; Jer. 5.12-13; 6.13-15; Mic. 2.11), which furthers the association of Jesus' ministry and message with that of the prophets for the implied reader.[27]

Third, the blessings in Matthew tend toward the spiritual attitude of the individual. The blessing and woe clusters in Lk. 6.20-26, on the other hand, are more oriented towards outward acts of social responsibility required of those who embrace the call to discipleship.[28] This falls in line with the overarching Lukan plotline of God dispensing salvation through the ministry of Jesus and through those who are his disciples.[29]

Finally, bipolarity of the blessing and woe clusters is not foreign to Luke-Acts; rather, the implied author shows a preference for composing opposites in pairs. Indeed, the use of opposites is an often used Greco-Roman rhetorical device; giving amplification to the argument, in terms of characterization and topoi.[30] Evidence in the introduction includes the

25. Lk. 3.7-14; 5.1-11; 5.27-32; 6.45-49; 9.57-62; 12.1-59; 14.25-35; 19.11-27; 24.13-49; Acts 3.11-26; 4.8-12; 7.2-53; 8.14-24; 13.13-52; 17.22-31; 20.17-35; 28.17-28. See Green, *Theology of the Gospel*, pp. 102–21, for an overview of the topos of discipleship.

26. However cf. Horsley ('Covenant Renewal', pp. 195–227) who contends that the parallels between Lk. 6.20-49 and LXX covenantal language such as that in Deut. 28, Lev. 19, and other texts go back to the earlier Q version of the speech; the inaugural speech in Q is the derivation of an oral covenantal renewal performance for village-based Christian communities in pre-70 CE Galilee.

27. Specifically, cf. Gerhard Lofink, *Die Himmelfahrt Jesu: Untersuchungen zu den Himmelfahrts- und Erhöhungstexten bei Lukas* (SANT, 26; Munich: Kösel, 1971); Thomas L. Brodie, 'Luke-Acts as an Imitation and Emulation of the Elijah-Elisha Narrative', in Earl Richard (ed.), *New Views on Luke and Acts* (Collegeville, Minn.: Liturgical Press, 1990), pp. 78–85.

28. Redaction critics (see, e.g., Paul S. Minear, 'Jesus' Audiences, According to Luke', *NovT* 16 [1974], pp. 81–109) see a change in audience between the introduction (vv. 20-26) and the remainder of the speech (vv. 27-49), with insiders as the audience for vv. 20-26 and outsiders for vv. 27-49. Such ignores the rhetorical nuances of the speech; these function as rhetorical markers – in contrast to rhetorical seams delineating changes in audience – and prompt the narrative audience and implied reader to engage the narrative discourse.

29. For a thoroughgoing overview of 'salvation to the ends of the earth' as the overarching plotline (or theme as he describes it) of Luke-Acts, see Green, *Theology of the Gospel*. Cf. also his 'Salvation to the End of the Earth', pp. 83–106.

30. Use of bipolarity encompasses Lukan characterization as well. Those who repudiate or fail to embrace Jesus' message and ministry are juxtaposed to those who adhere to his

extratextual connotations of μακάριοι and οὐαί, terms used to represent the cultural bipolar distinctions for honor and shame in Greco-Roman antiquity.[31] Hence, the narrative audience and the implied reader associate honor with those who part with possessions and wealth for the benefaction of others, all at the risk of bringing shame on themselves through their reckless allocation (cf. 6.20-23). In contrast, the narrative audience and the implied reader associate shame with those who fail to impart wealth and possessions for the fear of incurring shame on themselves (cf. 6.24-26).[32] This deductive paradigm forms an ironic argument for the narrative audience and the implied reader in that the person seeking honor – based on conventional modes of honor and shame associated with the use of wealth and possessions – incurs shame (at least from the standpoint of Jesus' rhetorical argument), whereas the person who is the recipient of shame – based on honor and shame cultural frameworks – is placed within the construct of honor. The narrative discourse, therefore, runs counter to cultural constructs of honor and shame and the use of wealth and possessions.

B. *Statement of Case (6.27-31)*

The conjunctive transition ἀλλὰ ὑμῖν λέγω in 6.27 marks the introduction to the next section, which specifies the statement of case of the speech (vv. 27-31) with the inclusion of τοῖς ἀκούουσιν ('the ones listening').[33] Those 'listening' include characters and character groups that associate themselves as 'disciples' within the Lukan narrative world as well as the

---

message and ministry (and, to take it a step further, the message and ministry of his disciples). See the extended discussion of this aspect of the narrative discourse in chapters eight and nine.

31. See K. C. Hanson, 'How Honorable! How Shameful! A Cultural Analysis of Matthew's Makarisms and Reproaches', *Semeia* 68 (1996), pp. 83–114.

32. Cf. Jerome H. Neyrey ('Loss of Wealth, Loss of Family and Loss of Honour: The cultural context of the original makarisms in Q', in Philip F. Esler (ed.), *Modelling Early Christianity: Social-scientific studies of the New Testament in its context* [London and New York: Routledge, 1996], pp. 139–58), who makes the argument that those who fail to use wealth and possessions in a strategic manner to accrue 'honor' on their families actually incur 'shame' on themselves and their families. In the case of the latter, the 'shame' brought upon the family brings about an estrangement between the individual and her or his family. Also, see George W. E. Nickelsburg, 'Riches, the Rich, and God's Judgment in 1 Enoch 92-105 and the Gospel according to Luke', *NTS* 25 (1978/79), pp. 324–44, who pinpoints the topos of apocalyptic judgment of the rich and poor from *1 Enoch* behind Luke.

33. This study's approach stands in contrast to the redaction-critical approaches that view the notation τοῖς ἀκούουσιν in v. 27a as a change in audience, envisioning a redactional seam between vv. 20-26 and vv. 27-49 (see, e.g., Minear, 'Jesus' Audiences', pp. 81–109; Betz, *Sermon on the Mount*, pp. 574–75; Bovon, *Luke 1:1-9:50*, pp. 216–17). Also, see the comments of Longinus, *On the Sublime*, 26: 'Change of person gives an equally powerful effect, and often makes the audience feel themselves set in the thick of the danger'.

implied reader.[34] The discourse of the speech ties 'listening' to 'doing'; both of which are inseparable. The implied reader concludes, as a result, that only those who act (ποιέω) qualify as real listeners. In addition, by means of the ensuing maxims and enthymemes in the statement of case and body of argument, the implied reader ascertains that the action expected on the part of a disciple is a new mode of social responsibility involving non-reciprocal benefaction.

Comprised of a series of maxims, the statement of case communicates the purpose of the speech. The anaphoric composition and presence of other rhetorical features in the introduction disappear from use in the statement of case. Though the speech in its entirety clearly qualifies as disjointed in style, the consecutive use of maxims – one on top of the other – accentuates the overall rhetorical impact of the statement of case.[35]

The maxims in the statement of case are general statements and concern material already familiar to the narrative audience and the implied reader. In particular, inclusion of maxims in the statement of case imbues it with an ethical quality (ethos), an element present in most, if not all, of the speeches of Luke-Acts.[36] With this in mind, the use of maxims, in addition to associating an ethical base to the logos of Jesus' argument, bolsters the ethos of Jesus. Further, in terms of pathos, the implied author skillfully guides the implied reader to a favorable actualization of the narrative discourse by means of using familiar statements, elements comprising the extratextual repertoire of the implied reader.

1. Overarching Topos: Loving Your Enemies (6.27-28)
The statement of case consists of nine maxims. The first eight (vv. 27-30) pertain to actions demanded of a disciple faced with behavior contrary to traditional modes representative of honor and shame. These are situations where behavior exhibited towards a disciple function as an affront to her or

---

34.   As discussed in Chapter two, there are different vistas from which to view narrative. There are four modes of interaction that revolve around the heuristic constructs of author, text, and reader: (1) the narrative world of Luke-Acts; (2) the fictive world of exchange between the implied author and implied reader; (3) the 'plausible' world of the authorial audience – enmeshed within an ideological matrix of cultural issues encompassing gender, ethnicity, sex, religion, social codes, etc.; and (4) the world of the real reader.

35.   The implied author changes to a more elaborate style in the body of argument with the use of inductive reasoning (i.e., examples) interspersed with deductive reasoning (i.e., both enthymemes and maxims). Cf. Demetrius (*On Style*, 12–35) who delineates four different styles, with the suggestion that most of the four can be used together to form even more alternatives: (1) the grand (or elevated) style, described as frigid; (2) the elegant style, described as affected; (3) the plain style, described as arid; and (4) the forceful style, described as unpleasant.

36.   For a detailed discussion of maxims and ethos, see Aristotle, *Rhetoric*, 2.21.13–2.21.16.

his cultural honor. The final maxim (v. 31) provides the rationale to the preceding eight maxims and serves as a transition to the body of argument.[37]

The first four maxims (vv. 27-28) of the statement of case closely correspond in form, with the present active imperative employed as the directive for each. The first maxim functions (v. 27b) as an overarching summary for the subsequent three (vv. 27c-28), which clarify what it means to 'love your enemies' (i.e., those displaying an affront, as depicted in the last three maxims, are deemed as 'enemies' by cultural standards). Antistrophic use of ὑμᾶς also functions to tie together the last three maxims and to distinguish them from the initial maxim:

Love your enemies
   Do good to the ones who hate *you* (ὑμᾶς)
   Bless the ones who curse *you* (ὑμᾶς)
   Pray for the ones who abuse *you* (ὑμᾶς)

Through analeptic processing, the implied reader identifies τοὺς ἐχθροὺς ὑμῶν with the Jewish groups in 5.27–6.1 that exhibit hostility towards Jesus and his disciples (also addressed in the final enthymemic blessing [vv. 22-23]).[38] The identity of τοὺς ἐχθροὺς ὑμῶν is broader, however, than just the groups represented in 5.27–6.1, as elaborated on in the next four maxims in vv. 29-30.[39] Specifically, the first two maxims (v. 29) address the actions

37. Cf. Bovon (*Luke 1:1-9:50*, p. 231) proposes a chiastic structure for vv. 27-38:
   A Introduction (v. 27a)
     B Love of enemies (vv. 27b-28)
       C Renunciation of resistance (vv. 29-30)
         D The Golden Rule (v. 31)
           E Comparison with sinners (vv. 32-34)
           E' Peculiar characteristic of Christans (v. 35)
         D' Call to compassion (v. 36)
       C' Not judging (v. 37ab)
     B' Giving (vv. 37c-38b)
   A' Measuring (v. 38c)
Also, see R. Conrad Douglas, '"Love Your Enemies": *Rhetoric, Tradents, and Ethos*', in *Conflict and Invention*, pp. 116–31, who proposes that Q 6.27-36 resembles a chreia tradent and comprised part of the first Q stratum. He proposes the following chreia parts: (1) encomium/introduction (v. 27a); (2) chreia (v. 27b); (3) paraphrase (vv. 28b-31, 35a); (4) rationale (v. 31); (5) converse (vv. 32-34); (6) analogy (v. 35b); (7) example (v. 36); (8) judgment (missing); and (9) exhortation (missing).

38. Attempts to uncover a Sitz im Leben for Luke-Acts based on the final blessing (vv. 22-23) and reference to τοὺς ἐχθροὺς ὑμῶν (vv. 27ff.) fail to consider the larger context of the speech; most who 'peel back' the redactional layers posit the expulsion of Jewish Christians from the synagogue as the historical context (see, e.g., Bovon, *Luke 1:1-9:50*, p. 227; Betz, *Sermon on the Mount*, pp. 579–81; Schürmann, *Lukasevangelium*, vol. 1, p. 333). However, as this chapter demonstrates, the parts, when assembled as a whole, prompt the implied reader to define 'enemy' as individuals or groups who dispense cultural dishonor upon disciples.

39. Green (*Gospel of Luke*, p. 272) makes a similar contention, although he does not pick up on the twofold identification of 'enemy' by means of the rhetorical positioning of the four maxims following the initial directive.

demanded of a disciple when confronted by an 'enemy' doling out calculated opposition, whereas the final two (v. 30) pertain to the actions expected when a disciple encounters a 'different' type of enemy; a situation where someone outside the patronal boundaries of companionship and kinship is afforded the honor due to only a companion or kin.[40] In the case of the first 'enemy' type, the typical response would be adverse reciprocity. As to the second 'enemy' type, an individual simply did not show generosity to those outside of patronal boundaries in Greco-Roman antiquity. In both instances, the narrative discourse overturns traditional mores: disciples are prompted to accept an inversion in social codes of friendship and kinship.[41]

2. *What It Means to Love Your Enemies (6.29-30)*

The four maxims in vv. 29-30 are more specific and elaborate than the initial four and delve into greater detail on the established topos: what it means to 'love your enemies'.[42] Each maxim corresponds closely in form; the obligatory action follows the enemy to which it is due. Antithesis is employed in the first two (v. 29), as two contrasting ideas are brought together.[43] While there is some difference in form and content between the first two (v. 29) and the second two sets of maxims (v. 30), there is symmetry as well: (1) the preposition τῷ serves as a connective for the first maxim in both sets; (2) the second maxim in both sets exhibits antistrophe (καὶ ἀπὸ τοῦ); and (3) the directive in the second maxim of both sets is given in terms of a negative (μὴ).

---

40. For an analysis of the plausible Sitz im Leben of vv. 29-30 (Mt. 5.38-42) and the historical Jesus, see Walter Wink, 'Neither Passivity nor Violence: Jesus' Third Way (Matt 5:38-42//Luke 6:29-30)', *Forum* 7 (1991), pp. 5–28.

41. Cf. Marius Reiser, 'Love of Enemies in the Context of Antiquity', *NTS* 47 (2001), pp. 411–27, though he does not consider the rhetorical context of Matthew or Luke in pinpointing the identity of 'enemy' ('enemies' equal those who oppose another). Cf. also Martin Ebner, 'Feindesliebe – ein Ratschlag zum Überleben? Sozial- und religionsgeschichtliche Überlegungen zu Mt 5,38-47 par Lk 6,27-35', in Jon M. Asgeirsson, et al. (eds), *From Quest to Q* (Festschrift James M. Robinson; BETL, 146; Leuven: Leuven University Press, 2000), pp. 119–42, who sees the 'rich' from within the Lukan congregation as the designate. Ebner's approach is overly reductionistic and falsely assumes that the world of the text mirrors the world of the reader.

For a general discussion of friendship in Greco-Roman antiquity and its social mores, see W. H. Adkins, ' "Friendship" and "Self-Sufficiency" in Homer and Aristotle', *Classical Quarterly* 13 (1963), pp. 30–45; Andrew Wallace-Hadrill, *Patronage in Ancient Society* (London: Routledge, 1989); Richard Saller, *Personal Patronage under the Early Empire* (Cambridge: Cambridge University Press, 1982). For friendship and its relevance to the New Testament, see Frederick W. Danker, *Benefactor: Epigraphic Study of a Graeco-Roman and New Testament Semantic Field* (St. Louis: Clayton, 1982); Bruce J. Malina, 'Patron and Client: The Analogy behind Synoptic Theology', *Forum* 4 (1988), pp. 2–32.

42. See W. C. van Unnik, 'Die Motivierung der Feindesliebe in Lukas VI 32-35,' *NovT* 8 (1966), pp. 284–300, for an overview of the principles of Greco-Roman reciprocity of showing generosity towards one's friends and hostility towards one's enemies.

43. See *Rhetorica ad Herennium*, 4.15; Quintilian, *Institutio Oratoria*, 9.3.81, for a description of antithesis as rhetorical argument.

To (τῷ) the one who strikes you on the cheek,
  offer also the other (cheek).
And from the (καὶ ἀπὸ τοῦ) one who takes away your garment,
  do *not* (μὴ) also withhold your shirt.
To (τῷ) everyone who begs from you,
  give (listener must fill in the predicate).
And from the (καὶ ἀπὸ τοῦ) one who takes away your things (τά) (listener
  must fill in the predicate),
  do *not* (μὴ) ask (listener must fill in predicate).

The first pair of maxims (v. 29) are embedded in Greco-Roman cultural language, with the actions described as a direct affront to an individual's honor. The requisite response – codified within Greco-Roman cultural mores – was retaliation, which would enable erasure of the shame incurred and recovery of the lost honor. But the directives given by Jesus are in contradistinction to the expected.[44] Specifically, the deductive argument of the maxims positions non-reciprocal benefaction as the requisite behavior (viz., actions) of a disciple.[45]

The second pair of maxims (v. 30) contain less verbiage than the first pair – specifically the absence of a predicate following the directive (viz., the imperative). The implied reader – and for that matter, the narrative audience – is required to identify the predicate in both cases using intratextual (viz., by means of analeptic and proleptic actualization) and extratextual data.[46] The first maxim (v. 30a) relates to the proactive actions of a disciple, whereas the second maxim (v. 30b) relates to the reactive actions of disciple. In the case of the first maxim, the implied reader knows that Jesus has come to deliver salvation to those on the margin from the birth narratives (Lk. 1–2), his initial speech of Jesus (4.14-30), and his inaugural ministry activities (4.31–6.19). Processing of the remaining narrative augments this picture further for the implied reader; specific implications include sharing table

---

44. Cf. Bruce J. Malina and Jerome H. Neyrey, 'Honor and Shame in Luke-Acts', pp. 25–65, for a discussion of honor and shame in Luke-Acts. Also, see Alan C. Mitchell, ' "Greet the Friends by Name": New Testament Evidence for the Greco-Roman *Topos* on Friendship', in John T. Fitzgerald (ed.), *Greco-Roman Perspectives on Friendship* (SBLRBS, 34; Atlanta: Scholars Press, 1997), pp. 236–57.

45. Reiser, 'Love of Enemies', pp. 411–27; Douglas, ' "Love Your Enemies" ', pp. 122–25. However cf. Betz, *Sermon on the Mount*, pp. 591–600, who argues that the maxim to 'love your enemies' in vv. 27-28, while 'seemingly absurd' (591), makes sense in terms of Greco-Roman ethics (via vv. 29-38). Further, according to Betz, the 'golden rule' maxim has an inadequate (vv. 32-34) and adequate (v. 35) understanding. Betz's analysis fails in that there is significant evidence that the discourse of Luke-Acts frequently modifies or challenges conventional Greco-Roman reciprocity practices (see, e.g., Malina and Neyrey, 'Honor and Shame', pp. 25–65).

46. Here it is important to note that the implied reader has a position of advantage in contrast to the narrative audience of Luke-Acts; the narrative audience, which has witnessed Jesus' ministry and heard his message since Lk. 3.7, whereas the implied reader is privilege to the entire narrative discourse and moreover can assimilate the 'gap' through multiple lenses that include intratextual, extratextual, and intertextual data.

fellowship with those traditionally excluded,[47] using possessions and wealth to assist those in need,[48] healing those afflicted with disease and possessed by demonic spirits,[49] and more. As to the second maxim, there are two 'gaps' that the implied reader is prompted to fill. First, rather than noting the specific item in question (viz., that which has been taken), the implied author simply uses the article τά, a term to which the implied reader can ascribe a range of elements. In particular, within the discourse of the speech as well as the narrative discourse of Luke-Acts, τά can denote both physical and non-physical possessions; the former include belongings such as possessions, property, and other means of wealth,[50] whereas the latter include cultural status such as power and honor.[51] The second 'gap' is intertwined with the first; the implied reader must ascertain the predicate to μὴ ἀπαίτει ('do not ask'). Hence, in the case of physical possessions, a disciple does not take action to recover them and, in the case of non-physical possessions, a disciple does not retaliate to regain honor.

3. *Rationale for the Statement of Case (6.31)*
The final maxim (v. 31) is different in content than the previous eight, providing a rationale for the directives specified in the eight preceding maxims through an appeal to individual personal honor and serving as a transition to the argument in the body of argument.[52] The ambivalent

47. Cf. Lk. 5.27-32; 7.36-50; 14.15-24; 16.19-31; 19.1-10; Acts 10.1–11.18; 16.39-40.

48. Cf. Lk. 8.1-3; 10.25-37; 12.13-48; 16.1-13, 14-18, 19-31; 18.18-30; 19.1-9, 11-27; 21.1-4; Acts 2.41-47; 4.32–5.11; 6.1-7; 9.36-43; 16.15, 40; 21.7-9, 16; 28.7-10, 11-16.

49. Cf. Lk. 7.1-10; 7.11-17; 8.26-39; 8.40-56; 9.37-43; 13.10-17; 14.1-6; 17.11-19; 19.35-43; Acts 3.1-10; 5.12-16; 8.4-8; 9.32-35; 9.36-43; 14.8-18; 19.11-20; 20.7-12; 28.7-10.

50. Cf. Lk. 6.32-36; 8.1-3; 10.25-37; 12.13-48; 16.1-13, 14-18, 19-31; 18.18-30; 19.1-9, 11-27; 21.1-4; Acts 2.41-47; 4.32–5.11; 6.1-7; 9.36-43; 16.15, 40; 21.7-9, 16; 28.7-10, 11-16. Also, see Moxnes, *Economy of the Kingdom, passim,* who argues that Luke stipulates the need for economic redistribution in which the needy are cared for and the wealthy give without expecting anything in return. Douglas ('"Love Your Enemies"', pp. 122–25) argues that this trident can be traced back to the first stratum of Q.

51. Cf. Lk. 4.25-27; 5.27-32; 7.36-50; 8.41b-48; 10.25-37; 14.7-14, 15-24; 15.11-32; 19.1-10; Acts 2.41-47; 4.32–5.11; 8.9-24; 8.26-40; 10.1–11.18; 16.15, 40.

52. The apparent dissonance between the 'Golden Rule' in v. 31 and the surrounding context purporting a dynamic of reciprocity is well attested – namely, the maxim directing 'love of enemies' (v. 27b) does not mesh with the reciprocity 'golden rule' maxim (v. 31). Plausible resolutions range from envisioning vv. 32-34 as a critique of reciprocity via construing v. 31 as an indicative statement (cf. Albrecht Dihle, *Die Goldene Regel: Eine Einführung in die Geschichte der antiken und früchristlichen Vulgärethik* [NTAbh, 28; Göttingen: Vandenhoeck & Ruprecht, 1962], pp. 72–80; Victor Paul Furnish, *The Love Command in the New Testament* [Nashville: Abingdon Press, 1972], pp. 57–58), to the presence of two separate sources – sayings on love of enemy and sayings on reciprocity – that were aggregated separately in Q (cf. Paul Hoffmann, *Tradition und Situation: Studien zur Jesusüberlieferung in der Logienquelle und den synoptischen Evangelien* [Münster: Aschendorff, 1995], pp. 19–42), to associating the golden rule maxim of reciprocity with an ethic of equivalence and classifying 'love of enemy' as a supra-ethic (Paul Ricoeur, 'The Golden Rule: Exegetical and Theological Perplexities', *NTS* 36 [1990], pp. 392–97).

nature of the maxim also opens up a virtual endless range of recipients for ethical action. The maxim summarizes the ethical behavior delineated in the preceding eight maxims, while, at the same time, serves as an introduction to topoi about to be covered in the body of argument (vv. 32-45). The maxim, in particular, 'limits permissible actions to those one would wish visited upon oneself, with one's actions not necessarily predicated upon the previous behavior or prospective reaction of others'.[53] In addition, in contrast to the argument of the first eight maxims, where a disciple is charged to embrace actions antithetical to cultural systems, the argument of the final maxim coincides with cultural norms. This represents a rhetorical movement from a texture of disorientation to a texture of orientation.[54]

C. *Body of Argument (6.32-45)*

The body of argument (vv. 32-45), which breaks into three rhetorical segments, is a mixture of deductive and inductive argumentation. The content of the first two segments revolves around the two topoi established in the statement of case: that of showing unconditional patronage, even to those who repudiate traditional modes of cultural honor (vv. 32-36), and that of embracing all individuals, regardless of social status and adherence to cultural norms (vv. 37-42).[55] The first segment consists of a series of three examples in the form of maxims (vv. 32-34) followed by a rationale in the form of two supporting enthymemes (vv. 35-36). The initial enthymeme provides the rationale for desired patronage (v. 35), whereas the second enthymeme functions as a paraenetic summary (v. 36). The second segment is comprised of a series of four maxims (vv. 37-38a) followed by a supporting enthymemic rationale (v. 38b) and a parabolic example (vv. 39-42). The final segment consists of two examples and functions as a rationale for the actions required of a disciple in the two previous segments (vv. 43-45).

However, rather than envisioning the golden rule maxim as standing in contrast with the topos of reciprocity, Alan Kirk (' "Love Your Enemies," The Golden Rule, and Ancient Reciprocity (Luke 6:27-35)', *JBL* 122 [2003], pp. 667–86) proposes that they are complementary: 'The golden rule, expressing the foundational, all-pervasive social norm of reciprocity, functions as a "starting mechanism" that stimulates the kind of interaction necessary to bring into existence the envisioned social relations. Without the reciprocity motif, the command to love enemies remains orphaned from a social context; it is just an emotive slogan, not the inaugural note of a comprehensive vision' (686).

53. Kirk, ' "Love Your Enemies" ', p. 685.

54. However cf. John Topel, 'The Tarnished Golden Rule (Luke 6:31): The Inescapable Radicalness of Christian Ethics', *Theological Studies* 59 (1998), pp. 475–85, who argues that the 'golden rule' maxim in v. 31 goes beyond other Jewish and Greco-Roman reciprocity maxims. Nevertheless, as Kirk notes (' "Loving Your Enemies" ', pp. 670–71), Topel's reading of Jewish and Greco-Roman reciprocity maxim parallels is questionable.

55. Kirk, (' "Love Your Enemies" ', pp. 673–82) makes the same connection.

1. Unconditional Patronage: First Segment (6.32-36)

All three segments exhibit careful attention to the use of rhetorical style, though the first segment is perhaps the most replete with rhetorical elements. The design of the three examples, posed as rhetorical questions, is constructed with an aim of moving the listener to action.[56] The pleonastic association of sinners with the actions specified in each of the three rhetorical questions prompts the implied reader as well as the narrative audience (the latter who would have been averse to being associated with sinners) to embrace a different mode of patronage. The use of χάρις situates the discourse in the context of cultural relationships, prompting the listener to interpret the discourse through an extratextual repertoire of credit and payment – specifically, concrete favors friends do for each other and the gratitude shown in exchange, including the action of a debtor attempting to pay off a previous debt by returning benefit for benefit.[57] In particular, the inductive nature of the examples prompts the implied reader and the narrative audience to assume a more active role in making meaning from the discourse. And the impetus for the specified action is delineated by means of the subsequent two enthymemes.[58]

The three maxims (vv. 32-34) exhibit careful rhetorical construction on the part of the implied author. Various modes of repetition play a key role in rhetorical amplification, including: (1) pleonastic use of the phrase (καὶ γὰρ) οἱ ἁμαρτωλοὶ following each question; (2) anaphoric use of καὶ εἰ at the beginning of each question; (3) antistrophic use of ποία ὑμῖν χάρις ἐστίν at the end of each question; (4) pleonastic use of ἀγαπάω in the first example, ἀγαθοποιέω in the second question, as well as δανίζω and λαμβάνω in the third question; (5) pleonastic use of ὑμᾶς at the same location in each question; and (6) duplicate positioning of ἁμαρτωλοὶ ἁμαρτωλοῖς in the third question.[59]

And if (καὶ εἰ) you *love* (ἀγαπᾶτε) those who *love* (ἀγαπῶντας) *you* (ὑμᾶς), *what credit is that to you* (ποία ὑμῖν χάρις ἐστίν)?
  for even the sinners (καὶ γὰρ οἱ ἁμαρτωλοὶ) *love* (ἀγαπῶσιν) those who *love* (ἀγαπῶντας) them.
(*For*) *and if* (καὶ γὰρ ἐὰν) you do *good* (ἀγαθοποιῆτε) to the ones who do *good* (ἀγαθοποιοῦντας) to *you* (ὑμᾶς), *what credit is that to you* (ποία ὑμῖν χάρις ἐστίν)?
  for even the sinners (καὶ γὰρ οἱ ἁμαρτωλοί) *do* (ποιοῦσιν) the same.

56. See Quintilian, *Institutio Oratoria*, 9.2.6–9.2.7; Demetrius, *On Style*, 279 for a discussion of rhetorical questioning in ancient Greco-Roman rhetoric.

57. For a discussion of χάρις in Greco-Roman antiquity, see David Konstan, 'Reciprocity and Friendship', in Christopher Gill, et al. (eds), *Reciprocity in Ancient Greece* (Oxford: Oxford University Press, 1998), pp. 279–301; Kirk, ' "Love Your Enemies" ', pp. 678–81.

58. The conjunctive πλήν serves as a marker for the implied reader, denoting a change from inductive to deductive argumentation.

59. See *Rhetorica ad Herennium*, 4.38.28, for an explanation of reduplication; the repetition of one or more words for the purpose of amplification.

And if (καὶ ἐὰν) you *lend* (δανίσητε) to the ones from whom you hope to *receive* (λαβεῖν), what credit is that to you (ποία ὑμῖν χάρις ἐστίν)? Even *sinners* (καὶ ἁμαρτωλοὶ) *lend* (δανίζουσιν) to *sinners* (ἁμαρτωλοῖς) to *receive* (ἀπολάβωσιν) as much.

Keeping with stipulations of Greco-Roman rhetoric to avoid verbatim repetition and thus boredom on the part of the listener by maintaining some divergence in the employment of repetition,[60] the implied author includes a somewhat obtrusive γάρ at the beginning of the second example,[61] drops the connective γάρ at the beginning of the pleonastic conclusion for the third example, and omits the verb ἔστιν from the final question.[62] In addition, the final example stands out from the previous two, as it is more elaborate in detail and in its use of repetition. It also makes a turn towards a specific issue (v. 36).[63] All of the above compels the implied reader to acknowledge repetitive disruption, which, rather than detracting from, amplifies the rhetorical repetition. In addition, in the first of a series of rhetorical repetition, the implied author employs a rhetorical 'hook' to the proceeding discourse of the speech with the pleonastic use of ποιέω at the end of the second example (v. 33).[64] Specifically, the use of ποιέω hearkens back to its use in the enthymematic summary (v. 31) of the statement of case, further accentuating the importance of action on the part of a disciple and marking the need for a disciple to perform actions that extend beyond traditional norms.

A complex enthymeme (v. 35) followed by a simple enthymeme forms the supporting rationale of the body's first segment (v. 36). The minor premises

60. See the instruction on the avoidance of repetition verbatim in *Rhetorica ad Herennium* (4.42.54): 'We shall not repeat the same thing precisely – for that, to be sure, would weary the hearer and not elaborate the idea – but with changes'. Cf. also Kennedy (*Through Rhetorical Criticism*, pp. 21–22), who pinpoints the fundamental basis of rhetoric as amplification of a speaker's positions, arguments, or theses.

61. The reading likely representative of the earliest manuscript tradition is that of καὶ γάρ ἐάν. This claim is supported by several arguments: (1) it is certainly the more difficult reading – versus καὶ ἐάν; (2) its attestation is supported by the oldest, most reliable manuscripts (viz., P75, ℵ2, B); and (3) a scribe deleted γάρ from ℵ (ℵ*). Nevertheless, it is unclear as to why the implied author choose to include γάρ and what rhetorical effect this decision may have had on the narrative discourse.

62. It is unlikely that ἐστίν can be traced back to the original text. While it is found in several of the older and more reliable manuscripts (viz., A, ℵ), its omission is supported by several other manuscripts that are comparable in terms of date and authenticity (viz., B, P45, P75) and it is certainly the more difficult reading. This claim is also supported by the disjointed style of the overall narrative discourse of Luke-Acts, whereby the exclusion of connectives, articles, verbs, and so forth serve as rhetorical amplification.

63. Betz (*Sermon on the Mount*, p. 602) points out that the move to a specific topos in a third rhetorical question (v. 34) serves to keep the listener alert.

64. The first to use the attribution, 'hook word', for the repetition between narrative sections is Joanna Dewey (*Markan Public Debate: Literary Technique, Concentric Structure, and Theology in Mark 2:1-3:6* [SBLDS, 48; Chico, California: Scholars Press, 1980], p. 32). Also, see Tolbert, *Sowing the Gospel*, pp. 109–110.

for both enthymemes, which the implied reader is compelled to fill using abduction, equates those who follow the directives given by Jesus as being in accordance with the divine.[65]

Enthymematic Rationale: Enacting the Three Examples (v. 35)
Conclusion: Love your enemies, and do good and lend, expecting nothing in return like God.
Major Premise: God is kind to the ungrateful and selfish.
Minor Premise: Those whose reward is great and are sons of the Most High emulate the behavior and actions of the Most High.

Concluding Enthymematic Directive (v. 36)
Conclusion: Disciples are to show mercy, emulating the actions of the Father.
Major Premise: The Father is merciful.
Minor Premise: Those who show mercy are like the Father.

The first enthymeme (v. 35) delivers a rationale that coincides, almost verbatim, with the three preceding examples. In particular, its conclusion serves as a recitation of the three examples through its use of the action verbs contained in each (viz., ποιέω, ἀγαθοποιέω, δανίζω). It also links to the overall speech by means of the pleonastic use of ἀγαπᾶτε τοὺς ἐχθροὺς ὑμῶν, hooking back to the overarching theme of the statement of case (v. 27). The abbreviated style of the enthymeme's conclusion – repetition of καί between the imperatives and the lack of predicate descriptions following the last two imperatives – accentuates the impact of the directives. The minor premise exhibits the use of similar sounds that heighten the rhetorical impact of the enthymeme – specifically paronomasia[66] and homoeoteleuton.[67] In the case of paronomasia, the predicate of divine action – χρηστός – closely corresponds in sound with the word used for the first recalcitrant recipient of that action – ἀχαρίστους (v. 35c). In particular, juxtaposition of these two very similarly sounding words increases the significance of the divine's action. The presence of paronomasia does not end with the context of the enthymeme but rather extends to the threefold repetition of the phrase ποία ὑμῖν χάρις ἐστίν (viz., the subject χάρις). The implied author distinguishes, as a result, between those who abide according to the mores of Greco-Roman patronal society and those who emulate, in a proactive manner, actions of the divine.[68] As to

---

65. And herein is the rhetorical impact of the argument (which draws upon abduction): repudiation of Jesus' directives equates to being in opposition to the divine.

66. *Rhetorica ad Herennium*, 4.21.29.

67. *Rhetorica ad Herennium*, 4.21.28.

68. Green (*Gospel of Luke*, pp. 274–75) and Betz (*Sermon on the Mount*, pp. 610–11) identify the wordplay between χάρις, χρηστός, and ἀχαριστία and reach a similar conclusion.

homoeoteleuton, the article plus the two recipients of the divine action have the same ending – ους (i.e., τοὺς ἀχαρίστους καὶ πονηρούς).[69]

The segment is immersed in language of Greco-Roman commerce and benefaction – specifically μισθός, χάρις, and δανίζω. The use of μισθός ('payment') – by means of the extratextual repertoire of the implied reader – forms a parallel to that of χάρις ('credit') in the three preceding rhetorical questions (vv. 32-34) and links to its earlier use in the final woe (v. 26). The implied reader, through analeptic processing, constructs the following topos: disciples who embrace Jesus' message will receive more than credit (χάρις) – namely, payment (μισθός). Viewed from the lens of Greco-Roman benefaction, the recipients of χάρις and μισθός stand at opposite ends of the friendship spectrum: a client receives χάρις with the obligation to show μισθός to the patron in return.[70] However the rhetorical argument deconstructs this cultural order: a client receives χάρις without the need to discharge μισθός to the patron.[71] In this scenario a disciple (viz., patron) should not extend χάρις with the expectation of receiving μισθός (and thus honor) from a client; rather, the reciprocal μισθός will come from the divine.[72] The period breaks into the following structure:

> But (πλὴν) *love your enemies* (ἀγαπᾶτε τοὺς ἐχθροὺς ὑμῶν), and *do good* (ἀγαθοποιεῖτε) and *lend* (δανίζετε), expecting nothing in return
>   and your payment (μισθός ← χάρις) will be great,
>   and you will be sons of the Most High;

---

69. Note the instructions on the use of homoeoptoton, homoioteleuton, and paronomasia in *Rhetorica ad Herennium*, 4.22.29:

> These last three figures ... are to be used very sparingly when we speak in an actual cause, because their invention seems impossible without labor and pains. Such endeavors, indeed, seem more suitable for a speech of entertainment than for use in an actual cause ... [T]he grand and beautiful can give pleasure for a long time, but the neat and graceful quickly sate the hearing ... ; but if we insert them infrequently and scatter them with variations throughout the whole discourse, we shall illuminate our style agreeably with striking ornaments.

70. A 'hook' with the statement of case in the speech is also evoked by means of μισθός, where it appears in the final blessing (v. 23). Part of the intercalated enthymeme in v. 23, the importance of μισθός, is thus heightened further.

71. See Betz (*Sermon on the Mount*, pp. 604–8) who argues that the 'lending' (δανίζω) in question relates to 'loan' (μισθός) interest.

72. Cf. the similar conclusion of Green, *Gospel of Luke*, p. 274:

> Those who act without expectation of return, even on behalf of their enemies, will be rewarded. Now, however, their reward does not consist of acts of gratitude from the recipients of their benefaction; rather, God rewards them. In the ethics of the larger Lukan world, a patron solidifies his or her position in the community by 'giving,' by placing others in his or her debt, and receiving from them obliged acts of service and reverence. In this new economy, however, the patron gives without strings attached, yet is still repaid, now by a third party, God, the great benefactor, the protector and the benefactor of those in need.

for (ὅτι) God is kind (χρηστός) to the ungrateful and selfish (τοὺς ἀχαρίστους καὶ πονηρούς).

The concluding enthymeme (v. 36) manifests a very simplified directive. Intertextual connections with LXX texts such as Pss. 25.8; 86.5, Zech. 1.16, Isa. 63.15, and Wis 15.1 supplement the major premise that God is merciful. Like the concluding maxim at the end of the state of case (v. 31), the concluding enthymematic directive (v. 36) serves as both a summary for the first segment of the speech's argument as well as a transition to the following segment (vv. 37-42) of argument. The rhetorical impact of the enthymeme falls on the pleonastic use of οἰκτίρμος, which appears in both the conclusion and the major premise:[73]

Be *merciful* (οἰκτίρμονες),
just as even (καθὼς καὶ)[74] your Father is *merciful* (οἰκτίρμων).

In particular, use of οἰκτίρμος prompts the implied reader to draw upon the aforementioned intertextual repertoire, where it is used in the context of describing divine sympathy towards humankind: non-reciprocal benefaction of disciples emulates the actions of the divine. The brevity of the enthymeme's conclusion guides the implied reader to use information from the major premise, not only to construct the minor premise but to sketch out the conclusion in full.

Use of ὕψιστος ('Most High') in v. 35 to represent the divine creates an analeptic echo to Gabriel's prediction of Jesus' birth to Mary (Lk. 1.32), where Jesus is described as a υἱός of ὑψίστου. The change in reference to πατήρ ('Father') rather than ὕψιστος in v. 36 heightens the rhetorical effect of this intertextual linkage. In particular, these intratextual connections prompt the implied reader to conclude that Jesus and his disciples – just as υἱός ('children') aspire to imitate the actions of their fathers (viz., ὕψιστος) – imitate the actions of the divine (in this case οἰκτίρμος).

2. Friendship without Boundaries: Second Segment (6.37-42)
The second segment of the speech's body (vv. 37-42) begins with four maxims followed by a supporting enthymeme (vv. 37-38). Two parabolic examples with an enclosed enthymeme conclude the segment (vv. 39-42), which posits the need for disciples to embrace others regardless of social and religious standing. The four maxims (vv. 37-38a) and supporting

73. Redactional activity on the part of the implied author is evident here: thematic interest in hospitality is found elsewhere in the narrative discourse (e.g., Lk. 1.50; 10.37) (cf. Ben Witherington III, 'Editing the Good News: some synoptic lessons for the study of Acts', in *History, Literature and Society*, p. 333).

74. As to whether καί should be included as part of the text is unclear. The manuscript tradition is split, with its omission supported by B, א, among others and its inclusion by A, D, f[13], the Latin and Syriac manuscript tradition, among others. While it only complicates the reading slightly, the more difficult reading is καθὼς καί. All that can be said, as a result, is that a much more detailed analysis of the manuscript tradition is required before an accurate assessment can be made.

enthymeme (v. 38bc) exhibit a number of rhetorical features that heighten their impact on the listener. The following are some of the more obvious rhetorical features of the four maxims. First, the first two maxims (v. 37ab) are negative, whereas the latter two are positive (vv. 37c-38a). The rhetorical division coincides with a separation of content; the first two pertaining to avoidance of negative actions and the latter two concerning the exhibition of proactive behavior.[75] Second, while the entire speech contains a number of disjointed periods, the maxims here contain even less language, evoking a heightened awareness on the part of the listener. Third, deviation in the form of the final maxim (v. 38a) from that of the preceding three (v. 37) – namely, the change from second person to first person – places the emphasis on the directive within the final maxim of the series. The culmination of the four consecutive maxims also falls on the enactment of unconditional social and religious reciprocity by means of the final maxim. As regards to the first three maxims, they set the stage by codifying the thought processes that corroborate actions: the decisions leading a disciple to embrace those outside of the boundaries of cultural companionship and kinship.

For the major premise of the supporting enthymeme (v. 38bc), the implied author employs a metaphor – μέτρον καλόν – and accompanying metaphoric language – in the form of three consecutive descriptive adjectival participles – πεπιεσμένον, σεσαλευμένον, ὑπερεκχυννόμενον. The even more disjointed style than the preceding discourse of the body, coupled with the elevated impact of the three consecutive participles as well as the fourfold sequential repetition of -μενον (in addition to the fivefold sequential use of -ον), serves as a rhetorical signal to the implied reader that the enthymeme is to receive heightened notice.[76] The use of μέτρον καλόν and the three adjectival participles following it evokes a rural, agrarian extratextual repertoire, in addition to an intertextual repertoire. Though there is not an extant text containing an amalgamated combination of the words, the subject μέτρον καλόν likely denotes a measure used for grain, whereas the adjectival participles convey eschatological inklings through their typical use in the LXX and elsewhere.[77] The implied reader compiles these connections and deduces that the measure is filled beyond capacity; hence, the reason for the grain overflowing. The conclusion of the enthymeme elicits an extratextual repertoire concerning grain contracts that stipulate the

---

75. See, e.g., Nolland (*Luke*, vol. 1, pp. 300–1) and I. Howard Marshall (*The Gospel of Luke: A Commentary on the Greek Text* [NIGTC; Grand Rapids, Mich.: William B. Eerdmans Publishing Company, 1978], p. 265) for a similar conclusion, though not on the basis of rhetorical analysis.

76. The consecutive deployment of the same ending is designated as homoeoteleuton; a rhetorical device that accentuates the impact of the discourse (*Rhetorica ad Herennium*, 4.21.28).

77. Cf. the use of ὑπερεκχύννω in Joel 2.24 and the scattered use of σαλεύω in the LXX (e.g., Hab. 2.16; Zech. 12.2; Jer. 10.10; Ezek. 12.18; Isa. 63.19; Sir. 16.18).

requirement to measure the delivered grain and corresponding payment with the same instrument.[78]

Use of three consecutive perfect participles in the supporting enthymeme – πεπιεσμένον, σεσαλευμένον, and ὑπερεκχυννόμενον – serves as a discourse marker for the implied reader. In particular, the change to perfect tense raises the enthymeme above the rest of the discourse.[79] As a complex rhetorical structure comprises the enthymeme, the discourse prompts the implied reader to draw upon information from the preceding four maxims, in addition to the enthymeme contained in the initial segment of the speech's body, to fulfill the deductive reasoning warranted by the implied author.[80]

Conclusion: Those who do not judge, do not condemn, forgive, and give will receive good measure.	*Conclusion:* Those who judge, condemn, do not forgive, and do not give will *not* receive good measure.
Major Premise: The measure a disciple gives will be the measure a disciple gets back.	*Minor Premise:* Good measure is equated with not judging, not condemning, forgiving, and giving.

The final portion of the second segment of the speech's body consists of an intercalation: two parabolic examples (vv. 39, 41-42) surrounding an enthymeme (v. 40). The insertion by the narrator (i.e., 'he spoke to them also a parable' in v. 39a) intrudes upon the discourse by interrupting the narrative flow. It serves, therefore, as a rhetorical marker for the implied reader. Specifically, an indirect reference to the narrative audience by means of αὐτοῖς in the narrative aside pulls the implied reader back to the beginning of the speech (vv. 17-19 and then v. 20), where the exact identity of the 'disciple' character group is unclear. In addition, while the identity of a 'disciple' is much more apparent at this point in the speech than at its beginning, it is not until the conclusion of the speech (vv. 46-49) that the implied reader reaches the understanding that 'disciples' are those characters who enact Jesus' teachings.

The first parable (v. 39) invokes an extratextual repertoire rooted in Greco-Roman rhetoric, one that had achieved proverbial status. In

---

78. See H. P. Rüger, 'Mit welchem Mass ihr messt, wird euch gemessen werden (Mt 7:2, Gen 38:25-26)', *ZNW* 60 (1969), pp. 174–82; B. Couroyer, 'De la mesure dont vous mesurez il vous sera mesuré', *RB* 77 (1970), pp. 366–70. The receptacle for dispensing the grain – κόλπος – is either the fold in the garment at the girdle that serves as a pocket or the actual skirt of the garment (when large quantities are represented). An intertextual allusion to the use of κόλπος in Isa. 65.6-7 would suggest to the implied reader that those who fail to dispense the 'good' measure risk evoke the wrath of the divine as exhibited in Deutero-Isaiah (e.g., 59.1-20; 64.1-12; 65.1-16; 66.14-16).

79. For the change in verbal tense to the perfect tense, see Stanley E. Porter, *Idioms of the Greek New Testament* (Biblical Languages Greek, 2; Sheffield: Sheffield Academic Press, 2nd ed., 1994), pp. 298–307, esp. pp. 301–2.

80. Vernon K. Robbins, 'From Enthymeme to Theology in Luke 11:1-13', in *Literary Studies*, pp. 196–98, 200–1, recognizes the enthymematic argument of Lk. 6.38, and, though he does not delineate a twofold set of major premises and conclusions, he identifies a connection with the preceding four maxims.

addition, it contains intratextual connotations through the use of ὁδηγέω ('blind') to denote those who lack faith or insight.[81] For the implied reader the inductive result is the rejection of characters and character groups that fail to understand Jesus' teaching and exhibit faithlessness. The rhetorical impact of the parable is accentuated by means of the repetition of τυφλός τυφλὸν. The central point of the narrative unit is found in the enthymeme (v. 40), with the implied author departing from the metaphorical language of the parable and the change from indirect references to disciples to direct references (via the use of μαθητής). In addition to the direct reference to disciple, the implied reader equates the identity of the 'teacher' with Jesus; the actions of those who purport to be teachers in the previous narrative run directly counter to the inductive conclusions prompted by the preceding parable. The implied reader deductively concludes, in particular, that those characters and character groups that attempt to elevate themselves above their teachers (viz., Jesus in this context) are blind. Based on the prior narrative, the implied reader places the Pharisees and lawyers in this category; they are shown in several scenes elevating themselves above Jesus (cf. 5.17-26; 6.1-5, 6-11). The minor premise of the enthymeme, which the implied reader must deduce, conveys additional meaning: a teacher aspires to elevate disciples to the same status level by seeking an egalitarian relationship, with the result being that disciples exemplify the characteristics embodied by the teacher (viz. Jesus).

Intercalated Enthymeme (v. 40)
Conclusion: A disciple becomes like the teacher when fully taught.
Minor Premise: A teacher aspires to elevate disciples to the same level of status.
Major Premise: A disciple never considers himself above one's teacher.

The narrative discourse in the second parabolic example (vv. 41-42) suddenly changes to the second person, from the first-person discourse of the first parabolic example and enthymeme. This change has a rhetorical function, bringing the discourse closer to the implied reader and arranging the discourse so that the two questions are posed directly to the narrative audience and the implied reader. The twofold rhetorical questioning necessitates activity on the part of the narrative audience and the implied reader, answers that are predetermined by means of the meshing of the parables in well-known sayings.[82] Shifting of the verb to the end of each clause in the case of both questions, in contrast to the earlier positioning in the first clause, also serves a rhetorical function, disallowing activity on the

81. The proverb of 'the blind leading the blind' is well known in antiquity, with the 'blind leader' (ὁδηγὸς τυφλός) used as a descriptive for exposing incompetence on the part of a leader. For this observation, see Betz, *Sermon on the Mount*, pp. 620–21; Bovon, *Luke 1:1–9:50*, p. 248.
82. Some of the more notable examples from Greco-Roman literature who condemn the shortcoming of reproving others when suffering from the same shortcoming include Aristotle, *Rhetoric*, 3.18.16–17; Plutarch, *De curios*, 515d; Horace, *Satire*, 1.3.25.

part of the implied reader until all of the argument has been heard.[83] The addition of the appellation ἀδελφέ, which represents language used to designate community relationships, focuses the discourse on the interaction within the Christian community.

It is important to note here that the corrective action on the part of a disciple is nowhere condemned in the discourse. Those who recognize their own shortcomings when correcting fellow disciples are not in purview, but rather those who take corrective action without recognizing their own shortcomings.[84] Extratextual connotations surrounding the nomenclature ὑποκριτής corroborate this understanding. Two definitions are possible for ὑποκριτής in the context of the discourse: the notation of someone whose behavior is not determined by the divine or someone playing a role by acting a part in a Greco-Roman theater. Both connotations are possible, as each form part of the extratextual repertoire of the implied reader and narrative audience.[85] Either one or a combination of both suggests that the one who fails to acknowledge her or his shortcomings while judging others is incongruent with the demeanor stipulated by the divine and moreover simply camouflages shortcomings by acting out a part. This understanding coincides with preceding rhetorical texture in the speech – namely, stereotyping and judging on the basis of social, ethnic, and religious location is inconsistent with the teachings of Jesus.[86]

3. *Rationale for the Body: Third Segment (6.43-45)*

The final section of the speech's body (vv. 43-45) provides the rationale for the reasoning of the first two sections in the form of three parabolic examples. The first two parables are shrouded in extratextual and intertextual meaning, encapsulating well-known agrarian symbols as well as language from the LXX. Intratextual linkage to the summary of John the Baptist's message in Lk. 3.7-14 also exists through the metaphorical use of (καρπός) 'fruit' as representative of human conduct.[87] All three parables resemble complex enthymemes. The first two enthymemes share the same minor premise (v. 44a). Unlike most other enthymemes in the Lukan discourse, the conclusions must be completed by the implied reader, a rhetorical maneuver by the implied author that helps accentuate the

---

83. Asyndeton – namely, the omission of the connective ἤ – at the start of the second question in v. 42 also serves a rhetorical function, creating a disjunctive gap in the discourse that results in the accentuation of the argument. The omission of the connective is of some question in the manuscript tradition. However, asyndeton is corroborated by the oldest and most reliable manuscripts, and, in addition, there is a viable rhetorical reason for the omission of the connective ἤ.

84. See, e.g., Betz, *Sermon on the Mount*, pp. 626–28.

85. For the latter, see Job 34.30; 36.13; 2 Macc. 6.21-25; *4 Macc.* 6.15-23; *Pss. Sol.* 4.5-6, 22. For a more in-depth analysis of the extratextual connotations of 'hypocrite', see Robert H. Smith, 'Hypocrite', in Joel B. Green and Scott McKnight (eds), *Dictionary of Jesus and the Gospels* (Downers Grove and Leicester: InterVarsity, 1992) 351–53.

86. Green, *Gospel of Luke*, p. 279.

87. See Green (*Gospel of Luke*, p. 279), who also identifies this intratextual connection.

importance of the closing rhetorical argument of the speech's body. The enthymeme resembles the following structure:

Conclusion: A good tree produces good fruit and is known for it.
Major Premise: No good tree   *Major Premise:* No bad tree
produces bad fruit.   produces good fruit.
Minor Premise: Each tree is known for its fruit.

The second enthymeme (v. 44) is a reversal in reasoning. Unlike the first enthymeme, where the implied reader concludes that each tree is known for its fruit (by means of the minor premise), the implied reader is prompted to construe both the ἄκανθα ('thorn bush') and the βάτος ('bramble bush') by what is not produced. Also of interest is that both enthymemes share the same minor premise (v. 44). Hence, the implied reader anticipates the same structure for the second enthymeme as in the case of the first enthymeme: the minor premise will come at the end of the enthymeme. This parallel structure prompts the implied reader to use the minor premise from the first enthymeme (v. 43) to build coherence when processing the second enthymeme. The second enthymeme breaks into the following parts:

Conclusion: A thorn is known for   *Conclusion:* A bramble bush is
producing bad fruit, not good fruit   known for producing bad fruit, not
such as figs.   good fruit such as grapes.
Major Premise: Figs are not   *Major Premise:* Grapes are not
gathered from thorns.   picked from a bramble bush.
Minor Premise: Each is known for their fruit.

The enthymemes in vv. 43-44 display some rhetorical features that heighten the discourse. The most obvious is the use of repetition, which is evident in several instances. The first is the use of homoioteleuton in both of the major premises of the first enthymeme: δένδρον καλὸν ποιοῦν καρπὸν σαπρόν in v. 43a and δένδρον σαπρὸν ποιοῦν καρπὸν καλόν in v. 43b. The minor premise also exhibits homoioteleuton by means of the repetition of τοῦ ἰδίου καρποῦ in v. 44a. The second is the anaphoric construction of the two enthymemes: both begin with οὐ γάρ, and οὐδέ serves as the transition between the two major premises. An additional rhetorical feature of the two enthymemes resembles synkrisis. The first enthymeme uses the metaphor of δένδρον as a means to place both of the major premises in contrast (i.e., a good tree bears good fruit and a bad tree bears bad fruit in v. 43a). The second enthymeme draws upon two comparable examples (i.e., figs do not come from thorns and grapes do not come from a bramble bush in 44bc) to accomplish a similar rhetorical result – namely, juxtaposition of the metaphors produces the dual conclusions.

The implied author in the final enthymeme (v. 45) moves the parabolic language – and thus the topos – closer to the implied reader by making a transition from the agrarian world to that of humankind. The narrative texture retains rhetorical similarity with the two preceding enthymemes by employing the same format: two conclusions and major premises and a shared minor premise. Yet the 'gap' the implied reader is required to fill narrows: the analogies in the major premises do not necessitate processing. Accordingly, unlike the previous two enthymemes where the implied reader needs to deduce the contrast (viz., if a good/bad tree cannot produce bad/good fruit, then it must produce good/bad fruit), no action is required on the part of the implied reader (viz., a good/bad person produces a good/bad treasure). The structure of the enthymeme is as follows:

Conclusion: The substance of a good person is exemplified by the good treasure of her or his heart.

Major Premise: A good person produces good from the good treasure of her or his heart.

Conclusion: The substance of an evil person is exemplified by the evil treasure of her or his heart.

Major Premise: An evil person produces evil from the evil treasure of her or his heart.

Minor Premise: The actions of a person are predicated on the substance of her or his heart.

Like the previous two enthymemes, the concluding enthymeme in v. 45 draws on repetition, including several instances of homoioteleuton and a parallel rhetorical construction for both major premises: (1) the threefold use of ἀγαθός followed by the threefold use of πονηρός in the two major premises; (2) the repetition of προφέρω to describe the action that eventuates from both the good and evil person; and (3) the focus of the minor premise and conclusions on καρδία as the origin for a person's action. Also consistent with ancient rhetorical style, θησαυρός is implied in the second enthymeme, a maneuver requiring the implied reader to fill the subject of the genitive clause ἐκ τοῦ πονηροῦ. Another rhetorical nuance relates to the ambiguous meaning of προφέρω, as the implied reader is prodded to look elsewhere for its reference. The search for meaning is not a long quest; the agricultural intratext of the preceding enthymemes (vv. 43-44) supplies the information the implied reader needs in order to fill the missing verbal 'gap' – ποιέω.

D. *Conclusion (6.46-49)*

The conclusion (vv. 46-49) of the speech is carefully crafted for maximum rhetorical impact. A perplexing conundrum for the implied reader is posed in the conclusion of the enthymeme from the body of the speech (v. 45c): biological norms dictate that a person speaks from the mouth, not from the heart. This rhetorical ploy melds into the building crescendo of the discourse, accentuating the importance of a disciple's action versus actual speech. The implied reader is led to this conclusion by means of the discourse: the 'successful' disciple is the one who listens to Jesus' words and responds with appropriate action, whereas the unsuccessful disciple is the one who does not listen to Jesus' words and responds with inappropriate action. The implied reader concludes that praxis entails more than corresponding speech; action is a non-negotiable requisite.

The conclusion of the speech departs from the enthymematic argument representative of most of the preceding speech. Rather, the implied author directly confronts the implied reader by posing a question for which there is no correct answer. The use of ποιέω in the rhetorical question (v. 46) and its repetition at the beginning of each example (vv. 47, 49) forms an intratextual connection with the preceding argument of the speech's body, particularly the concluding rationale in vv. 43-44. The prior enthymematic argument in vv. 43-45, when combined with the rhetorical discourse of the conclusion, ensnares Jesus' audience in a rhetorical trap. The prior extratextual repertoire that places the interaction between disciples and other members of society in the context of patron–client relations also carries over into the speech's conclusion by means of the appellative κύριε.[88] As a result, Jesus situates himself in the position of a patron and the disciples (both 'real' and 'would be') in the position of clients. The effect of this rhetorical maneuver is that honor and shame protocols associated with the patron–client relationship necessitate that disciples respond to Jesus with more than words; they must reciprocate with action.

The ethical dimensions of Jesus' instruction are couched by the use of ὑποδεικνύω, a term employed in Hellenistic and Rabbinical ethical instruction.[89] Use of rhetorical contrast in the two examples (vv. 47-49) is a common construction in Greco-Roman rhetoric.[90] Close resemblance in the form of both examples heightens the rhetorical impact of the discourse and prompts the implied reader and narrative audience to compare the details of each example: (1) θεμελίος as the essential building element needed in the construction of a house (vv. 48b, 49a); (2) ὅμοιος to begin each example; (3) ἀκούω to describe the receptive activity of the disciple equated with each example; (4) ποιέω to denote the response of each disciple upon hearing Jesus' instructions; (5) οἰκοδομέω (accompanied by οἶκός) to describe the activity of the subject; (6) a change from the present to past tense for οἰκοδομέω; and (7) exclusion of the descriptive noun πλημμύρης in the second example.

Further comparison of the rhetorical arrangement of the two examples evinces several other noteworthy features: the predicates of ἀκούω and ποιέω – namely, μου τῶν λόγων for ἀκούω and αὐτούς for ποιέω – are absent in the second example (v. 49a). John the Baptist's prediction in Lk. 3.17 that Jesus would bring division and strife is confirmed as the speech comes to a close. Specifically, ethical contrast translates into taxonomic characterization: characters and character groups who listen and enact Jesus' words versus those who listen but fail to act. The implied author continues to build on this taxonomic characterization in the fourth speech of the Lukan Galilean ministry, which is discussed in chapters seven and nine.

88. As noted by Green, *Gospel of Luke*, p. 280.
89. For a discussion of the extratextual repertoire, see Harvey K. McArthur and Robert M. Johnston, *They Also Taught in Parables: Rabbinic Parables from the First Centuries of the Christian Era* (Grand Rapids: Zondervan Publishing Company, 1990), pp. 184–85.
90. Aristotle, *Rhetoric*, 2.19.1; *Rhetorica ad Herennium*, 4.40–4.43.

IV. *Concluding Summary*

The rhetorical situation of the second speech of the Galilean ministry, through intertextual echoes and intratextual linkages, builds upon earlier discourse. It bolsters Jesus' ethos by situating the speech within the context of Moses' dissemination of the law. In addition, its topoi coincide with many of those established in the first speech (4.14-30), which compels the implied reader to bring coherence to the narrative. The speech aims, in particular, to persuade the narrative audience to a new mode of ethical action – specifically non-reciprocal benefaction.

In contrast to the assessment of some scholars, the speech exhibits a significant degree of attention to rhetorical argument, both inductive and deductive, that includes examples, maxims, rhetorical questioning, and enthymemes. In addition to the speech's rhetorical texture, redaction of Q by the implied author reveals attention to the formation of rhetorical argument that engenders and buttresses larger narrative trajectories. From a rhetorical standpoint, the implied author includes various 'gaps' and 'blanks' in the discourse, largely by means of enthymematic argument, that the implied reader must 'fill' in order to make sense of the narrative. This activity accentuates certain narrative trajectories, including the importance of ethical action and, in particular, the mode of non-reciprocal benefaction, both of which will be discussed in Chapter eight.

Much of the investigation of Jesus' third speech in the Lukan Galilean ministry (7.24-35) revolves around redactional analysis – the identification of Lukan interests through modifications made to Q.[1] Recently, several scholars have examined the narrative from the standpoint of how the discourse contributes to the construction of characterization for John the Baptist.[2] Regardless, few scholars, if any, pay attention to the rhetorical texture of the narrative discourse. This chapter investigates the narrative for its rhetorical argument and lays the groundwork for the identification of narrative trajectories that extend from the speech and play a role in shaping the narrative discourse of Luke-Acts.

I. *Rhetorical Situation*

The transition from the second speech to the next healing episode in 7.1 exhibits several rhetorical features that heed reference. First, reference to the narrative audience (i.e., λαός) points the implied reader back to the beginning of the second speech in 6.17-19, where the same audience was identified by the narrator. In contrast to 6.17-19, disciples are absent, which serves a rhetorical purpose: the implied author guides the implied reader to distinguish between disciples (viz., those whose actions embody the message and ministry of Jesus) and those who are not disciples (viz., those whose actions fail to coincide with Jesus' ministry and message). The second involves the close resemblance between Jesus' words (ῥήματος) in 7.1 and the demise (ῥῆγμα) met by those who do not heed Jesus' words in the second example of the conclusion (6.49), a rhetorical 'pun' (known as paraonomasia)[3] emphasizing the importance of adherence to Jesus' teaching. Finally, association of the narrative audience with those who just heard the preceding speech with the use of ἀκούω accentuates the connection between listening to Jesus' words and the act of appropriation: the implied author

1. See, e.g., Bovon, *Luke 1:1-9:50*, pp. 276–88; John S. Kloppenborg, *The Formation of Q: Trajectories in Ancient Wisdom Collections* (Studies in Antiquity and Christianity; Philadelphia: Fortress Press, 1987), pp. 107–21.
2. See, e.g., Darr, *Character Building*, pp. 60–84.
3. *Rhetorica ad Herennium*, 4.21; Aristotle, *Rhetoric*, 3.11.7

leaves 'little excuse' for the narrative audience – and for that matter the implied reader – not to listen to Jesus' teaching and to follow with action.

Both temporal and spatial markers demarcate to the implied reader that 7.1ff. initiates a new section. The end of the section is also signaled by temporal and spatial markers in 8.1. The message communicated in the initial two speeches of the Galilean ministry and depicted in various action scenes embedded between the two speeches coalesces in 7.1-50, which consists of three 'example' stories (vv. 1-10; vv. 11-17; vv. 36-50), a chreia (vv. 17-23), and a speech (vv. 24-35). The first two exemplary stories form an intertextual intersection with the Elisha and Elijah LXX narratives, an intratextual link back to the inaugural ministry speech (4.24-27). The first example (7.1-10), the healing of the centurion's slave, articulates a prophetic ministry exercised to the Gentiles and parallels the Naaman episode (2 Kgs 5.1-19).[4] The second example (7.11-17), the raising of the widow's son at Nain, closely mirrors Elijah's ministry to the disenfranchised within Israel through parallels with the raising of the son belonging to the widow at Zarephath in Sidon (1 Kgs 17.8-24). In sum, the intertextual association of Jesus' ministry with that of Elisha and Elijah is given further impetus by the analeptic reference to the first speech (4.25-27): their ministries to the Gentiles and the disenfranchised.[5]

II. *Rhetorical Texture*

The section preceding the speech (vv. 17-23) resembles an amplified chreia. The narrative introduction (vv. 17-18) establishes the context for the quaestio (vv. 19-20). Duplication of the questioning in the quaestio (seeking rationale) – first John the Baptist to his disciples (v. 19) and then his disciples to Jesus (v. 20) – serves to elongate narrative time, which accentuates the importance of Jesus' response to the implied reader. The chreia (v. 21) is followed by a paraphrase (v. 22). Repetition between the chreia and the paraphrase heightens the rhetorical significance of the argument, with Isaianic intertextual connections (29.18; 35.5-6; 42.18; 61.1) providing the implied reader with an analeptic link to the inaugural speech (4.18-20). This connection with the inaugural speech provides confirmation to the implied reader that Jesus is doing what he previously indicated he would do. The conclusion (v. 23), which is in the form of a maxim, provides

4. However cf. Thomas L. Brodie, 'Not Q but Elijah: The Saving of the centurion's Servant (Luke 7:1-10) as an Internationalization of the Saving of the Widow and Her Child (1 Kings 17:1-16)', *IBS* 14 (1992), pp. 54–71, who sees an intertextual connection with 1 Kgs 17.1-16 rather than 2 Kgs 5.1-19.

5. For a description of the intertextual connections between Elisha's and Elijah's ministries (viz., Elijah's encounter with the widow from Zarephath and Elisha's encounter with Naaman) and Jesus' encounters with the centurion and the widow from Zarephath in Lk. 7.1-17, see Thomas L. Brodie, 'Towards an Unravelling of Luke's Use of the Old Testament: Luke 7.11-17 as an *Imitatio* of 1 Kings 17.17-24', *NTS* 32 (1986), pp. 247–67; Green, *Gospel of Luke*, pp. 284–85.

a dramatic finish for the implied reader and narrative audience (viz., the disciples of John the Baptist) and sets the stage for the next speech.[6] The rhetorical argument of vv. 17-23 is deductive and requires the implied reader and narrative audience to answer the question posed by John the Baptist and his disciples. The implied author does not include an affirmative response by Jesus but rather a description of Jesus' ministry and a corresponding summary by Jesus: an embodiment of the prophetic principles found in Isaiah, where the expected Messiah would deliver 'salvation' to the disenfranchised.[7]

The speech is replete with ecphrasis and synkrisis. The rhetorical argument is directed at persuading the implied reader and narrative audience to judge the ethos of John the Baptist and, though in a much less direct manner, the ethos of Jesus in a positive light.[8] The intratextual context for the third speech is set at the end of the second example with the raising of the widow's son at Nain (7.11-17): Jesus is recognized as a 'great prophet', one imbued with the divine, by those attending the miraculous resurrection of the widow's son (vv. 16-17). This marks growing narrative momentum: all present identify Jesus and his ministry as representative of the prophets, and the report extends not only to the surrounding region but to Judea (i.e., versus the earlier report in 4.37 that simply spread to the surrounding region and, in addition, did not specifically note the subject matter).

A. *An Amplified Chreia*

Like Jesus' first two Galilean ministry speeches, the third speech embodies a number of rhetorical devices. Specifically, it exhibits close affinity with the pronouncement story, with the amplified chreia in the previous section expanded to an elaborated response-chreia.[9] The preceding scene –

---

6. The elaborate chreia in Lk. 7.17-23 resembles the following parts: (1) narrative introduction (vv. 17-18); (2) quaestio (vv. 19-20); (3) chreia (v. 21); (4) paraphrase (v. 22); and (5) conclusion (v. 23).

7. However cf. Cameron, '"What Have You Come Out to See?" Characterizations of John and Jesus in the Gospels', pp. 35–69, who argues that Lk. 7.18-35 resembles an elaborate chreia: (1) praise (missing); (2) chreia (vv. 18-19, 22); (3) rationale (v. 23); (4) statement of the opposite (vv. 24-26); (5) statements by an authority (vv. 27-28); (6) statement from analogy (vv. 31-32); (7) statement from example (vv. 33-34); and (8) concluding periodization (v. 35). Not all pieces of the chreia are present, however, and the individual pieces do not all fit together exactly – for example, the chreia breaks into two parts (vv. 18-19 and v. 21) and is separated by material (v. 20) that does not fit into the arrangement of the chreia.

8. See Patrick J. Hartin, '"Yet Wisdom Is Justified by Her Children" (Q 7:35): A Rhetorical and Compositional Analysis of Divine Sophia in Q', in *Conflict and Invention*, pp. 151–64; Cameron, 'Characterization in the Gospels', pp. 50–63.

9. See, e.g., Vernon K. Robbins, 'Pronouncement Stories from a Rhetorical Perspective', *Forum* 4 (1988), pp. 1–31, for an overview of pronouncement stories as an evolution of chreia.

specifically the chreia and its paraphrase (vv. 21-23) – establishes the rhetorical situation. Inclusion of a narrative aside (7.29-30), a strategy employed in various places of the Luke-Acts narrative, allows the narrator to intervene in the story and provides the implied reader with information relevant to the story that is unknown to the narrative audience.[10] The introduction in vv. 24-27 introduces the topos, with the help of a narrative description in v. 24a: the ethos of John the Baptist and his relationship to Jesus. The chreia occurs in the final part of the introduction, where Jesus cites an amalgamated form of Mal. 3.1 and Exod. 23.20: 'Behold, I send my messenger before you who shall prepare your way before you' (7.27). The speech's statement of case (v. 28), accompanied by a narrative aside (vv. 29-30), posits the purpose of the speech. In particular, the intervening narrative aside serves as a narrative digressio and provides the implied reader with information to use in processing the body of the speech (vv. 31-34): the identity of the individuals from the contemporary generation. The body corresponds with the chreia argument; it includes an example (v. 31-32) followed by the rationale behind the example (vv. 33-34). The conclusion (v. 35) confirms the argument of the body and, as a succinct aphorism, provides for a dramatic finish to the speech. In all, the third speech breaks into the following chreia-like arrangement:

1. Narrative Introduction (vv. 17-23)   5. Digressio (vv. 29-30)
2. Quaestio (vv. 24-26)   6. Statement by Analogy (vv. 31-32)
3. Chreia (v. 27)   7. Statement by Example (vv. 33-34)
4. Rationale (v. 28)   8. Conclusion (v. 35)

The focus of the speech centers on the ethos of John the Baptist, and the narrative transition prior to the introduction in v. 24a helps focus the implied reader on John the Baptist. In particular, the narrative transition is needed, as the preceding scene in 7.17-23 addresses the ethos of Jesus. Regardless, despite the change in focus from the ethos of Jesus to the ethos of John the Baptist, there is a close narrative relationship between the inquiry from John the Baptist about the ethos of Jesus in vv. 17-23 and Jesus' oration on the ethos of John the Baptist in 7.24-35. The rhetorical result is a positive judgment of both characters, with Jesus and his followers receiving greater importance, a topos previously found in the intertwined birth accounts of John the Baptist and Jesus in 1.5–2.52.[11] Intratextual linkages with the inaugural speech in 4.16-30 occurs by means of the close correspondence in language between the inaugural speech and the preceding narrative that describes the ministry of Jesus (cf. 7.23-24 = 4.18).[12] In addition to the more obvious intratextual connections with the inaugural

10. See Steven M. Sheeley, *Narrative Asides in Luke-Acts* (JSNTSup, 72; Sheffield: Academic Press, 1992), pp. 97–185.

11. Green, *Theology of the Gospel*, pp. 51–55.

12. See Suzanne Marie Kearney, 'A Study of Principal Compositional Techniques in Luke-Acts based on Lk. 4:16-30 in Conjunction with Lk 7:18-23' (Ph.D. diss, Boston University, 1978).

speech, including near verbatim repetition and intertextual usage, there is significant linkage with Jesus' second speech (6.20-49) in the Galilean ministry.[13]

B. *Narrative Introduction: Quaestio and Chreia (7.24-27)*

The ambivalence of John the Baptist and his disciples regarding the ethos of Jesus is prompted by the report about Jesus' ministry to Judea and all of the surrounding countryside (7.17). The derivation is understandable considering the ostensible differences in the ministries of John the Baptist and Jesus: the former prophesies severe punishment and a coming one who would bring judgment, whereas the latter proclaims a message of inclusion and forgiveness. Nevertheless, because the implied reader possesses knowledge not available to the narrative audience, the diminutive position of John the Baptist and his followers is only perceived by the implied reader, not the narrative audience. Specifically, the narrative audience does not have access to the analeptic linkage in 3.1-18, where John the Baptist's ministry to the people and tax collectors and his rejection by the Pharisees and lawyers is detailed.

The narrative introduction in v. 24a suggests to the implied reader that Jesus is about to deliver an oration. The rhetorical arrangement – questioning followed by the corresponding answer – is a common Greco-Roman rhetorical device.[14] The threefold repetition of the question τί ἐξήλθατε ἰδεῖν (θεάσασθαι) in the first question in v. 24b builds to an inexorable conclusion, with the initial two questions leading the narrative audience to the determination that John the Baptist was a figure of great significance – a prophet, the Elijah figure who would forerun the coming of the Messiah.[15] The addition of the conjunctive ἀλλά to the second and third inquiries as well as the permutation in the infinitive from θεάσασθαι to ἰδεῖν for the second and third queries heightens the rhetorical impact of the introduction. The implied reader, privy to the preceding narrative, already associates John the Baptist with the anticipated Elijah figure by means of the birth accounts (1.16-17, 76). Corroboration of the claim is made through the intertextual citations of Mal. 3.1 and Exod. 23.20. In particular, the bulk of the citation is contingent on Mal. 3.1, with the primary deviation resulting in the redaction of the first-person pronoun ('before me') to the second

13. The most notable instance would be the use of μακάριος in v. 23, which recalls the introduction of the second speech (6.20-23). In addition, some of the recipients of Jesus' ministry in 7.21-22 coincide with personages specified in the introduction of the speech (6.17-19).

14. Aristotle, *Rhetoric*, 3.18; *Rhetorica ad Herennium*, 4.22-24; Quintilian, *Institutio Oratoria*, 9.3.98.

15. For a discussion of intertextual connections between the characterization of John the Baptist and Elijah, see Robert J. Miller, 'Elijah, John, and Jesus in the Gospel of Luke', *NTS* 34 (1988), pp. 611–22.

person ('before you').[16] This change results in greater existential urgency for both the narrative audience and the implied reader.

C. *Statement of Case: Rationale (7.28)*

The statement of case (v. 28) defines the purpose of the speech: John the Baptist was a prophetic figure of great consequence, yet those who exemplify the teachings of Jesus and, as a result, are members of the kingdom of God are more important than him. The addition of λέγω ὑμῖν at the beginning of the statement of case heightens the rhetorical emphasis, directing the narrative audience and the implied reader to afford special attention to the period. Further, the greater-to-lesser and lesser-to-greater argument is an often used Greco-Roman rhetorical device that prompts ecphrasis and synkrisis.[17]

A rhetorical reading of the statement of case surfaces an enthymemic argument, one in which the narrative audience and implied reader must deduce (or 'fill') the minor premise. The enthymeme disorients – in terms of biological logos – the narrative audience and the implied reader: all humans are born of women. Specifically, the enthymeme prompts the narrative audience and the implied reader to question the derivation of those who belong to the kingdom of God. The only prior reference to the 'kingdom of God' is found in 4.42-44, where the people of Capernaum seek to retain Jesus but are told that he must preach the 'kingdom of God' to other cities in Galilee. The message communicated by Jesus is couched within the context of casting out unclean spirits and healing the disenfranchised. In the case of the speech in 7.24-35, this intratextual detail is available to the implied reader but not the narrative audience. The implied reader concludes, as a result, that those who belong to the kingdom of God are individuals and groups who receive salvation from Jesus (viz., those from the social and religious margin).

Identification of those who belong to the kingdom of God, however, does not resolve the *origination* of those who belong to the kingdom of God. The implied reader identifies the answer through an analeptic connection: the implied reader draws upon previous instruction dispensed by John the Baptist in 3.8, where he informs the crowd that God is able to raise up 'new' children (τέκνον) for Abraham in response to their claim that they are the chosen children of Abraham. This is corroborated by the conclusion of the speech (7.35), where the narrative audience and implied reader identify 'wisdom' – using the intertextual repertoire – with the divine.[18] As a result, the implied reader is able to fill the gap: those who belong to the 'kingdom of God' originate from the divine.

---

16. The permutation of τὴν ὁδόν to τὴν ὁδόν σου falls into this realm of reasoning as well (cf. Green, *Gospel of Luke*, p. 299).

17. Aristotle, *Rhetoric*, 2.23.4-2.23.5.

18. The association of the feminine 'wisdom' with the divine is corroborated by multiple LXX texts (cf. Prov. 8.1-9.6; Wis. 7.22-30; Sir. 24).

Statement of Case: Dual Enthymemes (7.28)

Conclusion: John the Baptist is the greatest among those born of women (i.e., naturally) (7.28a).

Major Premise: Members of the kingdom of God are greater than John the Baptist (7.28b).

Minor Premise: Members of the kingdom of God are born of the divine (3.8; 7.35).

Conclusion: Jesus is greater than John the Baptist, as he was born of the divine, not from a woman (i.e., naturally) (1.26-38; 3.21-22).

Major Premise: Jesus is greater than John the Baptist.

Minor Premise: John the Baptist was born of a woman (7.28a).

Also embedded within the statement of case is an enthymeme addressing the relationship of Jesus and John the Baptist, a deductive argument tethered to the preceding inquiry about Jesus' ethos (7.18-23). As with the other enthymeme in the statement of case, the implied reader must go beyond the context of the speech in order to 'fill' the missing minor premise. In this case, analeptic deductive activity to the scene depicting the foretelling of Jesus' birth in 1.26-38 and Jesus' baptism in 3.21-22 provides the implied reader with the data needed to complete the enthymemic argument. This information is not available, however, to the narrative audience: the implied reader construes two enthymemes from the statement of case, whereas the narrative audience perceives only one. This divergence is one of many instances in the discourse where the implied reader possesses information not available to the characters and character groups within the narrative (one form of irony). In particular, construction of characterization occurs at this narrative level: the implied reader is able to make judgments about different characters and character groups contained therein.

D. *Narrative Aside: Digressio (7.29-30)*

In the middle of the speech, the implied author elects to employ a narrative aside in 7.29-30, which provides a direct means of instructing the implied reader regarding two character groups that normally appear as antagonists: the Pharisees and lawyers, and the tax collectors. In particular, the narrative aside functions as an analeptic commentary on 3.1-18. And while the implied author could have provided the implied reader with this information in 3.1-18, the implied author does not disclose it until this point in the narrative. The rhetorical effect heightens its importance for the implied reader.[19] Disclosure of this information at this point in the narrative works to unite the ministries of Jesus and John the Baptist: both are inextricably related to the purpose of God, with the result being that those who jettison the baptism of John the Baptist reject the purpose of God. Withholding judgment on the character groups until this point in the narrative also gives the discourse greater validity: the implied reader has 'digested' several

19. See Sheeley, *Narrative Asides*, pp. 114-15, 167, who argues that the implied author withholds the narrative judgment for rhetorical effect.

interactions between Jesus and the Pharisees and lawyers (i.e., that stand in contrast to 3.1-18, the first reference to both character groups, where no judgment – positive or negative – is given by the implied author). The narrative aside also plays an essential role in the rhetorical texture of the speech, as the dual enthymemes resulting from the statement of case (7.28) cannot be completed without the intratextual connection with the episode in 3.1-18.

E. *Body of Argument: Statement by Analogy and Example (7.31-34)*

The body of the speech (7.31-34) returns to the rhetorical style of the conclusion, posing a rhetorical question to the narrative audience. The subject matter relates to the ethos of a group to which the narrative audience belongs – namely, the 'people of this generation'. However, their ethos stands in stark contrast with the ethos of John the Baptist who is depicted in the threefold inquiry about the ethos of John the Baptist. Inclusion of τίνι οὖν provides a transition from the statement of case to the actual body of the speech and accentuates the magnitude of the ensuing argument. The rhetorical texture of the body contains a number of features. Foremost is the use of synkrisis, embodied in the repetitive of the comparative ὅμοιοι and ὁμοίῳ (vv. 31-32).

'Members of this generation' serves as a generic reference to the people (λαός or, more specifically, the narrative audience). For the implied reader, the reference indirectly extends to encompass potential disciples. Intertextual connotations also accompany the designation; its use in the LXX is frequently associative of a negative portrayal: a stiff-necked, rebellious people.[20] The narrative audience, as well as the implied reader, therefore expects a similar disposition by means of the ensuing comparison in v. 32 and the description of their reciprocal actions in vv. 33-34. The comparative equivalent of 'members of this generation' coincides with the 'children' (παιδία) in the marketplace. As a result, the disposition of the 'members of this generation' parallels the activity of the children calling to one another to play games. This comparative example is couched in the form of a popular rhyme,[21] resulting in a unique intertextual combination. The two periods of the rhyme coincide as simplistic enthymemes: the 'children' (παιδον) want to play games, but the other 'children' (παιδον) to whom they inquire decline to do so.

20. See, e.g., Exod. 32.9; 33.3, 5; Deut. 10.16. Association of 'members of this generation' with negative connotations corresponds with intertextual interpretive use of 'members of this generation' elsewhere in Luke-Acts – specifically Stephen's speech in Acts 7.51-52. An alternative approach, as taken by Bovon (*Luke*, pp. 285–86), accounts for the intratextual use of this LXX appellation and argues that the rhetorical discourse of the speech's body solicits the narrative audience and implied reader to make this intertextual connection.
21. See Herodotus 1.141; Aesop *Fables* 27.

Rhyme as Enthymeme (7.32)

Conclusion: The other children (i.e., John and Jesus) did not dance when the children sitting in the marketplace piped.

Major Premise: The children sitting in the marketplace piped and wanted the other children (i.e., John and Jesus) to dance.

Conclusion: The other children (i.e., John and Jesus) did not wail when the children sitting in the marketplace wept.

Major Premise: The other children (i.e., John and Jesus) did not want to weep when the children sitting in the marketplace wail.

Minor Premise: The other children (i.e., John and Jesus) do not comply with the pleas of the children sitting in the marketplace.

The dispositions attributed to John the Baptist and Jesus brand both as deviant, individuals outside of the boundaries of acceptable social and religious discourse.[22] The parabolic imagery in vv. 31-34 assumes legal language representative of the court setting.[23] This extratextual repertoire prompts the narrative audience and implied reader, to exonerate the ethos of Jesus and John in the court of law and to envision the scribes and Pharisees as sitting and addressing each other as if in court. Use of derogatory rhetorical categorization is not foreign to Greco-Roman narrative, but rather is a common means of depicting opponents in a negative light. In both instances (vv. 31-32), the portrayal is a deductive interpretation of the ethos of each character, capturing elements of reality to convey veracity. Indeed, the accusation against Jesus is ironic: the implied reader – but not the narrative audience – knows that Jesus has formed friendships with tax collectors and sinners (in particular, Levi in 5.27-32; the centurion in 7.1-10) – by offering to establish reciprocal patron–client relationships with them.

The two periods describing the 'caricatures' of John the Baptist and Jesus are juxtaposed in their rhetorical representations: John the Baptist is depicted as not eating (ἐσθίων) and not drinking (πίνων), whereas the 'Son of Man' (i.e., Jesus) is portrayed as eating (ἐσθίων) and drinking (πίνων).[24]

22. However cf. Wendy Cotter, ' "Yes, I Tell You, and More Than a Prophet": The Function of John in Q', in *Conflict and Invention*, pp. 135–50, who argues that the ethos of John the Baptist, which is viewed favorably by the narrative audience and implied reader, serves to 'protect' the ethos of Jesus.

23. See Wendy Cotter, 'Parable of the Children in the Market Place, Q (Lk) 7:31-35: An Examination of the Parable's Image and Significance', *NovT* 29 (1987), pp. 289–304.

24. The interpretive judgment given to the ethos of a character or character group – whether in antiquity, modernity, or post-modernity – is subjective. Further, albeit the linkage between the implied author and implied reader places constraints on the actualization process, this does not necessitate that a real reader – whether one from antiquity or one today – opts to embrace the ideological boundaries as represented in the narrative discourse. Hence, in the case of the 'false' caricatures attributed to John the Baptist and Jesus, a real reader could opt to view both characters according to the false portrayal ascribed by their adversaries. This interpretive decision does not minimize the importance of the intertwined

The narrative audience and implied reader attribute little truth to the claims as result of the rhetorical juxtaposition, viewing the interpretative conclusions as illogical. An inductive (allegorical) construal of the rhyme paints a vivid picture of the rhetorical argument:[25] John the Baptist and Jesus refuse to embrace the sociological and religious conventions held by the 'members of this generation' and, as a result, are labeled as individuals with dispositions that reside outside the realms of social acceptance.[26]

F. *Conclusion (7.35)*

The conclusion of the speech (v. 35) is in the form of an aphorism. Albeit somewhat laconic in construction, the conclusion exhibits skillful construction. Several observations can be made. First, the implied author employs a different word for 'children' (τέκνον) than previously used in the rhyme (παιδίον), thereby avoiding association of the two designates by the narrative audience and the implied reader.[27] Second, while there is no prior intratextual use of 'wisdom' (σοφία) in the narrative, equating the divine with σοφία forms the basis of a rich intertextual repertoire for the implied

---

relationship that exists between the implied author and implied reader. Real readers who fail to account for the implied author display an unethical disregard for the text, obviating the value of encountering the 'textual' other by constructing a self-centered mirrored image.

25.   The aversion to an allegorical reading of the rhyme and its relationship to John the Baptist and Jesus is based on modernistic sensitivities that have been overturned. On the contrary, an important component of Greco-Roman rhetorical argument involves induction, which encompasses allegory. Those who embrace the interpretative view espoused here include Joachim Jeremias, *The Parables of Jesus*, (London: SCM Press, 3rd edn., 1972), pp. 160–62; D. A. Carson, 'Matthew 11:19b/Luke 7:35: A Test Case for the Bearing of Q Christology on the Synoptic Problem', in Joel B. Green and Max Turner (eds), *Jesus of Nazareth: Lord and Christ: Essays on the Historical Jesus and New Testament Christology* (Grand Rapids, Mich.: William B. Eerdmans Publishing Company, 1994), pp. 138–41; Olof Linton, 'The Parable of the Children's Game: Baptist and Son of Man (Matt xi,16-19 = Luke vii,31-35): A Synoptic Text-Critical, Structural, and Exegetical Investigation', *NTS* 22 (1975/76), pp. 159–79. Perhaps the most compelling reason in favor of an allegorical understanding is the rhetorical arrangement, that is, the enthymematic argument compels the narrative audience and implied reader to construe the discourse in an allegorical manner.

26.   See Green (*Gospel of Luke*, pp. 303–4) for a similar understanding.

27.   Use of different words for the same subject for rhetorical and narrative purpose occurs elsewhere in New Testament narrative. See, e.g., my discussion in 'Narrative Echoes in John 21', p. 60, involving the use of ἰχθύς for the cooked fish and ὀψάριον for the catch of fish in John 21.9-13. As such, while Jesus tells the disciples to bring him some of the fish (ἰχθύδια) they had just caught (v. 10), he feeds them the fish (ὀψάρια) he cooked on the charcoal fire (v. 13). The accentuation of the cooked fish (ὀψάρια) prompts the implied reader to identify Eucharistic connotations via intratextual linkage with John 6 – namely, the fish Jesus feeds the crowd and his disciples in John 6 is described by the narrator with the same word used in John 6 (i.e., ὀψάριον – vv. 9, 11).

reader.[28] Third, with that equivalent in the foreground, inclusion of the narrative aide from earlier in the speech is given a heightened sense of importance by means of the conclusion. The rhetorical result is a chiasm united by the repetition of δικαιόω.

Tax collectors and all the people justify (ἐδικαίωσαν) God (v. 29)
Wisdom is justified (ἐδικαιώθη) by her children (v. 35)

As a result of the chiastic arrangement, the implied reader concludes that the justification afforded to the divine by those exhibiting faithfulness corroborates the ethos of John the Baptist and Jesus.[29] This presents an ironic twist for the implied reader: those baptized by John assume a status greater than John himself. Finally, the rhetorical argument shifts from deduction and induction to abduction: the topos turns towards the divine (viz., σοφία).

The disparity between the narrative audience and the implied reader is brought to the forefront in the rhetorical argument of the conclusion: the implied reader, in contrast to the narrative audience, is in a privileged reading position, privy to the information delineated in the narrative aside. As a result, the implied reader is able to construct and then make sense of the chiasm in relationship to the narrative's characterization. Based on the deductive argument of the chiasm, the implied reader ascertains that the children of God include the tax collectors and the people and exclude the Pharisees and the lawyers. The deductive argument also tethers the baptism of John, the will of God, and the vindication of God together. In addition, while the narrative discourse concurrently closes ('fills') several gaps, it remains open concerning the inclusion of the 'people' as part of the children of God. The faithfulness (or faithlessness) of that particular character group is ambiguous, helping to move the plot along. This allows the implied author to present characters and character groups as the narrative progresses that exhibit varying degrees of faithfulness, all of which coincide with the various taxonomies presented in the final speech of the Galilean ministry (8.4-18). Certainly familiar with the story of the Israelite people in Exodus and Deuteronomy from which the intertextual echo 'members of this generation' derives, the implied reader also recognizes that not all the Israelites were considered faithless. Further, through the intertextual echo,

28. Representation of the divine with 'wisdom' (σοφία) is evinced in a number of Jewish texts from antiquity (see, e.g., James D. G. Dunn, *Christology in the Making: A New Testament Inquiry into the Origins of the Doctrine of the Incarnation* [Philadelphia: Westminster Press, 1980], pp. 168–76).

29. For a slightly different interpretive approach to 7.35, cf. Simon Gathercole, 'The Justification of Wisdom (Matt 11.19b/Luke 7.35)', *NTS* 49 (2003), pp. 476–88, who concludes that the aorist δικιαόω is best translated as 'has been disassociated' and moreover the subject of τέκνον refers to those who reject Jesus and John the Baptist. The result is that the aphorism ('And Wisdom has been dissociated from her children') stands as a bitter complaint from Jesus concerning the lack of a positive response to ministries of John the Baptist and himself.

the implied reader understands that the Israelites' journey of faith was ongoing. Within the context of the narrative discourse, the rhetorical texture of the third speech places Jesus and John the Baptist in continuity with the will of God and those opposed to them in contradistinction.

The episode featuring Jesus' encounter with a woman of disrepute at the house of a Pharisee (7.36-50) exemplifies the rhetorical topos conveyed in the preceding speech. The social and religious qualities associated with tax collectors would also encompass those embodied by the woman who approaches Jesus. The implied author uses the episode, as a result, to persuade the implied reader to regard the woman as a child of God. The representation of Simon, the Pharisee, is more nebulous and is not necessarily a mirror representation of the Pharisees and the lawyers identified in the prior narrative aside.[30] While Simon certainly abrogates normal hospitality protocol, which is fulfilled by the actions of the woman, he is not presented by the narrator as attempting to entrap Jesus in a premeditated plot (in contrast to the Pharisees in the episodes contained in 5.17-26; 6.6-11). Indeed, his initial characterization is seemingly favorable: he invites Jesus to his house for a banquet – perhaps on Jesus' behalf – and acknowledges him as a religious teacher. Indeed, most scholars concur that the focus of the episode is not on Simon but rather on the woman and on whether the community will accept her as a member.[31] The question regarding the taxonomic characterization of Simon and the banquet guests is ultimately resolved by the fourth speech, which I will discuss in greater detail in chapters seven and nine.

---

30.   The view embraced here operates on the premise that characterization in Luke-Acts is not always linear and individuals or groups of a character group can extend beyond the boundaries delineated for that character group. See Chapter nine for a more in-depth discussion. In the case of Simon, the Pharisee, versus the view of many in recent years that Simon is stereotypical of the Pharisaic attitude presented throughout the narrative (see, e.g., Darr, *Character Building*, pp. 101–3; John T. Carroll, 'Luke's Portrayal of the Pharisees', *CBQ* 50 [1988], pp. 604–21), his characterization is open-ended and likely embraces many of the concerns felt by the implied reader concerning the woman (see, e.g., Green, *Gospel of Luke*, pp. 305–15; Robert C. Tannehill, 'Should We Love Simon the Pharisee? Hermeneutical Reflections on the Pharisees in Luke', *CurTM* 21 [1994], pp. 424–33).

An additional element in favor of this argumentation is that the presence of the 'lawyers' (οἱ νομικοί) results in the carte blanche negative categorization; the implied author places the blame for Jesus' death on the priests and the other authorities serving in the temple (not the Pharisees), which would have included 'lawyers'. For this argument, see, e.g., Frank J. Matera, 'The Death of Jesus According to Luke: A Question of Sources', *CBQ* 47 (1985), pp. 469–85; Joel B. Green, 'The Death of Jesus', in *Dictionary of Jesus*, pp. 146–63.

31.   The latter is corroborated by the closing narrative notation in 7.49 that turns the focus of the implied reader from the foibles of Simon, by means of his interior monologue, to the narrative audience.

III. *Concluding Summary*

The rhetorical texture of the third speech uses ecphrasis and synkrisis and focuses on bolstering the ethos of Jesus and John the Baptist. Various enthymemes – which require the implied reader to locate information in the preceding narrative in order to complete the argument – play an integral role in the construction of meaning. Specifically, the enthymematic argument prompts the narrative audience and implied reader to place Jesus and his followers in a position superior to that of John the Baptist and his followers. At the same time, the implied author employs several instances of irony – wherefore the implied reader possesses information not known by the narrative audience – that prompts the implied reader to make certain judgments regarding the narrative audience. An extratextual repertoire of LXX concepts is assumed by the implied author as topoi for rhetorical argument – namely, representation of the divine as 'wisdom' and representation of the antagonists of Jesus and John the Baptist with 'members of this generation'. This intertextual repertoire plays an important role in the overall rhetorical strategy of the speech: the comparison of Jesus and John the Baptist to Elisha and Elijah and the completion of the enthymematic argument. In the end, like Elisha and Elijah, Jesus and John the Baptist do not comply with the ideological beliefs embraced by the 'members of their generation', but rather embody that which is commensurate with the divine will.

CHAPTER 7: THE FOURTH GALILEAN MINISTRY SPEECH (LK. 8.4-18):
SOWING CHARACTER TAXONOMIES FOR THE IMPLIED READER

Jesus' fourth and final speech of the Lukan Galilean ministry falls within a
section (8.1-56) comprised of a number of intertwined episodic encounters
between Jesus and various characters seeking his divine power. It also marks
a movement in the narrative towards greater emphasis on the involvement
of the twelve disciples in Jesus' ministry. The final section of the Galilean
ministry actually makes a further move in that direction, as it contains
several episodes that focus on the faithfulness (or faithlessness) of the twelve
disciples (9.1-46). A section that has received significant attention in recent
years, 8.1-3, serves as a transition from the preceding section in 7.1-50 to the
one in 8.1-56. It depicts the integral role women played in Jesus' Galilean
ministry, a theme that continues throughout the rest of Luke and into Acts.[1]
The discourse has been building on the presence of traveling companions,
with the twelve disciples, starting with 6.12-16, frequently appearing with
Jesus. With 8.1-3 not only are women now accompanying Jesus, but they are
fulfilling the role of patronage through their provision of financial support.
In addition, as noted in 8.1-3, Jesus' success continues to grow as his group
of disciples expands, which sets the stage for the fourth speech of the
Galilean ministry. In particular, 8.1-3 serves as a narrative transition,
helping to propel the narrative forward. This coincides with the use of
transitions and summaries elsewhere in Luke-Acts.[2]

I. *Rhetorical Situation*

The final speech (8.4-18) provides a framework that the implied reader
proleptically utilizes throughout the remainder of the narrative to assess
characters and character groups. It also prompts the implied reader to
analeptically evaluate characters and character groups from the prior
narrative. Much already has been written on the rhetorical dimensions of

1. See, e.g., Turid Karlsen Seim, *The Double Message: Patterns of Gender in Luke and
Acts* (Nashville: Abingdon Press, 1994), esp. pp. 72–76. In particular, for 8.1-3, see Ben
Witherington III, 'On the Road with Mary Magdalene, Joanna, Susanna, and Other
Disciples – Luke 8:1-3', *ZNW* 70 (1979), pp. 243–48; David Sim, 'The Woman Followers of
Jesus: The Implications of Luke 8:1-3', *HeyJ* 30 (1989), pp. 51–62.
2. Cf. Lk. 1.5; 2.39-40, 52; 4.14-15; 4.42-44; 6.12-16; 9.51; 12.1; 17.11; 19.11, 28, 41; 20.1;
22.1, 39, 66; 23.44, 49-51; 24.1,13; Acts 1.12-14; 2.43-47; 4.32-37; 5.12-16; 6.7; 8.4-8, 25; 9.31;
11.26b-30; 12.24-25; 15.36–16.10; 18.18-23; 19.20; 26.30-32; 28.30-31.

the speech – at least as it occurs in Mark – by Mary Ann Tolbert upon which this study draws.[3] Up until this point in the narrative discourse the implied author has provided significant detail on the disposition exhibited by a disciple as well as the characteristics of non-disciples. The basis for this is presented in the second speech (6.20-49), where the implied author articulates various characteristics, coupled with resulting behaviors of those who belong to and participate in the kingdom of God. These topoi from the second speech provide a backdrop from which the implied reader evaluates the faithfulness or faithlessness of characters and character groups.

The importance of 'hearing', which forms an integral component of the conclusion of the second speech (6.46-49), carries over into the final speech (8.4-18), where it becomes an overarching rhetorical element.[4] The fourth speech builds upon the concept of 'hearing', demonstrating that while it represents a favorable disposition towards discipleship in Luke-Acts, it does not result in one being automatically placed in the taxonomic category of true discipleship. Instead, the true test of discipleship is in the production of 'fruit' (καρπός). All characters and character groups are potential disciples and 'hear' the message proclaimed. The decisive factor is the manner in which they respond: with actions consistent with the message preached by Jesus, or with misdirected attempts.[5]

As regards to the people (λαός), the implied author does not demarcate a decisive portrayal, but rather leaves their characterization open. This narrative 'gap' functions as a rhetorical device in the narrative discourse, helping to move the plot along and pull the various narrative themes together.

The speech aims to persuade the audience about future events: specifically how the disciples and the people will listen to the message of Jesus. It also employs significant elements of synkrisis. The implied reader and narrative audience are led to compare the various sowing activities and the outcome of those sowing efforts with the exhibition of faith on the part of individuals. The largest audience thus far in the ministry of Jesus gathers to hear the speech per the narrative notation in v. 4a. Specifically, the narrator not only indicates that the audience was a 'great crowd' (ὄχλου πολλοῦ), which was used to describe the audience attending the second speech in the Galilean speech (6.17b), but includes the notation that the narrative audience came

---

3. *Sowing the Gospel*, pp. 176–230; eadem, 'Mark Builds Characterization', pp. 347–57. However, despite the attention paid to the speech in its Marcan form, rhetorical analysis of the Lukan version is largely non-existent.

4. See Green, *Gospel of Luke*, pp. 322–23, who identifies 'hearing' as an integral theme in the speech. Derivations of ἀκούω occur in vv. 8, 10, 12, 13, 14, 15, 18, 21. The connection between 'hearing' and Jesus' message (the 'word') is noted by Bernard Brandon Scott, *Hear Then the Parable: A Commentary on the Parables of Jesus* (Minneapolis: Fortress Press, 1989), p. 349: 'The key words 'hear' (vv. 8, 10, 12, 13, 14, 15, 18, 21) and 'word' (vv. 11, 13, 15, 21) hold the passage together like glue'.

5. Note the redaction-critical comments of Bovon (*Luke 1:1-9:50*, p. 307) regarding the implications of 'hearing' in the speech: 'What concerns Luke is the how of hearing and no longer the what, as in Mark'.

from every town (καὶ τῶν κατὰ πόλιν), a description that emphasizes the enormity of the crowd.

II. *Rhetorical Texture*

The actual parable serves as the introduction to the speech (8.5-8a), with Jesus' response to the inquiry from the disciples about the meaning of the parable (8.8b-10) taking the form of the statement of case. Jesus' corresponding explanation of the parable functions as the body of the speech (8.11-15), and the concluding parable serves as the conclusion (8.16-18). The implied author combines both inductive and deductive argumentation throughout the speech, using parabolic example as the former and various rhetorical devices as the latter.

A. *Introduction (8.5-8a)*

The example Jesus utilizes for the parable, which forms the introduction, is firmly rooted in agrarian culture, and the narrative audience would have been familiar with the activities he describes. The implied author, likely from an urban environment, is not as well versed in the intricacies of agrarian society. As a result, as some scholars contend, this might explain the apparent profligate and haphazard planting technique employed and moreover the oversight of certain components of planting and tilling processes.[6] Nevertheless, a better explanation for this apparent lack of care by the implied author is an attempt by the implied author to focus the implied reader on the outcomes of sowing, versus the actual sowing processes. The rhetorical argument employed in the introduction certainly points in that direction. The fourfold repetition of the noun and verbal derivatives of 'sow' (σπείρω, σπειρός) at the beginning of the introduction orient the attention of the narrative audience and the implied reader on the planting activity. The infinitival participle in v. 5a establishes the foreground for the four sowing examples: a farmer planting a crop, with the ultimate objective being a bountiful harvest. The repetition of the relative pronoun ἕτερος to introduce the final three examples and the cadence in the sowing of the seed, which is represented by the repetition of the two derivative forms of 'fell' (i.e., πίπτω and καταπίπτω),[7] serve to bring the introduction to a crescendo with the fourth example. Homoeoteleuton, in the form of fourfold repetition of the suffix -ήν (viz., τὴν γῆν τὴν ἀγαθήν) also functions to distinguish the fourth sowing instance from the previous three. Redactional emendation by the implied author by means of the deletion of ὅπου οὐκ εἶχεν γῆν πολλήν in Mark (parallel in Lk. 8.6) also helps ensure

---

6. See, e.g., Philip B. Payne, 'The Order of Sowing and Ploughing in the Parable of the Sower', *NTS* 25 (1978/79), pp. 123–39.

7. Keeping with good rhetorical style, the implied author avoids verbatim repetition (*Rhetorica ad Herennium*, 4.42.54).

that the focus of the implied reader remains the actual outcome of the sowing process rather than the encumbrances that inhibit the production of fruit.

The aforementioned attention to repetition is offset by the use of four different prepositions to describe the consequence of the farmer's sowing:

> some fell *along* the way (παρά)...
> some fell *on* the rock (ἐπί)...
> some fell *in the midst of* (ἐν μέσῳ)...
> some fell *into* (εἰς)...

The primary difference in the four prepositions is in the penetration and maturation of the seed: the first three do not reach the point of bearing fruit, which stand in contrast to the fourth example, where the seed finds its way into the soil to produce a substantial crop.[8] Hence, the distinguishing characteristic of the 'good soil' – versus the soil on the path, the rocky soil, and the soil full of thorns – is twofold: first, the seed penetrates the surface and, second, the seed undergoes a period of maturation and growth, with the outcome being a bountiful harvest.[9] The types of soil are not in the purview of the implied author: the hazards presented are not solely indicative of the soil type with which they are associated. In particular, good soil is only recognized when its fruitfulness becomes evident.[10]

Intrusion by the narrator at the end of the introduction (v. 8a), coupled with the nature of Jesus' proclamation, signals to the implied reader that the 'speech' is simply a parabolic example and has reached an apparent conclusion. Jesus' exclamation (v. 8b) – 'the one who has ears to hear (ἀκούειν), let that one hear (ἀκουέτω)' – serves as an intratextual echo for the implied reader (and possibly the narrative audience). Specifically, the reference to 'hearing' (ἀκούω) in v. 8a links the introduction with the end of the second speech (6.46-49), where 'hearing' (ἀκούω) serves as the central topos (viz., true disciples 'hear' versus false disciples who do not 'hear'). This intertwines the disposition and behavior of a disciple, as previously delineated in the second Galilean ministry speech, with the assimilation and

---

8. A redactional analysis of the discourse of the statement of case evinces only a handful of discrepancies between the Lukan and Marcan discourses. One of interest is the exclusion of the notation in the third parabolic example (Lk. 8.7 and Mk 4.7) that the seed produced no fruit (καὶ καρπὸν οὐκ ἔδωκεν – Mk 4.7) by the Lukan implied author. The likely reason for the omission is connected to the focus on the 'fruit' (καρπός) as the objective of the sowing activity in the narrative discourse. Inclusion of this notation in the case of the third sowing example would stifle the rhetorical impact of the fourth example (Lk. 8.8), whereby the production of 'fruit' is given cumulative emphasis.

9. See Charles W. Hedrick, *Parables as Poetic Fictions: The Creative Voice of Jesus* (Peabody, Mass.: Hendrickson Publishers, 1994), pp. 172–74, who posits that the harvest is the focus of the parable, not the types of soil. He also details that the threats as well as the anticipation of comparable harvests by Jesus in the parable are commonplace in Greco-Roman antiquity and thus formed an integral element of the extratextual repertoire of the implied reader.

10. As noted by Green, *Gospel of Luke*, p. 325.

enactment of Jesus' message. This intratextual connection is given added emphasis through the narrative marker ταῦτα λέγων ἐφώνει, which would have prompted the reader/performer of Luke to shout out ὁ ἔχων ὦτα ἀκούειν in a loud voice while pointing to her or his ears.[11]

B. *Statement of Case (8.9-10)*

The precise identity of the 'disciples' who approach Jesus in v. 9 is ambiguous; 'disciples' thus far in the narrative simply represent those who associate themselves with Jesus by accompanying him in his ministerial encounters. A change in narrative audience for the statement of case and the remainder of the speech is not evident: the identity of the character distinction 'disciples' is open; the implied author leaves this narrative element open, a 'gap' the implied reader must fill. This open-ended question is of particular relevance in that the language of the statement of case confronts the narrative audience and the implied reader with insider-outsider categories. Exclusion of the larger audience assembled to listen to Jesus' speech (8.5) is not indicated by the narrator (viz., the remainder of the speech does not serve as private instruction to a select group of 'disciples'). Likewise, it is not abnormal for Luke to portray Jesus in scenes where he answers questions posed by disciples and others within the hearing of a larger audience.[12]

Use of the perfect passive δέδοται in the statement of case serves as a discourse marker, highlighting the importance of the words about to follow.[13] In particular, the open-ended characterization of 'disciples' plays an important role in helping the narrative audience and the implied reader interpret the statement of case within the intratextual context. Though the occurrence of μυστήριον ('mystery') is a *hapax legomenon* for Luke-Acts, the topos of the divine purpose being hidden and then disclosed is a thread that can be traced through the Luke-Acts corpus.[14]

Substantiation for Jesus' insider-outsider claim is corroborated with the intertextual echo with Isa. 6.9-10 in v. 10. The implied reader and narrative audience conclude that interpretation, as denoted by means of the intertextual use (as part of the citation from Isa. 6.9-10) of συνίζω, is an integral component in a disciple's production of a 'bountiful harvest'. The

---

11.   For a discussion of narrative markers associated with delivery, see Nadeau, 'Delivery in Ancient Times', pp. 53–60; Olbricht, 'Delivery and Memory', pp. 159–67; Shiner, *Proclaiming the Gospel*, pp. 77–101, 127–42.

12.   See, e.g., Lk. 6.20, 12.1, 16.1.

13.   Use of the perfect verbal tense typically serves as a rhetorical marker, an indication to the listener and reader that the ensuing material is of particular importance (see Porter, *Idioms*, pp. 20–23).

14.   Cf. Dan. 2.18-19, 27-30, 47; Wis. 2.22; 6.22. For elaboration, see Joseph A. Fitzmyer, *The Gospel according to Luke*, vol. 1 (AB, 28; Garden City, New York: Doubleday, 5th edn., 1981), p. 708; John T. Squires, *The Plan of God in Luke-Acts* (SNTSMS, 76; Cambridge: Cambridge University Press, 1993), pp. 30–31; Green, *Theology of the Gospel*, pp. 23–42.

importance of interpretation is not a novel concept at this juncture of the narrative, but rather the topos of interpretation extends back to the prologue (1.4). The aim of the implied author, and ultimately the narrative audience and implied reader, is an accurate interpretation of Jesus' ministry and the actions of the early Christian community.[15] This topos receives significant attention as the narrative progresses: the implied reader concludes that Jesus' message (that which is 'heard') cannot be understood without interpretation. The message Jesus conveys to his audience and that which the implied author delineates to the implied reader is that the production of a 'bountiful harvest' by a disciple does not result without interpretation: 'hearing' is simply the initial act in the journey of discipleship.[16] In addition, Jesus' message is understandable for those able to interpret it, whereas it remains a 'mystery' (μυστήριον) for those who are not able to interpret it. Likewise, construction of meaning surrounding the 'kingdom of God' continues to progress: the implied reader reaches the understanding that the 'kingdom of God' is a reality to which one cannot belong unless correct interpretation occurs, interpretation with a resulting disposition and behavior (as delineated in earlier discourse – especially the second speech in 6.20-49).[17]

C. *Body of Argument (8.11-15)*

The argument of the speech's body (vv. 11-15) closely mirrors the categories put forth in the introduction and it actually replicates much of the language therein, following the four sowing activities. The descriptive interpretation that Jesus establishes functions to bolster the aphoristic claim of the speech's statement of case. The rhetorical style of the body also replicates certain rhetorical features from the introduction – specifically, the conjunction and article (οἱ ἀκούσαντες for the first two and οὗτοι for the latter two) followed by the preposition used in the introduction to describe each sowing activity.[18] Further rhetorical emphasis results in the parallel construction of the four periods: the fourfold repetition of the participle (οἱ ἀκούσαντες) preceded by the plural demonstrative pronoun οὗτοι. Deviation from this framework, in contrast to those who claim the implied author displays poor rhetorical style, heightens the impact of the discourse: the seed that fails to

---

15. This topos continues throughout the narrative discourse of Luke-Acts (cf. Lk. 24.45; Acts 8.26-40). For the importance of interpretation as related to the oral/aural processing in Greco-Roman antiquity, see, e.g., F. Gerald Downing, *Doing Things with Words in the First Christian Century* (JSNTSup, 200; Sheffield: Sheffield Academic Press, 2000).

16. See Green, *Gospel of Luke*, pp. 326–27, for a similar approach.

17. The permanent separation of those who fail to interpret Jesus' message is diluted by the implied author of Luke: the last clause of the intertextual citation from LXX Isa. 6.10 that is included in Mark (4.12c) – μήποτε ἐπιστρέψωσιν καὶ/ ἀφεθῇ αὐτοῖς – is excluded in Luke (8.10).

18. The only exception would be the preposition employed for the third example, as εἰς is changed to ἐν μέσῳ. This modification by the implied author can be attributed to rhetorical style, in that verbatim repetition is something to be avoided in good rhetoric.

initiate growth receives no designation (i.e., the demonstrative pronoun οὗτοι is not employed in the first example [v. 12]).

Before embarking on providing a more direct answer to the inquiry from the disciples, the implied author situates the response within an interpretative framework by identifying that which was being sown as the 'word of God'. The discourse, as a result, with the implied reader construing Jesus' message with the 'word of God', grounds it within the historical tradition of Israel's past, which serves to authenticate Jesus' message.[19]

Like the argument of the introduction, the argument of the body does not focus on the types of soil but on the outcomes of sowing. And while the resulting outcomes break into three 'growth' interpretive classifications – (1) no growth, (2) some growth but no fruit, and (3) sustained growth bearing fruit[20] – the center of the argumentation is on the descriptive growth (or lack thereof) activity. The implied reader construes, as a result, four character taxonomies. Repetition of verbal derivations of ἀκούω – a participial form in the case of the first, third, and fourth examples and an action verb in the case of the second – ties together the rhetorical argumentation and continues to keep hearing at the forefront of the discourse. This rhetorical maneuvering steers the narrative audience and the implied reader to the understanding that while Jesus' message is broadcast to a large audience, the decisive factor is in regard to the response.[21]

Lukan emphasis on the sequential maturation of faith is evident in the redactional activity of the implied author. This is manifest by means of several aspects of the narrative discourse. First, the urgency of the narrative discourse in Mark is downplayed through the omission of the adjective εὐθύς by the Lukan implied author (Mk 4.15; cf. Lk. 8.12). Second, concentration on producing fruit (i.e., the ongoing display of a disposition and behavior representative of a disciple) – rather than the actual outcome (viz., the exclusion of the specific measure of harvest reaped) – is apparent in the discourse of Luke. Specifically, the measure of 'thirtyfold and sixtyfold and a hundredfold' in Mark (4.20) disappears in Luke (8.15). Third, the addition of ἐν ὑπομονῇ by the Lukan implied author (Lk. 8.15 versus Mk 4.20) emphasizes the ongoing nature of discipleship (versus that in the Marcan discourse). Fourth, the Lukan implied author amends Marcan apocalyptic terminology (θλῖψις and διωγμός in Mk 4.17) to terminology with ethical connotations (πειρασμός in Lk. 8.13).[22] Finally, the Lukan implied author redacts ἄκαρπος γίνεται to τελεσφοροῦσιν (Mk 4.19; cf. Lk. 8.14) to give the discourse a teleological emphasis.[23]

---

19. Green, *Gospel of Luke*, p. 327.

20. See I. Howard Marshall, 'Tradition and Theology in Luke (Luke 8:5-15)', *TynBul* 20 (1969), p. 74, for this observation.

21. 'Growth' is linked to the maturation and sustenance of faithfulness (see, e.g., Marshall, 'Luke 8:8-15', pp. 56–75).

22. See Bovon (*Luke 1:1-9:50*, pp. 309–10) for this observation.

23. For other redactional refinements of Mark by the implied author of Luke, see Bovon, *Luke 1:1-9:50*, pp. 303–15.

1. *First Example: Sowing Along the Path*

The first example (v. 12) places the cause for the inability of the disciples to 'hear' on the devil (διάβολος), a designation that culls intratextual allusions for the implied reader to the earlier temptation episode (4.1-13). The connotation of this connection for the implied reader is that the struggle between the divine representatives of good and evil extends to that of the human realm. Yet, though the 'potential' disciples in the case of the first example are lured away by the devil, the implied reader simultaneously knows that Jesus withstood a temptation of great magnitude, and thus such can be overcome with divine guidance. A metaphorical connection between the devil and the 'birds of the air' (τά πετεινά τοῦ οὐρανοῦ) in the parabolic rendition of the first example is heightened by intertextual connotations, where the 'birds of the air' represent the devil.[24] Referential linkage to the interpretative framework established in the initial period of the body occurs in the form of Jesus' notation that the failure to produce a harvest is due to the 'word' (λογός) being taken from the hearts of potential disciples. The discourse also places the maturation of faith at the core of the disciple – namely, the heart. Specifically, the cause for the inability of the disciples to hear is identified as failure to believe – the initial mode of discipleship. The consequences of not 'hearing' appropriately and 'believing' are contained in the ἵνα + subjunctive clause at the end of the period: salvation does not come to those personages.[25] The ongoing nature of the 'disbelief' is conveyed by the use of the present tense rather than the aorist tense for the participle (πιστεύσαντες).

2. *Second Example: Sowing on the Rock*

Intratextual connectivity with the earlier temptation episode (4.1-13) continues in the second example (v. 13) with the reference to πειρασμός ('temptation'). While the narrative audience does not have access to this scene, it resides in the foreground for the implied reader. Actualization of this intratextual nexus engenders several images for the implied reader. First, disciples can fall prey to the 'temptation' of the devil even though Jesus overcame 'temptation' earlier. Second, disciples can draw upon Jesus' earlier triumph as an exemplar when encountering 'temptation from the devil'. Finally, since the disciples represented in this example are unable to overcome 'temptation' from the devil, in contrast to Jesus in 4.1-13, the implied reader concludes that disciples portrayed herein lack the faith and disposition of Jesus.

In addition to the analeptic intratextuality involving the use of πειρασμός, the second sowing example provides the implied reader with a

---

24. Metaphorical representation of the 'devil' as 'birds of the air' is part of the extratextual repertoire of the implied reader and the narrative audience (cf. *Jub.* 11.11; *Apoc. Abr.* 13.3-7; *1 En.* 90.8-13).

25. The aim of the implied author comes into view here, as the ἵνα + subjunctive result clause is a redaction. Reason for this redaction likely is tied to the integral role of 'salvation' in the plot of the narrative discourse.

proleptic referent to the scene at the Mount of Olives in Lk. 22.39-46, where πειρασμός forms an inclusio; the scene begins and ends with Jesus instructing the disciples to pray that they not to fall into temptation (πειρασμός).[26] Through retrospective actualization, the implied reader concludes that failure to pray gives rise to succumbing to temptation. Building further coherence, the implied reader also pinpoints connections through the combination of both προσευχῇ ('prayer') and πειρασμός ('temptation') with Jesus' instructions regarding prayer in Lk. 11.1-13. Specifically, Jesus' question to the disciples prior to his admonition of them at the close of the Mount of Olives scene (τί καθεύδετε in 22.46b) evinces imagery with the parabolic example in Lk. 11.5-13: the narrative implies that the friend and his family are 'sleeping' and had to be awakened ('at night' [v. 5]; 'my children are with me in bed' [v. 7]).[27] Linkage with the 'Lord's' Prayer' in Lk. 11.2-4, which is intertwined with the parabolic example in Lk. 11.5-13, directs the implied reader to construe prayer (viz., the 'Lord's Prayer') as the means of thwarting temptation. The implied reader, through this intratextual maneuvering, in addition to identifying the content of the 'Lord's Prayer' (11.1-4) as comprising the core subject matter for the prayer of disciples, delineates the parameters of temptation: the need to embrace the realized eschatological presence of the kingdom of God, which, in the case of Luke-Acts and within the contextual boundaries of Lk. 11.1-13, concerns issues of non-reciprocal benefaction and friendship without the constraints of honor and shame.[28]

Unlike the seed in the first example, the seed in the second example progresses; it actually begins to grow. The failure occurs in that it does not establish a root system from which to sustain ongoing growth. Specifically, the repetition of καιρός ('time') serves as a temporal marker, demarcating the period of initial growth and then that of the shriveling.

3. *Third Example: Sowing Among the Thorns*
Progression in growth and maturation continues with the third example; the seed produces fruit, but it does not mature.[29] Rhythmic repetition of the conjunction καί delivers rhetorical suspense to the discourse: elongation of the teleological result of the seed's growth. The style of the period sets it

26. 'Pray that you not enter into temptation (πειρασμός)' in 23.40 and 'rise and pray that you may not enter into temptation (πειρασμός)' in 23.46. I am grateful to Dr. Stephen C. Barton for suggesting this connection to me.
27. The mirroring of ἀναστάς in 11.8 to describe what the friend must do in order to enact the benefaction his friend is seeking with Jesus' admonition to the disciples to 'arise' (ἀναστάντες) in 22.46 creates an additional intratextual allusion between the two scenes.
28. For a discussion of honor and shame protocols in Lk. 11.1-13, see Herman C. Waetjen, 'The Subversion of "World" by the Parable of the Friend at Midnight', *JBL* 120 (2001), pp. 703-21.
29. A redactional analysis of Lk. 8.7, 14 and Mk 4.7, 18-19 corroborates the Lukan interest in faith as a maturation process: the process in Luke emphasizes the need for ripening (τελεσφορέω), whereas Mark is focused on the end result (ἄκαρπος γίνεται). See Bovon (*Luke 1:1-9:50*, p. 310) for a similar observation.

apart from the previous two examples and the last example. In particular, the rhetorical effect caused by the extended ending of the period builds suspense in the discourse. The redactional inclusion of ἀδονέω represents an emphasis, found elsewhere in the Lukan narrative, on faith as a sequential process. The addition of ἡδονῶν τοῦ βίου ('pleasures of life') to the list of reasons impeding growth coincides with the Lukan topos that emphasizes the importance of using possessions and wealth (and power) to enact non-reciprocal benefaction (per the second speech in 6.20-49), while concurrently posing how possessions and wealth are potential obstacles to discipleship (viz., in the reluctance to embrace the new mode of benefaction espoused by the narrative discourse of Luke-Acts).

4. *Fourth Example: Sowing into Good Soil*

Those represented by the 'good soil' exhibit authentic hearing that leads to actions commensurate with the message and ministry of Jesus. Continuation of the emphasis on faith as a progressive maturation by the implied author is evident in several ways. First, the implied author inserts ἐν ὑπομονῇ at the very end of the parabolic example (in contrast to Mk 4.20). The implied reader concludes, therefore, that those disciples who produce fruit do so over an extended period of time, often faced by some of the same adversities that confronted those in the preceding three examples.[30] Second, the implied author replaces the Marcan (4.20) παραδέχομαι with κατέχω. The resulting action changes from a demand for immediate action in Mark to ongoing in Luke. The redactional addition that disciples represented by the 'good soil' reflect upon Jesus' message in their hearts (ἐν καρδία καλῇ καὶ ἀγαθῇ), coupled with the dual adjectives καλός and ἀγαθός, has a similar rhetorical effect.[31] Finally, the implied author eliminates the reference to the bountiful harvest 'hundredfold' (as noted in the fourth sowing example of the introduction [v. 8a]) – in contrast to Mark (4.20). This focuses the discourse on the creation of fruit, in contrast to the results depicted in the three previous examples.

---

30. Note the observation of Bovon (*Luke 1:1-9:50*, p. 311): 'But this evangelist always favors the anthropological side; thus the continuous responsibility of human beings (8:15) plays the main role (ὑπομονή is not only passive patience, but perseverance). This consists in loyalty to the divine transmission of the Christological word (ἀκούω, "to listen", and κατέχω "to hold fast") and in bearing of fruit (καρποφορέω, "to bear fruit"), which is understood in an ethical sense.'

31. The use of καλός as an adjectival descriptive of the heart of the disciple forms a rhetorical link for the narrative audience and the implied reader (i.e., the adjectival descriptive for the 'soil' in the fourth sowing activity [v. 8a] is καλός). In addition, the duplicate adjectival description results in an emphasis on the nature of a disciple's καρδία ('heart'). Actual placement of the dative preposition ἐν καρδία καλῇ καί ἀγαθῇ prior to κατέχω, the opposite construction of similar phrases in Luke-Acts, heightens the attention of the narrative audience and implied author on the nature of the disciples' hearts.

D. *Conclusion (8.16-18)*

The discourse in Luke diverges from the Marcan discourse: the 'Parable of Sowing' is followed by only one of the series of parables that comprise the Marcan parabolic discourse (4.1-34). This shift in rhetorical arrangement demonstrates attentiveness by the implied author to the importance of speeches as vehicles for delineating narrative plot and characterization. Retention of metaphoric agrarian language continues in the conclusion (8.16-18). But the metaphorical change in the conclusion evinces a rhetorical effect:[32] the narrative audience and the implied reader are prompted to embark upon a deductive activity, relating the connotations of the conclusion with the preceding rhetorical pieces of the speech. In addition, the conclusion is replete with rhetorical stylistic features, including several instances of repetition and wordplay. This also contributes to the heightened discourse and the rhetorical effects on the narrative audience and the implied reader.

Both metaphors exhibit enthymematic argument, which prompt the narrative audience and the implied reader to embark on a deductive journey. In both instances, they are prodded to actively engage the discourse.

Enthymeme #1 (v. 16)
Conclusion: No one who wants those entering a house to see places a lamp underneath a vessel or places it under a bed.
Major Premise: Those who light a lamp place it on a stand so that those entering the house can see.
Minor Premise: Without a lighted lamp, or at least one correctly positioned within the house, it is impossible to see.

Enthymeme #2 (v. 17)
Conclusion: It is impossible to keep that which is hidden concealed and that which is a secret undisclosed when light is present.
Major Premise: Light reveals those things hidden and secret.
Minor Premise: Without light it is possible to hide or conceal.

The deductive relationship between the two enthymemes leads the narrative audience and the implied reader to the incontrovertible conclusion that those who listen to the message of Jesus exhibit actions indicative of authentic hearing. The parallel understanding is that those who hear the message of Jesus manifest authentic hearing and, in doing so, appropriate behavior (and thus maturation leading to the production of 'fruit').

Pleonasm serves an important rhetorical function. This is manifest in several different ways. First, wordplay between λυχνός ('light') and λυχνία ('stand'), both of which are very similar in sound, links the various components of the argument in the first enthymeme (v. 16) together. Synkrisis of covering the light emitted by the lamp versus that of placing it on a stand so that its light illuminates the room in which it is contained

---

32. *Rhetorica ad Herennium*, 4.34; Quintilian, *Institutio Oratoria*, 8.6.4–8.6.8; Aristotle, *Rhetoric*, 3.2.

addresses the contrast between the two actions (v. 16). The absurdity of covering a lamp in the room of a house,[33] thus preventing its light from illuminating the expanses of the room, is corroborated by the second enthymeme (v. 17): the deductive conclusion by the narrative audience and the implied reader is that it is impossible to conceal the light of a lamp and, in the case of the disciple whose disposition and actions coincide with the fourth sowing example from the speech's body (v. 15), it is incomprehensible for those who authentically hear the message of Jesus to enact anything but representative behavior. Second, the use of φανερός in both enthymemes ties the rhetorical argument together, moving the narrative audience and the implied reader to the understanding that the argument of the second enthymeme pertains to the argument of the first enthymeme. The resulting conclusion is that authentic hearing evinces befitting behavior, and the corollary that unauthentic hearing results in unfitting behavior. Similarly, duplicate use of φανερός in the second enthymeme provides rhetorical emphasis, bringing illumination, as made possible by the light, into the forefront of the discourse. Finally, close correspondence between the two metaphors in the second enthymeme – κρυπτός ('hidden') and ἀπόκρυφος ('secret') – engenders connectivity as well as heightens the relevance of connotations conjured by the metaphors.

The narrative discourse brings together the conclusion and the statement of case through intratextual repetition: the result being both a heightened rhetorical emphasis on the introduction as the focus for the narrative audience and a prodding of the implied reader to return to the earlier statements contained within the speech. Both of these are evident in several ways. The first metaphorical enthymeme (8.16b) employs βλέπω – an intertext of Isa. 6.9 (in 8.9c) – to describe the 'enabling' activity of those entering the house. The topos of understanding extends to the conclusion (i.e., in the use of γινώσκω in 8.9a and 8.17b); authentic hearing results in that which is hidden becoming comprehensible. Additional emphasis on the rhetorical impact of the intratextual connection occurs in the use of the double negative (v. 17a: 'For there is nothing [οὐ] hidden that shall not [οὐ] be made known'). The implied reader and narrative audience conclude that the 'secrets of the kingdom of God' equate to the 'fruit' produced by the 'good soil'.

The ongoing topos of authentic and inauthentic hearing receives its rhetorical culmination in the final metaphor of the conclusion (8.18). It contains, in particular, a number of elements that heighten its rhetorical impact. Foremost is enthymematic arrangement – based on contraries[34] – that guide the narrative audience and the implied reader to a deductive conclusion: those who embody authentic hearing will receive more, whereas

---

33. The precise meaning of 'covering' the light or 'putting it underneath the bed' is unclear (see Bovon, *Luke 1:1-9:50*, p. 313, for the possible interpretations).

34. For a discussion of enthymemic argument, as based on contraries, in the New Testament, see Paul A. Hollaway, 'The Enthymeme as an Element of Style in Paul', *JBL* 120 (2001), pp. 329–42.

those who fail to hear in an authentic manner lose that which has been received. Second, the use of αἴρω prompts the narrative audience and the implied reader to recall the metaphorical symbolism of the devil 'taking away' the seed in the first soil example (v. 12): the devil is seen as the subject of the passive form in the conclusion. Third, intratextual connection with the statement of case – in the form of repetition, including ἀκούω and βλέπω – provides the implied reader with information needed to fill a gap left in the narrative discourse: the identity of that which is given to those who hear with authenticity and that which is taken away from those who fail to do so. Here, the implied reader identifies the kingdom of God as the missing 'gap', specifically continued growth in the disposition and behavior befitting the message delivered and enacted by Jesus. Finally, use of δοκέω demarcates between 'hearing' that is genuine versus that which simply *appears* to be genuine. In particular, some hearing may merely be short term: it does not yield any fruit but rather fails to maturate, as is the case with the second and third sowing examples.[35] The structure of the enthymeme is as follows:

Conclusion: A careful hearing of Jesus' message is important, for appropriate or inappropriate behavior and disposition to result.

Positive Premise: Those who hear (and understand) Jesus' message will increasingly embody the disposition and behavior delineated therein.

Negative Premise: Those who do not hear (do not understand) Jesus' message will increasingly fail to embody the disposition and behavior delineated therein.

E. *Inclusio: 8.1-3 and 8.19-20*

The episodic narrative encounter in 8.19-20 functions as an inclusio with the narrative preceding the speech in 8.1-3. Thus far the implied author has not portrayed Jesus' family as exemplary disciples (or followers). This enables the implied author to use their entry into the narrative in 8.19-20 for a rhetorical purpose, a means for further elaboration on the nature and meaning of patronage and kinship.[36] This depiction is given meaning in the reply Jesus issues, which employs two verbs endowed with intratextual connotations. The first verb, ἀκούω, ties the episode to the final Galilean ministry speech (8.4-18), where authentic hearing is the pivotal topos. The second verb, ποιέω, posits a connection with the second Galilean ministry speech and, in particular, its conclusion (6.46-49). Compilation of these various connections moves the implied reader to the understanding that the

35. See Green, *Gospel of Luke*, pp. 329–30, who makes a similar point in the use of δοκέω.

36. Jesus' family seeking him could be construed by the narrative audience and the implied reader as an endeavor to implore patronage from him. If that is the case, then their characterization at this juncture of the narrative discourse is ambivalent to negative and the implied reader associates them with the third sowing taxonomy.

women in 8.1-3 embody the characteristics of exemplary disciples. Movement towards an acceptance of kinship that stands in contrast to traditional first-century CE Greco-Roman cultural systems is introduced here as well. Elaboration of this topos occurs as the narrative progresses: physical descent is no longer a determining factor in the exchange of benefaction, but rather authentic hearing that results in action.[37]

III. *Concluding Summary*

The rhetorical texture of the final speech of Jesus in the Galilean ministry forms an interpretive grid from which the implied reader construes characterization throughout Luke-Acts. The rhetorical argument focuses the discourse on action (viz., production of 'fruit') versus different soil types, something that becomes even more obvious to a real reader through redactional analysis. The construction of characterization in Luke-Acts coincides with the actions of sowing rather than the qualities of soil as is the case in Mark. The implied reader analeptically and proleptically associates characters and character groups with one of the four sowing activities. In particular, the implied author uses enthymematic argument in speech's conclusion to prod the implied reader to make deductive conclusions regarding earlier instructions on discipleship (especially those from the second speech in 6.20-49) and the actions of disciples who exhibit (or fail to exhibit) characteristics of the fourth sowing example.

The rhetorical argument of the fourth speech focuses the implied reader on the fourth sowing example. Specifically, the implied author guides the implied reader to the conclusion that authentic discipleship requires persistence (action that occurs over an extended period of time). In addition, by means of the intertextual connection with Isa. 6.9-10 (Lk. 8.9-10), the implied reader determines that interpretation must accompany authentic hearing.

---

37. See Green, *Gospel of Luke*, p. 330, for a similar view. Cf. also Stephen C. Barton, *Discipleship and Family Ties in Mark and Matthew* (SNTSMS, 80; Cambridge: Cambridge University Press, 1994), who reaches a similar understanding regarding Mark and Matthew.

PART THREE: NARRATIVE TRAJECTORIES AND HERMENEUTICAL
APPROPRIATION BY AUTHORIAL READERS

CHAPTER 8: RHETORICAL TEXTURE AND NARRATIVE TRAJECTORIES:
GENERATION OF PLOT, CHARACTERIZATION, AND TOPOI

The philosophical underpinnings of more recent methodological endeavors in the study of Luke-Acts helped move the investigation of the construction of plot, characterization, and topoi (thematic motifs) beyond the vestiges of authorial intent.[1] Though the implied author, as represented by the narrative discourse, constrains possible construction of meaning, the potential modes of construction allow for the generation of multivalent meanings. Indeed, construction of the narrative discourse occurs as an ethical enactment between the implied author, the implied reader, and the real reader. This interaction occurs on three different levels: extratextual repertoire (e.g., cultural codes and ideological systems), intertextuality (e.g., type scenes, textual echoes, citations, etc.), and intratextual coherence (e.g., repetition, narrative structure, etc.).

The four speeches of Jesus in the Lukan Galilean ministry, through their rhetorical texture, project various trajectories – both backwards to the preceding narrative (i.e., analeptic) and forwards to the subsequent narrative (i.e., proleptic) – that facilitate the construction of narrative meaning by the implied reader. The implied reader works from the basis that the rhetorical texture of the speeches serves as the interpretive matrix for each. In addition, the implied reader approaches the narrative discourse with the expectation that the speeches, particularly those at the beginning of the narrative, are pivotal in providing the foundation for constructing key narrative components.[2]

Identification of the narrative trajectories that extend from each of the four Galilean ministry speeches is difficult – at least in terms of an accurate and complete identification – apart from processing of the rhetorical elements by the implied reader. This study melds narrative and reader-response criticisms together in order to move the discussion beyond rhetorical texture (which is where rhetorical criticism typically stops) to actual trajectories associated with the larger narrative while, at the same

1. However cf. Moore, *Literary Criticism*, pp. 3–24, 71–107, for a critique of the philosophical underpinnings of narrative and reader-response criticisms.
2. Readers (or listeners) in Greco-Roman antiquity would not approach a text in total ignorance but rather with certain assumptions and expectations based on extratextual repertoire (e.g., see M. J. Wheeldon, ‘“True Stories”: the Reception of Historiography in Antiquity’, in A. Cameron (ed.), *History as Text: The Writing of Ancient History* [Chapel Hill: University of North Carolina Press, 1990], pp. 33–63).

time, maintaining an ethical interaction with the implied author (often a failing of narrative and reader-response criticisms). Attempts to identify narrative trajectories based on the four speeches without consideration of their rhetorical texture run the risk of seeing only part of the narrative landscape and, in some instances, breaching the ethical obligations every reader should exhibit in relation to the implied author and implied reader.[3] This chapter identifies key elements of rhetorical texture from the four preceding chapters and how they help shape various narrative trajectories that guide the implied reader in the generation of plot, characterization, and topoi.

I. *A Methodological Basis and Framework*

Investigation of Luke-Acts over the past twenty-five years is replete with analysis of plot and characterization. The centrality of motifs common to both works was identified by some of the early pioneers of redaction criticism, who then used these to locate theological agendas for each of the Gospels.[4] Narrative and reader-response criticisms built upon the work of the redaction critics. The pivotal importance of 'salvation' to the overarching discourse of Luke-Acts actually goes back to the work of the redaction critics. Though classification of 'salvation' into three epochs has been critically discredited as insensitive to various aspects of the narrative discourse,[5] there is significant coalescence around the recognition that Lukan theology and thus plot centers on the thematic motif of 'salvation to the ends of the earth'.[6]

Per the discussion in Chapter two of this study, the narrative of Luke-Acts, like other Greco-Roman narrative (in contrast to modern and post-

3. See, e.g., Booth, *Company We Keep, passim*.

4. The concept of the implied author is not a concept utilized by the redaction critics. The first to propose examination of the presumed sources in Luke in order to identify the theological agenda of the 'implied' author was Hans Conzelmann, *The Theology of St. Luke* (trans. G. Buswell; London: Faber and Faber, 1960).

5. Conzelmann (*Theology, passim*) was the initial proponent of dividing Lukan salvation history into three periods – the period of Israel (from creation to the imprisonment of John the Baptist), the period of Jesus (from his baptism to ascension), the period of the church (from Jesus' ascension to his parousia). He is followed by other redaction critics, including Joseph A. Fitzmyer, *Luke the Theologian: Aspects of His Teaching* (New York: Paulist Press, 1989), pp. 59–63. There is now overwhelming argument against viewing Lukan 'salvation' as consisting of three epochs (e.g., see François Bovon, *Luke the Theologian: Thirty-three Years of Research [1950-1983]* [PTMS, 12; Allison Park, Pa.: Pickwick Press, 1987], pp. 25–29).

6. The ways in which 'salvation' is construed obviously varies. However, recognition of its primacy to Lukan theology is widely accepted (e.g., see Green, *Theology of the Gospel, passim*; Marshall, 'Story of Salvation', pp. 340–56; John T. Carroll, 'The God of Israel and the Salvation of the Nations: The Gospel of Luke and the Acts of the Apostles', in A. A. Das and F. J. Matera (eds), *The Forgotten God* [Festschrift Paul J. Achtemeier; Louisville: Westminster/John Knox Press, 2002], pp. 91–106).

modern narrative), is relatively unsophisticated in its presentation of plot.[7] Plotline consists of a selection and arrangement of the events and actions remembered and functions as an interaction between the implied author and implied reader.[8] In addition, consistent with narrative from the same time and cultural milieu, Luke-Acts establishes a single threaded plotline – in this case the extension of the narrative theme of 'salvation to the ends of the earth' – surrounded by supporting topoi and characterization.[9]

Also in contrast to modern narrative but in the same literary vein as Greco-Roman narrative, Luke-Acts employs characters and topoi to move the plot along. Complex characterization, including glimpses (or more) into the psychological makeup of the characters, of modern narrative is not present in the narrative discourse of Luke-Acts. Characters and character groups, through their actions and words, are evaluated based on rhetorical grids, which are embedded within the narrative texture by the implied author. The implied reader draws upon these in order to construct characterization in relationship with plot.[10] The various topoi that arise from the narrative such as patronage, hospitality, suffering through

7.   Note the comments of Aristotle (*Poetics*, 1453a.10-13): 'A well-constructed plot should, therefore, be single in its issue, rather than double as some maintain. The change of fortune should be not from bad to good, but, reversely, from good to bad. It should come about as the result not of vice, but of some great error or frailty, in a character'. Also (*Poetics*, 1456a.10–11): 'Again, the poet should remember what has been often said, and not make an epic structure into a tragedy – by an epic structure I mean one with a multiplicity of plots'.

8.   The selection and arrangement of events and actions as an interactive author-reader-text activity is described by Paul Ricouer as 'emplotment', which he explains, based on the observations of Aristotle, embodies a configurational character as an imitation of reality, at least that as constructed by the implied author (*From Text to Action*, pp. 1–20). Cf. Aristotle, *Poetics*, 1450a.2–4: 'Plot is the imitation of the action – for by plot I here mean that in virtue of which we ascribe certain qualities to the agents. Thought is required whenever a statement is proved, or, it may be a general truth enunciated.' Also, cf. the discussion of the cumulative effect of narrative events described as 'amplification' by Longinus, *On the Sublime*, 11.1–12.2.

9.   As discussed earlier, Prince (*Narrative as Theme*, pp. 3–7) differentiates between the overarching theme of a narrative discourse and plotline on the basis that 'theme' unifies all of the various textual elements in a narrative, including that of plot (also motifs and characterization). In particular, he contends that 'theme' – in contrast to plot – lacks narrative movement/action.

Nevertheless, while indicative of modern and postmodern narrative, plot assumes the characteristics of theme in ancient Greco-Roman narrative, positing a view that envisions a confluence of theme and plot. This understanding coincides with Aristotle's equation of plot with action/sequencing and the primacy of plot over all other narrative components (*Poetics*, 1450b.1–3, 1454a.15–35, 1454b.1–15). See Scholes and Kellogg, *The Nature of Narrative*, pp. 26–30, 207–39, for a discussion of the differences of plot in antiquity and modernity.

10.   Aristotle subsumes characterization to plot (*Poetics*, 1450a.15–23): 'The plot, then, is the first principle, and, as it were, the soul of a tragedy: character holds the second place. A similar fact is seen in painting. The most beautiful colors, laid on confusedly, will not give as much pleasure as the chalk outline of a portrait. Thus tragedy is the imitation of an action, and of the agents mainly with a view to the action.'

tribulation, and the relationship of Jesus and John the Baptist are a part of but not separate from the overarching plotline. To put it another way, the various topoi in Luke-Acts contribute to (i.e., follow) the plotline rather than run parallel or even against it (as is often the case with modern narrative).

Authors in Greco-Roman narrative employ frameworks, such as prefaces, transitional summaries, speeches, and epilogues, from which the implied reader constructs meaning.[11] For Luke-Acts, in addition to the prefaces of Luke and Acts and the first two chapters of Luke, Jesus' four speeches in the Galilean ministry are integral to the implied reader's construction of plot, characterization, and topoi. Speeches play a similar role in other Greco-Roman narratives, in particular helping to explain not only what happened but why the events took place. In the case of characterization, the implied reader is compelled to imitate the successful actions of characters or avoid their failings.[12]

II. *Framing the Narrative Discourse: Lukan Prologue*

The Lukan prologue (1.1-4) has received much attention and is seen by many as the key in establishing the literary genre of Luke-Acts as well as the purpose and aim of Luke-Acts. Several aspects of the Lukan prologue are relevant to this study. First, the use of a Greek-style preface was prevalent in Greco-Roman narrative, ranging from the technical to the non-technical narrative. Green explains that these prefaces share common elements 'such as the author's name; dedication and/or request; remarks regarding the subject matter, including its importance and implications; (often diminutive) mention of predecessors; a claim to appropriate methodology; and the transition to the work itself'.[13] Second, the sophisticated vocabulary and style of the prologue, coupled with the fact that a relative few were literate in antiquity, suggests an implied author of some education, probably from an urban environment.[14] Third, the correspondence of the Lukan corpus and middlebrow narrative (whether historiography or the scientific tradition) implies that the implied author had a general appreciation for the artisan class – free artisans and those with small businesses – which, based on recent investigation, comprised a significant part of the population in first-century

---

11. For an excellent discussion of the roles of frameworks in narrative, see Genette, *Palimpsests*.

12. See, e.g., Toohey, *Reading Epic*; Hunter, *Past and Process*. Cf. also Marion L. Soards, 'The Speeches in Acts in Relation to Other Pertinent Ancient Literature', *ETR* 70 (1994), pp. 65–90; Stanley E. Porter, 'Thucydides 1.22.1 and Speeches in Acts: Is There a Thucydidean View?' *NovT* 32 (1990), pp. 121–42. However, it is important to note that investigation of the relationship of speeches in Luke-Acts to those in Greco-Roman narrative largely focuses on the speeches of Acts and pays little attention to the speeches in Luke.

13. *Gospel of Luke*, p. 34.

14. *Gospel of Luke*, p. 35.

Christian communities.[15] Finally, as briefly discussed in chapter two, the implied author, rather than using the addressee 'Theophilus' in a symbolic manner to represent a larger audience (viz., 'dear to God' or 'lover of God') as some argue, recognizes the role of Theophilus in the writing of the corpus: Theophilus provides benefaction by facilitating the circulation of the document to his family and friends. Specifically, the implied author hopes that the narrative, through Theophilus' recommendation and circle of friends and corresponding influences, would gain a wider audience. This contextual understanding broadens the 'reading' location of the authorial audience, a textual construct like the implied reader but also a multidimensional, real life-and-blood construct.

III. *The First Galilean Ministry Speech*

Research on the relevance of the first speech of the Galilean ministry and its role in establishing overarching thematic unity in the narrative of Luke-Acts is vast. It is almost uniformly held to be programmatic in the quest to understand the narrative discourse of Luke-Acts.[16] This study concurs with these earlier findings and proposes that closer attention to the rhetorical texture of the speech both supplements as well as contributes to a deeper understanding of how and why the speech is a driving factor in shaping the narrative discourse of Luke-Acts.

A. *Constructing Meaning from the Rhetorical Texture*

The rhetorical argument of the first speech in the Galilean ministry draws upon examples from the past (viz., 4.24-27) that orient the implied reader and narrative audience to embrace the understanding that 'salvation' will extend to Gentiles (viz., as happened in the case of the widow from Zarephath and the Syrian Naaman). Rhetorical texture of the speech also attempts to persuade the implied reader concerning the identity of Jesus.[17] The implied reader is predisposed, as a result, to process the speech with two elements foregrounded: the speech provides detail relevant to the characterization and ethos of Jesus, and it elicits a new understanding of the two examples cited from the LXX.

The rhetorical arrangement of the speech steers the implied reader in the identification of narrative trajectories. In particular, the statement of case (4.22-23) provides the implied reader with the purpose of the speech, and thus it serves as the funnel for understanding overarching rhetorical

---

15. Specifically, Alexander, 'Luke's Preface', pp. 48–74; eadem, *Preface*, pp. 200–5.

16. Though much has been added in the past decade or more, for a detailed bibliographical overview, see Schreck, 'Nazareth Pericope', pp. 399–471. Most recently, see Neirynck, 'Luke 4,16-30', pp. 357–95.

17. If viewed from a theological standpoint, the former is soteriological in focus, whereas the latter is Christological in scope.

argument: in contrast to the well-known Greco-Roman proverb that Jesus cites – 'Physician, heal yourself' (4.22) – he will not be doing the expected course of 'religious' patronage in Nazareth.[18] The narrative delays in revealing the deeds Jesus conferred in Capernaum to the section following the speech (4.31-32). The implied reader must wait to fill the 'gap' in the discourse – that is, Jesus will not afford the same patronage to his relatives and hometown as was shown to those in Capernaum – until the speech is completed. Patronage beyond ethnic and kinship boundaries forms part of a core of the plotline – 'salvation to the ends of the earth' – in that Jesus and his followers break down ethnographical and spatial boundaries to proclaim salvation to all of humankind.[19] In particular, the implied reader draws an intratextual connection between the closing scene of Acts (28.17-31) and Jesus' hometown synagogue speech (Lk. 4.16-30). As a result, the implied reader uses analeptic processing to construe the speech as a framing device for interpreting the overarching narrative discourse.[20]

With the body of the speech (4.24-27), the discourse takes on meaning for the implied reader on two different levels: the narrative world and the world of the reader. Specifically, Jesus' actions, namely, moving the boundaries of 'salvation' beyond his kin and friends, represents the topos of proclamation of salvation to the Jewish people throughout Luke-Acts. Of course, at this juncture in the narrative, the implied reader does not have the knowledge to generate this connection; it is only in the 'to-and-fro' interaction between text and reader – analeptic activity in this case – that results in the construction of this topos. In contrast to the narrative audience, the implied reader is in an omniscient position, able to make judgments about the

18.   However cf. Richard L. Rohrbaugh, 'Legitimating Sonship – A Test of Honour: A social-scientific study of Luke 4:1-30', in *Modelling Early Christianity*, pp. 183–97, who argues that the synagogue crowd's quip to Jesus was offensive, and thus the reason for his combative response.

19.   For a different understanding of the topographical movement in Luke-Acts, in contrast to the view typically held, see Loveday C. A. Alexander, 'Narrative Maps: Reflections on the Toponymy of Acts', in M. D. Carroll, D. J. A. Clines, and P. R. Davies (eds), *The Bible in Human Society* (Festschrift John Rogerson; JSOTSup, 200; Sheffield: Sheffield Academic Press, 1995), pp. 17–57. Alexander contends that the topographical movement in Luke-Acts towards Rome reflects an extratextual repertoire that held Rome to be the center of the earth and places the exotic in the eastern reaches of the Roman Empire. Hence, since the reading location of the implied reader (or more accurately the authorial audience) is closer to Rome than Jerusalem, the implied reader perceives that the salvific proclamation reaches its climax in Rome (viz., as a movement towards the reading location of the implied reader). However *Pss. Sol.* 8.16 represents Rome as being at the 'ends of the earth'.

20.   Perhaps the first to note the numerous echoes between Lk. 4.16-30 and Acts 28.17-31 is Jacques Dupont, 'La conclusion des Actes et son rapport à l'ensemble de l'ouvrage de Luc', in J. Kremer (ed.), *Les Actes des Apôtres. Traditions, rédaction, théologie* (BETL, 48; Leuven: Leuven University Press, 1978), pp. 359–404. More recently, see Alexander, 'Back to Front', pp. 419–46, esp. pp. 433–36, who notes the connections and argues that both Acts 28.17-31 and Lk. 1.1–4.30 function as framing devices for the narrative discourse of Luke-Acts.

actions and words of characters and character groups. The two examples from the LXX form, as a result, a hermeneutical framework that the implied reader uses to evaluate characters and character groups (i.e., do their actions and speech place them in the same vein as Elijah and Elisha?).

B. *Narrative Trajectories Engender Characterization*

The initial speech in the Galilean ministry provides significant detail about Jesus and the characterization of those who oppose him as well as those who embrace him. These lines of demarcation between characters and character groups extend to the final scene in Acts.

1. *Details on Jesus' Characterization*

A Christological trajectory emerges from the initial speech, producing additional background for the implied reader to draw upon in constructing Jesus' characterization. The speech contributes to Jesus' ethos in the following: (1) Jesus' ministry and words parallel those of Elijah and Elisha, and thus he is to be considered as a prophet in the same lineage (i.e., he narrowly and miraculously escapes death and preaches to both Jews and Gentiles); (2) Jesus is blessed with the Spirit of God to proclaim 'salvation' to the disenfranchised; (3) Jesus goes against cultural protocols in bestowing salvific patronage – showing no nepotism to those from his ethnographic origination; and (4) Jesus is considered a skilled orator, at least by his relatives and hometown (4.22: ' ... gracious words that proceeded out of his mouth'). All four of these trajectories carry forward in the discourse of Luke-Acts, reoccurring in various scenes. The first two trajectories are found in the earlier narrative discourse,[21] and their inclusion in the first speech serves as a form of rhetorical amplification.

2. *Jesus' Hometown Synagogue and Those Who Repudiate 'Salvation'*

The characterization of Jesus' relatives and hometown prompts the implied reader to equate them with those in Israel's past: those who rejected and persecuted the prophets of old such as Elijah and Elisha and who were condemned by the Deuteronomist. Repudiation of those whose positions of honor are threatened by the extension of 'salvation' to those in the religious and social margins (i.e., those embodying 'shame') forms a tangential topos that complements the narrative plotline. This topos serves as a characterization matrix for the implied reader: characters or character groups that retain religious and social systems of honor at the expense of salvific

---

21. For the trajectory that places Jesus in the prophetic lineage, cf. among Lk. 1.46-56 (a hypertext of 1 Sam. 2.1-10) and 2.52 (a hypertext of 1 Sam 2.21, 26); for the second trajectory, cf. among Lk. 3.21-22; 4.1, 14. 'Hypertext' is a heuristic construct used as the descriptor for the text upon which the earlier text – designated as the 'hypotext' – is grafted. Hypertextuality is mode of intertextuality where two or more texts are linked without direct citation (specifically, see Genette, *Palimpsests*, pp. 5–15).

proclamation are associated with the character type represented by Jesus' relatives and hometown as well as those who opposed the ministries and messages of Elijah and Elisha. As the narrative progresses, the implied reader associates other characters and character groups with this character taxonomy. Per the discussion in Chapter seven, the fourth speech of the Galilean ministry serves as a fourfold interpretive grid, providing the implied reader with a matrix for evaluating individual characters and character groups. In this context, Jesus' relatives and hometown coincide with the first sowing example: those who have the 'word' taken from them by the devil before they can act upon it (Lk. 8.12).

C. *Narrative Trajectories Engender Topoi*

The rhetorical texture of the first speech generates a number of topoi that corroborate and concurrently help move the plot along. In particular, these function as framing mechanisms, and the implied reader supplements additional detail as the narrative progresses and each receives more elaboration. As will be discussed below, the citation of Isa. 61.1-2 and 58.6 as the basis for the introduction (4.18-19) and reference to the stories in 2 Kgs 5.1-14 and 1 Kgs 17.17-24 in the body of the speech are interpretive keys found elsewhere in the narrative discourse of Luke-Acts.

1. *Forgiveness of Sin and Jubilee Legislation*

The introduction of the speech and the reference to the marginal – the poor, the captive, the blind, and the oppressed – as recipients (both direct and indirect) of divine deliverance has a rich intertextual background in the LXX.[22] Repetition of ἄφεσις ('release') by means of the redactional meshing of Isa. 61.1-2 and 58.6 functions as a rhetorical marker for the implied reader and emphasizes the importance of other occurrences of ἄφεσις in Luke-Acts where it is used to designate 'forgiveness' of sins: Lk. 5.20; 24.47; Acts 2.38; 5.31; 10.43; 13.38; 26.18. Within the context of Luke-Acts, sin assumes social implications and reflects the encumbrances that 'imprison' and 'oppress' characters (i.e., as denoted by the accusative prepositions of ἄφεσις in both clauses). Analeptic processing of the narrative discourse results in the implied reader identifying the disposition and actions of certain characters as representative of the connotations that form around both encumbrances. The consequence is that the implied reader construes these characters and character groups as a negative stereotype.

Though a change in the pattern of recitation occurs, as the first three clauses address specific entities (viz., the captives, the blind, and the oppressed), the final clause does not identify a group of recipients. In particular, the final clause serves as an interpretive key for the implied reader by means of its intertextual connections with Jubilee legislation (e.g.,

---

22. As noted by Roth, *Character Types*, pp. 80–141.

Lev. 25.10): the implied reader expects Jesus' ministry and proclamation to embrace social justice (in the form of Jubilee legislation).[23]

The chiastic framing of the introduction accentuates the reading of scripture at the center of the scene (i.e., v. 17b parallels v. 20a; cf. the discussion in Chapter four). The overriding topos is established in the form of an enthymeme (v. 18a), with the commissioning and the four consecutive infinitival clauses (vv. 18b-19) providing elaboration. Association of the Holy Spirit as representative of those who proclaim 'good news to the poor' – a deductive conclusion the implied reader reaches when filling the major premise of the enthymeme – is a topos upon which the implied author expands in the subsequent narrative.[24] The three infinitival clauses following the enthymeme provide guidance to the implied reader as to what it means to 'preach good news to the poor'.[25] The implied reader proleptically processes the ministry and speech of Jesus in Luke and the disciples in Acts against this framework. Specifically, the two LXX examples from the ministries of Elisha and Elijah provide the implied reader with a matrix for interpretation: characters and character groups representing the marginal in the narrative are compared (synkrisis) to the Zarephathian widow and the Syrian Naaman, and the actions shown to them are compared to what it means to 'preach good news'.

2. *A Type Scene: A Paradigm of Proclamation*

The fourfold flow of action – that is, (1) boldness of Jesus' proclamation; (2) an antithetical response by those listening to the rhetorical discourse; (3) a 'miraculous' escape by the one proclaiming the message of 'salvation' from listeners seeking to inflict harm; and (4) a renewed spread of 'salvation' – establishes a narrative framework (or 'type scene') that is replicated in various episodes in Acts: Peter and John in Acts 3.1–4.37; Peter in Acts 10.1–12.24; Paul and Barnabas in Acts 13.13-52; Paul and Barnabas in Acts 14.8-28; Paul and Silas in Acts 16.16-40; Paul in Acts 21.17-35; Paul and his companions in Acts 27.1–28.10. Construction of this type scene prompts the implied reader to associate the initial ministry and message of the early church and its leaders with the ministry and message of Jesus.[26] The implied

---

23. Ringe, *Biblical Jubilee*; Sloan, *Favorable Year*.

24. For characterization of the Holy Spirit, see, e.g., Shepherd, *Holy Spirit*; Hur, *Dynamic Reading*.

25. Per Roth (*Character Types*, pp. 95–141), the three groups (i.e., the imprisoned, the blind, and the oppressed), as depicted in the infinitival clauses, are seen by the implied reader as a constellation of stereotypical character types in the LXX. Clustering of the entities serves as a rhetorical heightening device.

26. Attempts of the Jewish antagonists to thwart Paul and Barnabas by casting them outside of the boundaries of the city or region (Antioch in Acts 13.48-52; Lystra in Acts 14.19-20) mirror the response of Jesus' hometown synagogue in the first Galilean speech (Lk. 4.16-30), who also attempt to cast Jesus outside the city (ἐξέβαλον αὐτὸν ἔξω τῆς πόλεως in Lk. 4.29 compared to ἐξέβαλον αὐτὸν ἀπὸ τῶν ὁρίων αὐτῶν in Acts 13.50 and ἔσυρον ἔξω τῆς πόλεως in Acts 14.19).

reader analeptically identifies similarities between remaining scenes and the fourfold action sequence of the type scene in Lk. 4.28-30.[27]

IV. *The Second Galilean Ministry Speech*

The second speech in the Galilean ministry is perhaps one of the most neglected sections of Luke-Acts. This is in large part due to the attention paid to its counterpart in Matthew (i.e., the Sermon on the Mount [Mt. 5.3–7.29]), which is seen as more authentic, more rhetorically appealing, and more influential to the overall Matthean narrative discourse. The examination of its rhetorical texture in Chapter fives shows significant attention to rhetorical argument on the part of the implied author. Indeed, even a redactional comparison of the Sermon on the Plain and the Sermon on the Mount pinpoints rhetorical formation.

A. *Constructing Meaning from the Rhetorical Texture*

The implied author locates the speech within the context of the giving of the law at Mount Sinai (Exod. 19.24; 24.3): like Moses, Jesus descends from the mountain to deliver divine instructions (Lk. 6.12-19), and thus the second Galilean ministry speech takes on a function similar to that of the law for Israel. An intertext of Isa. 40.3-5, which was used by John the Baptist to portend the ministry of Jesus in Lk. 3.4-6, appears in Lk. 6.17: τόπου πεδινοῦ ('level plain') prompts the implied reader to associate the second speech with the earlier pronouncement of John the Baptist.[28] In particular, this intratextual connection with John the Baptist's pronouncement compels the implied reader to associate the appearance of the 'salvation of God' (3.5) with the description of Jesus' ministry in 6.17-19. The implied reader uses this connection to construct further meaning around the plotline of 'salvation to the ends of the earth'. In addition, the naming of the twelve disciples in the prior episode (6.12-16) shrouds the second speech in the apocalyptic context of Israel's restoration.

Unlike the first speech, the identity of Jesus is not in the rhetorical foreground, but rather the ethical dimensions (ethos) of disciples. The rhetorical texture of the speech generates narrative trajectories in a number of ways. First, the bipolar argumentation of the speech's introduction creates a distinct line of demarcation between disciples and non-disciples. Second, rhetorical symmetry in the speech's introduction is marked by

27. For an overview of type scenes, see Alter, *Biblical Narrative*, p. 51; idem, 'Annunciation Type-Scene', pp. 115–30. The third part of the fourfold type scene framework undergoes permutation in the case of Stephen (Acts 7.1–8.3): the protagonist, Stephen, is not delivered from physical harm but rather receives eschatological salvation.

28. The editorial change by the implied author from καὶ ἡ τραχεῖα πεδία in Isa. 40.4 to καί αἱ τραχεῖαι εἰ ὁδούς λείας (Lk. 3.5) brings this intertext to the forefront of the aural/oral experience for the implied reader.

several places of deviation: the fourth blessing/woe pair, where the conclusion of the blessing contains more detail than that of the woe, including two enthymemes – versus one – that are intercalated, is a rhetorical signal to the implied reader of its heightened importance. Third, the speech's statement of case establishes the overarching elements of ethical behavior, while the body of the speech delves into the specifics of the behavior through deductive reasoning, augmented with inductive examples at its close. In particular, the statement of case includes two interrelated topoi that are elaborated upon in the body: the need to show unconditional patronage, even to those who repudiate traditional honor and shame constructs, and the requirement to embrace all individuals, regardless of their social status and adherence to accepted honor and shame stipulations. Fourth, the conclusion (6.46-49) departs from the largely deductive argument of the preceding discourse – as represented by maxims and enthymemes – through the use of rhetorical questioning: actions rather than speech distinguish a disciple from a non-disciple. Finally, rhetorical amplification occurs in the conclusion through the combination of synkrisis and ecphrasis. Much of the rhetorical argumentation assumes an intertextual knowledge of the LXX as well as an extratextual understanding of economic and, in particular, agronomical terminology. In addition, rhetorical mode of argumentation is deductive (viz., couched in the form of maxims and enthymemes), and thus directives are followed by a rationale.

B. *Narrative Trajectories Engender Characterization*

While the focus of the speech is not on establishing an ethos for Jesus, in contrast to the rhetorical discourse of the first speech, it does contain elements from which the implied reader builds characterization.[29]

1. *Jesus: Embodiment of Moses, Elijah, and Elisha*
The rhetorical situation for the second speech presents contextual data that spurs the implied reader to continue to build upon the characterization of Jesus. The actions of Jesus in 6.12-19 parallel those of Moses in Exodus, where Moses also secludes himself on the mountain and descends to proclaim a message from God (Exod. 3.1–4.17; 19.3-6; 24.9-18; 33.7-11; 34.29-35). Synkrisis with Moses results from analeptic and proleptic activity that brings prior narrative into the foreground: Jesus, like Moses, frequently withdraws into the 'wilderness' for prayerful contemplation (Lk. 4.42; 5.16; 9.28; 11.1). The narrative transition (Lk. 6.17-19) directly preceding the speech functions as a denouement to the narrative episodes 'sandwiched' between the first and second speeches, many of which are healing scenes (the Capernaum synagogue in 4.31-37; Simon's mother-in-law and subsequently crowds in 4.38-41; the leper in 5.12-15; the paralytic in 5.17-26; and the man with a withered hand in 6.6-11). Specifically, this characterization builds

---

29. However cf. Carruth, 'Strategies of Authority', pp. 98–115.

upon the earlier association of Jesus with Elijah and Elisha (4.24-27), both of whom were actively involved in healing.[30] Jesus' ability to administer healing to the afflicted is construed by the implied reader as a derivation of his possession of the Holy Spirit by means of the narrator's notation that δύναμις ('power') came forth from him (6.19b).[31] In all, the rhetorical situation places Jesus in the position of patron to the large audience that has gathered to listen to the speech as clients.[32]

2. *Opponents of Jesus*
Deviation in the fourth blessing/woe pair (6.22-23 versus 6.26) raises the identity of those who persecute disciples to the forefront, and, through synkrisis, the implied reader associates Jesus' interlocutors (i.e., the Pharisee and scribes) in the cycle of five controversies sandwiched between the first and second speeches (5.17-26; 5.27-32; 5.33-39; 6.1-5; 6.6-11) as well as his relatives and hometown with the adversaries depicted in the introduction of the fourth speech. Other characters encountered thus far in the narrative that coincide with this character type include Herod the tetrarch, because of his imprisonment of John the Baptist (3.18-20),[33] and the devil (4.1-13). Through proleptic activity the implied reader places various other characters and character groups into this same category: the chief priest (Lk. 22-23), the temple authorities and Sadducees (Acts 4.1–8.1), Saul (Acts 7.58b–8.3), the Jewish antagonists of Paul (Acts 13.1–28.31), Bar-Jesus (Acts 13.4-12), the owners of the slave girl (Acts 16.16-30), Demetrius the silversmith (Acts 19.23-41), the Jews from Asia, Ananias the high priest, the Jewish temple leaders, and the Jewish temple tribunal (Acts 21.27–26.32).

3. *True Disciples*
Just as the implied reader develops a stereotype for characters and character groups that appear as adversaries to John the Baptist, Jesus, and their disciples, the implied reader constructs a stereotype for characters and character groups who embrace Jesus' message. These are individuals and groups that embody the ethical conduct Jesus articulated in the second speech. Analeptic analysis guides the implied reader to associate characters and character groups such as the various persons from the birth narratives

30. See Craig A. Evans, 'Luke's Use of the Elijah/Elisha Narratives and the Ethic of Election', *JBL* 106 (1987), pp. 75–83.
31. Cf. the use of δύναμις in association with the Holy Spirit (4.14), which serves as an intratext for the implied reader. Also, see 5.17c: '. . . and the power (δύναμις) of the Lord was with him to heal'.
32. The series of the preceding healing episodes (4.31-41; 5.12-26; 6.6-11) coincide with this depiction: Jesus, as the one dispensing healing, is the patron, and the recipients of his healing activity are clients.
33. The characterization of Herod in Luke-Acts is the fullest in terms of adversarial/negative characters, functioning as a 'foil' to John the Baptist, Jesus, and even the Christian movement. However, Herod also embodies many of the actions and qualities of antipathetic characters and character groups (see, Darr, *Herod the Fox*).

(1.5–2.52); John the Baptist (3.1-22); Peter, John, and James (5.1-11); the friends of the paralytic (5.17-26); and Levi (5.27-32) as in compliance with the ethical behavior delineated in the speech. Proleptic construal of characters and character groups that the implied reader encounters later in the narrative is done through the ethical lens of the second speech.[34]

C. *Narrative Trajectories Engender Topoi*

The rhetorical texture of the second speech exhibits various topoi that serve a programmatic narrative function, demarcating actions representative of a true disciple. These are an extension of the Christological ethos set forth in the first speech: the speech and actions of Jesus are the foundational elements underlying the ethical dimensions of a disciple. The speech's rhetorical argumentation also compares the ethical demeanor of a disciple to the actions of the divine by means of the intercalated enthymematic rationale of the first segment of the body in 6.36. This rhetorical 'positioning' by the implied author places the implied reader and narrative audience in a rhetorical dilemma: failure to follow Jesus' instructions is tantamount to repudiation of the divine.

1. *Reversal of Fortunes*

The speech's introduction imposes an obligation upon the implied reader and the narrative audience to complete the major premises for each of the blessing and woe enthymemes. Each major premise (and the conclusions for each) runs counter to traditional Greco-Roman ideological systems – reversal of fortunes, a reoccurring topos in Luke-Acts.[35] This is not the first occurrence of this topos in the Lukan narrative; it is present in the prior characterization of Elizabeth and Mary (1.5–2.21), the two LXX examples Jesus cites in the first speech (4.24-27), and the healing Jesus dispenses to those from the social and religious margins of society (4.31-41; 5.12-26; 6.6-11). The topos recurs throughout the remainder of the narrative, with the culmination being that Paul's imprisonment diminishes from view in the closing scene of Acts (cf. 28.30: 'And he remained there two whole years at his own expense [ἐν ἰδίῳ]'). Reversal of fortune also occurs in the opposite direction, instances where individuals or groups go from positions of power and honor to positions of powerlessness and dishonor: Simon the Pharisee (Lk. 7.36-50), the profligate son (Lk. 15.11-32), the rich man (Lk. 16.19-31), and the demise of Herod (Acts 12.20-23).

2. *Material Benefaction*

There is an overriding focus on the use of economic (or material) means in the allotment of salvation in the speech's statement of case and body of argument. The implied author assumes that the extratextual repertoire of

---

34. For a more detailed discussion, see the examination of the fourth sowing example in this chapter.

35. York, *Reversal in Luke*.

the implied reader includes familiarity with economic benefaction, including terminology used in economic transactions: χάρις and μισθός, οἰκτίρμων and μέτρον, and κόλπος. The speech's statement of case also assumes knowledge of economic benefaction: the subject matter for its enthymematic argument is predicated on economic realities.[36] Concern for wealth and poverty is not new to the Lukan narrative; the implied reader draws connections with earlier narrative through analeptic echoes that include the Magnificat (1.46-56), connotations of poverty surrounding Jesus' birth (2.1-20), the preaching of John the Baptist (3.10-14), the first speech of the Galilean ministry (4.16-30), and the call of the first disciples (5.1-11). In particular, wealth and poverty become increasingly important in the narrative as the plotline progresses: disciples assume roles of benefaction to help elevate those in poverty to modes of new existence.[37]

3. *A New Mode of Benefaction: Ethical Comportment of Disciples*
The topos of reversal of fortunes in the introduction lays a hermeneutical framework for the implied reader and narrative audience: Jesus' teaching and actions reinterpret traditional social and religious ideological systems, with the recipients of 'salvation' being the disenfranchised. Use of the second-person address throughout the speech prompts the implied reader and the narrative audience to envision disciples as assuming the responsibility of enacting Jesus' salvific message. The rhetorical argument of the speech posits two interrelated topoi, ethical frameworks that guide disciples in their interaction with other individuals and groups: (1) the need to show benefaction to those who violate patronal boundaries (versus adverse reciprocity), and (2) the requisite to extend benefaction to those outside of the boundaries of kinship and friendship who do not have the capacity to reciprocate with corresponding benefaction.[38] The narrative of the second speech elaborates upon both of these topoi in the statement of case (the first topos from 6.27c-29 and the second topos from 6.30) and the body of

36. As corroboration, note that the Lukan implied author modifies the 'spiritual' blessings found in the blessings of the Matthean Sermon on the Mount to represent matters of wealth and poverty (Lk. 6.20-26).

37. For a discussion of wealth and poverty in Luke-Acts, see Luke T. Johnson, *The Literary Function of Possessions in Luke-Acts* (SBLDS, 39; Missoula, Montana: Scholars Press, 1977); Kyoung-Jin Kim, *Stewardship and Almsgiving in Luke's Theology* (JSNTSup, 155; Sheffield: Sheffield Academic Press, 1998); Joel. B. Green, 'Good News to Whom? Jesus and the "Poor" in the Gospel of Luke', in Joel B. Green and Max Turner (eds), *Jesus of Nazareth: Lord and Christ: Essays on the Historical Jesus and New Testament Christology* (Grand Rapids: William B. Eerdmans Publishing Company, 1994), pp. 59–74; David L. Balch, 'Rich and Poor, Proud and Humble in Luke-Acts', in L. Michael White and O. Larry Yarbrough (eds), *The Social World of the First Christians* (Festschrift Wayne A. Meeks; Minneapolis: Fortress Press, 1995), pp. 214–33; Moxnes, *Economy*.

38. Cf. Adriana Destro and Mauro Pesce, 'Fathers and Householders in the Jesus Movement: The Perspective of the Gospel of Luke', *BibInt* 11 (2003), pp. 211–38. Through the examination of household social codes, Destro and Pesce pinpoint household patronage without reciprocity as a topos comprising the Lukan model of discipleship.

argument (the first topos from the first segment [vv. 32-36] and the second topos from the second segment [vv. 37-42]).

Much of the Lukan narrative contains references to these two intertwined topoi, and the implied reader builds greater coherence through the to-and-fro activity of the reading process. In particular, the implied reader construes the ethos of characters and character groups – both analeptically and proleptically – based on their conformity or nonconformity with the stipulations of these two topoi. As regards to the plotline of 'salvation to the ends of the earth', both topoi play a key role in helping to define it: the implied reader constructs a more and more detailed view of ethical behavior and its relationship to salvific benefaction as the narrative progresses.

4. *Discipleship Equals Action*

Movement beyond simply hearing Jesus' instructions to putting them into action permeates much of the rhetorical argument of the second speech. Ambiguity around the identity of the disciples listening to the speech – namely, the implied reader is not given any information as to the individuals or groups comprising the designation 'disciples' (6.20a) – and the implied reader must fill the 'gap' by means of the speech's rhetorical texture. The speech's conclusion brings this rhetorical topos to its apex through the parabolic examples of the two builders. The synkrisis and ecphrasis in the two parabolic examples guide the implied reader to the following two conclusions: those who enact Jesus' directives build a house that will withstand the onslaught of flood waters, whereas those who do not act build a house that will experience destruction. The implied author has already conveyed the importance of ethical actions in the preaching of John the Baptist (3.1-14) and the calling of the first disciples (5.1-11). The centrality of this topos intensifies as Jesus progresses towards Jerusalem: it serves as a means for the implied reader to decipher disciples versus non-disciples. Characters and character groups such as the lawyer and the Good Samaritan (Lk. 10.25-37), the dishonest steward (Lk. 16.1-13), the rich ruler (Lk. 18.18-30), the poor widow (Lk. 21.1-4), the early Jerusalem community (Acts 2.41-47; 4.32-37), Barnabas (Acts 4.32-37), Ananias and Sapphira (Acts 5.1-11), and the Christian community that responds to Agabus' prophecy of famine (Acts 11.27-30) are evaluated by the implied reader on the basis of these two parabolic examples and their actions – or lack thereof. Elaboration of the topos is found in Jesus' teaching as well – for example, the instructions Jesus gives to the seventy 'missionaries' (Lk. 10.1-16) concentrate on actions versus speech.

5. *Ethical Actions Derive from the Heart*

The second speech makes it very clear that ethical behavior derives from the καρδία ('heart'). Interestingly, this topos is expressed alongside economic terminology – θησαυρός (i.e., a material equated with wealth)[39] – and as the

---

39.   Cf. the usage of θησαυρός in Lk. 12.33-34; 18.22.

final enthymeme of the speech's body (6.45). This heightens the importance of the topos to the implied reader: the actions of those who embody Jesus' teaching as well as the actions of those who are opposed to the new religious and social order Jesus preaches originate from the inner being of the person. Ethical transformation that conforms with or recalcitrant actions that contest Jesus' teaching on the new religious and social order stem from cognitive activity. The implied reader has already encountered instances of the two cognitive options in the prior narrative and draws upon the enthymematic argument behind the topos to make certain determinations about prior characterization. When construed in combination with the two preceding agronomical enthymematic examples (6.43-44), the implied reader concludes that those who resist Jesus' message have evil hearts (and are to be equated with thorns and bramble bushes), while those who listen and enact Jesus' instructions have good hearts (and are to be equated with fig trees and grape vines). This topos continues to play an important role throughout the remainder of the narrative, extending all of the way to the closing scene of Acts in the citation from Isa. 6.9-10 (Acts 28.27). In particular, the four character taxonomies established in the fourth speech provide the interpretive framework for the implied reader: characters and character groups that fall into the first three sowing taxonomies have – to varying extents – evil hearts, whereas those who coincide with the fourth sowing taxonomy have good hearts. In this context, those with evil hearts ultimately fail to embody the ethical dimensions of Jesus' message, whereas those with good hearts exemplify Jesus' message.

V. *The Third Galilean Ministry Speech*

The third speech of the Galilean ministry is replete with skillful rhetorical arrangement. Many scholars fail to equate Jesus' instructions as oratory on the basis that the episode is not a coherent whole (viz., because of the narrative aside separating the statement of case and body in 7.29-30). The speech is rarely examined, as a result, in its entirety but rather from a focus on redaction- and source-critical issues behind the text. However, the speech exhibits significant rhetorical coherence when examined as an amplified chreia, and the narrative aside serves as an interpretive key for the implied reader.

A. *Constructing Meaning from the Rhetorical Texture*

The rhetorical argument of the speech prompts the implied reader to make certain judgments concerning the ethos of John the Baptist and Jesus through the implied author's use of ecphrasis and synkrisis.[40] Their characterization contributes to the plotline: the implied author repudiates the accusations of Jewish adversaries, demonstrates the specious nature of

40.   See Cameron, 'Characterizations in the Gospels', pp. 35–69.

the accusations being cast upon John the Baptist and Jesus, and aligns John the Baptist and Jesus with the divine will. Ironic dissonance is created by the implied author through the use of the narrative aside (7.29-30): the implied reader is privy to information not available to the narrative audience, data that predisposes the implied reader to view the Pharisees and lawyers in a negative manner.

The two episodes following the second speech (7.1-10; 7.11-17) give rise to the inquiry from John the Baptist, made through his disciples, to Jesus about his ethos (7.18-23). The rhetorical situation establishes the ethos of Jesus and, in conjunction with the implied reader's processing of the statement of case (7.28), the ethos of John the Baptist. The result is the formation of the speech's topos: the relationship of Jesus and John the Baptist. The two prior episodes (7.1-10 and 7.11-17) evoke synkrisis and steer the implied reader to draw parallels between Jesus' ministry and those of Elijah and Elisha through intratextual linkages with the body of the first speech (4.24-27) and the intertextual type scenes in 7.1-10 (the healing of the centurion's servant; cf. 2 Kgs 5.19) and 7.11-17 (the raising of a widow's dead son at Nain; cf. 1 Kgs 17.10-24; 2 Kgs 4.32-37).[41] The amplified chreia preceding the speech – specifically the chreia (7.21) and its paraphrase (7.22) – provides the implied reader with analeptic referents to the first speech (4.18-19, 24-27), where Jesus' ministry (the character stereotypes spelled out in the chreia and its paraphrase) extends to those personages and groups on the religious and social marginal.[42]

The speech's rhetorical style reflects attentive construction by the implied author. The introduction (7.24-27) presents a threefold series of rhetorical questioning that repeats the same question with a different answer following each.[43] The only difference between the three rhetorical questions is in the answer to the first question: the answer is not followed with a rebuttal (cf. 7.25b, 26b-27). The rhetorical questioning reaches a crescendo with the third question and answer, a rhetorical effect that garners the attention of the implied reader.

The identity of John the Baptist is already known by the implied reader through prior intratextual information (cf. 1.16-17, 76) – namely, a prophet in the vein of Elijah – a reference unknown to the narrative audience. This information chasm enables the implied reader to make judgments about the narrative audience and their reactions to the messages and ministries of John the Baptist and Jesus. Heightening of the rhetorical address to the narrative audience occurs through emendations to the intertextual citation from Mal. 3.1 and Exod. 23.20 at the close of the introduction (7.27): the change from the third person to second person raises the response of the narrative audience to John the Baptist to the rhetorical foreground (for the response of the narrative audience, cf. 7.29-30).

---

41.   Green, *Gospel of Luke*, pp. 282–93; Kearney, 'Principal Compositional Techniques'.

42.   See Roth, *Character Types*, esp. pp. 80–206.

43.   Expolitio (viz., lingering on the same topos) has the rhetorical effect of amplification (*Rhetorica ad Herennium*, 4.54).

The statement of case (7.28) exhibits sophisticated enthymematic construction that necessitates the implied reader to evoke analeptic activity. The implied reader possesses information about John the Baptist and his disciples from prior narrative: the conception of John the Baptist (1.5-25; 3.21-22), the identity of his disciples (3.8), and his relationship to Jesus (1.26-38). The dual enthymemes of the speech's body (7.31-34) posits the ethos of Jesus and his disciples as well as John the Baptist and his disciples: Jesus and his disciples are conceived of the divine, but John the Baptist was born through natural means (i.e., 'born of a woman'). The result for the implied reader is that Jesus and his disciples receive greater status than John the Baptist and his disciples. Nevertheless, despite the elevation of Jesus and his disciples above John the Baptist and his disciples, all stand in contrast to the ethos of the Pharisees and lawyers, which is revealed in the narrative aside (7.29-30).

Inclusion of the narrative assessment of characters (7.28-30) that appeared in an earlier episode (3.1-18) is a narrative maneuver by the implied author that has the effect of rhetorical heightening. Characters extolled by the narrator in the narrative aside (7.28-30) are noted as comprising part of the narrative audience – that is, the people and tax collectors – who came out to hear John the Baptist's message in 3.1-18, while those condemned by the narrator – namely, the Pharisees and lawyers – are not mentioned as present. The implied reader seeks information that will enable the 'filling' of this narrative gap, and analeptic activity brings prior episodes involving the Pharisees and lawyers into the foreground. Indeed, the one episode where both are found together is the first instance in the Lukan narrative where Jesus' preaching and actions are outwardly contested (5.17-26).

The body of the speech (7.31-34) returns to the rhetorical mode of questioning (cf. the introduction for the same style in 7.24-27). Intertextual echoes to the rebellious, hard-hearted people of the LXX, created by the inclusion of 'members of this generation' (7.31), predisposes the implied reader to construe the comparative corollary – namely, 'children' (7.32) – in an unfavorable manner. In addition, rhetorical juxtaposition of the actions of John the Baptist and Jesus (7.33-34), when coupled with the interpretative conclusions derived from the preceding dual enthymeme (7.31-32), demonstrates a lack of logos behind the accusations of their interlocutors.

Use of τέκνα versus παιδία in the conclusion (7.35) as a designation for 'children' (παιδία is employed in the dual enthymeme of the body – 7.32) serves rhetorical purpose. In particular, the implied reader and the narrative audience are prodded to differentiate between the identity of τέκνα and παιδία: τέκνα denotes those who reject John the Baptist and Jesus, while παιδία represents those who embrace Jesus and John the Baptist. The latter occurs as a result of the inclusio between the first part of the narrative aside – 'tax collectors and all of the people *justified* God' (7.29) – and the conclusion – 'wisdom is *justified* by her children' (7.35). Precise identification of those who enact the directives of John the Baptist and Jesus is left open by the implied author through the use of λαός in the narrative aside (7.29-

30), which serves as an open-ended designation to which nearly any character or character group might correspond.[44] This mode of rhetorical argumentation coincides with the technique known as insinuation: a difficult problem is approached in an indirect manner.[45]

B. *Narrative Trajectories Engender Characterization*

The rhetorical texture of the speech places ethos in the foreground for the implied reader. In contrast to the second speech, which provides an interpretive grid for the implied reader to evaluate characters and character groups based on their actions, the third speech focuses on the characterization of Jesus and John the Baptist and the topos of their relationship. Characterization extends to the Pharisees and lawyers through their opposition to Jesus in preceding episodes (5.17-26) and the intrusion of the narrator into the speech in the form of the narrative aside (7.29-30). The most impugning aspect of the characterization of the Pharisees and lawyers revolves around the fallacies embedded in their logos against Jesus and John the Baptist. As the narrative progresses, characters and character groups whose actions embrace those of Jesus and John the Baptist are viewed in a positive light by the implied reader, while those whose thoughts and actions coincide with those of the Pharisees and lawyers are associated in a negative light.

1. *Characterization of John the Baptist*
John the Baptist plays an important role in the narrative discourse of Luke-Acts. The beginnings of the narrative in Luke (1.5–2.52) provide the implied reader with an analeptic reference for the synkrisis of John the Baptist and Jesus. Parallelism in the characterization of the two is not one of equals: the implied author, as evident in the rhetorical structuring of the narrative discourse, places Jesus in a position of greater prominence than John the Baptist. This occurs in the following ways: (1) Jesus' birth story receives almost twice as much space as that of John the Baptist; (2) two prophetic responses follow Jesus' presentation in the temple (that of Simeon in 2.22-35 and that of Anna in 2.36-38) compared to one for John the Baptist (that of Zechariah in 1.67-79); (3) the bulk of narrative attention is given to Mary versus Elizabeth when the two meet in 1.39-56; (4) Jesus is 'Son of the Most High' but John the Baptist is 'prophet of the Most High' (1.32, 76); and (5) John the Baptist, not Jesus, leaps in the womb when Elizabeth and Mary meet (1.41).[46] This continues in the rhetorical argument of the third speech of the Galilean ministry: Jesus, and now his disciples, is placed in a position

---

44. The sinful woman, who comes to Jesus at the house of Simon the Pharisee in the episode (7.36-50) following the third speech, per the interpretive grid the implied reader constructs, is understood as one of the τέκνα who justifies God.

45. Insinuatio is discussed in *Rhetorica ad Herennium*, 1.6.9–1.6.11; Quintilian, *Institutio Oratoria*, 4.1.42–4.1.50.

46. See Green, *Theology of the Gospel*, p. 54.

above John the Baptist and his disciples (cf. the statement of case in 7.28). Prioritization of Jesus' disciples over John the Baptist is new for the implied reader; coherence continues to form around the characterization of John the Baptist through rhetorical synkrisis.[47]

The third speech provides the implied reader with significant detail that is used to construct meaning around the characterization of John the Baptist and his disciples. Despite the fact that the implied author places Jesus and his disciples above John the Baptist and his disciples, the overarching characterization of both John the Baptist and his disciples is positive. Expansion of Jesus' ministry to a larger geographical, ethnographical, and social matrix prompts the inquiry; evidence that John the Baptist and his disciples associate Jesus' ministry and message with the awaited Messiah. In particular, correspondence between Jesus and Elijah and Elisha by means of the two preceding scenes (7.1-10; 7.11-17) elicits the questioning from John, an alignment between the ideological locations of the implied author and John the Baptist and his disciples. The questioning serves as an interpretive framework for other characters and character groups in the narrative that approach Jesus and then his disciples: Zacchaeus (Lk. 19.1-10), Gamaliel (Acts 5.33-42), the Ethiopian eunuch (Acts 8.26-39), the initial response from the Jews of Antioch of Pisidia (Acts 13.13-43), the Jerusalem Council (Acts 15.1-29), Lydia (Acts 16.11-15), the Jews of Beroea (Acts 17.10-12), the Athenians (Acts 17.16-34), among others. The ripostes to the first two questions that Jesus poses to the crowd about John the Baptist are ironic: the descriptions of John the Baptist are the very opposite of what the implied reader knows about him based on the preceding narrative. The ethos and logos of John the Baptist is unwavering (e.g., he was sent to prison for his condemnation of Herod; cf. 3.18-20) and his message runs counter to the lifestyle of the wealthy (viz., those who would clothe themselves in 'soft clothing'; cf. 3.7-14). As a result, though the implied author does not include a response from the crowd to Jesus' initial two queries, the implied reader fills the narrative 'gap' with a definitive 'no' in both instances.

2. *Characterization of Jesus*
In contrast to the first speech, Christological ramifications of Jesus' characterization are largely not in purview in the case of the third speech, though the first and third speeches are intertwined with the answer Jesus gives to the disciples of John the Baptist (7.22-23; cf. 4.18-19). This answer is actually at the heart of Jesus' characterization in the speech: the accusations Jesus notes are being cited against him (7.34) parallel the answer he gave to the disciples of John the Baptist (7.21-22), which hearkens back to the introduction of the first speech (4.18-19). Jesus is not an ascetic, a trait

---

47.   The implied author pays significant attention to John the Baptist throughout both Luke and Acts: the synkrisis of Jesus and John the Baptist (Lk. 1.5–2.52; 3.1-20; 7.29-30; Acts 13.24-25) and that of their disciples (Acts 18.25; 19.1-4) is always in the foreground of the narrative discourse.

associated with John the Baptist, but embraces a ministry that brings relief to those on the social and religious margins. The other aspect of Jesus' characterization was discussed above: the rhetorical argumentation of the speech places Jesus and his disciples above John the Baptist and his disciples.

3. *Characterization of the Pharisees and Lawyers*

Prior narrative represents the Pharisees and lawyers as opposing Jesus' words and ministry (5.17-26, 27-32, 33-39; 6.1-5, 6-11). The narrative aside (7.29-30) discloses to the implied reader that their opposition even extends to John the Baptist and his disciples. The rhetorical construction of the speech, specifically the conclusion (7.35), prompts the implied reader to equate tax collectors and sinners with the children (τέκνα) of God, and the Pharisees and lawyers, at least in the context of the narrative discourse until this point, as not children of God. Just as the Pharisees and lawyers oppose Jesus in prior episodes because of his embrace of those from the social and religious margin and repudiation of Jewish legal traditions, the rhetorical argument of the body (7.31-34) prods the implied reader to associate those who reject Jesus and John the Baptist (i.e., announce that John the Baptist has a demon and that Jesus is a glutton and drunkard) with the Pharisees and lawyers. Regardless, despite the fact that the Pharisees and lawyers are lumped together in the third speech, the implied author seems to distinguish between the two groups, with distinct characterization for both; specifically, Jesus' pronounced remonstration addresses the Pharisees (11.37-42) and the lawyers (11.45-52) separately. The characterization of the lawyers is closed for the implied reader,[48] whereas the characterization of the Pharisees contains possible 'cracks', particularly the few who are named by the implied author: Simon the Pharisee (7.36-50), Joseph of Arimathea (Lk. 23.50-56), and Gamaliel (Acts 5.33-42).

The body (7.31-34) establishes a topos – stereotypical behavior for those who oppose Jesus – that extends to the end of Acts. In particular, scattered throughout the narrative discourse are episodes where interlocutors – primarily comprised of the Pharisees – attempt to push Jesus to embrace their ideological systems (or at least 'confirm' his ideological system) or to entrap him in situations where he is in violation of those systems. As the narrative progresses, their attempts to entrap Jesus grow while their interest in persuading him to embrace their position diminishes. Here the narrative takes on allegorical meaning for the implied reader: Jesus' – and to a lesser extent John the Baptist's – rejection of traditional social and religious beliefs corresponds with the refusal of the παιδία to dance and weep.

---

48. Νομικός ('lawyer') appears in a few instances in Luke (and not at all in Acts) and, in all instances, in a very negative light (5.17-26; 7.29-30; 10.25-37; 11.45-52; 14.1-24).

4. *Characterization of All the People and the Tax Collectors*

'All the people and tax collectors', through the use of δικαιόω in 7.29 and 7.35 (an inclusio), stand in contrast to the 'Pharisees and lawyers' (cf. 7.29 and 7.35). In particular, the people and tax collectors are an open-ended, ambiguous designation that enables the implied reader to associate characters and character groups who arise in the narrative as 'children of God'. The implied reader, familiar with the story of the Israelite people as contained in Exodus and Deuteronomy, the source for the intertextual echo 'members of this generation' (Exod. 32.9; 33.3, 5; Deut. 10.16), knows that not all the 'members of this generation' were considered as faithless and that the journey of faith was ongoing. Hence, the implied reader views πᾶς ὁ λαός ('all the people') as an open referent. This rhetorical tactic allows the implied author to present characters and character groups that exhibit varying degrees of faithfulness and that coincide with the various taxonomic sowing categories presented in the final speech of the Galilean ministry (8.4-18).

C. *Narrative Trajectories Engender Topoi*

The rhetorical situation of the third speech is established by the questioning from John the Baptist and his disciples about Jesus' ethos and Jesus' response to the inquiry. The rhetorical situation not only builds upon the two previous narrative summaries of Jesus' ministry in 4.18-19 and 6.17-19 but actual incidents where benefaction has become a reality in Jesus' ministry (and will become in terms of proleptic connections): cleansing of the unclean and demonic possessed (4.31-37; 5.12-16), healing of the sick (4.38-39, 40-42; 5.17-26; 6.6-11; 7.1-10), and resurrection of the dead (7.11-17).[49] When the content from the narrative summaries is combined, it forms an intertextual matrix with the LXX from which the implied reader deduces a constellation of stereotypical characters: entities on the outer edges of social and religious systems.[50] As a result, the implied reader does not construe Jesus' benefaction to different characters throughout the narrative as individual acts but rather as part of a larger topos: Jesus delivers benefaction to characters and character groups on the social and religious margin (viz., viewed by the implied reader and narrative audience as shameful) to bring them back within the parameters of honor.

The final part of Jesus' response to the inquiry from John the Baptist and his disciples posits another topos (7.23: 'And blessed is the one who takes no offense at me.'): characters and character groups are defined by the narrative discourse by means of their response to Jesus and then the Christian movement. This is evident in various instances, places where the implied author withholds definitive judgment about certain characters or

---

49. There is a progression in the miraculous benefaction of Jesus prior to the third speech, with the incident involving the raising of the widow's son at Nain (7.11-17) as the final episode before the amplified chreia (7.18-23) preceding the speech.

50. See Roth, *Character Types*, pp. 95–141.

character groups because they refrain from renouncing Jesus or his disciples. Several of the more notable examples include Jesus' instructions to the seventy-two disciples (Lk. 10.1-12), Gamaliel (Acts 5.33-42); Gallio, the proconsul of Achaia (Acts 18.12-17), and Agrippa and Bernice (Acts 25.13–26.32).

VI. *The Fourth Galilean Ministry Speech*

The Marcan version of the final speech in the Galilean ministry (8.4-18) has received significant attention concerning its rhetorical texture and narrative that shows it to be a pivotal element in the narrative discourse, providing an interpretive matrix from which the implied reader construes characterization.[51] This study demonstrates that it serves a similar function in the narrative discourse of Luke-Acts: it builds upon earlier character grids found primarily in Jesus' three earlier speeches and delineates four distinct character taxonomies based on the four sowing activities. The topos of the speech focuses on action (ποιέω) and the outcomes of that action (καρπός).

A. *Constructing Meaning from the Rhetorical Texture*

A significant amount of contextual information is supplied by the implied author in the speech. Jesus continues to attract growing crowds of curious followers, per comments from the narrator prior to the speech (8.4), an entity that is larger in mass than the one that assembled for the second speech (6.17-19). In terms of rhetorical context, benefaction is at the forefront by means of the preceding episode at the house of Simon the Pharisee (7.36-50) and the transition summary (8.1-3). The sinful woman, in lieu of the hospitality expected of Simon as a host, shows hospitality in the lavishness of her actions[52] and receives salvific benefaction from Jesus in return. The women disciples, who were traveling with Jesus and the twelve apostles and had received healing benefaction from Jesus, provide material benefaction to Jesus and the twelve apostles. Both instances corroborate the topos established earlier in the second speech of the Galilean ministry: benefaction is to be given without expectation of reciprocity.

The implied author employs a rhetorical style of repetition, which accentuates 'hearing' as the thematic center to the speech, though the rhetorical texture denotes that disciples must go enact what they hear in order to exhibit authentic discipleship. The different taxonomies in the

51. Especially, Tolbert, *Sowing the Gospel*, 148–63; eadem, 'Builds Character', pp. 347–57.

52. The initial reaction of the implied reader and narrative audience is the same concerning the actions of the sinful women: she shamelessly exhibits sexual advances towards Jesus by taking down her hair and then fondling his feet (see, e.g., Kathleen E. Corley, *Private Women, Public Meals: Social Conflict in the Synoptic Tradition* [Peabody, Mass.: Hendrickson Publishers, 1993], pp. 124–25; Green, *Gospel of Luke*, pp. 305–15).

speech draw upon detail on the disposition and actions of disciples previously delineated in the second speech (6.20-49), which serve as an interpretive framework for the implied reader in the evaluation of characters and character groups per the four character taxonomies.

The speech's introduction (8.5-8a) consists of a parabolic example rooted in agrarian culture. Its lack of attention to details of planting and tilling is an indication to the implied reader that the aim of the sowing process centers on the outcome of the activity. The introduction abounds in repetition that climaxes with the fourth example, which employs homoeoteleuton for added emphasis. Repetition serves to accentuate the different consequences of the sowing activity that is represented by the four prepositions παρά, ἐπί, ἐν μέσῳ, and εἰς. The first three sowing instances fail to penetrate the surface of the soil, which likely contributes to their failure to produce fruit, whereas the fourth penetrates the soil, undergoes maturation, and ultimately produces a substantive crop. As the production of καρπός is a process that occurs over a period of time, the implied reader also construes discipleship as a process of maturation and growth.[53]

Intrusion by the narrator following the fourth instance of sowing (8.8b) heightens the importance of Jesus' final instruction. The narrative aside – ὁ ἔχων ὦτα ἀκούειν ἀκουέτω – forms a rhetorical bridge to the second Galilean ministry speech (particularly its conclusion – 6.46-49) through the verb ἀκούω. The implied author leaves the identity of the disciples who approach Jesus following the parable open-ended (8.9-10). This ambiguity coincides with other instances in the Lukan narrative where the identity of certain characters is left open and serves as a rhetorical prompter: the implied reader must ascertain which characters and character groups qualify as disciples and which ones do not qualify, with the fourth speech serving as the interpretive key. The intertextual citation by Jesus in the statement of case (Isa. 6.9-10 in 8.10), which forms part of his response to the inquiring disciples, elicits an intratextual connection to the Lukan prologue (1.4) in the form of συνίζω. As a result, the implied reader deduces that Jesus' message (and the 'kingdom of God') is only understandable to those who 'interpret' (συνίζω) it.[54] For those who fail to enact the interpretive process, the message of Jesus remains a 'mystery' (μυστήριον).

Like the introduction (8.5-8a), the body of the speech (8.11-15) does not focus on the types of soil but on the outcomes of sowing. This is evident in several ways. First, deviation in the parallel construction of the four periods

---

53. This coincides with conversion in Greco-Roman antiquity (e.g., Thomas M. Finn, *From Death to Rebirth: Ritual and Conversion in Antiquity* [New York: Paulist Press, 1997], *passim*). As argued by Charles H. Talbert ('Conversion in the Acts of the Apostles: Ancient Auditors' Perceptions', in *Literary Studies*, pp. 141–53), conversion in Luke-Acts is both moral and cognitive.

54. Moessner ('Appeal and Power', p. 108) contends that Apollos' accurate (καθεξῆς) interpretation of the Christian message (Acts 18.24–19.7) 'prefigures a Theophilus, Luke's readers, who must follow the two-volume narrative καθεξῆς to gain the firmer grasp of the Way of the Lord'.

in the fourth example serves to accentuate its rhetorical impact to the implied reader: the demonstrative pronoun (οἷτος), which is used in the first three examples (8.11-14), falls from use in the final example (8.15). Second, rhetorical repetition of ἀκούω in all four examples underscores the topos of the statement of case: an appropriate understanding of the kingdom of God, and thus Jesus' message, must go beyond hearing to interpretation. Third, deductive activity on the part of the implied reader is culled by the implied author through intratextual connections: the first and second sowing examples (8.5-6, 12-13) echo the episode of Jesus' temptation with the devil in 4.1-13. Based on the intratextual echo, the implied reader concludes that the devil tempts Jesus' disciples just as he tempted Jesus, yet the disciples lack Jesus' faith and fail to spurn the seduction of the devil. Finally, sequential maturation of faith is evident in the teleological progression of each example, including full maturation in the last sowing instance.[55]

Repetition of elements of the statement of case (8.9-10) in the speech's conclusion prompts the implied reader and the narrative audience to connect 'the secrets of the kingdom of God' with the 'fruit' produced in the fourth sowing example. This intratextual intertwining of the statement of case and the conclusion also places hearing and understanding in the foreground for the implied reader. The first two metaphors Jesus cites in the conclusion are enthymemes, both of which are linked through their use of φανερός. By means of the rhetorical argument, the absurdity of concealing a lamp within a house is the corollary of hearing Jesus' message and not bringing it to full maturation, the implied reader concludes that disciples are compelled to embody a disposition and actions representative of Jesus' message. The final metaphor heightens the relationship between the integrated relationship between hearing, interpretation, and action: interpretation helps ensure genuine hearing and facilitates action.

B. *Narrative Trajectories Engender Characterization*

The Parable of the Sower (Mk 4.1-20) is an essential ingredient in the construction of characterization in Mark. Character types in Mark roughly correspond with the four different taxonomies of soil.[56] The speech remains pivotal to Lukan characterization, though with some differences. Specifically, redactional activity by the Lukan implied author changes the rhetorical focus to the resulting activities ('fruit') of the four taxonomies versus a concentration on the actual 'seed' in the Marcan narrative. Disinterest (and even misrepresentation) in the sowing process in Luke is possible corroboration of this redactional element. Subsequent episodes in the narrative provide additional fodder for this emphasis on results (καρπός). One such instance is the Parable of the Barren Fig Tree (Lk. 13.6-9), where the production of 'fruit' is established as the discerning

55.   The emphasis on teleological progression in Luke is underscored further by means of a redactional comparison of Luke and Mark.

56.   Tolbert, *Sowing*, pp. 148–63; eadem, 'Builds Character', pp. 347–57.

measurement. Characters and character groups that correspond with the first three sowing examples and then the final sowing example break into two groups: those who fail to see (βλέπω) and understand (συνίζω) fall into one of the first three character taxonomies, while those who see and understand fall into the final character taxonomy (8.9-10).

The speech initiates analeptic as well as proleptic activity: the implied reader examines characters and character groups from prior narrative and then following narrative by means of these newly introduced character taxonomies. In particular, as the narrative progresses, the reading activity becomes more and more retrospective for the implied reader: characters and character groups from earlier in the narrative are reevaluated based on new characters and character groups.[57]

1. The First Sowing Example: Sowing Along the Path
The first sowing example depicts a situation where the seed does not even sprout. Imagery in the introduction and the body of the speech attributes the failure to the devil. The Lukan narrative is replete with examples where the devil prompts action not representative of Jesus' message and ministry. Individuals and groups include Herod the tetrarch (Lk. 3.19-20; 9.7-9), those who fail to show benefaction to Jesus' disciples (Lk. 10.10-15), the priest and Levite from the Parable of the Good Samaritan (Lk. 10.25-37), Sadducees and temple leaders (Lk. 20.20-47; 22.47–23.25; Acts 4.1-22; 5.17-42; 6.8–8.1; 22.30–23.35; 24.1-9; 25.1-12), Jewish opposition in Acts (9.23-24; 12.1-5; 13.44-52; 14.1-7; 14.19-20; 17.1-9, 10-15; 18.12-17; 20.3; 21.27-36; 24.9; 25.27; 25.1-12); the Jewish false prophet Bar-Jesus (Elymas, the magician; Acts 13.4-12, the seven sons of Sceva (Acts 19.11-20), Demetrius, the silversmith, and his fellow Ephesian craftworkers (Acts 19.23-41), and the high priest Ananias (Acts 24.1-8). There are some overarching attributes of this character taxonomy that the implied reader constructs from the narrative discourse. Foremost is that many of the characters and character groups exhibit animosity towards Jesus or his followers. This ranges from rhetorical challenges to actual infliction of physical harm – even death. At the same time, there is a topos connected to the characterization of these individuals that traces a journey ending in spiritual – and even physical – condemnation. Specifically, while those who actively oppose Jesus and his followers initially escape spiritual and physical punishment, they ultimately face apocalyptic judgment. The characterization of Herod is one such instance. His social and political standing remains unaffected, if not grows in stature, despite his imprisonment and murder of John the Baptist (Lk. 3.19-20; 9.7-9), implication in Jesus' trial (Lk. 23.6-12), and murder of James

---

57. See Stephen Halliwell, 'Traditional Greek Conceptions of Character', in Christopher Pelling (ed.), *Characterization and Individuality in Greek Literature* (Oxford: Clarendon Press, 1990), pp. 32–59; Christopher Gill, 'The Question of Character and Personality in Greek Tragedy', *Poetics Today* 7 (1986), pp. 251–73.

and arrest of Peter (Acts 12.1-5). Indeed, immediately before he is smitten by God he ostensibly ascends to the apex of social and political success (Acts 12.20-23).

2. *The Second Sowing Example: Sowing on the Rock*

Growth progresses further with the second sowing example: the seed germinates but withers away due to the lack of moisture. The devil, though not mentioned by name, remains in purview for the implied reader through the use of intratextual irony: the use of πειρασμός in the introduction and body (8.6, 13) mirrors its earlier use in the temptation episode between Jesus and the devil (4.2, 12-13). However, Jesus, unlike the characters and character groups represented by this taxonomy, does not succumb to the devil's temptation (πειρασμός). Though initially embodied by enthusiastic reception (viz., the sowing activity was received with χαρίς), the ultimate failure of the seed to produce καρπός ('fruit') revolves around two related issues: 'lack of moisture' (8.6) and failure to 'take root' (8.13). Analeptic processing by the implied reader pinpoints one character group as exhibiting the character traits of the second example: Jesus' hometown synagogue crowd initially gives him a positive reception but then violently rejects him because of the threat his message poses to their positions of honor (Lk. 4.28-30). Except for the tragic betrayal of Jesus by the disciples – particularly Judas and Peter (Lk. 22.31-34, 47-53, 54-62) – additional characters and character groups that the implied reader associates with the second taxonomy do not appear in the narrative until Acts. Simon the Magician (8.4-24) is the first character in Acts who exhibits the traits of the second sowing example. His succumbing to temptation centers on his desire for spiritual honor and his fallacious thinking that spiritual honor could be purchased. The mercurial actions of the Lycaonian crowd (ὄχλος) also resembles the second character taxonomy (Acts 14.8-20): ranging from their initial reaction in which they identify Paul and Barnabas as Greek gods, to an emphatic attempt to offer sacrifice to them (even after Paul's response to their initial reaction), to utter rejection and an attempt to kill (which they thought was successful; cf. v. 19d) both Paul and Barnabas (upon being persuaded by Jews from Antioch and Iconium).

3. *The Third Sowing Example: Sowing Among the Thorns*

Progression towards the bearing of fruit continues with the third sowing example, where fruit is produced but does not ripen. The impetus for the failure of those embodying the traits of this sowing activity involves the desire for honor in the form of wealth and, in particular, the ability to achieve honor through its possession (8.14). Through associative accumulation the implied reader determines that characters and character groups who represent this sowing activity conform with the rhetorical dimension of tragedy: the rich fool (Lk. 12.13-21), the rich man (in the Parable of the Rich Man and Lazarus – Lk. 16.19-31), the rich ruler (Lk. 18.18-30), Ananias and Sapphira (Acts 5.1-11), the disciples of Antioch (Acts 11.27-30), and the owners of the slave girl (Acts 16.16-24). The antithesis of this sowing type is exemplified in a number of instances in the narrative through characters or character groups who abandon positions of honor in exchange for embracing the word of God. Analeptic examples include Levi (5.27-32), the centurion with an ill servant (7.1-10), and the women followers of Jesus (8.1-3). Proleptic association places others such as the Good Samaritan (Lk. 10.25-37), Martha (Lk. 10.38-42), Zacchaeus (Lk. 19.1-10), the widow in the temple (Lk. 21.1-4), the early Christian community in Jerusalem (Acts 2.43-47; 4.32-37; 6.1-6), Barnabas (Acts 4.32-37), Tabitha (Acts 9.36-43), the disciples of Antioch (Acts 11.27-30), Lydia (Acts 16.11-15), the Philippian jailor (Acts 16.25-40), and Publius and the inhabitants of Malta (Acts 28.7-10) into the third character taxonomy as well. A topos that comes to the forefront in the comparison of these antithetical types is that characters whom the implied reader classifies as representing the third character taxonomy use possessions as a means to secure honor for themselves (or their social, political, religious groups), whereas those opposite the character taxonomy use possessions to confer honor upon those lacking honor as a result of their lack of possessions.

4. The Fourth Sowing Example: Sowing into the Good Soil
The final sowing activity focuses the implied reader on the production of 'fruit' (καρπός), a process that occurs over a period of time with an exerted effort in order for the maturation to reach completion. The emphasis on this topos by the implied author is corroborated by two redactions. The first is the deletion of the Markan threefold yield (4.8) to the highest yield ('hundredfold') in Luke (8.15). The second is the addition of the adjectival preposition ἐν ὑπομονῇ and the modification of παραδέχομαι to κατέχω (Lk. 8.15; cf. Mk 4.8), which serves to underline the need for enduring faith. While the implied reader is not cognizant of the redactional activity of the implied author, the implied reader does ascertain the rhetorical results: an emphasis on persevering discipleship.

Characters and character groups the implied reader associates with the fourth character taxonomy encompass a broad canvas of the Lukan narrative discourse. The foremost characters in Luke are God and Jesus: the former exhibits everlasting, compassionate love for humankind throughout history and the latter shows unwavering endurance unto death. This mode of characterization continues in Acts. Like the characterization of God and Jesus, characterization of the Holy Spirit as the conduit for the divine to humankind also bridges both volumes.[58]

Luke is replete with character examples of the fourth character taxonomy. Analeptic referents include the Jewish actors in the birth narratives (Zechariah, Elizabeth, Mary, Simeon, and Anna in Lk. 1.5–2.38), John the Baptist (Lk. 3.1-20; 7.18-35), the twelve disciples, as represented by Simon Peter, John, and James (Lk. 5.1-11; 22.31-34, 47-62), the friends of

58. Cf. Shepherd, *Holy Spirit*; Hur, *Dynamic Reading*.

the paralytic (Lk. 5.17-26), and the sinful woman who approaches Jesus at the house of Simon the Pharisee (Lk. 7.36-50). Proleptic referents include the menstruating woman (Lk. 8.42c-48), the Good Samaritan (Lk. 10.25-37), the dishonest steward (Lk. 16.1-13), the widow in the Parable of the Widow and Judge (Lk. 18.1-8), the blind beggar from Jericho (Lk. 18.35-43), Zacchaeus (Lk. 19.1-10), and the faithful servants in the Parable of the Ten Pounds (Lk. 19.11-27). Leading protagonists in the narrative discourse of Acts include the twelve disciples, as represented by Simon Peter, John, and James, and other leaders such as Stephen, Barnabas, Philip, and Paul and his companions. Lesser characters in the narrative of Acts also coincide with the final sowing taxonomy, which include the early Christian community in Jerusalem (2.41-47; 4.32-37), the Ethiopian eunuch (8.26-40), Ananias (9.10-19), Tabitha (9.36-43), Cornelius (10.1-48), Rhoda (12.12-17), Lydia (16.11-15), the Philippian jailor (16.25-40), the Beroean Jews (17.10-15), Dionysius the Areopagite and Damaris the Athenian (17.16-34), Apollos (18.24-28; 19.1-7), Aquila and Priscilla (18.1-4, 24-28), the Ephesian church (19.1-41; 20.17-38), and Julius the centurion (27.1-3, 30-44).

Several character groups exemplifying the fourth character taxonomy receive enhanced attention in the narrative discourse. The result is the implied reader, through the rhetorical activity of synkrisis, associates the disposition and actions of these characters with other characters of the same character type. One instance is the faith of the twelve disciples, as largely exemplified through Simon Peter, John, and James, ranging from their initial calling (Lk. 5.1-11), to pronouncements of faith (Lk. 9.28-36), to denunciation (Lk. 22.31-34, 47-62), to reconciliation (Lk. 24.12-53), to reconstitution (Acts 1.3-26), to continued discipleship (Acts 2.1-6.6; 9.32-12.17; 15.1-29). As a result, the implied reader understands discipleship within this more detailed contextual framework as a journey and not something that occurs at one point in time.

Journeying forms an important topos in both Luke and Acts and assumes allegorical meaning for the implied reader: it represents both the physical journey (in the case of Jesus in Lk. 9.51–19.44 and in the case of Paul and his companions in Acts 13.1–14.28, 16.1–21.16, and 23.12–28.16) as well as the spiritual journey of discipleship.[59] Naturally, it is not a mere coincidence that the Christian movement is designated as 'the Way' (ὁδός) in Acts (9.2; 19.9, 23; 22.4; 24.14, 22). The narrative discourse utilizes several character examples to demonstrate the importance of discipleship as a journey rather than a destination. One instance is the failure of John, the one called Mark, to complete the initial Gentile missionary journey. The implied reader construes his actions as exemplifying traits of the third character taxonomy

---

59. See James L. Resseguie, *Spiritual Landscape: Images of the Spiritual Life in the Gospel of Luke* (Peabody, Mass.: Hendrickson Publishers, 2004), pp. 29–43; Paul Borgman, *The Way according to Luke: Hearing the Whole Story of Luke-Acts* (Grand Rapids: William B. Eerdmans Publishing Company, 2006), *passim*; Green, *Theology of the Gospel*, pp. 102–9.

(Acts 13.5c; 15.36-41).[60] Characterization of Eutychus, who falls asleep and drops from the third-story window, symbolically, through antithesis, represents the importance of persistent discipleship and the dangers of failing to sustain enduring discipleship (Acts 20.7-12).[61]

Another case where this mode of characterization receives elaboration is that of the women disciples (Lk. 8.1-3; 10.38-42; 23.27, 49, 55; 24.1-11). The narrative transition in Lk. 8.1-3 places women as benefactors who symbolically help make the 'journey' topos possible. The women disciples reappear at the end of the narrative in Luke, where they stand in contrast, on the one hand, to the crowds and multitudes who initially embrace Jesus and his message but ultimately reject him in favor of Barabbas (Lk. 23.18-25)[62] and, on the other hand, to the disciples who reject Jesus upon his arrest. Indeed, the narrator reveals to the implied reader that the women benefactors in 8.1-3 followed Jesus all of the way to the crucifixion (from Galilee; cf. 23.49), a notation that certainly stands out to the implied reader as a model of true discipleship. Following Jesus' death and burial, the characterization of the women disciples is juxtaposed against the male disciples: the women demonstrate 'interpretation' representative of 'true' disciples (8.10) by understanding the meaning of the 'empty tomb' (cf. 24.8), whereas the men do not believe and dismiss the report based on cultural systems opposed to women as reliable witnesses (cf. 24.11). The positive portrayal of women followers continues in Acts through disciples such as Tabitha (9.36-43), Rhoda (12.12-17), Lydia (16.11-15), the Athenian Damaris (17.34), and Priscilla (18.24-28).

C. *Narrative Trajectories Engender Topoi*

The growing size of the crowds seeking to hear Jesus teach and to receive healing from him, the largest to gather before Jesus at this point of the narrative, forms the rhetorical situation for the speech. The rhetorical argument of the speech supplies the implied reader with an interpretive framework for discerning characteristics of 'true' disciples and those who fail to embody those characteristics. This dampens the perceived momentum of Jesus' ministry for the implied reader, who, through analeptic interpretation recognizes that many of the characters encountered thus far in the narrative coincide with one of the first three character types rather than the fourth sowing category. The fourth speech is rich in topoi that either directly

---

60. For a discussion of John Mark's characterization, see C. Clifton Black, 'John Mark in the Acts of the Apostles', in *Literary Studies*, pp. 101–20.

61. The implied reader likely identifies an intratextual link to Jesus' admonition to the sleeping disciples in Lk. 23.46: Eutychus, like the disciples before Jesus' arrest, engenders danger by falling asleep (which allegorically alludes to a failure to demonstrate enduring discipleship).

62. Through extratextual repertoire the actions of the crowds and multitudes likely take on a secondary, allegorical meaning for the implied reader. They represent the eventual demise of Jerusalem and those who rebelled against the authority of Rome (cf. Lk. 21.10-36).

derive from the attributes of the four character taxonomies or are constructed indirectly by the implied reader by means of synkrisis (comparison and contrast). As many of these were discussed in detail in the above discussion, only a short overview is needed.

1. *Maturation, Production of Fruit, and the Importance of 'Doing'*

Perhaps the most evident topos is the emphasis on the actual production of fruit. Correct interpretation is not simply an intellectual exercise but a lasting journey, one that results in a bountiful harvest. Characters and character groups from the fourth character taxonomy serve as the basis for helping the implied reader to define this topos. The characteristics of this character stereotype include willingness to use positions of honor to bestow honor upon others. In particular, there is significant emphasis on the use of material possessions to discharge honor. This topos appears as early as John the Baptist's preaching in Lk. 3.1-14, where he exhorts the multitudes to use their possessions to bestow honor on those who are lacking possessions (and thus honor), and it remains as a pertinent part of Jesus' preaching and ministry in Luke and then the preaching and ministry of the early church in Acts. In contrast, those who fail to use their positions of honor (or possessions) to empower others are not considered as 'true' disciples and correspond with the third character taxonomy.

2. *Condemnation of and Triumph over Divination and Magic*

An underlying topos connected to the use of honor enters the narrative once the story turns towards the Gentile mission in Acts: divination and magic are embraced as modes of social and spiritual elevation, frequently at the loss of honor as regards to gender, spiritual, and social standing. Characters and character groups that fit this construct are not only Gentiles but Jews as well. Disciples triumph when facing characters that enact divination and magic as modes of social and spiritual elevation and often administer punishment upon these same individuals. Some of the most notable examples include Bar-Jesus, the Jewish false prophet and magician serving Proconsul Sergius Paulus (Acts 13.4-12), the owners of the divining slave girl at Philippi (Acts 16.16-24), and the sons of Sceva (Acts 19.11-20).[63]

3. *Repudiation and Persecution Results in Apocalyptic Condemnation*

Eventual apocalyptic demise for those who repudiate and persecute true disciples forms a topos that extends from Luke to Acts. Characters and character groups that coincide with this stereotype, despite possessing social, religious, and political power, exhibit the most egregious failures around the misuse of honor in the Lukan narrative. Examples include Herod the tetrarch (Acts 12.20-24), the temple authorities as represented by

---

63. See Susan R. Garrett, *The Demise of the Devil: Magic and the Demonic in Luke's Writings* (Minneapolis: Augsburg/Fortress Press, 1989).

the chief priest, priests, scribes, and Sadducees (extratextual repertoire = annihilation with the destruction of Jerusalem in 70 CE – Lk. 21.5-36), and the seven sons of Sceva (Acts 19.11-20).

The narrative discourse also steers the implied reader to rhetorical irony: the persecution inflicted by these characters on disciples, rather than quelling spiritual formation and growth, generates renewed success and expansion. Examples include the attempt by Jesus' hometown synagogue to kill him and the immediate success he achieves in Capernaum afterwards (Lk. 4.14-30; cf. 4.37); condemnation of the scribes and Pharisees and their plotting against Jesus (Lk. 11.37-54; cf. 12.1); arrest of the apostles, their release, and the ensuing growth of believers (Acts 4.1-31; cf. 4.32-37); the arrest of the apostles in the next episode followed with their miraculous escape from prison (Acts 5.17-40; cf. 5.41-42 and 6.7); the stoning of Stephen and the spread of Christianity to Samaria (Acts 7.54-8.3; cf. 8.4-8, 25); the murder of James, the brother of John, the imprisonment of Peter, and the death of Herod (Acts 12.1-23; cf. 12.24); and the persecution of Paul and his companions during their ministry and preaching (Acts 13.48-52; 14.19-20; 19.8-10, 11-20).[64]

4. *Discipleship and the 'Heart' (*Καρδία*)*

The fourth sowing example culls an earlier topos from the second speech (8.15; cf. 6.45): the connection between καρδία ('heart') and discipleship. In the case of the fourth speech, the topos, by means of the body of argument, is used as an ascription to the fourth character taxonomy. Connections with the second speech, where the implied reader associates those who possess 'good hearts' with fruit-producing fig trees and grape vines (versus association of those who possess 'evil hearts' with non-fruit producing thorn bushes and bramble bushes), and the fourth speech highlights the topos of a bountiful, ongoing harvest, which, by means of the fourth sowing example, is associated with the actions of a 'true' disciple.

VII. *Concluding Summary*

The preceding analysis demonstrates how the rhetorical texture of Jesus' four Galilean ministry speeches plays a pivotal role in the construction of plot, characterization, and topoi – both analeptically and proleptically – in Luke-Acts. Rhetorical texture generates narrative trajectories, helps to shape the narrative discourse, and steers the implied reader in the construction of meaning.

The four speeches also form the basis for much of the overarching narrative discourse of Luke-Acts. Coinciding with the nature of Greco-

---

64. See O. Wesley Allen, *The Death of Herod: The Narrative and Theological Function of Retribution in Luke-Acts* (SBLDS, 158; Atlanta: Scholars Press, 1997), who argues that the death of Herod, a tyrant, forms a topos in Luke-Acts, one that derives from Greco-Roman narrative type scenes.

Roman narrative, plot and topoi establish the parameters for the implied reader's construction of characterization. In particular, the implied reader's identification of plot and topoi is propelled by the rhetorical texture of the four speeches. Likewise, the interpretive framework for constructing characterization and evaluating characters and character groups also arises from the rhetorical texture of the four speeches.

CHAPTER 9: HERMENEUTICAL APPROPRIATION BY AUTHORIAL
READERS AND THEIR IDEOLOGICAL TRANSFORMATION

Interest in readers over the past decade by an increasing number of scholars in the field of biblical studies marks an important transition: movement from a formalistic hermeneutic to a much more dynamic, integrated hermeneutic. The former approach focuses on textual configurations, whereas the latter approach is interested in ideological systems and how these shape author, discourse, and readers. Of course, there are potential deficiencies with this directional change, including the risk of having the 'the baby thrown out with the bath water' by means of the utilization of various forms of post-structural and ideological criticisms that examine texts with little or no concern for intra-, inter-, and extratextual parameters.[1] On the contrary, as argued in Chapter two, an ethical hermeneutic constrains real readers to understand the interpretive obligations that exist between implied authors and implied readers.[2] It also compels real readers to ascertain how the narrative discourse both coincides with and runs counter to ideological systems.[3] The interpretive approach in this study aims not only to examine narrative texture as it relates to plot, theme, characterization, and topoi but to understand how these narrative elements define a discourse that both corresponds with as well as differs from existing ideological constructs of the implied reader. This hermeneutical endeavor moves beyond simply *reading with* to *critical reading* or even *reading against* – the three modes of reading as conduction (as discussed in Chapter two).[4]

A significant gap in the investigation of biblical texts also exists in the attention given to initial flesh-and-blood readers, not only in regard to their ideological locations but even more so to how their ideological locations affect appropriation of narrative discourse. Using the construct of the authorial audience, this study aims to beyond a one-dimensional textual

1. See, e.g., Kevin J. Vanhoozer, *Is There a Meaning in This Text? The Bible, the Reader, and the Morality of Literary Knowledge* (Grand Rapids: Zondervan Publishing, 1998); idem, 'Reader', pp. 301–28.

2. Booth, *Company We Keep*, esp. pp. 169–200.

3. Wuthnow (*Communities of Discourse*, pp. 1–21) describes this as the 'problem of articulation' – how narrative discourse can both be shaped by its cultural location while managing to disengage from and even challenge that very cultural context in which it was generated. Also, see Freadman and Miller, *Re-Thinking Theory*, pp. 229–33.

4. See Booth, *Company We Keep*, esp. pp. 70–77; idem, 'The Ethics of Forms: Taking Flight with *The Wings of the Dove*', in James Phelan and Peter J. Rabinowitz (eds), *Understanding Narrative* (Berkeley and Los Angeles: University of California Press, 1994), pp. 102–5, for reading as conduction and the threefold delineation.

construct to a multidimensional, living entity comprised of different cultural systems – religious, gender, political, ethnic, and social. As a result, meaning-making dimensions of the text expand as it is examined from the lens of different readerly locations.

I. *Getting from Implied Reader to Authorial Readers*

The contractual agreement between implied authors and implied readers sets the stage for the analysis of authorial readers. The construct 'implied reader' derives from reader-response criticism and as a structure of the text, embodies the various predispositions necessary for a literary work to exercise its effect.[5] While extremely valuable in defining rhetorical texture and the resulting narrative discourse, the implied reader constrains the hermeneutical enterprise, tethering it to the formalstic parameters of author and text. Hence, while the implied reader plays an important role in understanding the various dimensions of the Lukan narrative, a different construct is needed in order to move the discussion to one that aims to understand plausible modes of transformation resulting from the rhetorical effects of narrative discourse.[6]

The authorial audience, the hypothetical audience for which authors rhetorically designed their narratives, is a reading construct that has gained widespread acceptance over the past decade.[7] The authorial audience is multidimensional; narrative – and certainly Greco-Roman narrative – is written for flesh-and-blood readers. Members of the actual audience appropriate the narrative discourse in slightly different ways based on variables in their ideological systems, and, as a result, authorial readers generate different meanings from the same text.[8]

5. See, e.g., Iser, *Implied Reader, passim.*

6. For the limitations of 'implied reader' as a textual construct, see Peter J. Rabinowitz, 'Where We Are When We Read', in *Authorizing Readers*, pp. 1–28, esp. pp. 4–9.

7. First proposed by Rabinowitz ('Truth in Fiction', pp. 121–41; idem, *Before Reading*, esp. pp. 15–42).

8. This does not mean that the authorial audience consists of an infinite mixture of ideological systems. As regards to Greco-Roman narrative, in contrast to modern and post-modern narrative where the authorial audience might consist of an almost infinite number of ideological reading locations, the constructs of author and text constrain meaning by establishing an interpretive community much smaller than those assumed by author and text in modern and post-modern narrative. For example, in the case of Luke-Acts, an authorial reader from the upper reaches of society seems implausible based on the parameters delimited by both the intratextual and extratextual repertoire. Likewise, leaders of rabbinical Judaism, the outgrowth of Pharisaical Judaism, would fall outside of the boundaries of the authorial audience

Nevertheless, simply because potential readers comprising different social, ethnic, religious, and political elements are outside of the parameters of the authorial audience does *not* invalidate a reading from their perspective. As many of these reading positions would oppose the rhetorical strategy of the narrative discourse, a mode of what Booth describes as *reading against* would be necessitated ('Ethics of Forms', pp. 102–5).

In the prior analysis, this study demonstrates how the rhetorical texture of Jesus' four Galilean ministry speeches helps shape the narrative discourse through various trajectories – plot, theme, characterization, and topoi. This chapter moves the interpretive exercise one step further by considering some of the potential ways authorial readers may have appropriated the narrative discourse: how the narrative discourse intersects with their ideological systems – confirming, reinterpreting, and even confronting.

II. *Appropriation by Authorial Readers*

Appropriation of narrative discourse takes place when readers connect the world of the text with their lives: the fictive world of the text is metaphorically transposed into the realm of the imaginary.[9] Authors use ideological conventions, which are shared with the authorial audience, as interpretive protocols. These same ideological conventions are used to provoke transformation on the part of readers, providing the means for the reinforcement or even the modification of social, religious, and political protocols.

A shared convention between author and reader, rhetorical argument consists of ideological systems that not only help guide the authorial audience in making sense of the text but serve as a means for ethical transformation. The narrative discourse compels the authorial audience to construe a fictive world containing systems different than those they embrace, which prompts them to evaluate their social, religious, and political systems. The impetus for driving change occurs in the form of what is described as rhetorical power.[10] In the case of Luke-Acts, the implied author employs deductive and inductive argument based on divine action as a means of rhetorical power. The authorial audience either accepts the ideological location espoused by the narrative or finds itself juxtaposed to the divine.

III. *Identifying Different Authorial Readers*

Some of the fallacies associated with attempts to identify the precise contours of the communities addressed by the implied authors of the four Gospels were summarized in Chapter two. In particular, it was demon-

---

9. Iser, *Fictive and the Imaginary*. Also, see Scholes, *Protocols of Reading*, pp. 89–155; Herman C. Waetjen, 'Social Location and the Hermeneutical Mode of Integration', in Fernando F. Segovia and Mary Ann Tolbert (eds), *Reading from this Place: Social Location and Biblical Interpretation in the United States*, vol. 1 (Minneapolis: Fortress Press, 1995), pp. 75–94.

10. For a discussion of rhetorical power, see Steven Mailloux, *Rhetorical Power* (Ithaca and London: Cornell University Press, 1989), pp. 3–18; Seymour Chatman, *Coming to Terms: The Rhetoric of Narrative in Fiction and Film* (Ithaca and London: Cornell University Press, 1990), pp. 90–108, 184–204.

strated that these attempts are founded on a flawed methodology: it is not possible to postulate a complete correlation between a text and the social group that carries and receives it.[11] Authorial readers of Luke-Acts that fall within the social network of Theophilus and thus cover a broad range of personages: from men and women, to masters and slaves, to patrons and clients, to Gentile and Jew, to political officials and mere residents, to Roman citizens and non-Roman citizens, to varying degrees of wealth and poverty. That said, there is sufficient intratextual and extratextual evidence to identify an audience located in a Hellenistic urban setting and one that likely did not include the upper and lower extremities of society.[12] Reflecting the composition of most Hellenistic urban environments, the authorial audience likely consisted of an ethnic mixture – Jews, Godfearers, and Gentiles. Situated somewhere at the end of the first century CE, and certainly post-70 CE, separation of Jewish Christians from the synagogue, both voluntarily and forcibly, had taken place or was in the process of occurring.[13] The apologetic aim of the narrative, with a primary trajectory aimed at demonstrating the validity of the Christian movement within the Jewish heritage and a lesser offshoot at positioning Christianity within political and social boundaries of honor,[14] implies an authorial audience concerned about the legitimacy of Christianity – particularly its relationship to its Jewish lineage and its standing within Hellenistic culture at large.[15] In addition, the authorial audience, if not Christian, s irrefutably predisposed to the Christian movement. Interpretive protocols include an extratextual

11. This is more so with narrative than with epistolary texts: the latter contain many more rhetorical markers that assist in uncovering the rhetorical situation (cf. Dennis L. Stamps, 'Rethinking the Rhetorical Situation: The Entextualization of the Situation in New Testament Epistles', in *Rhetoric and the New Testament*, pp. 93–210).

12. Attempts to identify a specific Hellenistic city are fruitless (in contrast to Esler, *Community and Gospel*, pp. 25–26). Indeed, the very nature of travel and communication networks between communities, with a specific focus on Christian communities, in Greco-Roman antiquity leaves open the possibility that the authorial audience could have spanned more than one urban setting (see, e.g., Alexander, 'Ancient Book Production', pp. 71–105; Michael B. Thompson, 'The Holy Internet: Communication Between Churches in the First Christian Generation', in *Gospels for All Christians*, pp. 49–70).

13. The debate on the significance of the *Birkat ha-minim* for Jewish Christians and the extent to which it contributed to the separation of Jewish Christians from the synagogue is vast and cannot be resolved in this study. In addition, questions around the evangelistic interest of first-century CE Judaism are extensive, with significant proponents on both sides of the issue. What can be said is that the narrative of Luke-Acts depicts the Jewish opponents of Christianity in a mode of missionary rivalry (cf. Acts 13.48-52; 14.1-7, 19-20; 17.5-9).

14. See, e.g., Alexander, 'Acts of the Apostles', pp. 15–44; Gregory E. Sterling, ' "Athletes of Virtue": An Analysis of the Summaries in Acts (2:41-47; 4:32-35; 5:12-16)', *JBL* 113 (1994), pp. 679–96; idem, *Historiography*, pp. 357–87.

15. However cf. Paul W. Walaskay, *'And So We Came to Rome': The Political Perspective of St. Luke* (Cambridge: Cambridge University Press, 1983), *passim*, who argues that the narrative of Luke-Acts is a pro-Roman apologia targeted at an anti-Roman audience. The deficiencies of his investigation are numerous and have been pinpointed by many.

repertoire consisting of knowledge that the gospel had been preached to Gentiles and to Jews as well as the existence of an intra-communal Jewish debate (in which they may be participants) about the inclusion of Gentiles and the formation of a heterogeneous community.[16] As such, the focus of the narrative is not on *what* happened but *how* it happened.

The authorial audience is multidimensional, with readers of different ideological locations and cultural backgrounds, reflecting various social, gender, ethnic, political, and religious roles that might affect hermeneutical appropriation. In this context, the hermeneutical encounter between the ideological systems of authorial readers and the ideological systems represented by the narrative discourse engenders different modes of appropriation. For example, authorial readers endowed with power because of material possessions versus authorial readers lacking power because of the lack of material possessions each accentuate different meaning-making dimensions of the same text: the narrative discourse prompts discomfort for those with power and wealth, and assurance for those lacking in power and wealth.[17] This study examines the narrative discourse of Luke-Acts, with Jesus' four Galilean ministry speeches in the foreground, from the standpoint of five different reading taxonomies: (1) Gentile, Jew, and Godfearer; (2) men and women; (3) the honored and shamed; (4) the wealthy and poor; and (5) disciples of Jesus and disciples of John the Baptist. It is important to note that these taxonomies are not finite boundaries for all of the plausible locations from which appropriation of the narrative discourse of Luke-Acts can take place. Rather, the taxonomies draw from ideological systems of Greco-Roman antiquity and reflect a construct of the authorial readership.

IV. *Authorial Readers and Ideological Transformation*

Hermeneutical appropriation takes place on a number of different ideological levels: (1) de-familiarization of honor and shame protocols; (2) reshaping of benefaction – namely, extension of salvation to the ends of the earth; (3) expansion of religious and ethnic boundaries; (4) elevation of Jesus and his followers over John the Baptist and his followers; and (5) evaluation of gender and its relationship to the narrative discourse.

A. *Defamiliarization of Honor and Shame Protocols*

Cultural interaction in Greco-Roman antiquity was heavily dependent upon the constructs of honor and shame. Both ascribed and acquired, honor and

---

16. The authorial audience is in a superior position to the implied reader: authorial readers possess prior knowledge (e.g., what happened to Paul versus the open ending of Acts [28.30-31]) not known to the implied reader.

17. However cf. Scholes (*Protocols of Reading*, pp. 104–9) who points out that *identity* and *experience* are not equivalents.

shame determined modes of exchange between individuals. Sensitive to public judgments and reproach, individuals from birth were taught to seek honor and avoid shame. Successful adherence to cultural norms determined honor, and those who spurned cultural norms brought shame upon themselves which even extended to family members and friends.[18] Greco-Roman rhetoric draws upon these cultural codes, using the audience's desire for honor and aversion to shame to achieve rhetorical persuasion.[19]

1. *Honor and Shame and the Narrative Discourse of the First Galilean Ministry Speech*

The first speech of the Galilean ministry presents a construct at odds with common cultural frameworks: Jesus' failure to show benefaction to his hometown synagogue, in contrast to the benefaction he doled out to those outside of his boundaries of kinship and friendship, disorients the authorial audience. The LXX intertextual examples of Elijah and Elisha (Lk. 4.25-27) re-enforce this disorientation: both depict benefaction toward individuals outside of ethnic and even religious boundaries. For an authorial reader, Jesus brings disgrace upon himself by repudiating the members of his hometown synagogue through his speech and actions. In the case of authorial readers in positions of honor, the rhetorical discourse confronts modes of interaction – within and without his or her community: benefaction, whether spiritual or material, is no longer determined by cultural dimensions. In addition, like Jesus, the ultimate exemplar in Luke-Acts, authorial readers are compelled to assume positions of shame in order to extend benefaction to those outside of their social or religious boundaries.

Non-reciprocal benefaction is not simply shown to those within the confines of kinship and companionship. For authorial readers in positions of shame, a status deriving from various deviations related to ethnicity, gender, wealth (or lack of it), or religion, the discourse extends divine benefaction while building the premise for an inclusive community. As delineated in the fourth character taxonomy, discipleship serves as the discerning factor of faithfulness.

Analeptic and proleptic narrative trajectories coalesce around the importance of inclusion, which includes actions by God,[20] Jesus, and

18. The breadth of research is significant; see, e.g., Halvor Moxnes, 'Honor and Shame', *BTB* 23 (1993), pp. 167–76; idem, 'Honor and Shame', in Richard L. Rohrbaugh (ed.), *The Social Sciences and New Testament Interpretation* (Peabody, Mass.: Hendrickson Publishers, 1996), pp. 19–40; David A. deSilva, 'Honor and Shame', in Craig A. Evans and Stanley E. Porter (eds), *Dictionary of New Testament Background* (Downers Grove, Ill.: InterVarsity Press, 2000), pp. 518–22. For honor and shame in Luke-Acts, see Bruce J. Malina, 'Honor and Shame in Luke-Acts', pp. 25–66.

19. David A. deSilva, *The Hope of Glory: Honor Discourse and New Testament Interpretation* (Collegeville, Minn.: Liturgical Press, 1999); idem, 'Investigating Honor Discourse: Guidelines from Classical Rhetoricians', in Kent H. Richards (ed.), 36, *SBLSP* (Atlanta: Scholars Press, 1997), pp. 491–525.

20. The characterization of God is constructed from both the narrative world of Luke-Acts and from intertextual LXX examples cited within the Lukan narrative.

disciples. Many of the individuals and groups to whom salvation is offered are from the cultural margin and represent varying degrees of shame. Just as God and Jesus do not exclude the marginalized from salvation, authorial readers are prompted by the narrative discourse not only to include those from the cultural periphery within their circumference of fictive kinship and companionship but to avoid adverse judgments about the honor of a person or group of personages based on typical modes of disposition and conduct.

Largely through rhetorical argument, the narrative discourse uses symbolic systems of honor and shame to disorient and even challenge authorial readers to reevaluate actions typically deemed as honorable or shameful. This narrative trajectory takes various forms in Luke-Acts, ranging from gender (e.g., the women who provide benefaction to Jesus in Lk. 8.1-3; Mary in Lk. 10.38-42), to ethnicity and religion (e.g., the centurion in Lk. 7.1-10; the Hellenistic widows in Acts 6.1-6; Cornelius in Acts 10.1–11.18; the Jerusalem Council in Acts 15.1-35), to sex (e.g., the sinful woman in Lk. 7.36-50; the Ethiopian eunuch in Acts 8.26-40), to politics (e.g., the embrace of tax collectors by Jesus and John the Baptist in Lk. 3.12; 5.27-32; 7.29-30; Zacchaeus in Lk. 19.1-10), to poverty (e.g., the widow in Lk. 21.1-4; the inclusion of widows in Acts 6.1-6), to uncleanness (e.g., the Good Samaritan in Lk. 10.25-37; Simon, the tanner, in Acts 10.1-8).

2. Honor and Shame and the Narrative Discourse of the Second Galilean Ministry Speech

The narrative discourse of the second speech also confronts traditional constructs of honor and shame: the introduction (6.20-26) reversing the roles of honor and shame – the powerful become weak and the weak become powerful. Failure to recognize the honor of an individual or group is not an affront to social position and power. Instead, rather than riposte or retaliation, the rhetorical argument of the second speech establishes benefaction as the response of an authentic disciple: the one who provides the act of benefaction loses honor and, in many instances, the group to which she or he belongs. Indeed benefaction to individuals and groups outside of kinship or friendship erases cultural boundaries, redefining ideological systems – both inside and outside of the Christian community – using the roles of honor and shame.

From the standpoint of the second speech, benefaction is no longer an act initiated with the intent of acquiring honor. As a result, ethical behavior is defined as a mode of interaction without respect for boundaries demarcated by material possessions, ethnicity, religious orientation, or gender. In particular, interaction is no longer controlled by kinship and friendship and the corresponding requirements of reciprocal benefaction. In this sense, kinship and friendship extend beyond their traditional boundaries, encompassing individuals and groups that fall outside of those parameters. The implied author exercises a form of rhetorical power to accentuate the importance of enacting this new mode of benefaction: the actions of God are commensurate with this new mode of benefaction (Lk. 6.36). The implied reader and authorial readers conclude, therefore, that those who maintain interaction based honor and shame structures do so in contradistinction with the divine.

Authorial readers in positions of power are confronted by the narrative discourse to embrace benefaction not enacted on the basis of the desire to secure reciprocation (6.27-36). Affronts to honor, and thus shameful behavior, do not necessitate riposte or retaliation in order to regain the lost honor. Instead, the utter lack of concern for and even abdication of honor in favor of benefaction are directed at the well-being and needs of the offending party (cf. the episode involving the sinful woman at the house of Simon the Pharisee in Lk. 7.36-50). This ethical framework dissolves cultural boundaries, and association with and interaction between different individuals and groups are no longer dictated by modes of friendship, purity, kinship, and other honor-shame codes. In this context, requests by authorial readers for benefaction are not recognitions of shame but a legitimate frame of interaction within the new egalitarian community.[21]

3. *Honor and Shame and the Narrative Discourse of the Third Galilean Ministry Speech*

The third speech continues the topos of reversing honor and shame. Its rhetorical argument positions the Pharisees and lawyers as upholders of the status quo (7.29-30), and intratextual connections – both analeptic and proleptic – corroborate this understanding. In particular, Jesus and his followers, and to a lesser extent John the Baptist and his followers, embody a symbolic system that reinterprets the one embraced by the Pharisees and lawyers: their actions and message reorient honor and shame constructs, despite pleas and challenges from those possessing honor (cf. the speech's body in 7.31-34). Insiders become outsiders, while outsiders become insiders.[22] And the narrative is replete with irony: the inclusio links the conclusion (7.35) with the narrative aside (7.29-30), and the implied reader concludes that the divine is justified not by those possessing honor but by those who are recognized as shameful (viz., the people and tax collectors mentioned in v. 29).[23]

The rhetorical argument of the third speech challenges authorial readers in positions of honor to emulate the words and actions of Jesus and John the

---

21. Lk. 11.1-13; 17.11-19; 18.1-8; 18.35-43; 19.1-10; Acts 6.1-7; 9.36-43. See Green, *Theology of the Gospel*, 117–21, for a discussion of the 'egalitarian community' in Luke-Acts.

22. See York, *Rhetoric of Reversal*.

23. The precise identity of πάντων τῶν τέκνον is disputed, ranging from Jesus and John (e.g., Hartin, 'Justified by Her Children', pp. 154–55), to those who adhere to the teachings of John and Jesus (e.g., Bovon, *Luke 1:1-9:50*, pp. 287–88), to the Pharisees and scribes (Green, *Gospel of Luke*, pp. 302–05). When viewed through the lens of rhetorical texture, narrative trajectories, and readerly concerns, the most plausible identification is with 'all the people and tax collectors' in vv. 29-30 (by means of the inclusio between vv. 29-30 and v. 35 as denoted by the repetition of δικιαόω).

Baptist: constructs of honor and shame are not determining factors in their social and religious interactions. Pressure to maintain honor by adhering to cultural norms when interacting with other individuals and groups is positioned by the rhetorical argument as invalid. The topos of salvation for authorial readers in positions of shame takes further shape in the third speech: their actions and words justify the divine and, in turn, Jesus and John the Baptist. In particular, their shame, whether deriving from ethnic, sexual, health, gender, or political issues,[24] does not prevent them from sharing in divine benefaction and friendship, which is done alongside those in positions of honor.

4. *Honor and Shame and the Narrative Discourse of the Fourth Galilean Ministry Speech*

The fourth speech does not directly address the topos of honor and shame. What it does highlight is the need for action: the need for authorial readers to demonstrate discipleship through enduring enactment of Jesus' message and ministry. This ethical comportment includes the requirement to embrace an egalitarian community without concern for protecting one's own honor or the honor of one's group.

B. *Reshaping Material Benefaction*

Much has been written on the topos of wealth and poverty in Luke-Acts.[25] Though some persist in arguing that the narrative equates renunciation of possessions with the need for disciples to make themselves poor,[26] narrative evidence suggests otherwise. In particular, the rhetorical argument posits a topos focused on non-reciprocal benefaction: just as the divine shows benefaction to the poor, authentic disciples demonstrate benefaction to the poor.[27] In addition, by definition of the rhetorical argument in Lk. 4.18-19,

---

24.   See Jerome H. Neyrey, 'Clean/Unclean, Pure/Polluted, and Holy/Profane: The Idea and the System of Purity', in *Social Sciences*, pp. 80–105, for the correlation of these different locations and the construct of shame.

25.   For a summary, see Thomas E. Phillips, 'Reading Recent Readings of Issues of Wealth and Poverty in Luke and Acts', *CBR* 1 (2003), pp. 231–70; idem, *Reading Issues of Wealth and Poverty in Luke-Acts* (Studies in the Bible and Early Christianity, 48; Lewiston, Queenston, and Lampeter: Edwin Mellen Press, 2001).

26.   See, e.g., L. Schottroff and W. Stegemann, *Jesus von Nazareth: Hoffnung der Armen* (Stuttgart: Kohlhammer, 3rd edn., 1990) esp. pp. 101–19; Walter E. Pilgrim, *Good News to the Poor: Wealth and Poverty in Luke-Acts* (Minneapolis: Augsburg Press, 1981), esp. pp. 41–49.

27.   See the threefold argument of Roth (*Character Types*, pp. 165–66): (1) there is no change of addressee before Lk. 6.24 and the woe to the rich; (2) admonitions to share wealth later in the second speech of the Galilean ministry (6.30, 32-35) run counter to this claim (i.e., it would not make sense for disciples to share their wealth if they had become poor); and (3) consistency requires that if disciples are to be identified as the poor, they must also be identified as those hungry now and those weeping now (but disciples in Luke-Acts never go hungry [Lk. 5.33; 6.1-5; 8.3; 9.3-5, 11-17; 10.3-9; 22.14-38; Acts 2.43-47; 4.32-35; 6.1-7; 11.27-30] and are often joyful [Lk. 10.17; 24.52; Acts 5.41; 8.8, 39; 13.52]).

the concept of the 'poor' assumes a much broader definition in Luke-Acts, representing a composite of disadvantaged personages. This topos arises from the rhetorical texture of the second speech and extends back to the beginnings of the Gospel. The rhetorical argument dissolves ideological constructs around honor and shame and patron and client: interaction between individuals and groups is no longer governed by these cultural elements, and the use of honor and wealth for the benefit of power is replaced with a focus on empowering others – both inside and outside the Christian community.[28] Synkrisis plays a key role in the development of this topos: characters or character groups are juxtaposed to highlight character types representing the thesis and antithesis of the topos: the rich man versus Lazarus (Lk. 16.19-31), scribes versus the destitute widow (Lk. 20.45–21.4), Barnabas versus Ananias and Sapphira (Acts 4.32–5.11), and the Christian community versus Herod (Acts 11.27–12.5).

The rhetorical texture of the second speech disorients the symbolic world of authorial readers with material means and stands in stark contrast with cultural obligations and expectations concerning the use of wealth, which required those with material means to use their wealth to secure honor – whether social, political, or religious.[29] Authorial readers wanting to embrace a framework of discipleship must adopt a new model of friendship where possessions are used to provide benefaction without the expectation of reciprocity (cf. the speech's body in Lk. 6.32-45).[30] The rhetorical impetus to embrace this model of discipleship is found in the enthymematic rationale at the end of the first segment of the speech's body: authorial readers who do not embrace this new model of benefaction stand in contrast to the actions of God (cf. Lk. 6.36). The third speech provides further emphasis: the ministries of Jesus and John the Baptist to tax collectors and sinners involves non-reciprocal benefaction, with neither demanding – or even expecting – reciprocity from the clients. Hence, authorial readers who fail to share their possessions are at odds with not only God but Jesus and John the Baptist. This topos is corroborated by both positive and negative examples by means of characters or character groups that exhibit models of behavior to either emulate or reject. Authorial readers embody the words and actions of exemplars in the narrative when they provide benefaction without

28. Specific attention has been given to the summary statements in Acts (2.41-47; 4.32-37; 5.12-16) regarding the Jerusalem Christian community. See, e.g., Alan C. Mitchell, 'The Social Function of Friendship in Acts 2:44-47 and 4:32-37', *JBL* 111 (1992), pp. 255–72; Maria Anicia Co, 'The Major Summaries in Acts: Acts 2,42-47; 4,32-35; 5,12-16 Linguistic and Literary Relationship', *ETL* 68 (1992), pp. 49–85; Sterling, ' "Athletes of Virtue" ', pp. 679–96.

29. See, e.g., John H. Elliott, 'Patronage and Clientage', in *Social Sciences*, pp. 144–57; Halvor Moxnes, 'New Community in Luke-Acts', in *Social World of Luke-Acts*, pp. 241–68; Craig S. Keener, 'Friendship', in *New Testament Background*, pp. 380–88.

30. See, e.g., Mary Ann Beavis, ' "Expecting Nothing in Return": Luke's Picture of the Marginalized', *Int* 48 (1994), pp. 357–68; Balch, 'Rich and Poor', pp. 214–33; Green, *Theology of the Gospel*, pp. 76–94, 117–21.

concern for reciprocity,[31] whereas authorial readers who do not embody the words and actions of exemplars from the narrative correspond with the first three character taxonomies in the fourth speech.[32]

Authorial readers in positions of poverty welcome the narrative discourse and its dissolution of the encumbrances of traditional benefaction – specifically the need for reciprocity when benefaction is extended. As disciples offer fictive kinship and friendship to others without the stipulations of reciprocity accompanying traditional modes of patronage, authorial readers in need of material support expect to receive non-reciprocal benefaction from other members of the Christian community; fictive friends and kin are compelled to use their possessions to the benefit of others (cf. Acts 6.1-6).

C. *Expansion of Religious and Ethnic Boundaries*

Because of the volatility of religion and ethnicity in the first and second centuries CE, the religious and ethnic locations of authorial readers are an important facet for consideration in the appropriation of New Testament texts.[33] Whether an authorial reader is Jewish, a Godfearer,[34] or a Gentile affects the appropriation of the narrative discourse. Each of these three constructs, which can be broken down into further granularity (e.g., Hellenistic women, Godfearers with material possessions, and so forth), represent select ideological systems that have an effect on the intersection of textual and readerly horizons. In particular, the four speeches from the

---

31.   E.g., the centurion in Lk. 7.1-10; Zacchaeus in Lk. 19.1-10; the destitute widow in Lk. 21.1-4; Joseph of Arimathea in Lk. 23.50-56; the Jerusalem Christian community in Acts 2.41-47 and 4.32-37; Barnabas in Acts 4.32-37; the ministry to the Hellenistic widows in Acts 6.1-6; Tabitha in Acts 9.36-43; the Christian community in Antioch in Acts 11.27-30; Lydia in Acts 16.11-15; the Asiarchs in Acts 19.30-31; Mnason of Cyprus in Acts 21.15; Publius in Acts 28.7-10; the Christian communities surrounding Rome in Acts 28.11-16.

32.   E.g., the rich fool who stored his grain in Lk. 12.13-21; the rich ruler in Lk. 18.18-30; the scribes in Lk. 20.45-47; Judas in Lk. 22.1-6; Ananias and Sapphira in Acts 5.1-11; Simon the Magician in Acts 8.9-24; the owners of the Philippian slave girl in Acts 16.16-40; Demetrius and Ephesian craftsmen in Acts 19.23-41.

33.   The literature is vast on Judaism and Hellenism in the first century CE (e.g., see Martin Hengel, *Judaism and Hellenism: Studies in their Encounter in Palestine during the Early Hellenistic Period* [trans. John Bowden; Philadelphia: Fortress Press, 1974]; Mary E. Smallwood, *The Jews under Roman Rule: From Pompey to Diocletian* [Studies in Judaism in Late Antiquity, 20; Leiden: Brill, 1976]; John J. Collins, *Between Athens and Jerusalem: Jewish Identity in the Hellenistic Diaspora* [New York: Crossroad, 1986]).

34.   While the existence of Godfearers in the first century CE is debated, the majority of scholars now favor their existence, at least in some form (cf. James A. Overman, 'The God-Fearers: Some Neglected Features', *JSNT* 32 [1988], pp. 17–26; Max Wilcox, 'The "God-Fearers" in Acts – A Reconsideration', *JSNT* 13 [1981], pp. 10–22). For the opposing view, cf. A. Thomas Kraabel, 'The Disappearance of the "God-fearers"', *Numen* 28 (1981), pp. 113–23; R. S. MacLennan and A. T. Kraabel, 'The God-Fearers – A Literary and Theological Invention', *BARev* 12 [1986], pp. 46–53).

Galilean ministry display significant attention to religious and ethnic systems.

The synagogue background for the first speech is a familiar setting for Jewish and Godfearer authorial readers. The intertextual LXX examples Jesus cites buttress his refusal to show patronage to his family and friends (Lk. 4.25-27). For authorial readers attentive to ethnic and religious concerns, the speech places Jesus' message and actions and the message and actions of Elisha and Elijah in continuity with the realities of much of the Christian movement at the end of the first century CE, one increasingly comprised of Gentiles rather than Jews. The intertextual linkages to the LXX circumvent potential Jewish counter arguments opposed to a mixed community of Jews and Gentiles by laying claim to the topos (viz., the LXX) that could serve as the rhetorical basis for the opposing view. Characterization in the first speech draws a sharp distinction for authorial readers: those who repudiate Jesus' interpretation of the LXX Elisha and Elijah traditions, and consequently his message and ministry, affiliate themselves with the friends and family from his hometown synagogue. For a Jewish authorial reader this presents a perplexing rhetorical conundrum: how can she or he articulate an alternative or opposing view and remain in conformity with the LXX prophetic traditions?

The rhetorical argument of the first speech both disorients and confronts the ideological protocols and beliefs of a Jewish authorial reader. Disorientation occurs as a result of Jesus' failure to show appropriate honor in accordance with the cultural codes of benefaction. The seriousness of this violation is given greater magnitude by the fact that it took place in Jesus' hometown synagogue. The narrative discourse dissolves the divine preference for the Jewish people over Gentiles by means of the LXX examples of Elisha and Elijah, which confronts the ideological framework of a typical Jewish authorial reader.

Unlike the disorientation and the confrontation a Jewish authorial reader encounters, a Gentile authorial reader experiences confirmation; corroboration of her or his religious heritage, one that has precedence within the religious history of the Jewish people. Since a Godfearer authorial reader embraces the religious belief systems of Judaism, the disorientation and confrontation a Jewish authorial reader encounters also apply to the Godfearer authorial reader. At the same time, a Godfearer authorial reader experiences confirmation: Gentiles and Jews receive equal status in the Christian community.

The topos of the second Galilean ministry speech does not focus on religious or ethnic issues, but rather on cultural systems pertaining to benefaction. The rhetorical argument of the third speech includes, however, a remonstration against the Pharisees and lawyers, and the narrative discourse guides the implied reader to view both character groups in a negative light. For all three religious and ethnic authorial readers, the rhetorical discourse evokes a negative judgment towards rabbinic Judaism through its caricature of the Pharisees and lawyers. This certainly fits into a late first-century CE Jewish setting, where different constituents – the

Christian movement being one – were vying for recognition as the rightful heirs to the Jewish religious establishment that was extinguished with the destruction of Jerusalem in 70 CE.[35] The rhetorical result is a legitimization of the Christian movement as a genuine heir of Judaism.

Through its various character taxonomies, the final speech engenders metaphorical comparison for the authorial audience: each ethnic entity gravitates towards those characters and character groups representing their own ethnic background.[36] Jewish authorial readers envision characters and character groups such as Jewish actors in the birth narratives of John the Baptist and Jesus (Lk. 1.5–2.52), women disciples (Lk. 8.1-3), the Good Samaritan (Lk. 10.25-37), Barnabas (Acts 4.32-37), Philip (Acts 8.26-40; 21.8), Jews of Beroea (Acts 17.10-15), and Crispus, the synagogue ruler, and other Corinthians (Acts 18.1-11) as exemplars. Godfearer authorial readers embrace characters and character groups such as the centurion with the ill servant (Lk. 7.1-10), the Ethiopian eunuch (Acts 8.26-40), Cornelius (Acts 10.1–11.18), Lydia (Acts 16.11-15), and Timothy (Acts 16.1-3) as exemplars. Gentile authorial readers associate characters and character groups, which include those envisioned by Godfearer authorial readers in addition to others with no prior Jewish background, such as Sergius Paulus (Acts 13.4-12), the Gentiles of Antioch of Pisidia (Acts 13.13-52), the Athenians (viz., Dionysius the Areopagite and Damaris in Acts 17.16-34), and the Ephesian Christians (Acts 19.1-41; 20.17-38) as exemplars. All three ethnic and religious authorial readers dismiss certain characters and character groups as role models and, therefore, view them as stereotypes not to emulate – those who fall into the first three sowing activities as defined in the fourth speech.

D. *Jesus, John the Baptist, and Their Disciples*

The narrative discourse of Luke-Acts pays specific heed to the delineation of differences between Jesus and John the Baptist, with John the Baptist assuming a subservient role to Jesus. As there is evidence that the John the Baptist movement continued into the fourth century CE, it is quite possible that it could have been an issue for the authorial audience of Luke-Acts.[37]

35. The literature is vast – see, e.g., Stanley G. Wilson, *Related Strangers: Jews and Christians 70-170 CE* (Minneapolis: Fortress Press, 1995), esp. pp. 169–94; William Horbury, *Jews and Christians in Contact and Controversy* (Edinburgh: T&T Clark, 1998), esp. pp. 127–99.
36. Cf. Kenneth Burke, *Language as Symbolic Action: Essays on Life, Literature, and Method* (Berkeley and Los Angeles: University of California Press, 1966), esp. 359–79, who pinpoints the relevance of understanding reading *while* it happens.
37. See C. H. Scobie, *John the Baptist* (Philadelphia: Fortress Press, 1984), pp. 187–202, for an analysis of the John the Baptist movement to the fourth century CE. As regards to the relevance of the John the Baptist movement for the authorial audience, see Luke T. Johnson, *The Acts of the Apostles* (SP, 5; Collegeville: Minn.: Liturgical Press, 1992), p. 338; Tannehill, *Narrative Unity*, vol. 2, pp. 233–34.

The third speech serves a twofold apologetic function: it positions Jesus and his disciples above John the Baptist and his disciples, and then situates both Jesus, John the Baptist, and their disciples above the Pharisees and lawyers.

For authorial readers, whether simply those with questions regarding the relationship between the Christian movement and the John the Baptist movement or those actually with a heritage extending back to John the Baptist, the rhetorical argument of the third speech serves as an interpretive key. In the case of authorial readers with merely questions about the relationship of John the Baptist and Jesus, the rhetorical texture provides confirmation, highlighting the symbolic systems of Jesus' message and ministry as superior to those comprising the symbolic world of John the Baptist and his disciples. For authorial readers with a lineage rooted in the heritage of John the Baptist, the rhetorical texture both confirms and disorients. Confirmation occurs in the alignment of Jesus' message and ministry with the message and ministry of John the Baptist. Disorientation takes place at the level of the narrative as well as belief systems and actual practices. This occurs in several ways. First, in the case of the narrative, the birth stories place John the Baptist in a subservient role, a precursor to Jesus (Lk. 1.5–2.52), a thread that unravels throughout the Lukan narrative (Acts 1.5; 11.16; 13.25) and culminates in the episodes of Apollos (Acts 18.24-28) and the disciples of John the Baptist (Acts 19.1-7). In regard to belief systems and actual practices, until the third speech the implied author provides indirect detail about the belief systems and practices of John the Baptist and his followers. However, in the third speech, specifically the body (Lk. 7.31-34), the implied author distinguishes between Jesus and John the Baptist in the caricature attributed to both by the Pharisees and lawyers: John the Baptist is an ascetic, whereas Jesus is the exact opposite. Further elaboration on the differences between the Christian movement and the movement of John the Baptist is found in the episodes of Apollos (Acts 18.24-28) and the disciples of John the Baptist (Acts 19.1-7). The inadequacy is not in the ascetic lifestyle of John the Baptist and his disciples, but rather in the absence of the Holy Spirit in the conversion experience of his disciples, which per the implied author is proof that one is a Christian (cf. Acts 11.17). Hence, the rhetorical deduction for the implied reader is that the belief systems and practices of Jesus, who is superior to John the Baptist, take precedence over those of John the Baptist and are to be followed in the present day. In addition, through rhetorical power, the narrative discourse confirms that disciples of Jesus are superior to those of John the Baptist.

E. *Evaluation of Gender and the Narrative Discourse*

Much has been written on the role of gender in the New Testament during the past decade. While the methodological approaches range from narrative criticism, to ideological analysis, to deconstruction, interest in feminist criticism has spurred much of the investigation. With a significant amount of space dedicated to women characters and character groups, as well as topoi involving women-related activities, Luke-Acts has received notable attention.[38]

The rhetorical texture of the four Galilean ministry speeches contains very little in regard to gender – at least directly. The only instance of direct reference is the first LXX example Jesus cites in the first speech (4.25-26). The intertextual echo creates both retrospective and prospective appropriation and reveals two topoi: the first emphasizes non-reciprocal benefaction towards economically and socially disadvantaged women,[39] and the second depicts women as exemplars of faith.[40]

Women authorial readers in positions of economic and social disadvantage take comfort in knowing that the Christian community is tasked to provide them with material support. The LXX echo in the first speech to the episode of Elijah and the widow of Zarephath (4.25-26; cf. 1 Kgs 17.17-24) creates a topos focused on the need for benefaction to marginalized widows. Proleptic processing of the narrative builds upon this topos, starting with the episode of the widow of Nain (Lk. 7.11-17) and then the episode involving the apostolic decision and commissioning to show benefaction to the Hellenistic widows (Acts 6.1-6). According to the episode of Tabitha (Acts 9.36-43), benefaction to widows has no gender boundaries: action is required of both men and women.[41] At the same time, women authorial readers are emboldened by the narrative discourse to emulate women characters and character groups whose actions coincide with the fourth character taxonomy: non-reciprocal benefaction in the form of using possessions to support the Christian community (e.g., Lk. 2.36-39; 8.1-3;

38. The Lukan portrayal of women is contested and includes the following views: (1) the narrative discourse reflects traditional patriarchal structures (e.g., Jacob Jervell, 'The Daughters of Abraham: Women in Acts', in Jacob Jervell (ed.), *The Unknown Paul* [Minneapolis: Augsburg, 1984], pp. 146–57); (2) the narrative discourse is diminutive and suppresses the roles and stories of women (e.g., Robert M. Price, *The Widow Traditions in Luke-Acts: A Feminist Critical Scrutiny* [SBLDS, 155; Atlanta: Scholars Press, 1997]; Richter I. Reimer, *Women in the Acts of the Apostles* [Minneapolis: Fortress Press, 1996]); (3) the narrative challenges patriarchal structures (Corley, *Private Women, Public Meals*, pp. 24–117); and (4) the narrative discourse both reflects and challenges gender protocols – conforms with while challenges social codes (e.g., Seim, *The Double Message*; Witherington, *Acts*, pp. 334–39). The approach of this study adopts the fourth view: the portrayal of women, while embedded within cultural constraints, pushes for an expanded role for women.

39. Cf. Lk. 7.11-17; 7.36-50; 13.10-17; Acts 6.1-6; 16.16-19.

40. Cf. Lk. 1.5-25; 1.26-38, 46-56; 10.38-42; 18.1-8; 21.1-4; Acts 9.36-43; 12.12-17; 16.11-15, 40; 17.34; 18.1-4, 18-21.

41. Ostracizing of family members and friends who convert to Christianity is a possibility. The narrative situation behind Acts 6.1-6 may reflect a situation where kinship ties have been severed. On the farthest extremes of society, widows, who relied upon the benefaction of family and friends, would suffer the greatest in this scenario. In particular, ostracizing would have the greatest effect on the Hellenistic widows, who, with a much smaller ethnographic support network in the Christian community, would have been in the greatest need of support. See Craig S. Keener, *Bible Background Commentary* (Downers Grove, Ill.: InterVarsity Press, 1993), p. 338.

21.1-4; Acts 2.41-47; 4.32-37; 9.36-43; 12.12–19; 16.11-15, 40; 17.34; 18.1-4). Notwithstanding, women are also held responsible for their benefaction (or failure to do so), with the characterization of Sapphira (Acts 5.1-11) serving as the basis for judgment (cf. also Acts 13.50-52).[42]

What the four Galilean ministry speeches do not provide is a framework for understanding the roles of women in the Christian community beyond the context of female space. Discourse enforcing or challenging existing ideological systems in the female space must be sought beyond the four speeches.[43] The most that can be said is that the speeches present a topos where salvation is extended to the disenfranchised, the marginalized, which included, when construed from the ideological viewpoint of the first century CE, significant numbers of women.

V. *Concluding Summary*

While the constructs of author and text demarcate boundaries around hermeneutical appropriation, the authorial audience, as an entity consisting of different ideological locations, precludes identification of meaning as one-dimensional. Rather, in the case of Jesus' four speeches from the Galilean ministry, authorial readers, depending on their cultural frameworks, actualize the narrative in differing ways. Cultural systems involving gender, ethnicity, wealth, and other ideological constructs – all of which comprise the authorial audience – affect how the narrative discourse is assembled and then construed. A number of different questions are posed as part of this process. These questions include the following. What pieces are seen as most important? What actions are prompted by the rhetorical argument? Which

42. Much is written on the characterization of Sapphira (e.g., Daniel Marguerat, 'La mort d'Ananias et Saphira (Ac 5,1-11)', *NTS* 39 [1993], pp. 209–26; Henriette Havelaar, 'Hellenistic Parallels to Acts 5.1-11 and the Problem of Conflicting Interpretations', *JSNT* 67 [1997], pp. 62–82). The scene and her characterization extend from intertextual LXX parallels. The most likely hypotext is Josh. 7, where Achan is condemned for selfish accumulation of material possessions without concern for the larger community and deception when confronted with that behavior. Cf. also Adam and Eve in Gen. 3 and how they parallel Ananias and Sapphira in Acts 5.1-11.

43. Within the overall narrative of Luke-Acts, as discussed in Chapter eight, women disciples are depicted as exemplars of faith: their characterization coincides with the fourth character taxonomy and stands in contrast to other characters and character groups who fail to exhibit discipleship. The episode about women disciples and the female space that has received the most attention is the episode at the house of Mary and Martha (Lk. 10.38-42). There are disparate views as to whether the narrative texture bolsters male-centric ideological systems (see, e.g., Elizabeth Schüssler Fiorenza, *But She Said: Feminist Practices of Biblical Interpretation* [Boston: Beacon Press, 1992], pp. 52–76) or presents a more egalitarian view of women – namely, Mary's actions of engaging in the role of a student embodies a role ascribed to men and not women (Loveday C. A. Alexander, 'Sisters in Adversity: Retelling Martha's Story', in George J. Brooke [ed.], *Women in Biblical Tradition* [Studies in Women in Religion, 31; Lewiston, New York: Edwin Mellen Press, 1992], pp. 167–86; Green, *Gospel of Luke*, pp. 433–37).

individuals and groups are empowered (and which individuals and groups lose power)? In particular, the implied author draws upon enthymematic argument to guide the implied reader – and thus the authorial audience – in generating different modes of appropriation. Deductive gap filling in the enthymematic logic and metaphoric images culled by the narrative serves as the basis for corroborating and altering the existing symbolic systems of authorial readers. In addition, appropriation of the same narrative discourse varies based on the ideological makeup of the authorial reader: disorienting the ideological systems of one authorial reader, while concurrently confirming the ideological systems of another authorial reader.

The ideological systems that extend from the narrative discourse of Luke-Acts reinterpret cultural modes of benefaction, with an interest in bestowing honor on the shameful and non-reciprocal patronage to those in need. Personages in positions of disadvantage, whether because of gender, lack of possessions, or insufficient social standing (viz., power), are envisioned as the recipients of the aforementioned patronage under the framework of fictive kinship and friendship. The narrative discourse also presents an apologia that positions the Christian movement – in contrast to post-70 CE rabbinic Judaism (identified by the narrative discourse as the derivation of the Jewish religious leadership) – as standing in the lineage of LXX tradition. Interpretation of the LXX tradition by the Christian community, which includes both understanding and action, is juxtaposed with inter-pretation of the LXX tradition by the Jewish religious leadership. As regards to the Christian tradition, also articulated in the form of apologia, Jesus and his disciples are placed in a superior position to John the Baptist and his disciples.

PART FOUR: CONCLUDING SUMMARY – FROM GALILEE TO ROME

CHAPTER 10: CONCLUSION: RHETORICAL TEXTURE, NARRATIVE TRAJECTORIES, AND APPROPRIATION BY AUTHORIAL READERS

Few investigations of Jesus' four speeches from the Galilean ministry approach them from the standpoint of ancient Greco-Roman rhetorical texture. This study shows, however, that the four speeches exhibit discernible rhetorical texture that directly and indirectly feeds narrative movement in Luke-Acts. Analysis of the four speeches reveals an implied author who relies on modes of Greco-Roman rhetorical argument, and a rhetorical texture that plays a pivotal role in guiding the implied reader in the construction of trajectories. Narrative constructs such as plot, theme, characterization, and various topoi extend from these narrative trajectories. The rhetorical argument of the speeches is both deductive and inductive, and the implied reader builds consistency and coherence by means of processing the embedded maxims, enthymemes, rhetorical questioning, intratextual repetition, intertextual examples and echoes, and extratextual referents. In the end, the rhetorical texture and narrative trajectories of the four speeches propel the Lukan story from the 'backwaters' of the world (Galilee) to the very center of the world (Rome).[1]

Also largely absent in scholarly discussion is the hermeneutical step that goes beyond looking at the hypothetical audience as a one-dimensional construct to a multidimensional audience representing various ideological systems. In particular, differences in the cultural locations of authorial readers affect what meaning-making dimensions arise from the act of hermeneutical appropriation: the same narrative discourse might confirm the ideological systems of one authorial reader but challenge those of another authorial reader.

Several core facets of understanding about the implied author, the implied reader, and the authorial audience emerge from this study's analysis of Jesus' four speeches in the Galilean ministry. This chapter summarizes the prior analysis and examines some potential implications related to larger issues concerning Luke-Acts. The discussion breaks into the following areas: (1) the identification and appropriation of rhetorical texture; (2) the construction of narrative trajectories; (3) how the implied author redacts source materials for the sake of crafting more compelling rhetorical argument; (4) Luke-Acts unity: (5) representation of the Jewish people; (6) the Lukan community; and (7) methodological implications.

---

1. For a discussion of the narrative movement from Galilee to Rome, see Alexander, 'Narrative Maps', pp. 17–57.

I. *Concluding Comments on Rhetorical Texture*

A. *The First Galilean Ministry Speech*

The first speech establishes Jesus' ethos: it places his message and ministry within the context of the prophetic ministries and messages of Elijah and Elisha. The speech also delineates the parameters of Jesus' message and ministry: he adopts a new mode of patronage that reinterprets traditional boundaries of kinship and friendship by extending spiritual and material benefaction to the disenfranchised. Rhetorical arrangement of the speech, using chiasm (vv. 18-20) and parallelism (vv. 25-27), guides the implied reader to its rhetorical core. To begin, the chiastic center of the introduction focuses the implied reader on Jesus' identification of the lection and his reading of it in vv. 17b-19. This chiastic structuring positions the LXX citation (vv. 18-19) in the interpretive foreground for the implied reader. Second, the climax of both parallels in the body of argument centers on the repetition of εἰ μή and the subjects following each – the widow of Zarephath (v. 26) and Naaman the Syrian (v. 27). When the different pieces of the speech are assimilated, the implied reader concludes that preaching salvation to the poor (cf. vv. 18-19) equates to the material and spiritual benefaction Elijah showed to the widow of Zarephath and Elisha gave to Naaman the Syrian.

B. *The Second Galilean Ministry Speech*

The second speech, the longest and most elaborate of the four speeches, establishes a foundation for the disposition and behavior of disciples who aspire to embrace Jesus' ministry and message. A topos of reversal, which is formed in the introduction (vv. 20-26) and then receives elaboration in the statement of case (vv. 27-31) and body or argument (vv. 32-45), permeates the speech's largely deductive argument. Maxims and enthymemes comprise much of its rhetorical argument; only the rationale for the body (vv. 43-45) and the conclusion (vv. 46-49) tap the often-used Lukan inductive parabolic example. The speech breaks down the reciprocal boundaries surrounding benefaction in ancient Greco-Roman culture, an interaction between clients and patrons that demanded reciprocity – both negative (when faced with affronts to honor) and positive (when extending patronage and expecting reciprocity). In particular, the rhetorical argument addresses the need to demonstrate non-reciprocal benefaction to those who disrespect the reciprocal protocols of benefaction by failing to show honor (first segment of the body in 6.32-36) and the requisite to extend benefaction without any expectation of reciprocity (second segment of the body in 6.37-42). The end result of the rhetorical argument is egalitarian kinship and friendship without boundaries.

C. *The Third Galilean Ministry Speech*

The third speech serves as a commentary on the relationship (viz., ethos) of Jesus and John the Baptist as well as their disciples, both of which are designated as offspring (τέκνον) of the divine (σοφία). The rhetorical situation of the speech is rendered in the prior scene (7.18-23), an amplified chreia that addresses Jesus' identity. The rhetoric places Jesus and his disciples in a superior position to John the Baptist and his disciples. The rhetorical argument, through the inclusion of the narrative aside (vv. 29-30), also prompts the implied reader to compare Jesus, John the Baptist, and their disciples to the Pharisees and lawyers. In particular, the implied author uses logos to demonstrate the faulty nature of their logos (vv. 31-34): Jesus' actions mirror the accusations they cite against John the Baptist, whereas John the Baptist's actions coincide with the accusations they cite against Jesus.

D. *The Fourth Galilean Ministry Speech*

The final speech provides a fourfold characterization matrix that the implied reader uses to assess characters and character groups within the narrative of Luke-Acts. The overarching rhetorical argument of the speech exhibits a high degree repetition: similarities contribute to a crescendo in the fourth sowing example – both in the introduction (vv. 5-8a) and body of argument (vv. 11-15) – and variations provide the implied reader with 'gaps' that help highlight certain aspects of the discourse. In particular, repetition of ἀκούω ('hearing') and λόγος ('word'), a topos established in the conclusion of the second speech (6.46-49), defines listening as a true test of discipleship. However, discipleship involves much more than simply listening to Jesus' message: the statement of case (vv. 9-10) pinpoints the need for 'interpretation' (συνίζω), a topos that reaches back to the Lukan prologue (1.4), as a pivotal ingredient in the maturation process that leads to the production of fruit. The rhetorical argument guides the implied reader to categorize character and character groups, based on their words and actions, into one of four sowing activities. The speech's conclusion (vv. 16-18) uses deductive and inductive argument (two enthymemes in the form of examples) to highlight the incontrovertible logos of Jesus' argument: listening, interpreting, and doing are inseparably tethered.

E. *Assessing the Rhetorical Texture of the Four Galilean Ministry Speeches*

Use of rhetorical argument is evident in all four speeches, though it is subsumed beneath the immediate narrative context. In particular, stringent compliance with rhetorical conventions is sacrificed in favor of the need to move the narrative discourse forward. The most obvious example is in the case of the first speech: the vitriolic reaction of the hometown synagogue crowd (4.28-30) serves as a premature interruption to the speech; the end result being that Jesus is unable to deliver the conclusion of the speech due to the actions of the crowd. Another notable instance is that Jesus' speeches appear as riposte to questions posed by the narrative audience (e.g., 4.22; 7.18-23; 8.9). Not only does this help integrate the speeches into the overall narrative discourse, bringing continuance and sequential movement, but it contributes to the overall ethos of the implied author – breathing 'accuracy' (cf. ἀκριβῶς in Lk. 1.3) and 'veracity' (cf. ἀσφάλεια in Lk. 1.4) to the narrative world.

The four speeches also affirm the growing understanding that New Testament oratory differs from the oratory defined in the Greco-Roman rhetorical handbooks. Attempts to define New Testament rhetoric – and in this case the rhetorical argument of Luke-Acts – in terms of the invention and arrangement of the handbook tradition is fruitless.[2] Rather, it is more accurate to speak in terms of rhetorical texture, with rhetorical proof and style as the key components for analysis.

All three modes of rhetorical proof – pathos, logos, and ethos – are evident in the four speeches. In the case of the first speech, the rhetorical proof centers on pathos, with the culmination in the violent response of the narrative audience (i.e., their attempt to kill Jesus; 4.28-30). Logos is not absent from the rhetorical argument either: the implied author employs deductive and inductive reasoning to move the implied reader to equate Jesus with the figures of Elijah and Elisha. The second speech uses logos to compel the implied reader to embrace the disposition and behavior demanded by Jesus' message and ministry. The third speech uses logos as the basis of its argument by drawing heavily upon synkrisis and ecphrasis in its elevation of Jesus and John the Baptist and denunciation of those opposed to the ministries and messages of John the Baptist and Jesus. The final speech also uses synkrisis and ecphrasis, with a culmination in the rhetorical argument occurring in the fourth sowing activity (cf. 8.8, 15).

The rhetorical style of the four speeches uses repetition to facilitate intratextual cohesion that ties together each speech as well as links each speech to the larger narrative. Several aspects of rhetorical style are evident. First, in addition to heightening the impact of certain contextual expressions and statements, rhetorical style guides the implied reader to connect the rhetorical argument of each speech to textual constructs such as plot, theme, characterization, and topoi. Second, the speeches exhibit a tendency for both inductive reasoning, through the use of aphorisms and metaphoric examples, and deductive reasoning, through the use of rhetorical questioning, maxims, and enthymemes. And the implied author does not separate

---

2. See, e.g., the comment of Burton L. Mack (*Rhetoric and the New Testament* [Minneapolis: Fortress Press, 1990], p. 35): 'Most attempts to define precisely the issue of an early Christian argument fail, however, simply because the social circumstances of the early Christian movements did not correspond to the traditional occasions for each type of speech. Early Christian rhetoric was a distinctly mixed bag in which every form of rhetorical issue and strategy was frequently brought to bear simultaneously in an essentially extravagant persuasion.'

deductive and inductive argument: the discourse is replete with enthymemes embedded as components of parabolic examples. Finally, abduction forms part of the rhetorical argument of the speeches: it serves as the rationale for ethical enactment, which derives from the divine.[3] Argument by abduction functions as a mode of rhetorical power: authorial readers who are not willing to embrace the conclusions of the narrative discourse are rhetorically positioned as in opposition to the divine.

II. *Concluding Comments on Narrative Trajectories*

The first speech establishes Jubilee-like benefaction as a core element of the Lukan plotline. The rhetorical situation of the second speech (6.17-19) culls a ministry context reminiscent of the first speech (cf. 4.18-19). Specifically, the introduction, in its topos of reversal of fortunes, echoes the enactment of Jubilee legislation (6.20-26). The rhetorical situation of the third speech, as defined by the preceding amplified chreia (7.18-23), recalls the same topos couched in terms of a LXX intertext (cf. v. 22). The emphasis on listening and then the enactment of Jesus' message in the fourth speech forms an intratextual connection with the conclusion of the second speech (6.46-49). It is through this intricate connection of intratexts that the implied author leads the implied reader to build narrative coherence between each of the four speeches.

A. *Theme and Plot*

The theme of 'salvation to the ends of the earth' and the underlying plot substructure gains momentum and definition from the four speeches. The first speech pinpoints that salvific benefaction is to be extended to those who are materially and spiritually disenfranchised. This is a new ethical mode of benefaction: cultural and religious boundaries no longer determine who receives or does not receive benefaction. The second speech elaborates upon the dimensions of salvific benefaction: it is to be shown without regard for reciprocity. The ethos of Jesus – and thus his message – is confirmed in the third speech: Jesus, John the Baptist, and their disciples stand in contrast to the Pharisees and lawyers (viz., in accordance with the divine). Based on the final speech, salvific benefaction is something humans eventuate through actions shown to others (ποιέω) – it is more than a disposition of listening (ἀκούω) or even interpreting (συνίζω).

---

3.   For the rhetorical argument of abduction, see the rationale for the first segment of the body in the second speech (6.36) and the statement of case (7.28) and conclusion (7.35) of the third speech.

B. *Characterization*

1. *Jesus*

The Galilean ministry establishes the foundation for Jesus' characterization, and the first and third speeches are at the crux of the implied reader's construction. Synkrisis of Jesus' first speech (cf. 4.24-27) and his ensuing actions (cf. 7.1-10, 11-17) results in the implied reader locating Jesus in the prophetic lineage of Elijah and Elisha: the ministries of Elijah and Elisha to those outside cultural boundaries coincides with Jesus' salvific benefaction to the disenfranchised. Jesus also transcends traditional modes of kinship and friendship: his acts of benefaction are not toward family and friends (cf. 4.23) but to outsiders, those beyond the personages who would exhibit honor and patronage in response to the benefaction. The rhetorical situation of Jesus' second speech (6.17-19) places his actions alongside those of Moses and, in particular, Moses' giving of the law in Exodus. The third speech positions Jesus and his disciples in a superior position to John the Baptist and his disciples, and Jesus, John the Baptist, and their disciples in a position superior to the Pharisees and lawyers (cf. 7.29-30). The third speech bolsters the characterization of John the Baptist as an ascetic figure whose message and ministry contrasts with the message and ministry of Jesus and his followers. In addition, through deduction, prompted by the inquiry from John the Baptist to Jesus (7.18-20), the implied reader concludes that John the Baptist is unaware of Jesus' messianic status (cf. 3.22).[4]

2. *The 'Poor'*

The character stereotype of 'poor' – the recipients of salvific benefaction – coalesces around the widow of Zarephath and Naaman the Syrian, both of whom receive salvific benefaction from Elijah and Elisha respectively. Through synkrisis with other characters and character groups who receive salvific benefaction from Jesus and then his disciples, the implied reader constructs a characterization of the 'poor' that spans the narrative of Luke and Acts.[5] These individuals and groups range from those in need of material benefaction (such as the widows in Acts 6.1-6), to those in need of spiritual benefaction (such as Lydia in Acts 16.11-15), to those who are ethnically unclean (such as the centurion in Lk. 7.1-10 and Cornelius in Acts 10.1–11.18), to those in need of physical healing (such as the paralytic in Lk. 5.17-26 or the lame man at the gate of the temple in Acts 3.1-10), to social and/or religious deviants (such as the 'sinful' woman in Lk. 7.36-50 or Zacchaeus in Lk. 19.1-10).

3. *Opponents of Jesus and His Disciples*

Opponents of Jesus and his followers are described in the four speeches as constructing cultural boundaries that inhibit salvific benefaction. The hometown synagogue crowd in the first speech violently retaliates against

---

4. See Darr, *Character Building*, pp. 60–84.
5. See Roth, *Character Types*; Phillips, *Wealth and Poverty*, pp. 95–96, 106–15.

Jesus when he refuses to perform miraculous acts of benefaction that he readily doles out to non-kinsmen and non-friends at Capernaum (4.31-37). The narrative aside in the third speech (7.29-30) provides the implied reader with direct commentary about the characterization of the Pharisees and lawyers: they reject the purpose of God by not heeding the message and ministry of John the Baptist (3.1-20). Their characterization contrasts the characterization of the people and tax collectors who did heed the message of John the Baptist and were baptized. The first sowing taxonomy in the final speech (8.5, 11) – namely, the character stereotype representative of opponents of Jesus and his followers – depicts the devil as playing a pivotal role in their failure to exhibit discipleship. An accumulation of character attributes form around this character taxonomy by means of proleptic construction of the narrative by the implied reader: characters and character groups in this character taxonomy exhibit animosity toward Jesus and his followers and follow a journey that typically ends in spiritual and even physical condemnation.

4. *Failed Disciples*

Personages who fail to embody the characteristics Jesus ascribes to 'true' disciples are metaphorically compared in the second speech to a bad tree that produces bad fruit (first rationale of the body in 6.43-44), bramble bushes that produce thorns (second rationale of the body in 6.45), and a person whose house crumbles during a flood because he did not build a foundation (conclusion in 6.49). The final speech, through its characterization matrix, provides the implied reader with further information about these individuals who fail to embrace Jesus' call to discipleship. In particular these character stereotypes break into further granularity: each of the first three sowing activities represent a stereotype that is at odds with the character stereotype of 'true' discipleship (as exemplified by the final sowing activity; cf. 8.8, 15).

5. *Four Sowing Activities Delineate Four Character Taxonomies*

The implied reader builds coherence around each of the four character stereotypes delineated in the final speech. The disposition and actions of each stereotype is metaphorically represented by the sowing activity to which it is associated. The first stereotype (those sown along the path) represents characters who hear the message but fail to believe (with the failure attributed to the devil; cf. 8.5, 11). In the second sowing example, the seed initially grows but withers away due to the lack of moisture. The characters associated with the second stereotype initially demonstrate varying degrees of faithfulness but then fall away due to different temptations (cf. 8.6, 12). In the case of the third example (cf. 8.7, 13), maturation is inhibited and ultimately altogether thwarted. Characters corresponding with this stereotype exhibit interest in discipleship but, in the end, cannot adhere to the principles ascribed because of their desire for honor in the form of possessing wealth. The final sowing activity depicts maturation occurring over a lengthy period of time and ethical behaviors that eventuate from the heart (cf. 8.8, 15). This stereotype embodies characteristics that stand in contrast with the characteristics representative of the first three stereotypes. The cognitive and moral comportment of characters in the fourth character taxonomy coincides with the cognitive and moral comportment of God, the Holy Spirit, and Jesus.

C. *Topoi*

The four speeches carry forward topoi established in earlier scenes as well as form new topoi, both of which receive elaboration with narrative progression. In addition, a significant number of the topoi overlap between two or more of the four speeches, which results in a heightened awareness on the part of the implied reader.

1. *Topoi Overlapping All Four Galilean Ministry Speeches*
First and foremost, intertwined with the overarching theme and plotline of Luke-Acts, is the topos of reversal of fortunes (cf. 6.20-26) and, the topos of extending salvific benefaction to those outside of the parameters of kinship and friendship[6] (cf. the intertextual LXX linkages in the first speech to Jubilee legislation; Isa. 61.1-2; 58.6 and Lk. 4.18-19). As a result of these two topoi, the implied reader construes discipleship as a demonstration of spiritual and material benefaction to those in need – particularly those unable to show reciprocity (4.18-19, 25-27; 6.20-26, 27-45). This understanding of discipleship leads to a third topos of non-reciprocal benefaction (4.23, 25-27; 6.27-45). A fourth topos posits that discipleship requires perseverance and necessitates both listening (ἀκούω) and doing (ποιέω). The conclusion of the second speech accentuates the importance of following Jesus' directives concerning non-reciprocal benefaction by means of synkrisis – specifically the comparison of the two metaphorical examples (6.46-49). This topos of action (ποιέω) extends to the fourth speech, which compares discipleship with the maturation required to produce fruit and contrasts the stereotypes associated with the fourth sowing activity with the stereotypes of the preceding three sowing activities (8.5-8a, 11-15). In this context, discipleship corresponds with the cognitive aspects of conversion, a topos that spans both Luke and Acts and finds its derivation in the second and fourth speeches – whereby ethical actions (and thus 'true' discipleship) originate from the heart (6.45; 8.15).

2. *Topoi Found in One Speech Only*
There are several topoi with no overlap between the four speeches that remain integral to the narrative discourse. The first speech establishes a

---

6. Cf. the first and second speeches and their rhetorical argument that reinterpret traditional cultural codes of benefaction. Also key is the narrative aside addressing the ministry activity of Jesus and John the Baptist in the third speech (7.29-30).

fourfold paradigm of proclamation[7] that serves as a type scene for scenes involving followers of Jesus. Hence, the events are interpreted (by means of synkrisis) by the implied reader through the lens of this prior type scene. The fourth speech produces two topoi that are integral to the development of the narrative discourse. Both of the topoi are deductive derivations – indirect constructions based on proleptic processing of the narrative. The first topos involves the condemnation of and triumph over divination and magic, modes of benefaction used to generate honor and garner patronage. This topos is the deductive result of identifying character stereotypes in the fourth speech and then comparing the actions of these character stereotypes against the actions representative of disciples in the second speech. As a result, the implied reader condemns characters and character groups that partake in divination and magic and exemplifies characters and character groups that triumph over those individuals and groups that use divination and magic to their advantage. The second topos concerns the eventual apocalyptic demise for those who repudiate and persecute disciples. Irony also plays a role in the construction of this topos: persecution, rather than thwarting or altogether halting the progression of Jesus and then the Christian movement, produces renewed growth.

III. *Concluding Comments on Redactional Indicators*[8]

Redaction by the Lukan implied author reveals an interest in melding the four speeches into the surrounding narrative discourse – specifically so the rhetorical argument bolsters plot, theme, characterization, and topoi.[9] The redactional changes, whether additions or emendations, reflect four general categorical tendencies.

---

7. The type scene in 4.16-30 includes the following: (1) boldness of proclamation; (2) an antithetical response by the audience; (3) a 'miraculous' escape by the protagonist from an audience seeking to inflict harm; and (4) renewed spread of 'salvation'.

8. The redactional analysis of this study assumes the Two Source Document theory – specifically, that the Lukan implied author used two primary sources (Mark and Q) in the composition of his Gospel (see, e.g., Christopher M. Tuckett, *Q and the History of Early Christianity: Studies on Q* [Edinburgh: T&T Clark; Peabody, Mass.: Hendrickson Publishers, 1996]; Peter M. Head, *Christology and the Synoptic Problem: An Assessment of One Argument for Markan Priority* [SNTSMS, 94; Cambridge: Cambridge University Press, 1997]. For an alternative view to the Two Source Document theory, cf. Alan J. McNicol, David L. Dungan, and David B. Peabody, *Beyond the Q Impasse – Luke's Use of Matthew: A Demonstration by the Research Team of the International Institute for Gospel Studies* (Valley Forge, Pa.: Trinity Press International, 1996).

9. Redactional analysis of the inaugural speech (4.14-30) is more difficult since there are significant differences between it and the apparent source in Mk 6.1-6. For a discussion of the redactional issues, see, e.g., Robert C. Tannehill, 'The Mission of Jesus According to Luke IV 16-30', in Walter Eltester (ed.), *Jesus in Nazareth* (BZNW, 40; Berlin and New York: Walter de Gruyter, 1972), pp. 51–75. For the second (6.17-49) and third (7.24-35) speeches, the source identified is Q. In the case of the fourth speech (8.4-18), Mark is the precursor and derivative source.

The first category relates to a tendency to orient the rhetorical argument to the level of the narrative audience and implied reader. The most obvious examples of this are the changes in Lk. 6.20-26 from the third-person plural pronoun to the second-person pronoun (cf. Mt. 5.3-12). In addition, the implied author includes a narrative aside to direct the implied reader in making judgments about characters in the immediate narrative discourse (cf. Lk. 7.29-30 versus Mt. 11.7-19).

The second category pertains to an interest in fitting the speeches into the overall flow of the narrative discourse. For example, the implied author in forming an inclusio around the final speech (Lk. 8.1-3, 19-21) omits the final two parabolic examples and inclusio statement from the narrative in Mark (cf. 4.26-34).[10] Perhaps the most notable instance of this redactional tendency is the relocation of the entire segment on John the Baptist to an earlier place in the narrative sequence (in contrast to the later sequential occurrence in Q [cf. Mt. 11.7-19]). Finally, the implied author also conflates sources in a few instances in order to build rhetorical impact (e.g., combination of the traditions in Mt. 7.17 and 12.35 in 6.43-45, which accentuates the contrast between the 'good' and 'bad' trees and their produce).

Third, the implied author displays unique awareness in heightening the rhetorical impact of the discourse. This is evident in myriad ways. The most notable ones include: (1) inclusion of the temporal pronoun νῦν in 6.20-26; (2) insertion of corresponding woes (cf. 6.24-26) to coincide with the preceding blessings (cf. 6.20-23), which accentuates the topos of role reversal; (3) inclusion of 'hook' words that prompt a rhetorical transition to the ensuing sowing example in 8.5-8a, 11-15; and (4) downplaying or deleting semantic expressions likely unfamiliar to the implied reader (e.g., the contrast between the 'wise' and 'foolish' person from Mt. 7.24-27).[11]

Finally, redactional activity discloses a penchant to modify source material to draw attention to topoi inherent to the narrative discourse.[12] A good example is the addition of 'woes' (6.24-26) to the 'blessings' (6.20-23; cf. Mt. 5.3-12) that results in a parallel juxtaposition of 'blessings' (6.20-23) and 'woes' (6.24-26). This juxtaposition reflects a Lukan emphasis on reversal of fortunes, a bipolarity found in the theme of Luke-Acts ('salvation to the ends of the earth') as well as modes of characterization and even other topoi.

10. In an ironic twist, the implied author of Luke replaces the inclusio in Mark: 'many things in parables' (Mk 4.2) and 'with many such parables' (Mk 4.33), as noted by Tolbert, *Sowing the Gospel*, p. 148.

11. There is no instance of the implied author adding Jewish colloquial phrases (see Marshall, *Gospel of Luke*, p. 253).

12. See Witherington, 'Editing the Good News', pp. 324–47, who reaches this conclusion after examining the use of Mark and Q as well as use of the source behind the conversion experience of Saul/Paul in Acts 9, 22, and 26.

IV. *Luke-Acts Unity*

While most scholars admit the presence of some small 'cracks' in regard to the unity of Luke and Acts, few believe the reports of a decade ago that large ruptures had appeared.[13] Scholarly responses to the volleys challenging Luke-Acts unity showed that many of the 'cracks' pertained to narrative and readerly concerns.[14] In the case of the four Galilean ministry speeches of Jesus, as discussed earlier, the rhetorical texture forms various narrative trajectories – related to plot, theme, characterization, and topoi – that extend across Luke and into Acts. Indeed, a significant number of these saturate the narrative of Acts and help corroborate Luke-Acts unity. Some of the more obvious trajectories from the four speeches that arch over into Acts include: (1) parallels between Lk. 4.14-30 and Acts 13.14b-52, including the presence of a type scene that is echoed in several episodes in Acts; (2) correspondence between characterization in Acts and the character taxonomies delineated in Lk. 8.4-18 and, to a lesser extent, in the second speech, interpretive criteria for deciphering between faithful and unfaithful discipleship – an element of the narrative discourse that extends into the narrative of Acts; (3) potential redactional shortening of the LXX citation – Isa. 6.9-10 – in Lk. 8.9-10 (cf. Mk 4.12) and then its inclusion in Acts 28.28 in order to bring full emphasis on the explanation for the centripetal movement towards the Gentiles:[15]

13. In 1927 Henry Cadbury (*The Making of Luke-Acts* [London: McMillan Publishing Company, 1927]) put forward a cogent argument in favor of viewing Acts as the second volume in a two-work sequel on literary and stylistic grounds. As a result, the unity of Luke-Acts as a single corpus was largely the consensus of the scholarly community until the past decade and a half. This has been challenged by several scholars on the grounds of generic. narrative, theological, and stylistic incoherence. They conclude that the hyphen Cadbury inserted in Luke-Acts should be removed. The initial challenge to the unity of Luke-Acts was by Richard Pervo (*Profit with Delight: The Literary Genre of the Acts of the Apostles* [Philadelphia: Fortress Press, 1987]) who argued that Acts employs the generic conventions of the ancient novel. Stylistic peculiarities led James M. Dawsey ('The Literary Unity of Luke-Acts: Questions of Style – A Task for Literary Critics', *NTS* 35 [1989], pp. 48–66) to question the validity of claiming narrative unity. Shortly thereafter, Pervo teamed with Mikeal C. Parsons in a monograph to dispute the unity of Luke-Acts from the perspectives of genre, narrative, and theology (*Rethinking the Unity of Luke and Acts* [Minneapolis: Fortress Press, 1993]). The monograph, in addition to Pervo's dissertation, was preceded by Parson's 'The Unity of the Lukan Writings: Rethinking the *Opinio Communis*', in Raymond H. Keathley (ed.), *With Steadfast Purpose* (Festschrift Henry Jackson Flanders, Jr.; Waco, Tex.: Baylor University Press, 1990), pp. 29–53 and Pervo's 'Must Luke and Acts be Treated as One Genre?' in Kent H. Richards (ed.), 28, SBLSP (Atlanta: Scholars Press, 1989), pp. 306–17.

14. For a detailed summary of the discussion around Luke-Acts unity over the past decade and a half, see C. Kavin Rowe, 'History, Hermeneutics and the Unity of Luke-Acts', *JSNT* 28 (2005), pp. 131–57.

15. For a discussion of the implications of this redactional maneuver, see François Bovon, '"How Well the Holy Spirit Spoke Through the Prophet Isaiah to Your Ancestors!" (Acts 28:25)', *New Testament Traditions and Apocryphal Narrative* (trans. Jane Haapiseva-Hunter; PTMS, 36; Allison Park, Pa.: Pickwick Press, 1995), pp. 43–50.

(4) the need for a narrative frame – namely, through intratextual links – concerning John the Baptist and his disciples (cf. Lk. 1.5–2.52; 3.1-22; 7.18-35) in Acts 19.1-7; (5) discernible interest in speeches and rhetorical texture as vehicles for delineating important narrative signposts for the implied reader in Acts[16] is also visibly present in the four speeches; and (6) intratextual connections between Lk. 4.16-30 – particularly by means of elements associated with plot, theme, and topoi – and various scenes in Acts (2.17-40; 3.11-26; 9.19b-25; 10.34-43; 13.4-12, 14-52),[17] including the closing scene in 28.17-28.[18]

The most compelling linkages between the four Galilean ministry speeches and the narrative of Acts may be reflected in the four constructs typically associated with narrative discourse – plot, theme, characterization, and topoi. Narrative emplotment of these in the four speeches stretches into the narrative of Acts: the implied reader builds greater and greater coherence around each of these by means of processing the narrative. Hence, while it might be argued that some veritable cracks remain as regards to the question of Luke-Acts unity, the varied narrative trajectories that extend from the four speeches into the narrative of Acts is compelling evidence that weighs in favor of Luke-Acts unity.

V. *Representation of the Jewish People*

The ongoing scholarly debate about the representation of the Jewish people in Luke-Acts is not something that can be resolved within the parameters of this investigation. The rhetorical texture of the four speeches certainly corroborates the conclusion of most scholars that the portrayal of the Jewish people in Luke-Acts is both positive and negative. What an analysis of rhetorical texture – in this case in regard to a select group of speeches in the narrative – shows is that positive and negative portrayal of different characters and character groups is an embedded construct of the rhetorical argument. This is consistent with Greco-Roman narrative,[19] and there are several aspects of this study's investigation of the four Galilean ministry speeches that contributes to the discussion on the representation of the Jewish people in Luke-Acts.

---

16.   For the importance of speeches and their rhetorical texture to the narrative discourse of Acts, see Witherington, *Acts*, esp. pp. 39–50, 116–22; Soards, *Speeches in Acts*, pp. 18–207; idem, 'Speeches in Acts', pp. 65–90; Richard A. Horsley, 'Speeches and Dialogue in Acts', *NTS* 32 (1986), pp. 609–14.

17.   For an overview, see Neirynck, 'Luke 4,16-30', pp. 357–95.

18.   See Dupont, 'La conclusion des Actes', pp. 359–404, for an in-depth examination of the parallels between Lk. 4.16-30 and Acts 28.17-28.

19.   See Kenneth S. Sacks, 'Rhetorical Approaches to Greek History Writing', in Kent H. Richards (ed.), (SBLSP, 23 Chico: Scholars Press, 1984), pp. 123–33; Robbins, 'Narrative in Ancient Rhetoric', pp. 368–84.

A. *The First Galilean Ministry Speech*

Jesus' refusal to show the same type of benefaction he showed to individuals outside of the boundaries of his kinship and friendship in Capernaum to his friends and family in Nazareth (Lk. 4.14-37) is a rhetorical argument for the implied author: the salvation of God is not only for friends and family – per cultural protocols accepted by the narrative audience and the implied reader – but for all who are willing to embrace the 'way' (ὁδός) of discipleship. The discourse presents a negative view of the Jewish people, as represented by Jesus' hometown synagogue crowd: they oppose the permutation in ethnic, religious, and social boundaries and, as a result, oppose the divine – as represented by Jesus and his message and ministry.[20] The LXX examples of Elisha and Elijah (4.25-27), in accordance with the rhetorical mode of synkrisis, simply corroborate the basis of the speech (viz., the statement of case – 4.21-22) by demonstrating continuity with LXX traditions held as authoritative by both the narrative audience and the implied reader.

B. *The Second Galilean Ministry Speech*

The second speech does not directly address the characterization of the Jewish people. It does provide, however, a commentary on the first speech, delineating ethical behavior that corroborates the rhetorical discourse of the first speech – an ideological framework that embraces non-reciprocal benefaction. Like Jesus, the implied reader castigates the hometown synagogue crowd in Nazareth, not for their Jewishness, but rather for the fact that they espouse a model of benefaction that anticipates reciprocity: they exhibit honor to friends and family and shame towards those outside of the boundaries of kinship and friendship.

C. *The Third Galilean Ministry Speech*

The third speech follows two episodes (7.1-10, 11-16) that serve as type scenes. Specifically, these two episodes correspond with the Elisha and Elijah LXX examples found in the body of the first speech (4.25-27): the episode involving the healing of the centurion's servant echoes the Elisha hypotext (2 Kgs 5.1-19) and the raising of the widow's son at Nain mirrors the Elijah hypotext (1 Kgs 17.8-24). Both of these type scenes further define Jesus and his message and ministry for the implied reader and prompt association between Jesus and the prophetic figures of Elisha and Elijah. The questioning of John the Baptist and his disciples in the chreia preceding the third speech (7.17-23) does not depart from this narrative context: the ethos of Jesus and his ministry and message are in full purview. The negative

---

20. The rhetorical invention of proof uses ethos as a means of bolstering the character of the rhetor and denigrating the character of her or his opponents (see, e.g., William W. Fortenbaugh, 'Aristotle on Persuasion Through Character', *Rhetorica* 10 [1992], pp. 207–44).

characterization of the Pharisees and scribes in the speech is not an overarching nomenclature for the Jewish people but rather a taxonomy representing the Jerusalem religious leadership.[21] The implied reader inductively associates the 'children' (τέκνα) in the marketplace who mock both Jesus and John the Baptist with the Pharisees and scribes, particularly since those two groups appear together as antagonists in a prior scene (5.17-26) and then, through retrospective evaluation by the implied reader, several later scenes (10.25-37; 11.32-52; 14.1-24). In addition, as the parabolic example of the children in the marketplace represents a legal (court) setting,[22] the implied reader discerns an utter lack of logos in the argument of the Pharisees and scribes: they castigate John the Baptist for not exhibiting the behavior of Jesus and Jesus for not exhibiting the behavior of John the Baptist. Hence, as regards to the third speech, negative characterization pertains only to the Jewish leadership, as represented by the Pharisees and scribes.

D. *The Fourth Galilean Ministry Speech*

The redactional decision by the implied author to omit the final clause of the citation from Isa. 6.9 in the statement of case of the fourth speech (cf. Mk 4.12c: 'lest they should turn again and be forgiven'; Lk. 8.9-10) and then include it in the closing scene of Acts (28.25-27)[23] is viewed by some as a final closure and denunciation of the Jewish people: the final pronouncement against the Jewish people could not take place until the close of the narrative. However, other scholars see it as an open-ended statement that holds out future hope for the Jewish people.[24] The constraints of this study obviously cannot bring rapprochement to these two very disparate positions. What can be said is that the implied reader, as part of the process of building consistency and coherence and filling gaps in the narrative, identifies an intratextual linkage between the closing scene in Acts and the fourth speech. This retrospective activity of intratextual connectivity prompts the implied reader to reevaluate the various Jewish characters and character groups through the four character taxonomies delineated in the

21. As argued by Richard A. Horsley, 'The Kingdom of God as the Renewal of Israel', in *Whoever Hears You*, pp. 263–66.
22. See Wendy Cotter, 'Children Sitting in the Agora: Q (Luke) 7:31-35', *Forum* 5 (1989), pp. 63–82; eadem, 'Children in the Market Place', pp. 289–304.
23. It is important to note that the implied author reverts to the LXX for the citation in Acts 28.27 versus the redactional source of Lk. 8.9-10 (viz., Mk 4.12c): ἀφίημι is used rather than ἰάομαι. This reversion to the LXX version may simply reflect that the implied author was using the LXX versus Mark in composing Acts 28.17-28. However, Lukan interest in 'healing' could also be a reason for this redactional change (cf. Pilch, 'Sickness and Healing', pp. 181–209).
24. See, e.g., Robert C. Tannehill, 'Israel in Luke-Acts: A Tragic Story', *JBL* 104 (1985), pp. 69–85; Vittorio Fusco, 'Luke-Acts and the Future of Israel', *NovT* 38 (1996), pp. 1–17; David Ravens, *Luke and the Restoration of Israel* (Sheffield: JSOT Press, 1995); Wasserberg, *Israels Mitte*, pp. 179–89.

fourth speech. The result reinforces judgments made by the implied reader about the classification of those characters and character groups, which highlights the division between the Jewish people who fall into the fourth character taxonomy and those who fall into the three other character taxonomies.

VI. *The Lukan Community*

A number of attempts over the past two decades identify varied flesh-and-blood readers – or communities – for Luke-Acts. The proposed *Sitz im Leben* and corresponding community for the two-volume work run the gamut, from Jewish Christians, to Godfearers, to Gentile converts, and from Christians (insiders) to non-Christians (outsiders). As regards to the question of Christians or non-Christians, most scholars concur that Luke-Acts was directed to an audience of insiders – converted Christians. Nevertheless, several investigations of the apologetic nature of Luke-Acts point toward the possibility of an unconverted Jewish audience, at least as an element of the purported audience.[25] The ecclesiastical focus of the two-volume work remonstrates, however, against a monolithic evangelistic thrust and exclusively non-Christian audience.

Beyond the question of insider versus outsider, debate concerning the identity of the Lukan community becomes significantly murkier. Here are some of the more prominent attempts to identify the Lukan audience. First, utilizing a sect-based sociological model, Esler constructs a socio-historical setting reflecting the theological agenda represented by the narrative discourse.[26] He then argues that Luke-Acts addresses a Christian community largely comprised of Gentile Godfearers and Jewish converts seeking legitimacy during a time of adversity, a situation involving pressures from the Jewish synagogue and the wider Gentile society. Second, a number of scholars, best represented by the socio-historical analysis of Moxnes, contend that the symbolic systems represented within the narrative world create a window into the historical community of Luke-Acts.[27] Narrative interest in material benefaction and the binary opposites of rich and poor reflect a community struggling with the need for economic redistribution. Third, employing a similar methodological approach, Tyson argues that various Godfearers stand as symbolic representatives of the Lukan community.[28] The apologetic aim of the narrative is to persuade these

25. See Alexander, 'Acts of the Apostles', pp. 38–44, who concludes that 'it does not follow that Luke's primary readership is Gentile. Acts is a dramatized narrative of an intra-communal debate, a plea for a fair hearing at the bar of the wider Jewish community in the Diaspora, perhaps especially in Rome' (p. 43).

26. *Community and Gospel*, esp. pp. 220–23.

27. 'Social Context', pp. 379–89; idem, 'Social Relations', pp. 58–75; idem, *Economy of the Kingdom, passim*. Also, see David P. Seccombe, *Possessions and the Poor in Luke-Acts* (SNTSU, B6; Linz: Fuchs, 1983).

28. *Images of Judaism*, pp. 19–41; idem, 'Reading as a Godfearer', pp. 19–38.

Godfearers that Christianity is the true derivation of LXX prophetic tradition. Fourth, drawing on a methodological framework based on narrative and reader-response considerations, Wasserberg poses that the Lukan community is broader – encompassing Godfearers as well as Jewish converts. Like Tyson, he also proposes an apologetic purpose that places Jesus' ministry and message and the early Christian movement in continuity with the LXX traditions. In particular, the early Christian movement stands in contrast with Pharisaic Judaism that is represented by the Jewish characters and character groups opposing Jesus and then the early church.[29] Fifth, Johnson pinpoints a concerted focus in the narrative discourse on the Jewish people and their reception and rejection of Jesus and then the early church. He believes the outcome is a Gentile Christian readership concerned with the Jewish rejection of the gospel and its acceptance by Gentiles.[30] Luke-Acts serves, therefore, to provide the Gentile Christian audience with assurances involving the legitimacy of the Christian movement.

Optimism from the last couple of decades of the twentieth century that it is possible to identify specific communities behind each of the New Testament Gospels quickly turned to pessimism during the past decade on the basis of several concerns.[31] The first involves the definition of 'community', an ambiguous, slippery term that is difficult, if not impossible, to define. The concern pertains to the implausibility of a complete and positive correlation between a text and the social group that carries or receives it. In particular, construal of a text as a sociological mirror of the community to which it is addressed is fraught with reductionism. A third concern relates to the erroneous assumption of many that the methodological framework for uncovering the rhetorical situations behind the New Testament Epistles can be applied in a similar manner to narrative materials – specifically the four Gospels. While the writing of many of the New Testament Epistles was prompted by social and theological situations facing their addressees, the pastoral and theological concerns of the four Gospels do not mirror crises facing the recipients.[32] A final concern involves the tendency of many to use the label of sect in construing the sociological composition of the four Gospels. Classification of the early church as a sect is a gross oversimplification and assumes that Christianity largely did not share the ideological systems of the surrounding culture, an assumption that is far from correct.

So, with the above concerns in mind, what can be said regarding the

---

29. *Israels Mitte*, pp. 31–70, 179-90, 361–66.

30. *Gospel of Luke*, pp. 3–10. Also, see Robert J. Karris, 'Missionary Communities: A New Paradigm for the Study of Luke-Acts', *CBQ* 41 (1979), pp. 80–97.

31. These concerns are found in the various essays by Barton, 'Early Christianity', pp. 140–62; idem, 'Gospel Audiences', pp. 173–94; idem, 'Sociology and Theology', pp. 459–72. Also, see Spencer, 'Preparing the Way of the Lord', pp. 104–24.

32. Note the comments of Johnson ('Lukan Community', p. 90): 'Reading everything in the Gospel narratives as immediately addressed to a contemporary crisis reduces them to the level of cryptograms, and the evangelists to the level of tractarians'.

Lukan community? To begin, as demonstrated in Chapter two, the few who argue for a singular addressee – namely, Theophilus[33] – fail to comprehend fully the nature of literary patronage in Greco-Roman antiquity. Theophilus is not the only intended recipient but rather serves as the literary patron, circulating Luke and then Acts to his family and friends – perhaps Christians and non-Christians – as well as adopted brothers and sisters in Christ, a group that likely included various house churches. Second, a growing number of scholars acknowledge that it is virtually impossible to pinpoint a precise identity to the authorial audience: it is a mixed entity comprised of Gentiles, Jews, and Godfearers; various degrees of material possession; men, women, and children; and so forth.[34] They also concur that the narrative discourse exhibits a concern with legitimization and the apologetic, an ecclesiastical focus that positions the Christian movement as heirs of Jesus' ministry and message on the basis of the LXX traditions.[35] Third, on a related note and as recently shown, Luke-Acts, like other Greco-Roman narrative that espouses an ethnic mixing (or Romanization) of outsiders, constructs a new constitution that serves as an apology, legitimizing the formation of an early church comprised of Jews, Godfearers, and Gentiles.[36] In this context, emphasis on continuity with LXX traditions does not directly translate into a Jewish and Godfearer audience in need of legitimization. Rather, like other narrative texts from Greco-Roman antiquity, Luke-Acts simply uses the heritage of the authorial audience – namely, the LXX traditions and Jesus, the founder – to corroborate the legitimacy of their practices and beliefs.

Using the above conclusions as an interpretive lens, how do the four speeches from the Galilean ministry contribute to the ongoing discussion about the identity of the Lukan community? First, the speeches assume an intertextual repertoire that includes significant knowledge of LXX traditions. The implied reader cannot build coherence and consistency, including filling narrative gaps, without this intertextual knowledge. Hence, while this does not necessitate identification of an authorial audience comprised of individuals who have undergone full initiation to Judaism or Christianity, it does specify authorial readers with a general understanding of the LXX and

---

33. Witherington, *Acts*, esp. pp. 63–65; Nolland, *Luke 1-9:20*, pp. xxxii–xxxiii.

34. See, e.g., Joel B. Green, 'Acts of the Apostles', in Ralph Martin and Peter H. Davids (eds), *The Dictionary of the Later New Testament and Its Developments: A Compendium of Contemporary Biblical Scholarship* (Downers Grove, Illinois: InterVarsity Press, 1997), pp. 7–24; Moxnes, 'Social Context', pp. 379–89; Sterling, *Historiography*, pp. 139–59; Marguerat, *Christian Historian*, pp. 129–54; Downing, 'First Reading', pp. 91–109.

35. See, e.g., Green, 'Acts of the Apostles', pp. 7–24; Sterling, *Historiography*, pp. 139–59; Marguerat, *Christian Historian*, pp. 1–25, 129–54.

36. Note Balch's comment ('METABOAH ΠOAITEIΩN', pp. 139–88): 'Luke represents not only a group with little cultural power but also a group of pork-eating, uncircumcised Gentiles who do not rest on the Sabbath. Such radical discontinuity threatens to bring a loss of identity. So Luke must claim continuity on other grounds: the reception of foreigners such as Cornelius was prophesied, authorized by the ancient prophets Moses and Isaiah, as well as the Lukan founder, Jesus'.

willingness to attribute some authoritative value to it. In addition, as the rhetorical argument includes abduction (cf. Lk. 6.36) – namely, logos based on the divine nature or past action by the divine – the implied author assumes that the authorial audience believes in the monotheistic God of Judaism. This points to an authorial audience of converted insiders – both Jew and Gentile are possible – or Jewish outsiders. Non-Christian Gentiles without sufficient knowledge of Judaism or Christianity would fall outside of purview. Second, the speeches also assume extratextual knowledge regarding Greco-Roman texts (cf. Lk. 4.23; 7.32). Therefore, an authorial audience consisting of Jewish Christians without broad exposure to Hellenistic culture falls outside of the plausible parameters. Third, the rhetorical argument and narrative trajectories involving material benefaction (particularly the rhetorical texture and narrative trajectories of the second speech) infers that some authorial readers possess a certain degree of wealth. Finally, when synkrisis between John the Baptist and Jesus in the third speech is considered in conjunction with the larger narrative that addresses John the Baptist and his disciples, there seems to be a sufficient indication that some of the authorial readers may have been disciples of John the Baptist or, at the very least, required clarification about the relationship between Jesus and John the Baptist.

VII. *Methodological Implications*

Reading as conduction necessitates the use of an interdisciplinary methodological approach and an integrated hermeneutic.[37] Historically, biblical scholars have tended to apply methodological tools in a one-dimensional manner, looking at form, source, and redactional issues during the first part of the twentieth century and then narrative, rhetorical, readerly, and ideological concerns during the past two decades. In many instances, these are silo-based approaches: each methodological tool is applied separately. Though a comprehensive overview is not possible, the following are some hermeneutical implications that derive from this study.

A. *Redaction Criticism and the Integrated Hermeneutic*

Redactional analysis is not only useful in helping to identify historical issues and theological tendencies but in understanding different nuances of the

---

37. Reading as 'conduction' is discussed in detail in Chapter two (see, e.g., Booth, *Company We Keep*, pp. 70–77). As regards to the need for an interdisciplinary methodology and integrated hermeneutic, see Joel B. Green, 'Scripture and Theology: Uniting the Two So Long Divided', in Joel B. Green and Max Turner (eds), *Between Two Horizons: Spanning New Testament Studies & Systematic Theology* (Grand Rapids and Cambridge: William B. Eerdmans Publishing Company, 2000), pp. 23–43; Waetjen, 'Hermeneutic Mode of Integration', pp. 75–94.

rhetorical texture of speeches in the Gospels.[38] Indeed, in the earlier analysis, several redactional adjustments by the implied author of Luke-Acts were identified as bolstering the rhetorical argument of the speech in question. In addition, in some instances, in contrast to claims that the implied author exhibits little regard for rhetorical conventions of the day,[39] emendations of source material from Mark and Q show particular sensitivity for rhetorical texture. As a result, biblical scholars who employ methodologies that arose during the last two decades of the twentieth century – such as narrative, reader-response, rhetorical, and ideological criticisms – should take care in wholesale abandonment of methodologies such as redaction criticism. Rather, these methodologies are an extremely valuable component of a larger integrated, interdisciplinary hermeneutic.[40]

B. *Rhetorical Texture and Narrative Trajectories*

The rhetorical texture of the speeches aids in the construction of overarching narrative issues such as plot, theme, chararacterization, and topoi.[41] The implied reader draws upon the rhetorical argument of the speeches in order to build meaning – a proleptic and analeptic activity – around the surrounding narrative action. Some of the more prominent ways this occurs range from use of the statement of case in the speeches to identify the plotline, theme, and topoi, to understanding how the narrative discourse concurrently conforms with and reinterprets ideological systems, to different taxonomies used in interpreting modes of characterization, to use of logos, ethos, and pathos as a means of exercising rhetorical power over the implied reader and, ultimately, authorial readers. Analysis of rhetorical argument leads to the identification of instances where language – through synkrisis or ecphrasis – is used to place one ideological position over another (or one character or group of characters over another character or group of characters).

C. *Ideological Systems and Hermeneutical Transformation*

Covered in much greater detail in Chapter nine, narrative discourse not only corresponds with ideological systems but concurrently reinterprets and even challenges those same ideological frameworks. The rhetorical texture of the

---

38. However cf. Fowler, *Let the Reader Understand*, pp. 228–60, who uses redactional analysis to read Matthew through the intertextual lens of Mark.
39. See, e.g., the comment of Kennedy (*New Testament Interpretation*, p. 67): 'Luke 6 is not a very good speech'.
40. For a discussion, see John R. Donohue, 'The Literary Turn and New Testament Theology: Detour or New Direction?' *JR* 76 (1996), pp. 250–75; Max Turner, 'Historical Criticism and Theological Hermeneutics of the New Testament', in *Between Two Horizons*, pp. 44–70.
41. For a discussion of ancient rhetoric in ancient narrative, see Robbins, 'Narrative in Ancient Rhetoric', pp. 368–84.

four speeches is the key to unlocking these aspects of the narrative discourse: deductive argument, as reflected by rhetorical questioning, maxims, and enthymemes, frequently serves as a means of provoking the narrative audience and the implied reader to embrace an ideological location that differs from their existing cultural system. The narrative events surrounding the speeches – as well as inductive argument contained within the speeches in the form of parabolic examples – serve as commentary, representing situations that define the ethnic, religious, and social worldviews embodied in the speeches. For example, as discussed earlier, the two episodes in Lk. 7.1-10 and 7.11-17 illustrate the implications of Jesus' rhetorical argument in the first speech of the Galilean ministry for benefaction without concern for cultural reciprocity involving kinship and friendship.[42]

D. *Authorial Readers and Hermeneutical Appropriation*

Reader-response critics, coupled with the research of classical scholars around the nuances of literary patronage in antiquity, highlight the importance of understanding hermeneutical appropriation from different reading locations. While certainly not a dynamic construct consisting of a near infinite number of ideological systems as in the case of postmodern authorial readers, the authorial audience of narrative in Greco-Roman antiquity is more than simply a one-dimensional construct. As a result, while authorial readers of Greco-Roman narrative actualize meaning from a dominant ideological framework, differences in cultural location affect the hermeneutical implications that are drawn about the narrative discourse, namely, which narrative trajectories, characters or character groups, and topoi receive the greatest attention during the process of hermeneutical appropriation. In the case of the Jesus in the Galilean ministry speeches, differences in wealth, power, gender, and ethnicity play a role in the hermeneutical appropriation of the narrative discourse that arises from the rhetorical texture.

Over the past several years, a number of publications have appeared that address the need to examine the hermeneutical appropriation of biblical texts from varied reading locations. These studies primarily look at the construct of reader from the perspective of real flesh-and-blood readers of the twenty-first century.[43] This investigation demonstrates the relevance of examining biblical texts, though with the realization that authorial readers are a much more monolithic entity and comprise a more uniform set of

---

42. For an in-depth discussion, see Brodie, 'Towards an Unravelling', pp. 247–67; idem, 'Imitation and Emulation', pp. 78–85; Robbins, 'Socio-Rhetorical Role', pp. 81–93.

43. For an overview of these methodological inquiries, see, e.g., Fernando F. Segovia, 'Cultural Studies and Contemporary Biblical Criticism: Ideological Criticism as Mode of Discourse', in Fernando F. Segovia and Mary Ann Tolbert (eds), *Reading from this Place: Social Location and Biblical Interpretation in Global Perspective*, vol. 2 (Minneapolis: Fortress Press, 1995), pp. 1–17; Mary Ann Tolbert, 'Afterwords: The Politics and Poetics of Location', in *Biblical Interpretation in the United States*, pp. 311–17.

ideological systems than in the case of modern and postmodern authorial readers, from the lens of different authorial readers. In this vein, the same narrative discourse brings consolation to one group of authorial readers while confronting the beliefs and actions of another group.

VIII. *Concluding Summary*

It would be difficult, if not impossible, for the narrative of Luke-Acts to make the journey from Galilee to Rome without the four speeches of Jesus from the Galilean ministry. Each of the speeches plays an important function in propelling the narrative down the 'way' (ὁδός) and delineating 'sign-posts' that provide the implied reader with frameworks from which to construct the narrative discourse. Viewing the speeches from the standpoint of Greco-Roman rhetoric provides valuable insight on the different ways authorial readers would have understood them. Various trajectories associated with narrative conventions such as plot, theme, characterization, and topoi extend from the rhetorical texture. Hence the stage is set for hermeneutical appropriation when the implied reader combines the rhetorical texture and narrative trajectories. Authorial readers encounter the narrative discourse, which compels them to strengthen, alter, and even jettison certain ideological beliefs and protocols. In the end, the four speeches make the long, event-filled journey from Galilee to Rome a worthwhile venture and transformative experience.

Figure 1: A Hermeneutical Model:
Reading as Conduction

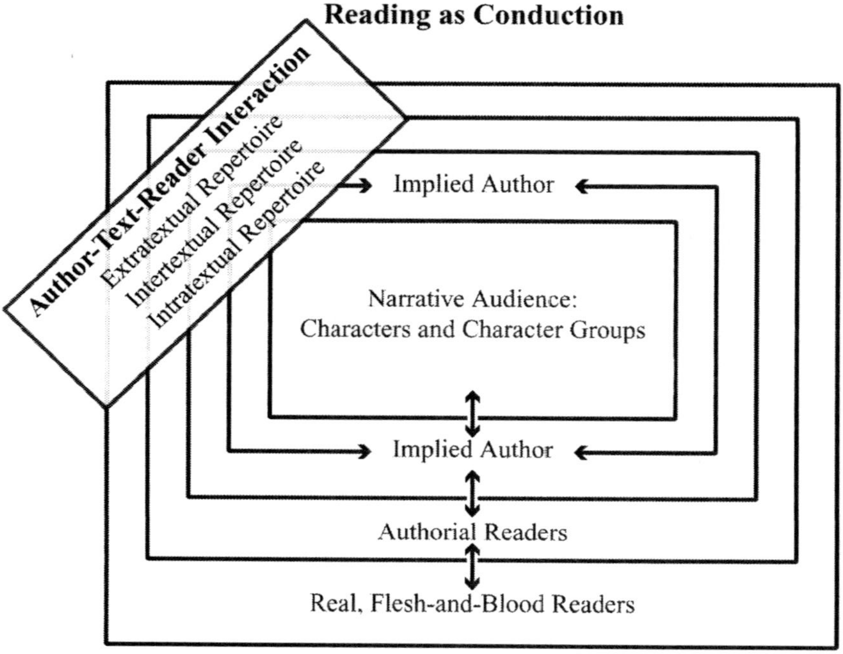

Figure 2: Sowing Four Character Taxonomies

First Character Taxonomy
(Sowing Along the Path)

1. Herod the tetrarch (Lk. 3.19-20; 9.7-9)
2. Those who fail to show Jesus' disciples benefaction (Lk. 10.10-15)
3. The priest and Levite from the Parable of the Good Samaritan (Lk. 10.25-37)
4. Sadducees and temple leaders (Lk. 20.20-47; 22.47–23.25; Acts 4.1-22; 5.17-42; 6.8–8.1, 22.30–23.35; 24.1-9, 25.1-12)
5. Jewish opposition in Acts (9.23-24; 12.1-5; 13.44-52; 14.1-7; 14.19-20; 17.1-9, 10-15; 18.12-17; 20.3; 21.27-36, 24.9, 25.27, 25.1-12)
6. The Jewish false prophet Bar-Jesus (Acts 13.4-12)
7. The seven sons of Sceva (Acts 19.11-20)
8. Demetrius the silversmith and his fellow Ephesian craftworkers (Acts 19.23-41)
9. Ananias the high priest (Acts 24.1-8)

Second Character Taxonomy
(Sowing on the Rock)

1. Jesus' hometown synagogue (Lk. 4.28-30)
2. Betrayal by Judas and Peter (Lk. 22.31-34, 47-53, 54-62)
3. Lycaonian crowd (Acts 14.8-20)
4. Simon the Magician (Acts 8.4-24)

Third Character Taxonomy
(Sowing Among the Thorns)

1. The rich fool (Lk. 12.13-21)
2. The rich man in the Parable of the Rich Man and Lazarus (Lk. 16.19-31)
3. The rich ruler (Lk. 18.18-30)
4. Ananias and Sapphira (Acts 5.1-11)
6. The disciples of Antioch (Acts 11.27-30)
7. John Mark (Acts 13.5c; 15.36-41)
8. Owners of the slave girl (Acts 16.16-24)
9. Eutychus (Acts 20.7-12)

Fourth Character Taxonomy
(Sowing into the Good Soil)

1. God
2. Jesus
3. Holy Spirit
4. Jewish actors in the birth narratives: Zechariah, Elizabeth, Mary, Simeon, and Anna (Lk. 1.5–2.38)
5. John the Baptist
6. Twelve disciples
7. Friends of the paralytic (Lk. 5.17-26)
8. Sinful woman at the house of Simon the Pharisee (Lk. 7.36-50)
9. Menstruating woman (Lk. 8.42c-48)
10. Good Samaritan (Lk. 10.25-37)
11. Dishonest steward (Lk. 16.1-12)
12. Widow in the Parable of the Widow and Judge (Lk. 18.1-8)
13. Blind Begger from Jericho (Lk. 18.35-43)
14. Zacchaeus (Lk. 19.1-10)
15. Faithful servants in the Parable of the Ten Pounds (Lk. 19.11-27)
16. Stephen
17. Barnabas
18. Philip
19. Paul and his companions
20. Early Christian Jewish community (Acts 2.41-47; 4.32-37)
21. Ethiopian eunuch (Acts 8.26-40)
22. Ananias (Acts 9.10-19)
23. Tabitha (Acts 9.36-43)
24. Cornelius (Acts 10.1-48)
25. Rhoda (Acts 12.12-17)
26. Lydia (Acts 16.11-15)
27. The Philippian jailor (Acts 16.25-40)
28. Beroean Jews (Acts 17.10-15)
29. Dionysius the Areopagite and Damaris the Athenian (Acts 17.16-34)
30. Apollos (Acts 18.24-28; 19.1-7)
31. Aquila and Priscilla (Acts 18.1-4, 24-28)
32. The Ephesian church (Acts 19.1-41; 20.17-38)
33. Julius the centurion (Acts 27.1-3, 30-44)

BIBLIOGRAPHY

Abrams, M. H., *The Mirror and the Lamp: Romantic Theory and Critical Tradition* (London and Oxford: Oxford University Press, 1953).
Achtemeier, Paul J., '*Omne verbum sonat*: The New Testament and the Oral Environment of Late Western Antiquity', *JBL* 109 (1990), pp. 3–27.
Adkins, W. H., '"Friendship" and "Self-Sufficiency" in Homer and Aristotle', *Classical Quarterly* 13 (1963), pp. 30–45.
Aichele, George, et al., *The Postmodern Bible: The Bible and Culture Collective* (New Haven: Yale University Press, 1995).
Aitkins, Douglas G., and Laura Morrow (eds), *Contemporary Literary Theory* (Amherst: University of Massachusetts Press, 1989).
Aletti, J.-N., *Quand Luc raconte: Le récit comme théologie* (Lire la Bible, 115; Paris: Cerf, 1998).
Alexander, Loveday C. A., 'Luke's Preface in the Context of Greek Preface-Writing', *NovT* 28 (1986), pp. 48–74.
—'Sisters in Adversity: Retelling Martha's Story', in George J. Brooke (ed.), *Women in Biblical Tradition*, pp. 433–37.
—(ed.), *Images of Empire* (JSOTSup, 122; Sheffield: Sheffield Academic Press, 1991).
—*The Preface to Luke's Gospel: Literary Convention and Social Context in Luke 1.1-4 and Acts 1.1* (SNTSMS, 78; Cambridge: Cambridge University Press, 1993).
—'Acts and Ancient Intellectual Biography', in Bruce W. Winter and Andrew D. Clarke (ed.), *Ancient Literary Setting*, pp. 31–64.
—'The Preface to Acts and the historians', in Ben Witherington III (ed.), *History, Literature and Society*, pp. 84–99.
—'Ancient Book Production and the Circulation of the Gospels', in Richard Bauckham (ed.), *Gospels for All Christians*, pp. 71–112.
—'Marathon or Jericho? Reading Acts in Dialogue with Biblical Historiography', in David J. A. Clines and Stephen D. Moore (eds), *Auguries*, pp. 92–125.
—'Fact, Fiction and the Genre of Acts', *NTS* 44 (1998), pp. 380–99.
—'Formal Elements and Genre: Which Greco-Roman Prologues Most Closely Parallel the Lukan Prologues?' in David P. Moessner (ed.), *Heritage of Israel*, pp. 9–26.
—'Reading Luke-Acts From Back to Front', in J. Verheydon (ed.), *Unity of Luke-Acts*, pp. 419–46.
—'The Acts of the Apostles as an Apologetic Text', in Mark Edwards, et al. (eds), *Apologetics in the Roman Empire*, pp. 15–44.

—'Narrative Maps: Reflections on the Toponymy of Acts', in M. D. Carroll, D. J. A. Clines, and P. R. Davies (eds), *Bible in Human Society*, pp. 17–57.

—'What If Luke Had Never Met Theophilus?' *BibInt* 8 (2000), pp. 161–70.

Allen, Wesley O., *The Death of Herod: The Narrative and Theological Function of Retribution in Luke-Acts* (SBLDS, 158; Atlanta: Scholars Press, 1997).

Alter, Robert, *The Art of Biblical Narrative* (New York: Basic Books, 1981).

—'How Convention Helps Us Read: The Case of the Bible's Annunciation Type Scene', *Prooftexts* 3 (1983), pp. 115–30.

Anicia Co, Maria, 'The Major Summaries in Acts: 2,42-47; 4,32-35; 5,12-16: Linguistic and Literary Relationship', *ETL* 68 (1992), pp. 49–85.

Argyle, A. W., 'The Greek of Luke and Acts', *NTS* 20 (1973/74), pp. 441–45.

Asgeirsson, Jon M., et al. (eds), *From Quest to Q* (Festschrift James M. Robinson; BETL, 146; Leuven: Leuven University Press, 2000).

Atkins, G. Douglas, and Laura Morrow (eds.), *Contemporary Literary Theory* (Amherst: University of Massachusetts Press, 1989) pp. 81–100.

Aune, David E., 'Septem Sapientium Convivium (*Moralia* 146B-164D)', in Hans Deiter Betz (ed.), *Plutarch's Ethical Writing's*, 51–105.

—*The New Testament in Its Literary Environment* (Library of Early Christianity, 8; Philadelphia: Fortress Press, 1987).

—(ed.), *Greco-Roman Literature and the New Testament* (Atlanta: Scholars Press, 1988).

—'Luke 1:1-4: Historical or Scientific *Prooimion*?' in Alf Christophersen, et al. (eds), *Paul, Luke and the Graeco-Roman World*, pp. 138–64.

—'The Use and Abuse of the Enthymeme in New Testament Scholarship', *NTS* 49 (2003), pp. 299–320.

—*The Westminster Dictionary of New Testament & Early Christian Literature & Rhetoric* (Louisville/London: Westminster John Knox Press, 2003).

Bakhtin, Mikael M., *The Dialogic Imagination: Four Essays* (trans. Caryl Emerson and Michael Holquist; Austin: University of Texas Press, 1981).

Bal, Mieke, *Narratology: Introduction to the Theory of Narrative* (trans. Christine van Boheemen; Toronto and Buffalo: University of Toronto Press, 1985).

—*On Meaning Making: Essays in Semiotics* (FFNT; Sonoma, Calif.: Polebridge Press, 1994).

Balch, David L., 'Comments on the Genre and a Political Theme of Luke-Acts: A Preliminary Comparison of Two Hellenistic Historians', in Kent H. Richards (ed.), SBLSP, 28 (Atlanta: Scholars Press, 1989), pp. 343–61.

Balch, David L., and Everett Ferguson and Wayne A. Meeks (eds), *Greeks, Romans, and Christians* (Festschrift Abraham J. Malherbe; Minneapolis: Fortress Press, 1990).

—'Rich and Poor, Proud and Humble in Luke-Acts', in L. Michael White and O. Larry Yarbrough (eds), *Social World of the First Christians*, pp. 214–33.

—'ἀκριβῶς...γράψαι (Luke 1:3): To Write the *Full* History of God's Receiving All Nations', in David P. Moessner (ed.), *Heritage of Israel*, pp. 229–50.

—'ΜΕΤΑΒΟΛΗ ΠΟΛΙΤΕΙΩΝ—Jesus as Founder of the Church in Luke-Acts: Form and Function', in Todd Penner and Caroline Vander Stichele (eds), *Contextualizing Acts*, pp. 139–88.

Bartholomew, Craig G., and Joel B. Green, and Anthony C. Thiselton (eds), *Reading Luke: Interpretation, Reflection, Formation* (Scripture and Hermeneutics Series, 6; Grand Rapids, Mich.: Zondervan, 2005).

Barton, Stephen C., 'Early Christianity and the Sociology of the Sect', in Francis Watson (ed.), *Open Text*, pp. 140–62.

—*Discipleship and Family Ties in Matthew and Mark* (SNTSMS, 80; Cambridge: Cambridge University Press, 1994).

—'Can We Identify the Gospel Audiences?' in Richard Bauckham (ed.), *Gospels for All Christians*, pp. 173–94.

—'Sociology and Theology', in I. Howard Marshall and David Peterson (eds), *Witness to the Gospel*, pp. 459–72.

Bauckham, Richard. 'The Acts of Paul as Sequel to Acts', in Bruce W. Winter and Andrew D. Clarke (eds), *Book of Acts in Its Ancient Literary Setting*, pp. 105–52.

—(ed.), *The Gospels for All Christians: Rethinking the Gospel Audiences* (Grand Rapids and London: William B. Eerdmans Publishing Company, 1997).

Bauer, David R., *The Structure of Matthew's Gospel: A Study in Literary Design* (Bible and Literature Series, 15; Sheffield: Almond Press, 1988).

Beavis, Mary Ann, ' "Expecting Nothing in Return": Luke's Picture of the Marginalized', *Int* 48 (1994), pp. 357–68.

Beck, Brian E., 'The Common Authorship of Luke and Acts', *NTS* 23 (1976/77), pp. 346–52.

Betz, Hans Dieter, *The Sermon on the Mount: A Commentary on the Sermon on the Mount, including the Sermon on the Plain (Matthew 5:3-7:27 and Luke 6:20-49)* (Hermeneia, Minn.: Fortress Press, 1995).

—(ed.) *Plutarch's Ethical Writings and Early Christian Literature* (Studia ad Corpus Hellenisticum Novi Testamenti, 3; Leiden: Brill Publishers, 1978).

Bieringer, R., and G. Van Belle and J. Verheyden (eds), *Luke and His Readers* (Festschrift A. Denaux; BETL, 182; Leuven: Leuven University Press/Peeters, 2005).

Bitzer, Lloyd F., 'The Rhetorical Situation', *Philosophy and Rhetoric* 1 (1968), pp. 1–14.

Black, Clifton, II, 'Keeping up with Recent Studies: Rhetorical Criticism and Biblical Interpretation', *ExpTim* 100 (1988/89), pp. 252–58.

—'John Mark in the Acts of the Apostles', in Richard P. Thompson and Thomas E. Phillips (eds), *Literary Studies in Luke-Acts*, pp. 191–214.

Bonz, Marianne Palmer, *The Past as Legacy: Luke-Acts and Ancient Epic* (Minneapolis: Fortress Press, 2000).

Booth, Wayne C., *The Rhetoric of Fiction* (Chicago: University of Chicago Press, 2nd edn., 1983.

—*The Company We Keep: An Ethics of Fiction* (Berkeley and Los Angeles: University of California Press, 1988).

—'The Ethics of Forms: Taking Flight with *The Wings of the Dove*', in James Phelan and Peter J. Rabinowitz (eds), *Understanding Narrative*, pp. 99–135.

Borgman, Paul, *The Way according to Luke: Hearing the Whole Story of Luke-Acts* (Grand Rapids, Mich.: William B. Eerdmans Publishing Company, 2006).

Bosend, William F. II., 'The means of absent ends', in Ben Witherington III (ed.), *History, Literature and Society*, pp. 348–62.

Bovon, François, *Luke the Theologian: Thirty-three Years of Research [1950-1983]* (PTMS, 12; Allison Park, Pennsylvania: Pickwick Press, 1987).

—'The God of Luke', in *New Testament Traditions*, pp. 67–80.

—'The Importance of Mediations in Luke's Theological Plan', in François Bovon, *New Testament Traditions*, pp. 51–66.

—' "How Well the Holy Spirit Spoke Through the Prophet Isaiah to Your Ancestors!" (Acts 28:25)', in *New Testament Traditions*, pp. 43–50.

— *New Testament Traditions and Apocryphal Narratives* (trans. Jane Haapiseva-Hunter; PTMS, 36; Allison Park, Penn.: Pickwick Press, 1995.

—*Luke 1: A Commentary on the Gospel of Luke 1:1-9-50* (trans. Christine M. Thomas; Hermenia, Minn.: Fortress Press, 2002).

Braet, Antoine C., 'Ethos, Pathos, and Logos in Aristotle's *"Rhetoric"*: A Re-examination', *Argumentation* 6 (1992), pp. 307–20.

Braumann, Gerhard, 'Die Lucanische Interpretation der Zerstörung Jerusalems', *NovT* 6 (1963), pp. 120–27.

Braun, Willi, *Feasting and social rhetoric in Luke 14* (SNTSMS, 85; Cambridge: Cambridge University Press, 1995).

Brawley, Robert L., *Centering on God: Method and Message in Luke-Acts* (Literary Currents in Biblical Interpretation; Louisville: Westminster/ John Knox Press, 1990).

—'The God of Promises and the News in Luke-Acts', in Richard P. Thompson and Thomas E. Phillips (eds), *Literary Studies in Luke-Acts*, pp. 279–96.

—*Text to Text Pours Forth Speech: Voices of Scripture in Luke-Acts* (Bloomington, Ind.: Indiana University Press, 1995).

Brodie, Thomas L., 'Towards an Unravelling of Luke's Use of the Old Testament: Luke 7.11-17 as an *Imitatio* of 1 Kings 17.17-24', *NTS* 32 (1986), pp. 247–67.

—'Luke-Acts as an Imitation and Emulation of the Elijah-Elisha Narrative', in Earl Richard (ed.), *New Views*, pp. 78–85.

—'Not Q but Elijah: The Saving of the Centurion's Servant (Luke 7:1-10) as an Internationalization of the Saving of the Widow and Her Child (1 Kings 17:1-16)', *IBS* 14 (1992), pp. 54–71.

Brooke, George J. (ed.), *Women in Biblical Tradition* (Studies in Women in Religious, 31; Lewiston, New York: Edwin Mellen Press, 1992).

Budick, Sanford, and Wolfgang Iser (eds), *Languages of the Unsayable: The Play of Negativity in Literature and Literary Theory* (Stanford: Stanford University Press, 1996).

Burke, Kenneth, *Language as Symbolic Action: Essays on Life, Literature, and Method* (Berkeley and Los Angeles: University of California Press, 1966).

Burnett, Frederick W., 'Characterization and Reader Construction of Characters in the Gospels', in Barry Callen (ed.), *Listening to the Word of God*, pp. 69–88.

—'Characterization and Reader Construction of Characters in the Gospels', *Semeia* 63 (1993), pp. 1–29.

Burridge, Richard A., *What Are the Gospels? A Comparison with Graeco-Roman Biography* (SNTSMS, 70; Cambridge: Cambridge University Press, 1992).

Cadbury, Henry, *The Making of Luke-Acts* (London: McMillan Publishing Company, 1927).

Cadzow, Hunter, 'New Historicism', in Michael Groden and Martin Kreiswirth (eds), *Johns Hopkins Guide*, pp. 534–39.

Callan, Terrance, 'The Preface to Luke-Acts and Historiography', *NTS* 31 (1985), pp. 576–81.

Callen, Barry (ed.), *Listening to the Word of God* (Festschrift Boyce W. Blackwelder; Anderson, Ind.: Warner Press, 1990).

Cameron, A. (ed.), *History as Text: The Writing of Ancient History* (Chapel Hill: University of North Carolina Press, 1990).

Cameron, Ron, '"What Have You Come Out to See?" Characterizations of John and Jesus in the Gospels', *Semeia* 49 (1990), pp. 35–69.

Camery-Hoggatt, Jerry, *Speaking of God: Reading and Preaching the Word of God* (Peabody, Mass.: Hendrickson Publishers, 1995).

Camp, Gregory Alan, 'Woe to You Hypocrites! Law and Leaders in the Gospel of Matthew' (Ph.D. dissertation. University of Sheffield, 2003).

Carras, George P., 'Observant Jews in the Story of Luke and Acts: Paul, Jesus and Other Jews', in J. Verheydon (ed.), in *Unity of Luke-Acts*, pp. 693–708.

Carroll, John T., 'Luke's Portrayal of the Pharisees', *CBQ* 50 (1988), pp. 604–21.

—'The God of Israel and the Salvation of the Nations: The Gospel of Luke and the Acts of the Apostles', in A. A. Das and Frank J. Matera (eds), *Forgotten God*, pp. 91–106.

Carroll, M. D., D. J. A. Clines and P. R. Davies (eds), *The Bible in Human Society* (Festschrift John Rogerson; JSOTSup, 200; Sheffield: Sheffield Academic Press, 2000.

Carruth, Shawn, 'Strategies of Authority: A Rhetorical Study of the

Character of the Speaker in Q 6:20-49', in John S. Kloppenborg (ed.), *Conflict and Invention*, pp. 98–115.

Carson, D. A., 'Matthew 11:19b/Luke 7:35: A Test Case for the Bearing of Q Christology on the Synoptic Problem', in Joel B. Green and Max Turner (eds), *Jesus of Nazareth*, pp. 138–41.

Chatman, Seymour, *Story and Discourse: Narrative Structure in Fiction and Film* (Ithaca and London: Cornell University Press, 1978).

—*Coming to Terms: The Rhetoric of Narrative in Fiction and Film* (Ithaca and London: Cornell University Press, 1990).

Christophersen, A., et al., *Paul, Luke and the Graeco-Roman World: Essays in Honour of Alexander J. M. Wedderburn* (JSNTSup, 217; Sheffield: Sheffield Academic Press, 2002).

Clayton, Jay, and Eric Rothstein (eds), *Influence and Intertextuality in Literary History* (Madison: University of Wisconsin Press, 1991).

—'Figures in the Corpus: Theories of Influence and Intertextuality', in Jay Clayton and Eric Rothstein (eds), *Influence and Intertextuality*, pp. 3–36.

Clines, David J. A., and Stephen D. Moore (eds), *Auguries: The Jubilee Volume of the Sheffield Department of Biblical Studies* (JSOTSup, 269; Sheffield: Sheffield Academic Press, 1998).

Collins, John J., *Between Athens and Jerusalem: Jewish Identity in the Hellenistic Diaspora* (New York: Crossroad, 1986).

Combrink, H. J. B., 'The Structure and Significance of Luke 4:16-30', *Neot* 7 (1973), pp. 27–47.

Conley, Thomas M., 'The Enthymeme in Perspective', *Quarterly Journal of Speech* 70 (1984), pp. 168–87.

Conzelmann, Hans, *The Theology of St. Luke* (trans. G. Buswell; London: Harper & Row, 1960).

Corbett, Edward P. J., *Classical Rhetoric and the Modern Student* (Oxford: Oxford University Press, 1965).

Corley, Kathleen E., *Private Women, Public Meals: Social Conflict in the Synoptic Tradition* (Peabody, Mass.: Hendrickson Publishers, 1993).

Cotter, Wendy, 'The Parable of the Children in the Market Place, Q (Lk) 7:31-35: An Examination of the Parable's Image and Significance', *NovT* 29 (1987), pp. 289–304.

—'Children Sitting in the Agora: Q (Luke) 7:31-35', *Forum* 5 (1989), pp. 63–82.

—' "Yes, I Tell You, and More Than a Prophet": The Function of John in Q', in John S. Kloppenborg (ed.), *Conflict and Invention*, pp. 135–50.

Couroyer, B., 'De la mesure dont vous mesurez il vous sera mesuré', *RB* 77 (1970), pp. 366–70.

Creech, Robert R., 'The Most Excellent Narratee: The Significance of Theophilus in Luke-Acts', in Raymond H. Keathley (ed.), *Steadfast Purpose*, pp. 107–26.

Crockett, Larrimore C., 'Luke 4:25-27 and Jewish-Gentile Relations in Luke-Acts', *JBL* 88 (1969), pp. 177–83.

D'Angelo, Mary Rose, 'The *ANHR* Question in Luke-Acts: Imperial

Masculinity and the Deployment of Women in the Early Second Century', in Amy-Jill Levine and Marianne Blickenstaff (eds), *Feminist Companion to Luke*, pp. 44–69.

Danker, Frederick W., *Benefactor: Epigraphic Study of a Greco-Roman and New Testament Semantic Field* (St. Louis: Clayton, 1982).

Darr, John A., *On Character Building: The Reader and the Rhetoric of Characterization in Luke-Acts* (Literary Currents in Biblical Interpretation; Louisville: Westminster Press, 1992).

—'Narrator as Character: Mapping a Reader-Oriented Approach to Narration in Luke-Acts', *Semeia* 63 (1993), pp. 43–60.

—*Herod the Fox: Audience Criticism and Lukan Characterization* (JSNTSup, 163; Sheffield: Sheffield Academic Press, 1998).

—'Irenic or Ironic? Another Look at Gamaliel before the Sanhedrin Acts 5:33-42)', in Richard P. Thompson and Thomas E. Phillips (eds), *Literary Studies*, pp. 121–40.

Das, A. A., and Frank J. Matera (eds), *Forgotten God* (Festschrift Paul J. Achtemeier; Louisville: Westminster/John Knox Press, 2002).

Dawsey, James M., 'The Literary Unity of Luke-Acts: Questions of Style – A Task for Literary Critics', *NTS* 35 (1989), pp. 48–66.

de Beaugrande, Robert, 'Discourse Analysis', in Michael Groden and Martin Kreiswirth (eds), *Johns Hopkins Guide*, pp. 207–10.

Deissmann, Adolf, 'Hellenistic Greek with Special Consideration of the Greek Bible', in Stanley E. Porter (ed.), *Language of the New Testament*, pp. 39–59.

Delobel, Joël (ed.), *Logia: Les Paroles de Jésus – The Sayings of Jesus. Mémorial Joseph Coppens* (BETL, 59; Leuven: Leuven University, 1982).

deSilva, David A., 'Investigating Honor Discourse: Guidelines from Classical Rhetoricians', in Kent H. Richards (ed.), SBLSP, 36 (Atlanta: Scholars Press, 1997), pp. 491–525.

—*The Hope of Glory: Honor Discourse and New Testament Interpretation* (Collegeville, Minnesota: Liturgical Press, 1999).

—'Honor and Shame', in Craig A. Evans and Stanley E. Porter (eds), *Dictionary of New Testament Background*, pp. 518–22.

Destro, Adriana, and Mauro Pesce, 'Fathers and Householders in the Jesus Movement: The Perspective of the Gospel of Luke', *BibInt* 11 (2003), pp. 211–38.

Dewey, Joanna, *Markan Public Debate: Literary Technique, Concentric Structure, and Theology in Mark 2:1-3:6* (SBLDS, 48; Chico, Calif.: Scholars Press, 1980).

Diefenbach, Manfred, *Die Komposition des Lukasevangeliums unter Berücksichtigung antiker Rhetorikelemente* (FTS; Frankfurt am Main: Verlag Josef Knacht, 1993).

Dihle, Albrecht, *Die Goldene Regel: Eine Einführung in die Geschichte der antiken und frühchristlichen Vulgärethik* (NTAbh, 28; Göttingen: Vandenhoeck & Ruprecht, 1962).

Donohue, John R., 'The Literary Turn and New Testament Theology: Detour or New Direction?' *JR* 76 (1996), pp. 250–75.

Douglas, Conrad R., '"Love Your Enemies": Rhetoric, Tradents, and Ethos', in John S. Kloppenborg (ed.), *Conflict and Invention*, pp. 116–34.

Downing, Gerald F., 'Theophilus's First Reading of Luke-Acts', in Christopher M. Tuckett (ed.), *Luke's Literary Achievement*, pp. 91–109.

—*Doing Things with Words in the First Christian Century* (JSNTSup, 200; Sheffield: Sheffield Academic Press, 2000).

Duff, Timothy, *Plutarch's Lives: Exploring Virtue and Vice* (New York: Oxford University Press, 1999).

Dunn, James D. G., *Christology in the Making: A New Testament Inquiry into the Origins of the Doctrine of the Incarnation* (Philadelphia: Westminster Press, 1980).

Dupont, Jacques, *Les béatitudes: Le problème littéraire: Les deux versions du Sermon sur la Montagne et des Béatitudes* (vol. 1; Bruges and Louvain: Abbaye de Saint-André/E. Nauwelaerts, 2nd edn., 1958).

—'La conclusion des Actes et son rapport à l'ensemble de l'ouvrage de Luc', in J. Kremer (ed.), *Les Actes des Apôtres*, pp. 359–404.

Ebner, Martin, 'Feindesliebe – a ein Ratschlag zum Überleben? Sozial- und religionsgeschichtliche Überlegungen zu Mt 5,38-47 par Lk 6,27-35', in Jon M. Asgeirsson, et al. (eds), *From Quest to Q*, pp. 119–42.

Eco, Umberto, *The Role of the Reader: Explorations in the Semiotics of Texts* (Bloomington: Indiana University Press, 1979).

Edwards, Mark, et al. (eds), *Apologetics in the Roman Empire: Pagans, Jews, and Christians* (Oxford: Oxford University Press, 2000).

Elliott, John H., 'Patronage and Clientage', in Richard Rohrbaugh (ed.), *Social Sciences*, pp. 144–57.

Eltester, Walther (ed.), *Jesus in Nazareth* (BZNW, 40; Berlin and New York: Walter de Gruyter, 1972).

Esler, Philip, *Community and Gospel in Luke-Acts: The Social and Political Motivations of Lucan Theology* (Cambridge: Cambridge University Press, 1987).

—(ed.), *Modelling Early Christianity: Social-scientific studies of the New Testament in its context* (London and New York: Routledge, 1996).

Evans, Craig A., 'Luke's Use of the Elijah/Elisha Narratives and the Ethic of Election', *JBL* 106 (1987), pp. 75–83.

Evans, Craig A., and Stanley E. Porter (eds), *Dictionary of New Testament Background* (Downers Grove, Ill.: InterVarsity Press, 2000).

Evans, Craig A., and James A. Sanders, *Luke and Scripture: The Function of Sacred Tradition in Luke-Acts* (Minneapolis: Fortress Press, 1993).

Evans, Craig A., and W. Richard Stegner (eds), *The Gospels and Scriptures of Israel* (JSNTSup, 104; Sheffield: Sheffield Academic Press, 1994).

Farrell, Thomas B., 'Aristotle's Enthymeme as Tacit Reference', in Alan G. Gross and Arthur E. Walzer (eds), *Rereading Aristotle's Rhetoric*, pp. 93–106.

Finn, Thomas M., *From Death to Rebirth: Ritual and Conversion in Antiquity* (New York: Paulist Press, 1997).

Fiorenza, Elizabeth Schüssler, *But She Said: Feminist Practices of Biblical Interpretation* (Boston: Beacon Press, 1992).

—(ed.), *Searching the Scriptures: A Feminist Introduction* (vol. 1; New York: Crossroad, 1993).

—(ed.), *Searching the Scriptures: A Feminist Commentary* (vol. 2; New York: Crossroad, 1994).

Fitzgerald, John T. (ed.), *Greco-Roman Perspectives on Friendship* (SBLRBS, 34; Atlanta: Scholars Press, 1997).

Fitzmyer, Joseph A., *The Gospel according to Luke I-IX* (AB, 28; New York: Doubleday & Company, 1981).

—*The Gospel according to Luke X-XXIV* (AB, 28A; New York: Doubleday & Company, 1985).

—*Luke the Theologian: Aspects of His Teaching* (New York: Paulist Press, 1989).

Fortenbaugh, William W., 'Aristotle on Persuasion Through Character', *Rhetorica* 10 (1992), pp. 207–44.

Fowl, Stephen, 'Texts Don't Have Ideologies', *BibInt* 3 (1995), pp. 15–34.

—'The Role of Authorial Intention in the Theological Interpretation of Scripture', in Joel B. Green and Max Turner (eds), *Between Two Horizons*, pp. 71–87.

Fowl, Stephen, and L. Gregory Jones, *Reading in Communion: Scripture and Ethics in Christian Life* (Grand Rapids and London: William B. Eerdmans Publishing Company, 1991).

Fowler, Robert M., *Let the Reader Understand: Reader-Response Criticism and the Gospel of Mark* (Minneapolis: Fortress Press, 1991).

Freadman, Richard, and Seumas Miller, *Re-Thinking Theory: A Critique of Contemporary Literary Theory and an Alternative Account* (Cambridge: Cambridge University Press, 1992).

Freund, Elizabeth, *The Return of the Reader: Reader-Response Criticism* (London and New York: Methuen, 1987).

Furnish, Paul Victor, *The Love Command in the New Testament* (Nashville: Abingdon Press, 1972).

Fusco, Vittorio, 'Luke-Acts and the Future of Israel', *NovT* 38 (1996), pp. 1–18.

Gadamer, Hans-Georg, *Truth and Method* (New York: Continuum, 2nd edn., 1992).

Gamble, Harry Y., *Books and Readers in the Early Church: A History of Early Christian Texts* (New Haven: Yale University Press, 1995).

Garrett, Susan R., *The Demise of the Devil: Magic and the Demonic in Luke's Writings* (Minneapolis: Augsburg/Fortress Press, 1989).

Gathercole, Simon, 'The Justification of Wisdom (Matt 11.19b/Luke 7.35)', *NTS* 49 (2003), pp. 476–88.

Gavrilov, A. K., 'Reading Techniques in Classical Antiquity', *Classical Quarterly* 47 (1997), pp. 56–73.

Geertz, Clifford, *The Interpretation of Cultures* (New York: Basic Books, 1973).

Genette, Gérard, *Palimpsests: Literature in the Second Degree* (trans. Channa Newman and Claude Doubinsky; Lincoln, Neb.: University of Nebraska Press, 1997).

Gerdhardsson, Birger, *Memory and Manuscript: Oral Tradition and Written Transmission in Rabbinic Judaism and Early Christianity* (Grand Rapids: William B. Eerdmans Publishing Company, 1998).

Gilbert, Gary, 'Roman Propaganda and Christian Identity in the Worldview of Luke-Acts', in Todd Penner and Caroline Vander Stichele (eds), *Contextualizing Acts*, pp. 233–56.

Gill, Christopher, 'The *Ethos/Pathos* Distinction in Rhetorical and Literary Criticism', *Classical Quarterly* 34 (1984), pp. 149–66.

—'The Question of Character and Personality in Greek Tragedy', *Poetics Today* 7 (1986), pp. 251–73.

—'The Character-Personality Distinction', in Christopher Pelling (ed.), *Characterization and Individuality* (Oxford: Clarendon Press, 1990), pp. 1–31.

Gill, Christopher, and Norman Postlewaite and Richard Seaford (eds), *Reciprocity in Ancient Greece* (Oxford: Oxford University Press, 1998).

Gill, D. W. J., and Conrad Gempf (eds), *The Book of Acts in Its Ancient Greco-Roman Setting: Volume Two* (The Book of Acts in Its First Century Setting. Grand Rapids: William B. Eerdmans Publishing Company, 1994).

Gilliard, Frank D., 'More Silent Reading in Antiquity: *Non omne verbum sonat*', *JBL* 112 (1993), pp. 689–96.

Gold, Barbara K., *Literary Patronage in Greece and Rome* (Chapel Hill: University of North Carolina Press, 1987).

Gowler, David M., 'Characterization in Luke: A Socio-Narratological Approach', *BTB* 19 (1989), pp. 57–62.

—*Host, Enemy, and Friend: Portraits of the Pharisees in Luke and Acts* (Emory Studies in Early Christianity, 2; New York: Peter Lang, 1991).

—'Text, Culture, and Ideology in Luke 7:1-10: A Dialogic Reading', in David B. Gowler, L. Gregory Bloomquist and Duane F. Watson (eds), *Fabrics of Discourse*, pp. 89–125.

Gowler, David M., and L. Gregory Bloomquist and Duane F. Watson (eds), *Fabrics of Discourse: Culture, Ideology, and Religion* (Harrisburg, PA: Trinity Press International, 2003).

Green, Joel B., 'The Social Status of Mary in Luke 1,5-2,52: A Plea for Methodological Integration', *Bib* 73 (1992), pp. 457–72.

—'The Death of Jesus', in Joel B. Green and Scot McKnight (eds), *Dictionary of Jesus and the Gospels*, pp. 146–63.

—'Good News to Whom? Jesus and the "Poor" in the Gospel of Luke', in Joel B. Green (ed.), *Jesus of Nazareth*, pp. 59–74.

—(ed.), *Jesus of Nazareth: Lord and Christ: Essays on the Historical Jesus and New Testament Christology* (Grand Rapids: William B. Eerdmans Publishing Company, 1994).

—*The Theology of the Gospel of Luke* (New Testament Theology; Cambridge: Cambridge University Press, 1995).
—'Discourse Analysis and New Testament Interpretation', in Joel B. Green (ed.), *Hearing the New Testament*, pp. 175–96.
—'The Practice of Reading the New Testament', in Joel B. Green (ed.), *Hearing the New Testament*, pp. 411–27.
—(ed.), *Hearing the New Testament: Strategies for Interpretation* (Grand Rapids: William B. Eerdmans Publishing Company, 1995).
—'The Problem of a Beginning: Israel's Scriptures in Luke 1-2', *BBR* 4 (1996), pp. 61–86.
—'Internal Repetition in Luke-Acts: Contemporary Narratology and Lukan Historiography', in Ben Witherington III (ed.), *History, Literature and Society*, pp. 283–99.
—*The Gospel of Luke* (NICNT; Grand Rapids: William B. Eerdmans Publishing Company, 1997).
—'Acts of the Apostles', in Ralph Martin and Peter H. Davids (eds), *Dictionary of the Later New Testament*, pp. 7–24.
—' "Salvation to the Ends of the Earth" (Acts 13:47): God as Saviour in the Acts of the Apostles', in I. Howard Marshall and David Peterson (eds), *Witness to the Gospel*, pp. 83–106.
—'Scripture and Theology: Uniting the Two So Long Divided', Joel B. Green and Max Turner (eds), *Between Two Horizons*, pp. 23–43.
Green, Joel B., and Scot McKnight (eds), *Dictionary of Jesus and the Gospels* (Downers Grove and Leicester: InterVarsity Press, 1992).
Green, Joel B., and Max Turner (eds), *Between Two Horizons: Spanning New Testament Studies & Systematic Theology* (Grand Rapids and Cambridge: William B. Eerdmans Publishing Company, 2000).
Greenblatt, Stephen, 'Culture' in Frank Lentricchia and Thomas McLaughlin (eds), *Critical Terms*, pp. 225–32.
Greenblatt, Stephen, and Giles Gunn (eds), *Redrawing the Boundaries: The Transformation of English and American Literary Studies* (New York: Modern Language Association, 1992).
Grimshaw, Jim, 'Luke's Market Exchange District: Decentering Luke's Rich Urban Center', *Semeia* 86 (1999), pp. 33–51.
Groden, Michael, and Martin Kreiswirth (eds), *The Johns Hopkins Guide to Literary Theory and Criticism* (Baltimore: Johns Hopkins University Press, 1994).
Gross, Alan, and Arthur E. Walzer (eds), *Rereading Aristotle's Rhetoric* (Carbondale and Edwardsville: Southern Illinois University Press, 2000).
Haenchen, Ernst, 'Judentum und Christentum in der Apostelgeschichte', *ZNW* 54 (1963), pp. 155–87.
—*The Acts of the Apostles* (Philadelphia: Westminster Press, 1971).
Halliwell, Stephen, 'Traditional Greek Conceptions of Character', in Christopher Pelling (ed.), *Characterization and Individuality*, pp. 32–59.
Hamilton, Paul, *Historicism* (London and New York: Routledge, 1996).

Hanson, K. C., 'How Honorable! How Shameful! A Cultural Analysis of Matthew's Makarisms and Reproaches', *Semeia* 68 (1996), pp. 83–114.

Harker, John W., 'Information Processing and the Reading of Literary Texts', *New Literary History* 20 (1989), pp. 465–81.

Hartin, Patrick J., ' "Yet Wisdom Is Justified by Her Children" (Q 7:35): A Rhetorical and Compositional Analysis of Divine Sophia in Q', in John S. Kloppenborg (ed.), *Conflict and Invention*, pp. 151–64.

Havelaar, Henriette, 'Hellenistic Parallels to Acts 5.1-11 and the Problem of Conflicting Interpretations', *JSNT* 67 (1997), pp. 62–82.

Hawthorne, Gerald F. (ed.), *Current Issues in Biblical and Patristic Interpretation* (Grand Rapids, Mich.: William B. Eerdmans Publishing Company, 1975).

Hays, Richard B., and Joel B. Green, 'The Use of the Old Testament by New Testament Writers', in Joel B. Green (ed.), *Hearing the New Testament*, pp. 222–38.

Head, Peter, *Christology and the Synoptic Problem: An Assessment of One Argument for Markan Priority* (SNTSMS, 94; Cambridge: Cambridge University Press, 1997).

Heath, Malcolm, 'Invention', in Stanley E. Porter (ed.), *Handbook*, pp. 89–119.

Hedrick, Charles W., *Parables as Poetic Fictions: The Creative Voice of Jesus* (Peabody, Mass.: Hendrickson Publishers, 1994).

Hengel, Martin, *Judaism and Hellenism: Studies in their Encounter in Palestine during the Early Hellenistic Period* (trans. John Bowden; Philadelphia: Fortress Press, 1974).

Hoffmann, Paul, *Tradition und Situation: Studien zur Jesusüberlieferung in der Logienquelle und den synoptischen Evangelien* (Münster: Aschendorff, 1995).

Hollaway, Paul A., 'The Enthymeme as an Element of Style in Paul', *JBL* 120 (2001), pp. 329–42.

Horbury, William, *Jews and Christians in Contact and Controversy* (Edinburgh: T&T Clark, 1998).

Horsley, Richard A., 'Ethics and Exegesis: "Love Your Enemies" and the Doctrine of Non-violence', *JAAR* 54 (1986), pp. 3–31.

—'Speeches and Dialogue in Acts', *NTS* 32 (1986), pp. 609–14.

—'Social Conflict in the Synoptic Sayings Source Q', in John S. Kloppenborg (ed.), *Conflict and Invention*, pp. 37–52.

—'The Covenant Renewal Discourse: Q 6:20-49', in Richard A. Horsley and Jonathan A. Draper (eds), *Whoever Hears You*, pp. 195–227.

—'The Kingdom of God as the Renewal of Israel', Richard A. Horsley and Jonathan A. Draper (eds), *Whoever Hears You*, pp. 260–82.

Horsley, Richard, and Jonathan A. Draper (eds), *Whoever Hears You Hears Me: Prophets, Performance, and Tradition in Q* (Harrisburg, Pa.: Trinity Press International, 1999).

Hunter, Virginia J., *Past and Process in Herodotus and Thucydides* (Princeton: Princeton University Press, 1982).

Hur, Ju, *A Dynamic Reading of the Holy Spirit in Luke-Acts* (JSNTSup, 211;
    Sheffield: Sheffield Academic Press, 2001).
Iser, Wolfgang, *The Act of Reading: A Theory of Aesthetic Response*
    (Baltimore: Johns Hopkins University Press, 1978).
—'The Interplay Between Creation and Interpretation', *New Literary
    History* 15 (1984), pp. 387–96.
—*Prospecting: From Reader Response to Literary Anthropology* (Baltimore
    and London: Johns Hopkins University Press, 1989).
—*The Fictive and the Imaginary: Charting Literary Anthropology* (Baltimore
    and London: Johns Hopkins University Press, 1993).
—'The Play of the Text', in Sanford Budick and Wolfgang Iser (eds),
    Languages of the Unsayable, pp. 325–39.
Jeremias, Joachim, *The Parables of Jesus* (London: SCM Press, 3rd edn.,
    1972.
Jervell, Jacob, *Luke and the People of God: A New Look at Luke-Acts*
    (Minneapolis: Augsburg Press, 1972).
—*The Unknown Paul: Essays on Luke-Acts and Early Christian History*
    (Minneapolis: Fortress Press, 1984).
—'The Daughters of Abraham: Women in Acts', in *Unknown Paul*, pp. 122–
    37.
Jobling, David, et al. (eds), *The Bible and the Politics of Exegesis* (Festschrift
    Norman K. Gottwald; Cleveland: Pilgrim Press, 1991).
Johnson, Luke T., *The Literary Function of Possessions in Luke-Acts*
    (SBLDS, 39; Missoula: Scholars Press, 1977).
—'On Finding the Lukan Community: A Cautious Cautionary Essay', in
    Kent H. Richards (ed.), SBLSP, 26 (Missoula: Scholars Press, 1987),
    pp. 87–100.
—*The Gospel of Luke* (SP, 3; Collegeville, Minnesota: Liturgical Press,
    1991).
—*The Acts of the Apostles* (SP, 5; Collegeville, Minnesota: Liturgical Press,
    1992).
Joubert, Stephan, 'Coming to Terms with a Neglected Aspect of Ancient
    Mediterranean Reciprocity: Seneca's views on benefit-exchange in *De
    beneficiis* as the framework for a model of social exchange', in John J.
    Pilch (ed.), *Social Scientific Models for Interpreting the Bible*, pp. 47–63.
Just, Arthur A., Jr., *The Ongoing Feast: Table Fellowship and Eschatology at
    Emmaus* (Collegeville, Minn.: Liturgical Press, 1993).
Karris, Robert J., 'Missionary Communities: A New Paradigm for the
    Study of Luke-Acts', *CBQ* 41 (1979), pp. 80–97.
Kavanagh, James H., 'Ideology', in Frank Lentricchia and Thomas
    McLaughlin (eds), *Critical Terms*, pp. 306–20.
Kearney, Suzanne Marie, 'A Study of Principal Compositional Techniques
    in Luke-Acts based on Lk 4:16-30 in Conjunction with Lk 7:18-23'
    (Ph.D. dissertation; Boston University, 1978).
Keathley, Raymond H. (ed.), *With Steadfast Purpose* (Festschrift Henry
    Jackson Flanders, Jr.; Waco: Baylor University Press, 1990).

Keck, Leander, and J. Louis Martyn (eds), *Studies in Luke-Acts* (Philadelphia: Fortress Press, 1966).

Keener, Craig S., *Bible Background Commentary* (Downers Grove, Ill.: InterVarsity Press, 1993).

—'Friendship', in Craig A. Evans and Stanley E. Porter (eds), *Dictionary of New Testament Background*, pp. 380–88.

Kennedy, George A., *Classical Rhetoric and Its Christian and Secular Tradition from Ancient to Modern Times* (Chapel Hill: University of North Carolina Press, 1980).

—*New Testament Interpretation Through Rhetorical Criticism* (Chapel Hill and London: University of North Carolina Press, 1984).

—'The Composition and Influence of Aristotle's *Rhetoric*', in A. O. Rorty (ed.), *Aristotle's Rhetoric*, pp. 416–24.

—*Progymnasmata: Greek Textbooks and Prose Composition and Rhetoric* (Writings from the Greco-Roman World, 10; Leiden and Boston: Brill, 2003).

Kern, Philip H., *Rhetoric and Galatians: Assessing an approach to Paul's epistle* (SNTSMS, 101; Cambridge: Cambridge University Press, 1998).

Kim, Kyoung-Jin, *Stewardship and Almsgiving in Luke's Theology* (JSNTSup, 155; Sheffield: Sheffield Academic Press, 1998).

Kingsbury, Jack Dean, *Conflict in Luke: Jesus, Authorities, Disciples* (Minneapolis: Fortress Press, 1991).

—'The Pharisees in Luke-Acts', in F. Van Segbroeck, et al. (eds), *The Four Gospels 1992*, (Leuven: Leuven University Press), pp. 1497–1511.

—'The Plot of Luke's Story of Jesus', *Int* 48 (1994), pp. 369–78.

—*Gospel Interpretation: Narrative-Critical & Social-Science Approaches*, (Harrisburg: Trinity Press International, 1997).

Kirk, Alan, ' "Love Your Enemies," The Golden Rule, and Ancient Reciprocity (Luke 6:27-35)', *JBL* 122 (2003), pp. 667–86.

Kitzberger, Ingrid Rosa, 'Mary of Bethany and Mary of Magdala – Two Female Characters in the Johannine Passion Narrative: A Feminist, Narrative-Critical, Reader-Response', *NTS* 41 (1995), pp. 564–86.

Klink, Edward W., 'The Gospel Community Debate: State of the Question', *CBR* 3 (2004), pp. 60–85.

Kloppenborg, John S., *The Formation of Q: Trajectories in Ancient Wisdom Collections* (Studies in Antiquity and Christianity; Philadelphia: Fortress Press, 1987), pp. 107–21.

—*Q Parallels: Critical Notes and Concordance* (Sonoma, Calif.: Polebridge Press, 1988).

—(ed.), *Conflict and Invention: Literary, Rhetorical, and Social Studies on the Sayings Gospel Q* (Valley Forge, Pa.: Trinity Press International, 1995).

Knight, Jonathan, *Luke's Gospel* (New Testament Readings; New York and London: Routledge Press, 1998).

Koet, Bernard, 'Simeons Worte (Lk 2,29-32c-35) und Israels Geschick', in Frans Segbroeck (ed.), *Four Gospels*, 1149-69.

Konstan, David. 'Reciprocity and Friendship', in Christopher Gill, Norman

Postlewaite, and Richard Seaford (eds), *Reciprocity in Ancient Greece*, pp. 279–301.

Kraabel, A. Thomas, 'The Disappearance of the "God-fearers" ', *Numen* 28 (1981), pp. 113–23.

Kremer, J. (ed.), *Les Actes des Apôtres. Traditions, rédaction, théologie*, (BETL, 48; Leuven: Leuven University Press, 1978).

Kristeva, Julia, *Desire in Language: A Semiotic Approach to Literature and Art* (trans. T. Gora, A. Jardine, and L. Roudiez; New York: Columbia University Press, 1980).

Kurz, William S., 'Narrative Approaches to Luke-Acts', *Bib* 68 (1987), pp. 195–20.

—'Narrative Models for Imitation in Luke-Acts', in David L. Balch, Everett Ferguson, and Wayne A. Meeks (eds), *Greeks, Romans, and Christians*, pp. 171–89.

—*Reading Luke-Acts: Dynamics of Biblical Narrative* (Louisville: Westminster Press, 1993).

—'Intertextual Use of Sir. 48.1-16 in Plotting Luke-Acts', in Craig A. Evans and W. Richard Stegner (eds), *Gospels and Scriptures of Israel*, pp. 308–24.

—'Effects of Variant Narrators in Acts 10-11', *NTS* 43 (1997), pp. 570–86.

LaFargue, Michael, 'Are Texts Determinant? Derrida, Barth, and the Role of the Biblical Scholar', *HTR* 81 (1988), pp. 341–57.

Lambrecht, Jan, S. J., 'Rhetorical Criticism and the New Testament', *Bijdragen* 50 (1989), pp. 239–53.

Lanigan, Richard L., 'From Enthymeme to Abduction: The Classical Law of Logic and the Postmodern Rule for Rhetoric', in Lenore Landsdorf and Andrew R. Smith (eds), *Recovering Pragmatism's Voice*, pp. 49–70.

Landsdorf, Lenore, and Andrew R. Smith (eds), *Recovering Pragmatism's Voice: The Classical Tradition, Rorty, and the Philosophy of Communication* (Albany, New York: SUNY Press, 1995).

Lentricchia, Frank, and Thomas McLaughlin (eds), *Critical Terms for Literary Study* (Chicago: University of Chicago Press, 2nd edn., 1995).

Lentz, John C., *Luke's Portrait of Paul* (SNTSMS, 77; Cambridge: Cambridge University Press, 1994).

Levine, Amy-Jill, Marianne Blickenstaff (eds), *A Feminist Companion to Luke* (London and New York: Sheffield Academic Press, 2002).

Linton, Olof, 'The Parable of the Children's Game: Baptist and Son of Man (Matt xi,16-19 = Luke vii,31-35): A Synoptic Text-Critical, Structural, and Exegetical Investigation', *NTS* 22 (1975/76), pp. 159–79.

Litwak, Kenneth Duncan, *Echoes of Scripture in Luke-Acts: Telling the History of God's People Intertextually* (JSNTSup, 282; London: T&T Clark, 2005).

Lofink, Gerhard, *Die Himmelfahrt Jesu: Untersuchingen zu den Himmelfarts-und Erhöhungstexten bei Lukas* (SANT, 26; Munich: Kösel, 1971).

Luomanen, Peter (ed.), *Luke-Acts: Scandinavian Perspectives* (Paderborner

Theologische Studien, 54; Helsinki and Göttingen: Vandenhoeck & Ruprecht, 1991).

MacDonald, Dennis R., 'Luke's Eutychus and Homer's Elphenor: Acts 20:7-12 and Odyssey 10-12', *JHC* 1 (1994), pp. 4–24.

—'The Shipwrecks of Odysseus and Paul', *NTS* 45 (1999), pp. 88–107.

—'Luke's Emulation of Homer: Acts 12:1-17 and Iliad 24', *Forum* 3 (2000), pp. 197–205.

Mack, Burton L., *Rhetoric of the New Testament* (Minneapolis: Fortress Press, 1990).

MacLennan, R. S., and A. T. Kraabel, 'The God-Fearers – A Literary and Theological Invention', *BARev* 12 (1986), pp. 46–53.

Mailloux, Steven, *Rhetorical Power* (Ithaca and London: Cornell University Press, 1989).

Malherbe, Abraham J., *Social Aspects of Early Christianity* (Philadelphia: Fortress Press, 2nd edn., 1983.

Malina, Bruce, 'Patron and Client: The Analogy behind Synoptic Theology', *Forum* 4 (1988), pp. 2–32.

—'Interpretation: Reading, Abduction, Metaphor', in David Jobling (ed.), *Politics of Exegesis*, pp. 253–66.

Malina, Bruce, and Jerome H. Neyrey, 'Honor and Shame in Luke-Acts: Pivotal Values in the Mediterranean World', in Jerome H. Neyrey (ed.), *Social World of Luke-Acts*, pp. 25–65.

Marguerat, Daniel, 'La mort d'Ananias et Saphira (Ac 5,1-11)', *NTS* 39 (1993), pp. 209–26.

—'Saul's Conversion (Acts 9-22-26) and the Multiplication of Narrative in Acts', in Christopher Tuckett (ed.), *Luke's Literary Achievement*, pp. 127–55.

—'The Enigma of the Silent Closing of Acts (28,16-31)', in David P. Moessner (ed.), *Heritage of Israel*, pp. 284–304.

—*The First Christian Historian: Writing the 'Acts of the Apostles'* (SNTSMS, 121; Cambridge: Cambridge University Press, 2002).

—'The End of Acts (28,16-31) and the Rhetoric of Silence', in Stanley E. Porter and Thomas H. Olbricht (eds), *Rhetoric and the New Testament*, pp. 74–89.

Marshall, I. Howard, 'Tradition and Theology in Luke (Luke 8:8-15)', *TynBul* 20 (1969), pp. 56–75.

—*The Gospel of Luke: A Commentary on the Greek Text* (NIGTC; Grand Rapids: William B. Eerdmans Publishing Company, 1978).

—*The Acts of the Apostles* (New Testament Guides; Sheffield: Sheffield Academic Press, 1992).

—' "Israel" and the Story of Salvation: One Theme in Two Parts', in David P. Moessner (ed.), *Heritage of Israel*, pp. 340–57.

Marshall, Howard I., and David Peterson (eds), *Witness to the Gospel: The Theology of Acts* (Grand Rapids and Cambridge: William B. Eerdmans Publishing Company, 1998).

Martin, Ralph, and Peter H. Davids (eds), *The Dictionary of the Later New*

Testament and Its Developments: A Compendium of Contemporary Biblical Scholarship (Downers Grove, Ill.: InterVarsity Press, 1997).

Matera, Frank J., 'The Death of Jesus According to Luke: A Question of Sources', *CBQ* 47 (1985), pp. 469–85.

Matson, David L., *Household Conversion Narratives in Acts: Pattern and Interpretation* (JSNTSup, 123; Sheffield: Sheffield Academic Press, 1996).

McArthur, Harvey K., and Robert M. Johnston, *They Also Taught in Parables: Rabbinic Parables from the First Centuries of the Christian Era* (Grand Rapids: Zondervan Publishing Company, 1990).

McNicol, Alan J., David L. Dungan and David B. Peabody, *Beyond the Q Impasse – Luke's Use of Matthew: A Demonstration by the Research Team of the International Institute for Gospel Studies* (Valley Forge, Pa.: Trinity Press International, 1996).

Mealand, David L., 'Hellenistic Historians and the Style of Acts', *ZNW* 82 (1991), pp. 42–66.

Meeks, Wayne A., *The First Urban Christians: Social World of the Apostle Paul* (New Haven: Yale University Press, 1983).

—'Assisting the Word by Making (Up) History: Luke's Project and Ours', *Int* 57 (2003), pp. 151–62.

Merenlahti, Petri, 'Characters in the Making: Individuality and Ideology in the Gospels', in David Rhoads and Kari Syreeni (eds), *Characterization in the Gospels*, pp. 49–72

Merenlahti, Petri, and Raimo Hakola, 'Reconceiving Narrative Criticism', in David Rhoads and Kari Syreeni (eds), *Characterization in the Gospels*, pp. 13–48.

Miller, Robert J., 'Elijah, John, and Jesus in the Gospel of Luke', *NTS* 34 (1988), pp. 611–22.

Minear, Paul S., 'Luke's Use of the Birth Stories', in Leander E. Keck and J. Louis Martyn (eds), *Studies in Luke-Acts*, pp. 111–30.

—'Jesus' Audiences, According to Luke', *NovT* 16 (1974), pp. 81–109.

Mitchell, Alan C., 'The Social Function of Friendship in Acts 2:44-47 and 4:32-37', *JBL* 111 (1992), pp. 255–72.

—' "Greet the Friends by Name": New Testament Evidence for the Greco-Roman *Topos* on Friendship', in John T. Fitzgerald (ed.), *Perspectives on Friendship*, pp. 236–57.

Mitchell, Margaret M., 'Patristic Counter-Evidence to the Claim that "The Gospels Were Written for All Christians" ', *NTS* 51 (2005), pp. 36–79.

Moessner, David P., ' "The Christ must suffer": New Light on the Jesus-Peter, Stephen, Paul Parallels in Luke-Acts', *NovT* 28 (1986), pp. 220–56.

—'And Once Again: What Sort of "Essence"? A Response to Charles Talbert', *Semeia* 43 (1988), pp. 75–84.

—'Re-reading Talbert's Luke', in Mikeal C. Parsons and Joseph B. Tyson (eds), *Cadbury, Knox, and Talbert*, pp. 229-40.

—(ed.), *Jesus and the Heritage of Israel: Luke's Narrative Claim Upon Israel's Legacy* (Harrisburg, Penn: Trinity Press International, 1999).

—'The Appeal and Power of Poetics (Luke 1.1-4): Luke's Superior Credentials (παρηκολουθηκότι), Narrative Sequence (καθεξῆς), and Firmness of Understanding (ἀσφάλεια) for the Reader', in David P. Moessner (ed.), *Heritage of Israel*, pp. 84–123.

—'The Lukan Prologues in the Light of Ancient Narrative Hermeneutics: Παρηκολουθηκότι and the Credentialed Author', in J. Verheyden (ed.), *Unity of Luke-Acts*, pp. 399–417.

—' "Managing" the Audience: Diodorus Siculus and Luke the Evangelist on Designing Authorial Intent', in R. Bieringer, G. Van Belle, J. Verheyden (eds), *Luke and His Readers*, pp. 61–80.

—' "Ministers of Divine Providence": Diodorus Siculus and Luke the Evangelist on the Rhetorical Significance of the Audience in Narrative "Arrangement" ', in Sharon H. Ringe and H. C. Paul Kim (eds), *Literary Encounters*, pp. 304–23.

Montrose, Louis, 'New Historicisms', in Stephen Greenblatt and Giles Gunn (eds), *Redrawing the Boundaries*, pp. 392–418.

Moore, Stephen D., *Literary Criticism the Gospels: The Theoretical Challenge* (New Haven and London: Yale University Press, 1989).

—*Mark and Luke in Poststructuralist Perspectives: Jesus Begins to Write* (New Haven: Yale University Press, 1992).

Moreland, Milton C., 'The Jerusalem Community in Acts: Mythmaking and the Socio-rhetorical Functions of a Lukan Setting', in Todd Penner and Caroline Vander Stichele (eds), *Contextualizing Acts*, pp. 285–310.

Moreland, Milton C., and James M. Robinson, 'The International Q Project: Work Sessions 23-27, 22-26 August, 17-18 November 1994', *JBL* 114 (1995), pp. 475–85.

Morgan, Robert, with John Barton, *Biblical Interpretation* (Oxford: Oxford University Press, 1988).

Morganthaler, Robert, *Lukas und Quintilian. Rhetorik al Erzählkunst* (Zurich: Gotthelf, 1993).

Mott, Charles Stephen, 'The Power of Giving and Receiving: Reciprocity in Hellenistic Benevolence', in Gerald F. Hawthorne (ed.), *Biblical and Patristic Interpretation*, pp. 60–72.

Moxnes, Halvor, *The Economy of the Kingdom: Social Conflict and Economic Relations in Luke's Gospel* (OBT, Philadelphia: Fortress Press, 1988).

—'Patron-Client Relations and the New Community in Luke-Acts', in Jerome H. Neyrey (ed.), *Social World of Luke-Acts*, pp. 241–70.

—'Social Relations and Economic Interaction in Luke's Gospel', in Peter Luomanen (ed.), *Luke-Acts*, pp. 58–75.

—'Honor and Shame', *BTB* 23 (1993), pp. 167–76.

—'The Social Context of Luke's Community', *Int* 48 (1994), pp. 379–89.

—'Honor and Shame', in Richard Rohrbaugh (ed.), *Social Sciences and the New Testament*, pp. 19–40.

—'Kingdom Takes Place: Transformation of Place and Power in the Kingdom of God in the Gospel of Luke', in John J. Pilch (ed.), *Social Scientific Models for Interpreting the Bible*, pp. 176–209.

Nadeau, Ray, 'Delivery in Ancient Times: Homer to Quintilian', *Quarterly Journal of Speech* 50 (1964), pp. 53–60.

Neirynck, Frans (ed.), *L'Evangile de Luc – The Gospel of Luke* (BETL, 100; Leuven: Leuven University Press, 1989).

—'Luke 4,16-30 and the Unity of Luke-Acts', in J. Verheydon (ed.), *Unity of Luke-Acts*, pp. 357–95.

Neyrey, Jerome H. (ed.), *The Social World of Luke-Acts: Models of Interpretation* (Peabody, Mass.: Hendrickson Publishers, 1991).

—'Ceremonies in Luke-Acts: The Case of Meals and Table-Fellowship', in Jerome Neyrey (ed.), *Social World of Luke-Acts*, pp. 361–88.

—'Luke's Social Location of Paul: Cultural Anthropology and the Status of Paul in Acts', in Ben Witherington III (ed.), *History, Literature and Society*, 251-79.

—'Loss of Wealth, Loss of Family and Loss of Honour: The cultural context of the original makarisms in Q', in Philip F. Esler (ed.), *Modelling Early Christianity*, pp. 139–58.

—'Clean/Unclean, Pure/Polluted, and Holy/Profane: The Idea and the System of Purity', in Richard Rohrbaugh (ed.), *Social Sciences*, pp. 80–105.

Nickelsburg, George W. E., 'Riches, the Rich, and God's Judgment in 1 Enoch 92-105 and the Gospel according to Luke', *NTS* 25 (1978/79), pp. 324–44.

Nolland, John, 'Classical Rabbinic Parallels to "Physician, Heal Yourself" (Luke iv 23)', *NovT* 21 (1979), pp. 193–209.

—*Luke 1-9:20* (WBC, 35a; Dallas: Word Books, 1989).

Noorda, S. J., ' "Cure Yourself, Doctor!" (Luke 4,23): Classical Parallels to an Alleged Saying of Jesus', in Joël Delobel (ed.), *Logia*, pp. 459–69.

Olbricht, Thomas H., 'An Aristotelian Rhetorical Analysis of 1 Thessalonians', in David L. Balch, et al. (eds), *Greeks, Romans, and Christians*, pp. 216–36.

—'Delivery and Memory', in Stanley E. Porter (ed.), *Handbook*, pp. 159–70.

Osiek, Carolyn, and David L. Balch, *Families in the New Testament World: Households and House Churches* (Louisville: Westminster/John Knox Press, 1997).

O'Toole, Robert F., 'Reflections on Luke's Treatment of Jews in Luke-Acts', *Bib* 74 (1993), pp. 547–55.

Overman, James A., 'The God-Fearers: Some Neglected Features', *JSNT* 32 (1988), pp. 17–26.

Palmer, David W., 'Acts and the Ancient Historical Monograph', in Bruce W. Winter and Andrew D. Clarke (eds), *Book of Acts in Its Ancient Literary Setting*, pp. 1–29.

Parsons, Mikeal C., 'The Unity of the Lukan Writings: Rethinking the *Opinio Communis*', in Raymond H. Keathley (ed.), *With Steadfast Purpose*, pp. 29–53.

—'Luke and the *Progymnasmata*: A Preliminary Investigation into the Preliminary Exercises', in Todd Penner and Caroline Vander Stichele (eds), *Contextualizing Acts*, pp. 43–64.

Parsons, Mikeal C., and Richard Pervo, *Rethinking the Unity of Luke and Acts* (Minneapolis: Fortress Press, 1993).

Parsons, Mikeal C., and Joseph B. Tyson (eds), *Cadbury, Knox, and Talbert: American Contributions to the Study of Acts* (Atlanta: Scholars Press, 1992).

Patte, Daniel, *Ethics of Biblical Interpretation: A Reevaluation* (Louisville: Westminster Press, 1995).

Payne, Philip B., 'The Order of Sowing and Ploughing in the Parable of the Sower', *NTS* 25 (1978/79), pp. 123–39.

Pelling, Christopher (ed.), *Characterization and Individuality in Greek Literature* (Oxford: Clarendon Press, 1990).

Penner, Todd, 'Contextualizing Acts', in Todd Penner and Caroline Vander Stichele (eds), *Contextualizing Acts*, pp. 1–22.

—'Civilizing Discourse: Acts, Declamation, and the Rhetoric of the *Polis*', in Todd Penner and Caroline Vander Stichele (eds), *Contextualizing Acts*, pp. 65–104.

Penner, Todd, and Caroline Vander Stichele, *Contextualizing Acts: Lukan Narrative and Greco-Roman Discourse* (SBLSS, 20; Atlanta: Scholars Press, 2003).

Pervo, Richard, *Profit with Delight: The Literary Genre of the Acts of the Apostles* (Philadelphia: Fortress Press, 1987).

—'Must Luke and Acts be Treated as One Genre?' in Kent H. Richards (ed.), SBLSP, 28 (Atlanta: Scholars Press, 1989), pp. 306–17.

—'Israel's Heritage and Claims upon the Genre(s) of Luke and Acts: The Problems of History', in David P. Moessner (ed.), *Heritage of Israel*, pp. 127–46.

Petersen, Norman R., *Literary Criticism for New Testament Critics* (Philadelphia: Fortress Press, 1978).

Phelan, James, *Reading People, Reading Plots: Character, Progression, and the Interpretation of Narrative* (Chicago: University of Chicago Press, 1989).

Phelan James, and Peter J. Rabinowitz (eds), *Understanding Narrative* (Berkeley and Los Angeles: University of California Press, 1994).

Phillips, Thomas E., *Reading Issues of Wealth and Poverty in Luke-Acts* (Studies in the Bible and Early Christianity, 48; Lewiston, Queenston, and Lampeter: Edwin Mellen Press, 2001).

—'Reading Recent Readings of Issues of Wealth and Poverty in Luke and Acts', *CBR* 1 (2003), pp. 231–70.

Phillips, Thomas E., 'The Genre of Acts: Moving Toward a Consensus?' *CBR* 4 (2006), pp. 365–96.

Pilch, John J. (ed.), *Social Scientific Models for Interpreting the Bible* (Festschrift Bruce J. Malina; Biblical Interpretation Series, 53; Leiden, Boston, and Köln: Brill, 2001).

—'Sickness and Healing in Luke-Acts', in Jerome H. Neyrey (ed.), *Social World of Luke-Acts*, pp. 181–209.

Pilgrim, Walter E., *Good News to the Poor: Wealth and Poverty in Luke-Acts* (Minneapolis: Augsburg Press, 1981).

Piper, Ronald A., 'The Language of Violence and the Aphoristic Sayings in Q: A Study of Q 6:27-36', in John S. Kloppenborg (ed.), *Conflict and Invention*, pp. 53–74.

Porter, Stanley E., 'Thucydides 1.22.1 and Speeches in Acts: Is There a Thucydidean View?' *NovT* 32 (1990), pp. 121–42.

—(ed.), *The Language of the New Testament: Classic Essays* (Sheffield: Sheffield Academic Press, 1991).

—'The Theoretical Justification for Application of Rhetorical Categories to the Pauline Epistolary Literature', in Stanley E. Porter and Thomas H. Olbricht (eds), *Rhetoric and the New Testament*, pp. 108–16.

—*Idioms of the Greek New Testament* (Biblical Languages Greek, 2; Sheffield: Sheffield Academic Press, 2nd edn., 1994).

—(ed.), *Handbook of Classical Rhetoric in the Hellenistic Period 330 B.C. - A.D. 400* (Leiden, New York, and Köln: Brill Publishing, 1997).

Porter, Stanley E., and Thomas H. Olbricht (eds), *Rhetoric and the New Testament: Essays from the 1992 Heidelberg Conference* (JSNTSup, 90; Sheffield: Sheffield Academic Press, 1993).

—(eds), *The Rhetorical Analysis of Scripture: Essays from the 1995 London Conference* (JSNTSup, 146; Sheffield: Sheffield Academic Press, 1997).

Powell, Mark Allan, *What Are They Saying About Luke?* (New York: Paulist Press, 1989).

—'The Religious Leaders in Luke: A Literary-Critical Study', *JBL* 109 (1990), pp. 93–110.

—*What Is Narrative Criticism?* (Philadelphia: Fortress Press, 1990).

Praeder, Susan Marie, 'Jesus-Paul, Peter-Paul, and Jesus-Peter Parallelisms in Luke-Acts: A History of Reader Responses', in Kent H. Richards (ed.), SBLSP, 23 (Chico, Calif.: Scholars Press, 1984), pp. 23–39.

—'Acts 27,1-28.16: Sea Voyages in Ancient Literature and the Theology of Luke-Acts', *CBQ* 46 (1984), pp. 683–706.

Price, Robert M., *The Widow Traditions in Luke-Acts: A Feminist Critical Scrutiny* (SBLDS, 155; Atlanta: Scholars Press, 1997).

Prince, Gerald, *A Dictionary of Narratology* (Lincoln and London: University of Nebraska Press, 1987).

—*Narrative as Theme: Studies in French Fiction* (Lincoln and London: University of Nebraska Press, 1992).

Rabinowitz, Peter J., 'Truth in Fiction: A Reexamination of Audiences', *Critical Inquiry* 4 (1977), pp. 121–41.

—*Before Reading: Narrative Conventions and the Politics of Interpretation* (Ithaca and London: Cornell University Press, 1987).

—'Whirl Without End: Audience-Oriented Criticism', in G. Douglas Aitkins and Laura Morrow (eds), *Contemporary Literary Theory*, pp. 81–100.

—'Where We Are When We Read', in Michael Smith and Peter J. Rabinowitz (eds), *Authorizing Readers*, pp. 1–28.

Räisänen, Heikki, 'The Redemption of Israel', in P. Luomanen (ed.), *Luke-Acts*, pp. 94–114.

Ravens, David, *Luke and the Restoration of Israel* (Sheffield: JSOT Press, 1995).

Reimer, Richter I., *Women in the Acts of the Apostles* (Minneapolis: Fortress Press, 1996).

Reiser, Marius, 'Love of Enemies in the Context of Antiquity', *NTS* 47 (2001), pp. 411–27.

Rese, Martin, 'The Jews in Luke-Acts: Some Second Thoughts', in J. Verheydon (ed.), *Unity of Luke-*Acts, pp. 357–95.

Resseguie, James L., 'Defamiliarization and the Gospels', *BTB* 20 (1990), pp. 147–53.

—*Spiritual Landscape: Images of the Spiritual Life in the Gospel of Luke* (Peabody, Mass.: Hendrickson Publishers, 2004).

Rhoads, David, 'Narrative Criticism: Practices and Prospects', in David Rhoads and Kari Syreeni (eds), *Characterization in the Gospels*, pp. 264–85.

Rhoads, David, and Kari Syreeni (eds), *Characterization in the Gospels: Reconceiving Narrative Criticism* (JSNTSup, 184; Sheffield: Sheffield Academic Press, 1999).

Richard, Earl (ed.), *New Views on Luke and Acts* (Collegeville, Minnesota: Liturgical Press, 1990).

Ricoeur, Paul, *Interpretation Theory: Discourse and the Surplus of Meaning* (Forth Worth: Texas Christian University Press, 1976.

—*Time and Narrative* (2 vols.; trans. Kathleen McLaughlin and David Pellauer; Chicago: University of Chicago Press, 1984).

—'The Golden Rule: Exegetical and Theological Perplexities', *NTS* 36 (1990), pp. 392–97.

—*From Text to Action: Essays in Hermeneutics, II* (trans. Kathleen Blamey and John B. Thompson; Evanston, Ill.: Northwestern University Press, 1991).

Ringe, Sharon, *Jesus, Liberation, and the Biblical Jubilee: Images for Ethics and Christology* (OBT; Philadelphia: Fortress Press, 1985).

Ringe, Sharon, and H. C. Paul Kim (eds), *Literary Encounters with the Reign of God* (Festschrift Robert C. Tannehill; New York: T&T Clark, 2004).

Robbins, Vernon K., 'By Land and By Sea: The We-Passages and Ancient Sea Voyages', in Charles H. Talbert (ed.), *Perspectives on Luke-Acts*, pp. 215–42.

—'Pragmatic Relations as a Criterion for Authentic Sayings', *Forum* 1 (1985), pp. 35–63.

—'The Chreia', in David E. Aune (ed.), *Greco-Roman Literature*, pp. 1–23.

—'Pronouncement Stories from a Rhetorical Perspective', *Forum* 4 (1988), pp. 1–31.

—'The Social Location of the Implied Author of Luke-Acts', in Jerome H. Neyrey (ed.), *Social World of Luke-Acts*, pp. 305–22.

—'Luke-Acts: A Mixed Population Seeks a Home in the Roman Empire', in Loveday C. A. Alexander (ed.), *Images of Empire*, pp. 202–21.

—'Introduction: Using Rhetorical Discussions of the Chreia to Interpret Pronouncement Stories', *Semeia* 64 (1993), pp. vii-xvii.

—'Social Scientific Criticism and Literary Studies: Prospects for Cooperation in Biblical Interpretation', in Philip F. Esler (ed.), *Modelling Early Christianity*, pp. 274–89.

—*The Tapestry of Early Christian Discourse: Rhetoric, Society, and Ideology* (London and New York: Routledge Press, 1996).

—'Narrative in Ancient Rhetoric and Rhetoric in Ancient Narrative', in Kent H. Richards (ed.), SBLSP, 35 (Atlanta, Scholars Press), pp. 368–84.

—'The Present and Future State of Rhetorical Analysis', in Stanley E. Porter and Thomas H. Olbricht (eds), *Rhetorial Analysis of Scripture*, pp. 32–41.

—'From Enthymeme to Theology in Luke 11:1-13', in Richard P. Thompson and Thomas E. Phillips (eds), *Literary Studies in Luke-Acts*, pp. 191–214.

—'The Claims of the Prologues and Greco-Roman Rhetoric: The Prefaces to Luke and Acts in Light of Greco-Roman Rhetorical Strategies', in David P. Moessner (ed.), *Heritage of Israel*, pp. 63–83.

—'The Socio-Rhetorical Role of Old Testament Scripture in Luke 4-19', in Hana Tonzarova and Petr Melmuk (eds), *Z Noveho Zakona*, pp. 81–93.

Robinson, James M., 'The International Q Project: Work Sessions 12-14 July, 22 November 1991', *JBL* 111 (1992), pp. 500–08.

Rohrbaugh, Richard L., 'The Pre-Industrial City in Luke-Acts', in Jerome H. Neyrey (ed.), *Social World of Luke-Acts*, pp. 125–49.

—'Legitimating Sonship – A Test of Honour: A social-scientific study of Luke 4:1-30', in Philip F. Esler (ed.), *Modelling Early Christianity*, pp. 183–97.

—(ed.), *The Social Sciences and New Testament Interpretation* (Peabody, Mass.: Hendrickson Publishers, 1996).

Rorty, A. O. (ed.), *Essays on Aristotle's Rhetoric* (Berkeley, Los Angeles, and London: University of California Press, 1996).

Rosenblatt, Marie-Eloise, *Paul the Accused: His Portrait in Acts of the Apostles* (Collegeville: Liturgical Press, 1995).

Roth, John S., *The Blind, the Lame, and the Poor: Character Types in Luke-Acts* (JSNTSup, 144; Sheffield: Sheffield Academic Press, 1997).

Rowe, Galen O., 'Style', in Stanley E. Porter (ed.), *Handbook*, pp. 121–57.

Rowe, Kavin C., 'History, Hermeneutics and the Unity of Luke-Acts', *JSNT* 28 (2005), pp. 131–57.

Rüger, H. P., 'Mit welchem Mass ihr messt, wird euch gemessen werden (Mt 7:2, Gen 38:25-26)', *ZNW* 60 (1969), pp. 174–82.

Sacks, Kenneth S., 'Rhetorical Approaches to Greek History Writing', in Kent H. Richards (ed.), SBLSP, 23 (Chico: Scholars Press, 1984), pp. 122–33.

Saller, Richard, *Personal Patronage under the Early Empire* (Cambridge: Cambridge University Press, 1982).

Sanders, Jack T., 'The Salvation of the Jews in Luke-Acts', in Charles H. Talbert (ed.), *Luke-Acts*, pp. 104–28.

Satterhwaite, Philip E., 'Acts Against the Background of Classical Rhetoric', in Bruce W. Winter and Andrew D. Clarke (eds), *Book of Acts in Its Ancient Literary Setting*, pp. 337–80.

Scholes, Robert, *Protocols of Reading* (New Haven and London: Yale University Press, 1989).

Scholes, Robert, and Robert Kellogg, *The Nature of Narrative* (London and New York: Oxford University Press, 1966).

Schottroff, Luise, and W. Stegemann, *Jesus von Nazareth: Hoffnung der Armen* (Stuttgart: Kohlhammer, 3rd edn., 1990).

Schreck, Christopher J., 'The Nazareth Pericope: Luke 4:16-30 in Recent Study', in Frans Neirynck (ed.), *L'Evangile de Luc*, pp. 399–471.

Schürmann, Heinz, *Das Lukasevangelium* (2 vols,; HTKNT, 3; Freiburg: Herder, 1984/94).

Schwartz, Saundra, 'The Trial Scene in the Greek Novels and Luke-Acts', in Todd Penner and Caroline Vander Stichele (eds), *Contextualizing Acts*, pp. 105–38.

Scobie, C. H., *John the Baptist* (Philadelphia: Fortress Press, 1984).

Scott, Bernard Brandon, *Hear Then the Parable: A Commentary on the Parables of Jesus* (Minneapolis: Fortress Press, 1989).

Scott, J. M., 'Luke's Geographical Horizon', in D. W. J. Gill and Conrad Gempf (eds), *Book of Acts in Its Ancient Greco-Roman Setting*, pp. 483–544.

Seccombe, David P., *Possessions and the Poor in Luke-Acts* (SNTSU, B6; Linz: Fuchs, 1983).

Segbroeck, Frans (ed.), *The Four Gospels 1992: Fetschrift Frans Neirynck* (vol. 2; Leuven: Leuven University Press, 1992).

Segovia, Fernando F., 'Cultural Studies and Contemporary Biblical Criticism: Ideological Criticism as Mode of Discourse', in Fernando F. Segovia and Mary Ann Tolbert (eds), *Interpretation in Global Perspective*, pp. 1–17.

Segovia, Fernando F., and Mary Ann Tolbert (eds), *Reading from this Place: Social Location and Biblical Interpretation in the United States* (vol. 1; Minneapolis: Fortress Press, 1995).

—(eds), *Reading from this Place: Social Location and Biblical Interpretation in Global Perspective* (vol. 2; Minneapolis: Fortress Press, 1995).

Seim, Turid Karlsen, *The Double Message: Patterns of Gender in Luke and Acts* (Nashville: Abingdon Press, 1994).

Sheeley, Steven M., *Narrative Asides in Luke-Acts* (JSNTSup, 72; Sheffield: Sheffield Academic Press, 1992).

Shepherd, William H., Jr., *The Narrative Function of the Holy Spirit as a Character in Luke-Acts* (SBLDS, 147; Atlanta: Scholars Press, 1994).

Shiner, Whitney, *Proclaiming the Gospel: First-Century Performance of Mark* (Harrisburg, Penn.: Trinity Press International, 2003).

Siker, Jeffrey S., ' "First to the Gentiles": A Literary Analysis of Luke 4:16-30', *JBL* 111 (1992), pp. 73–90.

Sim, David, 'The Woman Followers of Jesus: The Implications of Luke 8:1-3', *HeyJ* 30 (1989), pp. 51–62.

Sloan, Robert, *The Favorable Year of the Lord: A Study of Jubilary Theology in the Gospel of Luke* (Austin, Tex.: Schola Press, 1977).

Smallwood, Mary E., *The Jews under Roman Rule: From Pompey to Diocletian* (Studies in Judaism in Late Antiquity, 20; Leiden: Brill, 1976).

Smith, Dennis E., 'Table Fellowship as a Literary Motif in the Gospel of Luke', *JBL* 106 (1987), pp. 613–38.

Smith, Michael, and Peter J. Rabinowitz (eds), *Authorizing Readers: Resistance and Respect in Teaching of Literature* (New York and London: Teachers College Press, 1997).

Smith, Robert H., 'Hypocrite', in Joel B. Green and Scot McKnight (eds), *Dictionary of Jesus and the Gospels*, pp. 351–53.

Soards, Marion L., *The Speeches in Acts: Their Content, Context, and Concerns* (Louisville: Westminster/John Knox Press, 1994).

—'The Speeches in Acts in Relation to Other Pertinent Ancient Literature', *ETR* 70 (1994), pp. 65–90.

Spencer, Scott F., 'Acts and Modern Literary Approaches', in Bruce W. Winter and Andrew D. Clarke (eds), *The Book of Acts in Its Ancient Literary Setting*, pp. 381–414.

—'Neglected Widows in Acts 6:1-7', *CBQ* 56 (1994), pp. 715–33.

—*Acts* (Readings: A New Biblical Commentary; Sheffield: Sheffield Academic Press, 1997).

—'Preparing the Way of the Lord: Introducing and Interpreting Luke's Narrative: A Response to David Wenham', in Bartholomew, et al. (eds), *Reading Luke*, pp. 104–25.

—*Journeying Through Acts: A Literary-Cultural Reading* (Peabody, Mass.: Hendrickson Publishers, 2004).

—'Act and Modern Literary Approaches', in Bruce W. Winter and Andrew D. Clarke (eds), *Ancient Literary Setting*, pp. 382–14.

Spencer, Patrick E., 'Narrative Echoes in John 21: Intertextual Interpretation and Intratextual Connection', *JSNT* 75 (1999), pp. 49–68.

Squires, John T., *The Plan of God in Luke-Acts* (SNTSMS, 76; Cambridge: Cambridge University Press, 1993).

Staley, Jeffrey A., '"With Power of the Spirit": Plotting the Program and Parallels of Luke 4:14-37 in Luke-Acts', in Kent H. Richards (ed.), *SBLSP*, 32 (Atlanta: Scholars Press, 1993), pp. 281–302.

—'Narrative Structure (Self Stricture) in Luke 4:14-9:62: The United States of Luke's Story World', *Semeia* 72 (1995), pp. 173–213.

Stamps, Dennis L., 'Rethinking the Rhetorical Situation: Entextualization of the Situation in New Testament Epistles', in Stanley E. Porter and Thomas H. Olbricht (eds), *Rhetoric and the New Testament*, pp. 193–210.

Sterling, Gregory L., *Historiography and Self-Definition: Josephus, Luke-*

Acts, and Apologetic Historiography (NovTSup, 64; Leiden: Brill, 1992).

—' "Athletes of Virtue": An Analysis of the Summaries in Acts (2:41-47; 4:32-35; 5:12-16)', *JBL* 113 (1994), pp. 679–96.

Stichele, Caroline Vander, 'Gender and Genre: Acts in/of Interpretation', in Todd Penner and Caroline Vander Stichele (eds), *Contextualizing Acts*, pp. 311–30.

Stout, Jeffrey, 'What Is the Meaning of a Text?' *New Literary History* 14 (1982), pp. 1–12.

Suleiman, Susan R., and Inge Crosman (eds), *The Reader in the Text: Essays on Audience and Interpretation* (New Jersey: Princeton University Press, 1980).

Talbert, Charles H., *Literary Patterns, Theological Themes, and the Genre of Luke-Acts* (SBLMS, 20; Missoula: Scholars Press, 1974).

—(ed.), *Perspectives on Luke-Acts* (Edinburgh: T&T Clark, 1978).

—*Reading Luke: A Literary and Theological Commentary on the Third Gospel* (New York: Crossroad, 1982).

—*Reading Acts: A Literary and Theological Commentary on the Book of Acts* (New York: Crossroad, 1984).

—(ed.), *Luke-Acts: New Perspectives from the Society of Biblical Literature Seminar* (New York: Crossroad, 1984).

—'Once Again: Gospel Genre', *Semeia* 43 (1988), pp. 53–74.

—'Reading Chance, Moessner, and Parsons', in Mikeal C. Parsons and Joseph B. Tyson (eds), *Cadbury, Knox, and Talbert*, pp. 229–40.

—'The Acts of the Apostles: monograph or "bios"?' in Ben Witherington III (ed.), *History, Literature and Society*, pp. 58–71.

—'Conversion in the Acts of the Apostles: Ancient Auditors' Perceptions', in Richard P. Thompson and Thomas E. Phillips (eds), *Literary Studies on Luke-Acts*, pp. 141–53.

Talbert, Charles H., and John H. Hays, 'A Theology of Sea Storms in Luke-Acts', in David P. Moessner (ed.), *Heritage of Israel*, pp. 267–83.

Tannehill, Robert C., 'The Mission of Jesus According to Luke IV 16-30', in Walther Eltester (ed.), *Jesus in Nazareth*, pp. 51–75.

—'Israel in Luke-Acts', *JBL* 104 (1985), pp. 69–85.

—'Rejection by Jews and Turning to Gentiles: The Pattern of Paul's Mission in Acts', in Joseph B. Tyson (ed.), *Luke-Acts and the Jewish People*, pp. 83–101.

—*The Narrative Unity of Luke-Acts: A Literary Interpretation* (2 vols.; Philadelphia: Fortress Press, 1986/1990).

—' "Cornelius" and "Tabitha" Encounter Luke's Jesus', *Int* 48 (1994), pp. 347–56.

—'Should We Love Simon the Pharisee? Hermeneutical Reflections on the Pharisees in Luke', *CurTM* 21 (1994), pp. 424–33.

—*Luke* (Abingdon New Testament Commentaries; Nashville: Abingdon Press, 1996).

—'The Story of Israel within the Lucan Narrative', in David P. Moessner (ed.), *Heritage of Israel*, pp. 325–39.

Theissen, Gerd, *Social Reality and the First Christians: Theology, Ethics, and the World of the New Testament* (Edinburgh: T&T Clark, 1992).

Thiselton, Anthony C., *New Horizons in Hermeneutics: The Theory and Practice of Transforming Biblical Reading* (Grand Rapids: Zondervan Publishing House, 1992).

Thomas, Rosalind, *Literary and Orality in Ancient Greece* (Cambridge: Cambridge University Press, 1992).

Thompson, Michael B., 'The Holy Internet: Communication Between Churches in the First Christian Generation', in Richard Bauckham (ed.), *Gospels for All Christians*, pp. 49–70.

Thompson, Richard P., 'Christian Community and Characterization in the Book of Acts: A Literary Study of the Lukan Concept of the Church', (Ph.D. dissertation; Southern Methodist University, 1996).

—'Believers and Religious Leaders in Jerusalem: Contrasting Portraits of Jews in Acts 1-7', in Richard P. Thompson and Thomas E. Phillips (eds), *Literary Studies in Luke-Acts*, pp. 327–44.

Thompson, Richard P., and Thomas E. Phillips (eds), *Literary Studies in Luke-Acts: Essays in Honor of Joseph B. Tyson* (Macon: Mercer University Press, 1998).

Tiede, David L., ' "Glory to Thy People Israel": Luke-Acts and the Jews', in David P. Moessner (ed.), *Heritage of Israel*, pp. 21–34.

Tolbert, Mary Ann, *Sowing the Gospel: Mark's World in Literary-Historical Perspective* (Minneapolis: Fortress Press, 1989).

—'How the Gospel of Mark Builds Character', *Int* 47 (1993), pp. 347–57.

—'Afterwords: The Politics and Poetics of Location', in Fernando F. Segovia and Mary Ann Tolbert (eds), *Biblical Interpretation in the United States*, pp. 311–17.

Tompkins, Jane P. (ed.), *Reader-Response: From Formalism to Post-Structuralism* (Baltimore and London: Johns Hopkins University Press, 1980).

—'The Reader in History: The Changing Shape of Literary Response', in Jane P. Tompkins (ed.), *Reader-Response*, pp. 201–32.

Tonzarova, Hana, and Petr Melmuk (eds), *Z Noveho Zakona From the New Testament: Sbornik k narozeninam Prof. ThDr. Zdenka Sazavy* (Festschrift Zdenka Sazavy; Praha: Vydala Cirkev ceskoslovenska husitska, 2001).

Toohey, Peter, *Reading Epic: An Introduction to the Ancient Narratives* (New York: Routledge, 1992).

Topel, John, 'The Tarnished Golden Rule (Luke 6:31): The Inescapable Radicalness of Christian Ethics', *TS* 59 (1998), pp. 475–85.

Tracy, Stephen V., *The Story of the Odyssey* (Princeton: Princeton University Press, 1990).

Tuckett, Christopher M. (ed.), *Luke's Literary Achievement* (JSNTSup, 116; Sheffield: Sheffield Academic Press, 1995).

—*Q and the History of Early Christianity: Studies on Q* (Edinburgh: T&T Clark; Peabody, Mass.: Hendrickson Publishers, 1996).

Turner, Max, 'Historical Criticism and Theological Hermeneutics of the

New Testament', in Joel B. Green and Max Turner (eds), *Between Two Horizons*, pp. 44–70

Tyson, Joseph B., 'The Jewish Public in Luke-Acts', *NTS* 30 (1984), pp. 574–83.

—(ed.), *Luke-Acts and the Jewish People: Eight Critical Perspectives* (Minneapolis: Fortress Press, 1988).

—'The Birth Narratives and the Beginnings of Luke's Gospel', *Semeia* 52 (1991), pp. 103–20.

—*Images of Judaism in Luke-Acts* (Columbia: University of South Carolina Press, 1992).

—'Jews and Judaism in Luke-Acts: Reading as a Godfearer', *NTS* 41 (1995), pp. 19–38.

—*Luke, Judaism, and the Scholars: Critical Approaches to Luke-Acts* (Columbia: University of South Carolina Press, 1999).

—'From History to Rhetoric and Back: Assessing New Trends in Acts Studies', in Todd Penner and Caroline Vander Stichele (eds), *Contextualizing Acts*, pp. 23–42.

Vaage, Leif E., 'Composite Texts and Oral Mythology: The Case of the "Sermon" in Q (6:20-49)', in John Kloppenborg (ed.), *Conflict and Invention*, pp. 75–97.

Vanhoozer, Kevin J., 'The Reader in New Testament Interpretation', in Joel B. Green (ed.), *Hearing the New Testament*, pp. 301–28.

—*Is There a Meaning in This Text? The Bible, the Reader, and the Morality of Literary Knowledge* (Grand Rapids: Zondervan Publishing, 1998).

van de Sandt, H., 'Acts 28,28: No Salvation for the People of Israel?' *ETL* 70 (1994), pp. 341–58.

van Unnik, W. C., 'Die Motivierung der Feindesliebe in Lukas VI 32-35', *NovT* 8 (1966), pp. 284–300.

Verheydon, J. (ed.), *The Unity of Luke-Acts* (BETL, 112; Leuven: Leuven University Press, 1999).

Vison, Richard B., 'A Comparative Study of the Use of Enthymemes in the Synoptic Gospels', in Duane F. Watson (ed.), *Persuasive Artistry*, pp. 93–118.

Waetjen, Herman C., 'Social Location and Hermeneutical Mode of Integration', Fernando F. Segovia and Mary Ann Tolbert (eds), *Biblical Interpretation in the United States*, pp. 75–94.

—'The Subversion of "World" by the Parable of the Friend at Midnight', *JBL* 120 (2001), pp. 703–21.

Walaskay, Paul W., *'And So We Came to Rome': The Political Perspective of St. Luke* (Cambridge: Cambridge University Press, 1983).

Wall, Robert W, 'Successors to the 'Twelve' according to Acts 12.1-17', *CBQ* 53 (1991), pp. 628–43.

Wallace-Hadrill, Andrew, *Patronage in Ancient Society* (London: Routledge, 1989).

Wasserberg, Günter, *Aus Israels Mitte – Heil für die Welt: Eine narrativ-exegetische Studie zue Theologie des Lukas* (BZNW, 92; Berlin and New York: Walter de Gruyter, 1998).

Watson, Duane F. (ed.), *Persuasive Artistry: Studies in New Testament Rhetoric* (Festschrift George A. Kennedy; JSNTSup, 50; Sheffield: Sheffield Academic Press, 1991).

Watson, Francis (ed.), *The Open Text: New Directions for Biblical Studies?* (London: SCM Press, 1993).

Wenham, David, 'The Purpose of Luke-Acts: Israel's Story in the Context of the Roman Empire', in Bartholomew, et al. (eds), *Reading Luke*, pp. 79–103.

Wheeldon, M. J., '"True Stories": the Reception of Historiography in Antiquity', in A. Cameron (ed.), *History as Text*, pp. 33–63.

White, Michael L., and O. Larry Yarbrough (eds), *The Social World of the First Christians* (Festschrift Wayne A. Meeks; Minneapolis: Fortress Press, 1995).

Wilcox, Max, 'The "God-Fearers" in Acts – A Reconsideration', *JSNT* 13 (1981), pp. 10–22.

Wilson, Stanley G., *Related Strangers: Jews and Christians 70-170 CE* (Minneapolis: Fortress Press, 1995).

Wink, Walter, 'Jesus' Reply to John: Matt 11.2-6/Luke 7.18-35', *Forum* 5 (1989), pp. 121–28.

—'Neither Passivity nor Violence: Jesus' Third Way (Matt 5:38-42//Luke 6:29-30)', *Forum* 7 (1991), pp. 5–28.

Winter, Bruce W., and Andrew D. Clark (eds), *The Book of Acts in Its First Century Setting: Volume 1: Ancient Literary Setting* (The Book of Acts in Its First Century Setting; Grand Rapids: William B. Eerdmans Publishing Company, 1993).

Witherington, Ben III, 'On the Road with Mary Magdalene, Joanna, Susanna, and Other Disciples – Luke 8:1-3', *ZNW* 70 (1979), pp. 243–48.

—(ed.), *History, Literature and Society in the Book of Acts* (Cambridge: Cambridge University Press, 1996).

—'Editing the Good News: some synoptic lessons for the study of Acts', in Ben Witherington III (ed.), *History, Literature and Society*, pp. 324–47.

—*The Acts of the Apostles: A Socio-Rhetorical Commentary* (Cambridge and Grand Rapids: William B. Eerdmans Publishing Company, 1997).

Witherup, Ronald D., 'Functional Redundancy in the Acts of the Apostles', *JSNT* 48 (1992), pp. 67–86.

—'Cornelius Over and Over Again: "Functional Redundancy" in the Acts of the Apostles', *JSNT* 49 (1993), pp. 45–66.

Wolter, Michael, 'Israel's Future and the Delay of the Parousia, according to Luke', in David P. Moessner (ed.), *Heritage of Israel*, pp. 307–24.

Wuellner, Wilhelm, 'Where is Rhetorical Criticism Taking Us?' *CBQ* 49 (1987), pp. 448–63.

—'Hermeneutics and Rhetorics: From "Truth and Method" to "Truth and Power"', *Scriptura* 3 (1989), pp. 1–54.

—'Arrangement', in Stanley E. Porter (ed.), *Handbook*, pp. 51–88.

Wuthnow, Robert, *Communities of Discourse: Ideology and Social Structure in the Reformation, the Enlightenment, and European Socialism* (Cambridge and London: Harvard University Press, 1989).

York, John O., *The Last Shall Be First: The Rhetoric of Reversal* (JSNTSup, 46; Sheffield: Sheffield Academic Press, 1991).

INDEX OF REFERENCES

Old Testament

Genesis
3   179n42

Exodus
3.1–4.17   141
19   74n9
19.3–6   141
19.24   71, 140
21–23   71n2
23.20   104, 105, 147
24   74n9
24.3   71, 140
24.9-18   141
32.9   108n20, 152
33.3   108n20, 152
33.5   108n20, 152
33.7-11   141
34.29-35   141

Leviticus
19   72n2, 74n9, 80n26
25.10   67, 138–39
25.21   67n9

Deuteronomy
10.16   108n20, 152
13.1-11   69–70
22   72n2
28   72n2, 80

1 Samuel
2.1-10   137n21
2.21   137n21
2.26   137n21

1 Kings
17.8-24   68, 102, 195
17.10-24   147
17.17-24   138, 178

2 Kings
4.32-37   147
5.1-14   138
5.1-19   68, 102, 195
5.19   147

2 Chronicles
25.12   70n16

Nehemiah
9.26   80

Job
34.30   96n85
36.13   96n85

Psalms
25.8   92
86.5   92

Proverbs
8.1–9.6   106n18

Ecclesiastes
10.16-17   75n11, 80

Isaiah
3.10-11   75n11
6.1-10   72
6.9-10   25, 118, 127,
    145, 154, 193
6.9   125
6.10   119n17
29.18   102
35.5-6   102
40.3-5   140
40.4   140n28
42.18   102
57   67
58.6   72, 73, 138, 190
59.1-20   94n78
61   67

61.1   72, 102
61.1-2   73, 138, 190
63.15   92
63.19   93n77
64.1-12   94n78
65.1-16   94n78
65.6-7   94n78
66.14-16   94n78

Jeremiah
5.12-13   79, 80
6.13-15   79, 80
10.10   93n77

Ezekiel
2.1-7   79, 80
12.18   93n77

Daniel
2.18-19   118n14
2.27-30   118n14
2.47   118n14
9.24-27   67n8

Joel
2.24   93n77

Micah
2.11   79, 80

Habakkuk
2.6-20   80
2.16   93n77

Zechariah
1.16   92
12.2   93n77

Malachi
3.1   104, 105, 147

Tobit
13.12   75n11, 80

Wisdom of Solomon
2.22   118n14
6.22   118n14
7.22-30   106n18
15.1   92

Sirach (Ecclesiasticus)
16.18   93n77
24   106n18
48.1-16   16

2 Maccabees
6.21-25   96n85

New Testament

Matthew
5.1–7.29   73
5.3-12   79, 192
5.3–7.27   6
5.3–7.29   140
7.17   192
7.24-27   192
11.7-19   192
12.35   192

Mark
4.1-20   155
4.1-34   9, 124
4.2   192n10
4.7   117n8, 122n29
4.8   158
4.12   119n17, 193, 196
4.15   120
4.17   120
4.18-19   122n29
4.19   120
4.20   120, 123
4.26-34   192
4.33   192n10
6.1–6   191n9
16.8   59n48

Luke
1-2   85
1.1-4   26, 32, 34, 50,
    134
1.1–4.30   136n20
1.3   186
1.4   119, 154, 185, 186
1.5   114n2

1.5-25   148, 178n40
1.5–2.21   143
1.5–2.38   158
1.5–2.52   58, 63, 104,
    143, 149, 150n47, 176,
    177, 194
1.15   64
1.16–17   105, 147
1.26-38   63, 107, 148,
    178n40
1.32   92, 149
1.35   64
1.39–56   149
1.41   64, 149
1.46-55   77
1.46-56   137n21, 144,
    178n40
1.50   92n73
1.67   64
1.67-79   149
1.76   105, 147, 149
2.1-20   144
2.22-35   149
2.25   64
2.27   64
2.29-35   23
2.29-40   63
2.35   68n12
2.36-38   149
2.36-39   178
2.39-40   114n2
2.39-34   63
2.42   64
2.47   64
2.48-50   68
2.51-52   63
2.52   114n2, 137n21
3–4   25
3.1-14   145, 161
3.1-18   105, 107, 108,
    148
3.1-20   150, 158, 189
3.1-22   143, 194
3.4-6   140
3.5   140
3.7   85n46
3.7–14   80n25, 96, 150
3.8   106, 148
3.10–14   144
3.12   170
3.17   99
3.18–20   142, 150
3.19–20   156
3.21–22   137n21, 148

3.21–23   68, 107
3.22   64, 188
3.23   68n12
4.1   137n21
4.1-13   121, 142, 155
4.1-15   64
4.2   157
4.12-13   157
4.14   63, 137n21,
    142n31
4.14-15   72, 114n2
4.14-16   63, 64
4.14-30   4, 5, 6, 17, 63–
    70, 72, 77, 85, 100,
    162, 191n9, 193
4.14-37   195
4.14–9.50   4, 44
4.14–9.62   5
4.16-18   67n10
4.16-19   65
4.16-30   7, 10–11, 25,
    73, 77, 104, 136,
    139n26, 144, 191n7,
    194
4.17   139
4.17-19   184
4.18   104
4.18–19   56, 139, 147,
    150, 152, 172, 184,
    187, 190
4.18-20   66–7, 72, 102,
    184
4.19   69
4.20   65, 139
4.20–21   67n10
4.20-22   65, 67–8
4.21   67n10, 73
4.21-22   195
4.22   66, 136, 137, 186
4.22-23   135
4.23   65, 68, 70, 102,
    188, 190, 200
4.23-27   68–9
4.24   65, 68
4.24-27   102, 135, 136,
    142, 143, 147, 188
4.25-26   178
4.25-27   65, 69, 86n51,
    102, 169, 175, 184,
    190, 195
4.26   184
4.26-27   72
4.27   184
4.28-29   68

4.28-30   66, 68, 69–70, 140, 157, 185, 186
4.29   70n16, 139n26
4.30   73
4.31-32   136
4.31-37   141, 152, 189
4.31-41   142n32, 143
4.31-42   68
4.31–6.19   85
4.37   102, 162
4.38-39   72, 152
4.38-41   141
4.40-41   72
4.40-42   152
4.42   141
4.42-44   72, 106, 114n2
5.1-11   72, 74, 80n25, 143, 144, 145, 158, 159
5.12-15   141
5.12-16   152
5.12-26   142n32, 143
5.16   141
5.17   142n31
5.17-26   72, 77, 95, 112, 141, 142, 148, 149, 151, 152, 159, 188, 196
5.20   138
5.27-32   74, 77, 80n25, 86n47, 86n51, 109, 142, 143, 151, 158, 170
5.27–6.1   83
5.33   172n27
5.33-39   142, 151
6.1-5   77, 95, 142, 151, 172n27
6.6-11   72, 77, 95, 112, 141, 142, 142n32, 143, 151, 152
6.12-16   71, 114, 114n2, 140
6.12-19   140, 141
6.17-19   71, 72, 73, 94, 101, 152, 153, 187, 188
6.17–49   4, 5, 6–7, 11, 71–100, 184, 191n9
6.17   72, 140
6.19   72, 142
6.20   7, 76, 78, 94, 118n12, 145
6.20-21   76
6.20-23   75, 81, 105n13, 192
6.20-26   7, 56, 57, 58,

74, 75–81, 144n36, 184, 187, 190, 192
6.20-49   15, 44, 53, 71, 73, 115, 119, 123, 127, 154, 170
6.21   76, 78
6.22–23   76, 77, 83, 142
6.23   78, 91n70
6.24   75, 76, 78, 172n27
6.24–26   75, 81, 192
6.25   75, 76, 78
6.26   75, 76, 77, 90, 142
6.27   7, 81, 83, 85, 90
6.27-28   82–4
6.27-29   144
6.27-31   58, 74, 81–87, 184
6.27-36   74n9, 171
6.27-38   7
6.27-45   7, 74, 190
6.29   85
6.29-30   83, 84–6
6.30   84, 85, 144, 172n27
6.31   86–7, 89, 92
6.32-34   85n45, 87, 88, 91
6.32-35   172n27
6.32-36   86n50, 88–92, 145, 184
6.32-45   56, 58, 74, 87–98, 173, 184
6.33   89
6.34   89n63
6.35   85n45, 87, 89, 90, 92
6.35-36   87
6.36   57, 58, 87, 89, 90, 92, 143, 170–1, 173, 187n3, 200
6.37   93
6.37-38   86, 92, 93
6.37-42   74n9, 87, 92–6, 145, 184
6.37-49   73n6
6.38   87, 93, 94n80
6.39   7, 94
6.39-42   7, 87, 92
6.39–49   7
6.40   95
6.41-42   94
6.43   97
6.43-44   97, 98, 99, 146, 189

6.43-45   57, 74n9, 87, 96–8, 99, 184, 192
6.44   96, 97
6.45   97, 98, 146, 162, 190
6.45-49   80n25
6.46-49   7, 58, 74, 94, 98–9, 115, 117, 126, 141, 154, 184, 185, 187, 190
6.47-49   99
6.48   99
6.49   99, 101, 189
7.1   7, 53, 101
7.1-10   86n49, 102, 109, 147, 150, 152, 158, 170, 174n31, 176, 188, 195, 202
7.1-17   102n5
7.1-50   102
7.11-16   195
7.11-17   86n49, 102, 103, 147, 150, 152, 178, 188, 202
7.16-17   103
7.17   105
7.17-23   102, 103, 104, 195
7.18-20   188
7.18-23   107, 147, 152n49, 185, 186, 187
7.18-35   103n7, 158, 194
7.20   102
7.21   102, 147
7.21-22   105n13
7.21-23   104
7.22   147
7.22-23   150
7.22-24   104
7.23   105n23, 152
7.24   104, 105
7.24-27   53, 104, 105–6, 147, 148
7.24-35   4, 5, 8, 11, 101–13, 185, 161n9
7.25   147
7.26–27   147
7.27   104, 147
7.28   57, 58, 106–7, 108, 148, 150, 187n3
7.28-30   148
7.29   111, 148, 152, 171
7.29–30   104, 107–8,

146–7, 148–9, 151,
170, 171, 185, 188,
189, 190n6
7.31   148
7.31-32   104, 108, 109,
148
7.31-34   56, 108–10,
148, 151, 171, 177, 185
7.32   108, 109, 148, 200
7.32-34   53, 148
7.33-34   104, 108
7.34   150
7.35   104, 106, 110–12,
148, 151, 152, 171,
187n3
7.36-50   86n47, 86n51,
102, 112, 143, 149n44,
151, 153, 159, 170,
171, 178n39, 188
7.49   112n31
8.1-3   86n48, 86n50,
114, 126–7, 153, 158,
160, 170, 176, 178, 192
8.1-56   114
8.3   172n27
8.4   115, 153
8.4-18   4, 5, 8–9, 11,
111, 114–27, 152, 153,
185, 191n9, 193
8.5   118, 189
8.5-6   155
8.5-8   58, 116–18, 154,
185, 190, 192
8.6   117, 157, 189
8.7   117n8, 122n29, 189
8.8   115n4, 117, 123,
154, 186, 189, 190
8.8-10   58, 116, 193
8.9   118, 125, 186
8.9-10   118–19, 127,
154, 155–6, 185, 196
8.10   115n4, 118,
119n17, 154
8.11   115n4, 120, 121,
126, 138, 189
8.11-15   58, 116, 119–
21, 154–5, 185, 190,
192
8.12-13   155
8.12   115n4, 120, 121,
157, 189
8.13   115n4, 120,
122n29, 157, 189
8.14   115n4, 120,

123n30, 155, 158, 162,
186
8.15   124, 125, 189, 190
8.16-18   56, 58, 116,
124–6, 185
8.17   124, 125
8.18   115n4, 125
8.19-20   126–27
8.19-21   192
8.21   115n4
8.26-39   86n49
8.40-56   86n49
8.41-48   86n51
8.42-48   159
9.1-46   114
9.3-5   172n27
9.7-9   156
9.11-17   172n27
9.28   141
9.28-36   159
9.37-43   86n49
9.51   4, 114n2
9.51–19.44   159
9.57-62   80n25
10.1-12   153
10.1-16   145
10.3-9   172n27
10.17   172n27
10.25-37   86n48, 86n50,
86n51, 145, 151n48,
156, 158, 159, 170,
176, 196
10.37   92n73
10.38-42   158, 160, 170,
178n40, 179n43
11.1   141
11.1-4   122
11.1-13   122, 171n21
11.2-4   122
11.5   122
11.5–13   122
11.7   122
11.8   122n28
11.32-52   196
11.37-42   151
11.37-54   162
11.45-52   151n48
12.1   114n2, 118n12,
162
12.1-59   80n25
12.13-21   157, 174n32
12.13-48   86n48, 86n50
12.33-34   145n39
13.6-9   155–6

13.10-17   86n49, 178n39
14.1-6   86n49
14.1-24   151n48, 196
14.7-14   86n51
14.7-24   77
14.15-24   86n47, 86n51
14.25-35   80n25
15.11-32   86n51, 143
16.1   118n12
16.1-13   86n48, 86n50,
145, 159
16.14-18   86n48, 86n50
16.19–31   77, 86n47,
86n48, 86n50, 143,
157, 173
17.11   114n2
17.11-19   86n49, 171n21
18.1-8   159, 171n21,
178n40
18.9-14   77
18.18-30   86n48, 86n50,
145, 157, 174n32
18.22   145n39
18.35-42   159, 171n21
19.1–10   86n47, 86n48,
86n50, 150, 158, 159,
170, 171n21, 174n31,
188
19.11   114n2
19.11-27   80n25, 86n48,
86n50, 159
19.28   114n2
19.35-43   86n49
19.41   114n2
20.1   114n2
20.20-47   156
20.45-47   174n32
20.45–21.4   173
21.1-4   86n48, 86n50,
145, 158, 170, 174n31,
178n40, 179
21.10-36   160n62
22.1   114n2
22.1-6   174n32
22.14-38   172n27
22.30   71n1
22.31-34   157, 158, 159
22.39   114n2
22.39-46   122
22.46   122
22.47-53   157
22.47-62   158, 159
22.54-62   157
22.47–23.25   156

22.56   67n11
22.66   114n2
22-23   23, 142
22-24   77
23.6-12   156
23.18-25   160
23.27   160
23.40   122n26
23.44   114n2
23.46   122n26, 160n61
23.49   160
23.49-51   114n2
23.50-56   151, 174n31
23.55   160
24.1   114n2
24.1-11   160
24.8   160
24.11   160
24.12–53   159
24.13   114n2
24.13-49   80n25
24.45   119n15
24.47   138
24.52   172n27

John
21.9-13   110n27

Acts
1.1-2   32, 34, 50
1.3-26   159
1.5   177
1.10   67n11
1.12-14   114n2
1.12-26   71n1
2.1–6.6   159
2.17-40   194
2.38   138
2.41-47   18, 86n48,
    86n50, 86n51, 145,
    159, 173n28, 174n31,
    179
2.43-47   77, 114n2, 158,
    172n27
3.1-10   77, 86n49, 188
3.1–4.37   139
3.4   67n11
3.11-26   80n25, 194
3.12   67n11
4.1–8.1   142
4.1-22   156
4.1-31   162
4.8-12   80n25
4.32-35   172n27

4.32-37   77, 114n2, 145,
    158, 159, 162, 173n28,
    174n31, 176, 178
4.32–5.11   18, 86n48,
    86n50, 86n51, 173
5.1-11   77, 145, 157,
    174n32, 179
5.12-16   86n49, 114n2,
    173n28
5.16   77
5.17-40   162
5.17-42   156
5.41-42   162
5.31   138
5.33-39   23, 150
5.33-42   151, 153
5.41   172n27
6.1-6   174, 178, 188
6.1-7   18, 86n48, 86n50,
    158, 170, 171n21,
    172n27
6.7   114n2, 162
6.8-8.1   156
6.15   67n11
7.1-8.3   140n27
7.2-53   80n25
7.51-52   108n20
7.54-8.3   162
7.55   67n11
7.58-8.3   142
8.4-8   86n49, 114n2,
    162
8.4-24   157
8.8   172n27
8.9-24   86n51, 174n32
8.9-40   77
8.14-24   80n25
8.25   114n2, 162
8.26–40   86n51,
    119n15, 150, 159, 170,
    176
8.39   172n27
9   20, 192n12
9.2   159
9.10-19   159
9.19-25   194
9.23-24   156
9.31   114n2
9.32-35   86n49
9.32–12.17   159
9.36-43   18, 86n48,
    86n49, 86n50, 158,
    159, 160, 171n21,
    174n31, 178, 179

10–11   20
10.1-8   170
10.1-48   159
10.1–11.18   77, 86n47,
    86n51, 170, 176, 188
10.1–12.24   139
10.4   67n11
10.34-43   194
10.43   138
11.6   67n11
11.16   177
11.17   177
11.26-30   114n2
11.27-30   18, 145, 157,
    158, 172n27, 174n31
11.27–12.5   173
12.1-5   156, 157
12.1-23   162
12.12-17   159, 160,
    178n40
12.12-19   179
12.20-23   143, 157
12.20-24   151
12.24   162
12.24-25   114n2, 150n47
13.1–14.28   159
13.1–28.31   142
13.4-12   77, 142, 156,
    161, 176, 194
13.5   160
13.6   67n11
13.13-52   80n25, 139,
    150, 176
13.14-52   193, 194
13.25   177
13.38   138
13.44-52   156
13.48-52   139n26, 162,
    167n13
13.50-52   179
13.52   172n27
14.1-7   156, 167n13
14.8   67n11
14.8-18   77, 86n49
14.8-20   157
14.8-28   139
14.19   139n26, 157
14.19-20   139n26, 156,
    162, 167n13
15.1-29   150, 159
15.1-35   170
15.36-41   160
15.36–16.10   114n2
16.1-3   176

16.1–21.16   159
16.15   86n48, 86n50,
   86n51
16.11-15   77, 150, 158,
   159, 160, 174n31, 176,
   178n40, 179, 188
16.16-19   178n39
16.16-24   158, 161
16.16-30   142
16.16-40   77, 139,
   174n32
16.25-40   158, 159
16.39-40   86n47
16.40   86n48, 86n50,
   86n51, 178n40, 179
17.1-9   156
17.5-9   167n13
17.10-12   150
17.10-15   156, 159, 176
17.16-34   150, 159, 176
17.22-31   80n25
17.34   160, 178n40, 179
18.1-4   159, 178n40,
   179
18.1-11   176
18.12-17   153, 156
18.18-21   178n40
18.18-23   114n2
18.24-28   159, 160, 177
18.24–19.7   154n54
19.1-7   159, 177, 194
19.1-41   159, 176
19.8-10   162
19.9   159
19.11-20   77, 86n49, 156,
   161, 162
19.20   114n2
19.23   159
19.23-41   142, 156,
   174n32
19.30-31   174n31
20.3   156
20.7-12   86n49, 160
20.1–35   80n25
20.17-38   159, 176
21.7-9   86n48, 86n50
21.8   176
21.15   174n31
21.16   86n48, 86n50
21.17-35   139
21.27-36   156
21.27–26.32   142
22   20, 46, 192n12
22.4   159

22.30–23.35   156
23.1-10   23
23.3   23
23.12–28.16   159
24.1-8   156
24.1-9   156
24.9   156
24.14   159
24.22   159
25   46
25.1-12   156
25.13–26.32   153
25.27   156
26   20, 46, 192n12
26.18   138
26.30-32   114n2
27   13
27.1-3   159
27.1–28.10   21, 139
27.30-44   159
28.1-16   13
28.7-10   86n48, 86n49,
   86n50, 158, 174n31
28.11-16   86n48, 86n50,
   174n31
28.17-28   13, 59n48,
   80n25, 196n23
28.17-31   13, 23, 25, 136,
   136n20, 194
28.25-27   196
28.27   145, 196n23
28.28   193
28.30   143
28.30-31   114n2,
   168n16

**Pseudepigrapha and
Qumran Writings**

11QMelch   67n8

1QS
3.13–4.26   74n9

Apocalypse of Abraham
13.3–7   121n24

1 Enoch
90.8-13   121n24
96.1-8   75n11,
   80
97.1-10   75n11,
   80

Jubilees
11.11   121n24

4 Maccabees
6.15-23   96n85

Psalms of Solomon
4.5-6   96n85
4.22   96n85
8.16   136n19
11   67n8

Greek and Latin Authors

Aesop, *Fables*
27   108n21

Aphthonius
25b-27c   53n28

Aristotle, *Poetics*
1450a–1551b   40n59
1450a.2-4   133n9
1450a.15-23   133n10
1450b.1-3   133n8
1451a–1451b   36n44
1454a.15-35   133n8
1454b.1-15   133n8

Aristotle, *Rhetoric*
1.2.3–1.2.6   39n55
1.2.19–1.2.22   41n66
2.19.1   78n21,
   99n90
2.21.1–2.21.16   53n29,
   82n36
2.21.6   53n28
2.22.13–2.23.30   41n66
2.23.4–2.23.5   106n17
2.23.23   56n37
2.23.30   56n36,
   56n37
2.25.8–2.25.14   57n42
3.2   124n32
3.11.7   101n3
3.14.12   75n13
3.17.6–3.17.8   58n45
3.18   105n14
3.18.16–3.18.17   95n82

Cicero, *De inventione*
1.7   54n32

Cicero, *De Oratore*
2.42.182   75n13
3.54.207   52

Demetrius, *On Style*
8   53n29
12–35   82n35
30   55
32   55
30–33   55
34   54n32
222
  39n54
278–279   52n27
279   88n56

Dionysius, *Epistle ad Ammaeum*
1.6-9   54n32

Dionysius, *Letter to Gnaeus Pompeius*
3   39n54

Hermogenes
8b-10   53n28

Herodotus
1.141   108n21

Horace, *Satire*
1.3.25   95n82

Longinus, *On the Sublime*
11.1–12.1   36n44,
  133n9
25.1   78n19
26   81n33

Lucian, *How to Write History*
55   36n44

Nicolaus, *Progymnasmata*
25–29   53n28

Plutarch, *De curios*
515   95n82

Quintilian, *Institutio Oratoria*
3.8.36   75n13
4.1.7   75n13
4.1.42–4.1.50   149n45
5.14.25   56n38
5.14.27–5.14.32   58n45
8.6.4–8.6.8   124n32
9.2.6–9.2.7   88n56
9.3.81   84n43

9.3.90–9.3.98   52
9.3.98   105n14

Rhetorica ad Alexandrum
15   75n13

Rhetorica ad Herennium
1.2.3   75n13
1.6.9–1.6.11   149n45
4.13   78n20
4.15   84n43
4.16   52
4.18   53n29, 78n21
4.19   79n22
4.21   101n3
4.21.28   90n67
4.21.29   90n66
4.22–4.24   105n14
4.22.29   91n69
4.23   58n44
4.34   124n32
4.38.28   88n59
4.40-43   99n90
4.42.54   89n60, 116n7
4.54   147n43
4.59–61   78n21

Theon, *Progymnasmata*
61b   54n32
96–97   53n28

INDEX OF AUTHORS

Abrams, M.H. 28n2
Achtemeier, Paul J. 5n9, 30n11
Adkins, W.H. 84n41
Aletti, J.-N. 14n45
Alexander, Loveday C.A. 25–26, 32,
  34n30, 59n47, 135n15, 136n19,
  136n20, 167n12, 167n14, 179n43,
  184n1, 197n25
Allen, Wesley O. 162n64
Alter, Robert 41n65, 72n3, 140n27
Aune, David E. 26, 34n30, 41n64,
  54–58

Bakhtin, Mikhail 37n48
Bal, Mieke 10n28
Balch, David L. 26n95, 26n96,
  33n23, 34n31, 59n49, 144n37,
  173n30, 199n36
Barton, Stephen C. 14n47, 31n18,
  122n26, 127n37, 198n31
Bauer, David R. 3n4
Beavis, Mary Ann 173n30
Betz, Hans Dieter 7, 15, 74n10,
  76n15, 79n23, 81n33, 83n38, 85n45,
  89n63, 90n68, 91n71, 95n81, 96n84
Bitzer, Lloyd F. 47n6
Black, Clifton C. II 46n1, 160n60
Bonz, Marianne Palmer 38n50
Booth, Wayne C. 28n1, 132n3,
  164n2, 164n4, 165n8, 200n37
Borgman, Paul 159n59
Bosend, William F. II 25n92, 59n48
Bovon, François 19, 64n1, 67n9,
  70n16, 73n7, 74n9, 79n24, 81n33,
  83n37, 83n38, 95n81, 101n1, 108n20,
  115n5, 120n22, 120n23, 122n29,
  123n30, 125n33, 132n5, 171n23,
  193n15
Braet, Antoine C. 57n41
Brawley, Robert L. 18
Brodie, Thomas L. 80n27, 102n4,
  102n5, 202n42

Burke, Kenneth 176n36
Burnett, Frederick W. 38

Cadbury, Henry 193n13
Cameron, Ron 8n20, 103n7, 146n40
Camery-Hoggatt, Jerry 36n40
Camp, Greg Alan 4n4
Carroll, John T. 112n30, 132n6
Carruth, Shawn 75n13, 77n17,
  78n19, 141n29
Carson, D.A. 110n25
Chatman, Seymour 166n10
Clayton, Jay 37n47
Co, Maria Anicia 173n28
Collins, John J. 174n33
Combrink, H.J.B. 66n6
Conley, Thomas M. 58n43
Conzelmann, Hans 6, 132n4, 132n5
Corley, Kathleen E. 153n52, 178n38
Corbett, Edward P.J. 50n19
Cotter, Wendy 109n22, 109n23,
  196n22
Couroyer, B. 94n78
Creech, Robert R. 31n17
Crockett, Larrimore C. 69n15

Danker, Frederick W. 84n41
Darr, John A. 8, 11n35, 16–17, 33,
  101n2, 112n30, 142n33, 188n4
Deissmann, Adolf 50n21
deSilva, David A. 169n18, 169n19
Destro, Adriana 144n38
Dewey, Joanna 89n64
Diefenbach, Manfred 15n49, 46n4
Dihle, Alchrecht 86n52
Donohue, John R. 201n40
Douglas, Conrard R. 83n37, 85n45,
  86n50
Downing, Gerald F. 33n24, 119n15,
  199n34
Dungan, David L. 191n8
Dunn, James D.G. 111n28

Dupont, Jacques   74n10, 79n24, 136n20, 194n18

Ebner, Martin   84n41
Eco, Umberto   25
Elliott, John H.   173n29
Esler, Phillip   14–15, 31n17, 34n33, 167n12, 197
Evans, Craig A.   142n30

Farrell, Thomas B.   57n40
Finn, Thomas M.   154n53
Fitzmyer, Joseph A.   118n14, 132n5
Fortenbaugh, William W. 195n20
Fowl, Stephen E.   44n71
Fowler, Robert M.   37n46, 201n38
Freadman, Richard   43n69, 164n3
Furnish, Victor Paul   86n52
Fusco, Vittorio   196n24

Garrett, Susan R.   161n63
Gathercole, Simon   111n29
Gavrilov, A.K.   36n42
Genette, Gerard   37n47, 134n11, 137n21
Gerhardsson, Birger   48n13
Gilbert, Gary   41n62
Gill Christopher   40n57, 156n57
Gilliard, Frank D.   36n42
Gold, Barbara K.   32n19
Gowler, David   11
Green, Joel B.   4n8, 6n12, 7n14, 17n58, 23–25, 36n40, 37n49, 38n51, 40n58, 41n62, 43n70, 66n6, 70n16, 75n14, 77n17, 77n18, 80n25, 80n29, 83n39, 90n68, 91n72, 96n86, 96n87, 99n88, 102n5, 104n11, 106n16, 110n26, 112n30, 115n4, 117n10, 118n14, 119n16, 120n19, 126n35, 127n37, 132n6, 134n13, 134n14, 144n37, 147n41, 149n46, 153n52, 159n59, 171n21, 171n23, 173n30, 179n43, 198n30, 199n34, 199n35, 200n37
Greenblatt, Stephen   43n68
Grimshaw, Jim   34n28

Halliwell, Stephen   156n57
Hamilton, Paul   24n85
Hanson, K.C.   81n31
Hartin, Patrick J.   103n8, 171n23
Havelaar, Henriette   179n42
Hays, Richard B.   38n51
Head, Peter M.   191n8

Health, Malcolm   47n9
Hedrick, Charles W.   117n9
Hengel, Martin   174n33
Hoffmann, Paul   86n52
Hollaway, Paul A.   125n34
Horbury, William   176n35
Horsley, Richard A.   72n2, 73n6, 74n9, 80n26, 194n16, 196n21
Hunter, Virgina J. 58n46
Hur, Ju   18n62, 139n24, 158n58

Iser, Wolfgang   29, 33n26, 37n45, 42–43, 44n72, 165n5, 166n9

Jakobson, Roman   9
Jeremias, Joachim 110n25
Jervell, Jacob   72n1, 178n38
Johnson, Luke T.   71n2, 144n37, 176n37, 198n32
Johnson, Robert M.   99n89
Jones, Gregory L.   44n71

Karris, Robert J.   198n30
Kavanagh, James H.   30n12
Kearney, Suzanne Marie 104n12, 147n41
Keener, Craig S.   173n29, 178n41
Kellogg, Robert   39n53, 133n8
Kennedy, George A.   7, 46–7, 51n24, 54n32, 73, 89n60, 201n39
Kern, Philip H.   48n14, 49n16, 49n18, 50n22
Kim, Kyoung-Jin   144n37
Kingsbury, Jack D.   3n1, 12
Kirk, Alan   87n52, 87n53, 87n54, 87n55, 88n57
Kitzberger, Ingrid Rosa   30n13
Klink, Edward W. 32n18
Kloppenborg, John S.   79n24, 101n1
Knight, Jonathan   10n30, 73n6
Konstan, David   88n57
Kraabel, Thomas A.   174n34, 174n34
Kristeva, Julia   37n47
Kurz, William S.   16, 20n71

Lanigan, Richard L.   57n39
Lentz, John C.   19
Linton, Olof   110n25
Litwak, Kenneth D.   21n73, 33n27
Lofink, Gerhard   80n27

MacDonald, Dennis R.   21n75, 38n50
Mack, Burton L.   186n2
MacLennan, R.S. 174n34

Mailloux, Steven 166n10
Malherbe, Abraham J. 34n31
Malina, Bruce J. 35n37, 57n39,
  84n41, 85n44, 85n45, 169n18
Marguerat, Daniel 13–14, 59n48,
  179n42, 199n34, 199n35
Marshall, Howard I. 40n61, 93n75,
  120n20, 192n11
Matson, David Lertis 20n72
Matera, Frank J. 112n30
McArthur, Harvey K. 99n89
McNicol, Alan J. 191n8
Meeks, Wayne A. 34n31
Merenlathi, Petri 39n56
Miller, Carolyn R. 41n64
Miller, Robert J. 105n15
Miller, Seumas 43n69, 164n3
Minear, Paul S. 6n11, 80n28, 81n33
Mitchell, Alan C. 85n44, 173n28
Mitchell, Margaret M. 32n18
Moessner, David P. 19n66, 27n100,
  154n54
Morganthaler, Robert 15n49, 46n4
Moreland, Milton C. 79n24
Moore, Stephen D. 3n3, 10n30,
  131n1
Moxnes, Halvor 15, 34n28, 34n32,
  35n35, 35n38, 86n50, 144n37,
  169n18, 173n29, 197, 199n34

Nadeau, Ray 48n13, 118n11
Neirynck, Frans 65n2, 135n16,
  194n17
Neyrey, Jerome H. 19, 35n36, 35n37,
  49n17, 81n32, 85n44, 85n45, 172n24
Nickelsburg, George W.E. 81n32
Nolland, John 31n16, 66n6, 68n13,
  93n75, 199n33
Noorda, S.J. 68n13

Olbricht, Thomas H. 48n12, 50n22,
  118n11
Osiek, Carolyn 33n23, 34n31
Overman, James A. 174n34

Parsons, Mikeal 4n6, 46n4, 193n13
Payne, Philip B. 116n6
Peabody, David B. 191n8
Penner, Todd 10n29, 32n22
Pervo, Richard 4n6, 193n13
Pesce, Mauro 144n38
Petersen, Norman 9
Peterson, David 40n61
Phelan, James 39n57

Phillips, Thomas E. 26n98, 172n25,
  188n5
Pilch, John J. 72n5, 196n23
Pilgrim, Walter E. 172n26
Porter, Stanley E. 49n15, 50n20,
  94n79, 118n13, 134n12
Powell, Mark Alan 11–12
Praeder, Susan M. 21n74
Price, Robert M. 178n38
Prince, Gerald 41n63, 133n8

Rabinowitz, Peter J. 4n7, 28n3, 29–
  30, 35n39, 165n6, 165n7
Ravins, David 196n24
Reimer, Richter I. 178n38
Reiser, Marius 84n41, 85n45
Resseguie, James L. 43n69, 159n59
Ricoeur, Paul 29n5, 86n52, 133n9
Ringe, Sharon 67n8, 139n23
Robbins, Vernon K. 21n77, 35n38,
  46n1, 46n2, 65n3, 65n4, 76n16,
  77n17, 94n80, 103n9, 194n19,
  201n41, 202n42
Robinson, James M. 79n24, 79n24
Rohrbaugh, Richard L. 34n29,
  136n18
Rosenblatt, Marie-Eloise 19n68
Roth, John S. 7, 17–18, 67n7,
  138n22, 139n25, 147n42, 152n50,
  172n27, 188n5
Rothstein, Eric 37n47
Rowe, Galen O. 48n11
Rowe, Kavin C. 193n14
Rüger, H.P. 94n78

Sacks, Kenneth S. 194n19
Saller, Richard 84n41
Satterthwaite, Philip E. 4, 46n2
Scholes, Robert 30n9, 39n53, 133n8,
  168n17
Schottroff, L. 172n26
Schürmann, Heinz 79n23, 83n38
Schüssler Fiorenza, Elizabeth 3n3,
  179n42
Schwartz, Saundra 38n50
Scobie, C.H. 176n37
Scott, Bernard Brandon 115n4
Scott, J.M. 35n34
Schreck, Christopher J. 6n13, 135n16
Seccombe, David P. 197n27
Segovia, Fernando F. 202n43
Seim, Turid Karlsen 114n1, 178n38
Sheeley, Steven M. 104n10, 107n19

Shepherd, William H., Jr. 18, 139n24, 158n58
Shiner, Whitney 48n13, 118n11
Siker, Jeffrey S. 65n2, 67n10, 67n11, 69n14
Sim, David 112n1
Sloan, Robert 67n8, 139n23
Smallwood, Mary E. 174n33
Smith, Dennis E. 35n36
Smith, Robert H. 96n85
Soards, Marion L. 4n5, 46n3, 134n12, 194n16
Spencer, Patrick. E. 31n15, 110n27
Spencer, Scott F. 9n24, 10n29, 11n33, 15n52, 198n31
Squires, John T. 118n14
Stamps, Dennis L. 167n11
Staley, Jeffrey A. 5
Stegemann, W. 172n26
Sterling, Gregory A. 26n97, 167n14, 173n28, 199n34, 199n35
Stock, Augustine 66n6

Talbert, Charles H. 3n2, 9, 20, 72n4, 154n53
Tannehill, Robert C. 3n2, 7n14, 9–11, 30n13, 112n30, 176n37, 191n9, 196n24
Theissen, Gerd 34n32
Thomas, Rosalind 36n42
Thompkins, Jane P. 44n71
Thompson, Michael B. 167n12
Thompson, Richard P. 19–20
Tolbert, Mary Ann 9, 89n64, 115, 153n51, 155n56, 192n10, 202n43

Toohey, Peter 58n46, 134n12
Topel, John 87n54
Tracy, Stephen V. 40n60
Tuckett, Christopher M. 191n8
Turner, Max 201n40
Tyson, Joseph B. 6, 10n29, 12n40, 21–22, 34n33, 35n38, 197

van Unnik, W.C. 84n42

Vanhoozer, Kevin J. 164n1
Vison, Richard B. 55n35

Waetjen, Herman C. 122n28, 166n9, 200n37
Walaskay, Paul W. 167n15
Wallace-Hadrill, Andrew 84n41
Wasserberg, Günter 22–23, 68n12, 69n14, 196n24, 198
Wenham, David 15n52
Wheeldon, M.J. 131n2
Wilcox, Max 174n34
Wilson, Stanley G. 176n35
Wink, Walter 8, 84n40
Witherington, Ben III 4n5, 31n17, 41n62, 46, 72n5, 92n73, 112n1, 178n38, 192n12, 194n16, 199n33
Witherup, Ronald D. 20n71, 20n72
Wuellner, Wilhelm 48n10, 51n25
Wuthnow, Robert 29n4, 164n3

York, John O. 77n18, 143n35, 171n22